From

maranGraphics™

&

IDG Books Worldwide, Inc.
An International Data Group Company
Foster City, CA • Indianapolis, IN • Chicago, IL • New York, NY

Teach Yourself VISUALLY™ Networking, 2nd Edition

Published by
IDG Books Worldwide, Inc.
An International Data Group Company
909 Third Street
New York, NY 10022

Library of Congress Catalog Card No.: 00-107999

ISBN: 0-7645-3534-X

Printed in the United States of America
10 9 8 7 6 5 4 3 2 1

2K/RY/QR/QR/MG

Distributed in the United States by IDG Books Worldwide, Inc.

Distributed by CDG Books Canada Inc. for Canada; by Transworld Publishers Limited in the United Kingdom; by IDG Norge Books for Norway; by IDG Sweden Books for Sweden; by IDG Books Australia Publishing Corporation Pty. Ltd. for Australia and New Zealand; by TransQuest Publishers Pte Ltd. for Singapore, Malaysia, Thailand, Indonesia, and Hong Kong; by Gotop Information Inc. for Taiwan; by ICG Muse, Inc. for Japan; by Intersoft for South Africa; by Eyrolles for France; by International Thomson Publishing for Germany, Austria and Switzerland; by Distribuidora Cuspide for Argentina; by LR International for Brazil; by Galileo Libros for Chile; by Ediciones ZETA S.C.R. Ltda. for Peru; by WS Computer Publishing Corporation, Inc. for the Philippines; by Contemporanea de Ediciones for Venezuela; by Express Computer Distributors for the Caribbean and West Indies; by Micronesia Media Distributor, Inc. for Micronesia; by Chips Computadoras S.A. de C.V. for Mexico; by Editorial Norma de Panama S.A. for Panama; by American Bookshops for Finland.
For corporate orders, please call maranGraphics at 800-469-6616.
For general information on IDG Books Worldwide's books in the U.S., please call our Consumer Customer Service department at 800-762-2974.
For reseller information, including discounts and premium sales, please call our Reseller Customer Service department at 800-434-3422.
For information on where to purchase IDG Books Worldwide's books outside the U.S., please contact our International Sales department at 317-572-3993 or fax 317-572-4002.
For consumer information on foreign language translations, please contact our Customer Service department at 800-434-3422, fax 800-550-2747, or e-mail rights@idgbooks.com.
For information on licensing foreign or domestic rights, please phone 650-653-7000 of fax 650-653-7500.
For sales inquiries and special prices for bulk quantities, please contact our Sales department at 650-655-3200.
For information on using IDG Books Worldwide's books in the classroom or for ordering examination copies, please contact our Educational Sales department at 800-434-2086 or fax 317-572-4005.
For press review copies, author interviews, or other publicity information, please contact our Public Relations department at 650-653-7000 or fax 650-653-7500.
For authorization to photocopy items for corporate, personal, or educational use, please contact maranGraphics at 800-469-6616.

Trademark Acknowledgments

Permissions

ABOUT IDG BOOKS WORLDWIDE

Welcome to the world of IDG Books Worldwide.

IDG Books Worldwide, Inc., is a subsidiary of International Data Group, the world's largest publisher of computer-related information and the leading global provider of information services on information technology. IDG was founded more than 30 years ago by Patrick J. McGovern and now employs more than 9,000 people worldwide. IDG publishes more than 290 computer publications in over 75 countries. More than 90 million people read one or more IDG publications each month.

Launched in 1990, IDG Books Worldwide is today the #1 publisher of best-selling computer books in the United States. We are proud to have received eight awards from the Computer Press Association in recognition of editorial excellence and three from Computer Currents' First Annual Readers' Choice Awards. Our best-selling *...For Dummies®* series has more than 50 million copies in print with translations in 31 languages. IDG Books Worldwide, through a joint venture with IDG's Hi-Tech Beijing, became the first U.S. publisher to publish a computer book in the People's Republic of China. In record time, IDG Books Worldwide has become the first choice for millions of readers around the world who want to learn how to better manage their businesses.

Our mission is simple: Every one of our books is designed to bring extra value and skill-building instructions to the reader. Our books are written by experts who understand and care about our readers. The knowledge base of our editorial staff comes from years of experience in publishing, education, and journalism — experience we use to produce books to carry us into the new millennium. In short, we care about books, so we attract the best people. We devote special attention to details such as audience, interior design, use of icons, and illustrations. And because we use an efficient process of authoring, editing, and desktop publishing our books electronically, we can spend more time ensuring superior content and less time on the technicalities of making books.

You can count on our commitment to deliver high-quality books at competitive prices on topics you want to read about. At IDG Books Worldwide, we continue in the IDG tradition of delivering quality for more than 30 years. You'll find no better book on a subject than one from IDG Books Worldwide.

John Kilcullen
Chairman and CEO
IDG Books Worldwide, Inc.

Eighth Annual Computer Press Awards 1992

Ninth Annual Computer Press Awards 1993

Tenth Annual Computer Press Awards 1994

Eleventh Annual Computer Press Awards 1995

IDG is the world's leading IT media, research and exposition company. Founded in 1964, IDG had 1997 revenues of $2.05 billion and has more than 9,000 employees worldwide. IDG offers the widest range of media options that reach IT buyers in 75 countries representing 95% of worldwide IT spending. IDG's diverse product and services portfolio spans six key areas including print publishing, online publishing, expositions and conferences, market research, education and training, and global marketing services. More than 90 million people read one or more of IDG's 290 magazines and newspapers, including IDG's leading global brands — Computerworld, PC World, Network World, Macworld and the Channel World family of publications. IDG Books Worldwide is one of the fastest-growing computer book publishers in the world, with more than 700 titles in 36 languages. The "...For Dummies®" series alone has more than 50 million copies in print. IDG offers online users the largest network of technology-specific Web sites around the world through IDG.net (http://www.idg.net), which comprises more than 225 targeted Web sites in 55 countries worldwide. International Data Corporation (IDC) is the world's largest provider of information technology data, analysis and consulting, with research centers in over 41 countries and more than 400 research analysts worldwide. IDG World Expo is a leading producer of more than 168 globally branded conferences and expositions in 35 countries including E3 (Electronic Entertainment Expo), Macworld Expo, ComNet, Windows World Expo, ICE (Internet Commerce Expo), Agenda, DEMO, and Spotlight. IDG's training subsidiary, ExecuTrain, is the world's largest computer training company, with more than 230 locations worldwide and 785 training courses. IDG Marketing Services helps industry-leading IT companies build international brand recognition by developing global integrated marketing programs via IDG's print, online and exposition products worldwide. Further information about the company can be found at www.idg.com. 1/26/00

maranGraphics is a family-run business
located near Toronto, Canada.

At **maranGraphics**, we believe in producing great computer books–one book at a time.

Each maranGraphics book uses the award-winning communication process that we have been developing over the last 25 years. Using this process, we organize screen shots, text and illustrations in a way that makes it easy for you to learn new concepts and tasks.

We spend hours deciding the best way to perform each task, so you don't have to! Our clear, easy-to-follow screen shots and instructions walk you through each task from beginning to end.

Our detailed illustrations go hand-in-hand with the text to help reinforce the information. Each illustration is a labor of love–some take up to a week to draw!

We want to thank you for purchasing what we feel are the best computer books money can buy. We hope you enjoy using this book as much as we enjoyed creating it!

Sincerely,

The Maran Family

Please visit us on the Web at:
www.maran.com

CREDITS

Author:
Paul Whitehead

Director of Copy Editing:
Wanda Lawrie

Copy Editors:
Stacey Morrison
Roderick Anatalio
Cathy Benn
Luis Lee

Project Manager:
Judy Maran

Editors:
Teri Lynn Pinsent
Norm Schumacher
James Menzies

Layout Designer & Illustrator:
Treena Lees

Illustrators:
Russ Marini
Sean Johannesen
Steven Schaerer
Suzana G. Miokovic
Dave Thornhill
Natalie Tweedie

Indexer:
Teri Lynn Pinsent

Permissions Coordinator:
Jennifer Amaral

Senior Vice President and Publisher, IDG Books Technology Publishing Group:
Richard Swadley

Publishing Director, IDG Books Technology Publishing Group:
Barry Pruett

Editorial Support, IDG Books Technology Publishing Group:
Martine Edwards
Lindsay Sandman
Sandy Rodrigues

Post Production & Technical Consultant:
Robert Maran

ACKNOWLEDGMENTS

Thanks to the dedicated staff of maranGraphics, including Jennifer Amaral, Roderick Anatalio, Cathy Benn, Sean Johannesen, Kelleigh Johnson, Wanda Lawrie, Luis Lee, Treena Lees, Jill Maran, Judy Maran, Robert Maran, Ruth Maran, Russ Marini, Suzana G. Miokovic, Stacey Morrison, Teri Lynn Pinsent, Steven Schaerer, Norm Schumacher, Raquel Scott, Dave Thornhill, Natalie Tweedie, Roxanne Van Damme and Paul Whitehead.

Finally, to Richard Maran who originated the easy-to-use graphic format of this guide. Thank you for your inspiration and guidance.

TABLE OF CONTENTS

Chapter 1

INTRODUCTION TO NETWORKS

What is a Network 4
Types of Networks 6
Network Hardware 8
Network Software 10
Peer-to-Peer Networks 12
Client/Server Networks 16
Network Benefits 20
Network Considerations 22

NETWORK STRUCTURE

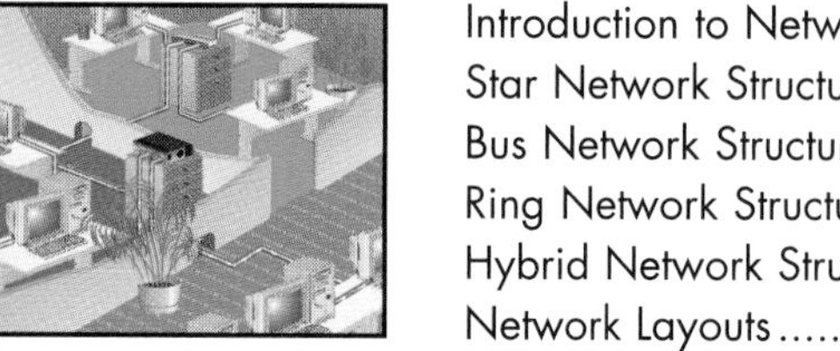

Introduction to Network Structure 26
Star Network Structure 28
Bus Network Structure 30
Ring Network Structure 32
Hybrid Network Structure 34
Network Layouts 36

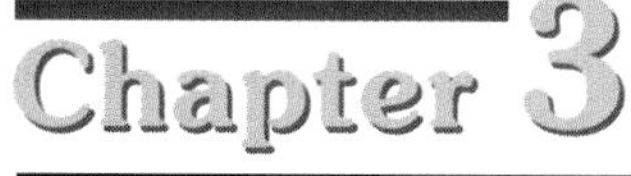

NETWORK HARDWARE

Servers 40
Storage Devices 44
Network Printers 46
Network Interface Cards 48
Hubs 50
Switches 52
Repeaters 54
Bridges 55
Routers 56
Brouters 60
Gateways 61
Modems 62
Digital Service and Channel Service Units 64
Multiplexers 65

Chapter 4 — TRANSMISSION MEDIA

Introduction to Transmission Media 68
Transmission Media Considerations 70
Coaxial Cable 72
Unshielded Twisted Pair Cable 74
Shielded Twisted Pair Cable.............................76
Fiber-optic Cable 78
Infrared Systems 80
Radio Systems 81
Microwave Systems...82
Satellite Systems 83

Chapter 5 — NETWORK ARCHITECTURE

Introduction to Network Architecture 86
Ethernet Architecture 88
Token-Ring Architecture 92
ARCnet Architecture 94
AppleTalk Architecture.....................................95

Chapter 6 — NETWORK SERVICES

Introduction to Network Services 98
File Services...99
Print Services 100
Database Services 101
Application Services 102
Message Services...103

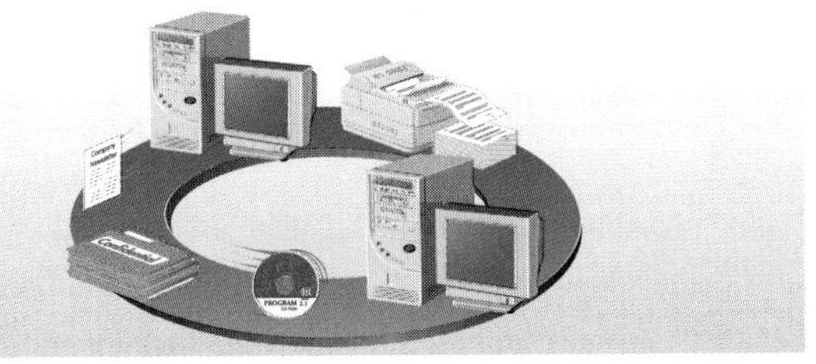

TABLE OF CONTENTS

NETWORK OPERATING SYSTEMS

Peer-to-Peer Network Operating Systems 106
Client/Server Network Operating Systems 108
NetWare 110
Windows NT 112
Windows 2000 114
UNIX 116
Linux 117

THE OSI MODEL AND PROTOCOLS

The OSI Model 120
OSI Model Layers 122
Protocols 124
IPX/SPX Protocols 126
NetBEUI Protocol 128
TCP/IP Protocols 130
Common TCP/IP Protocols 132

PROTECTING NETWORK DATA

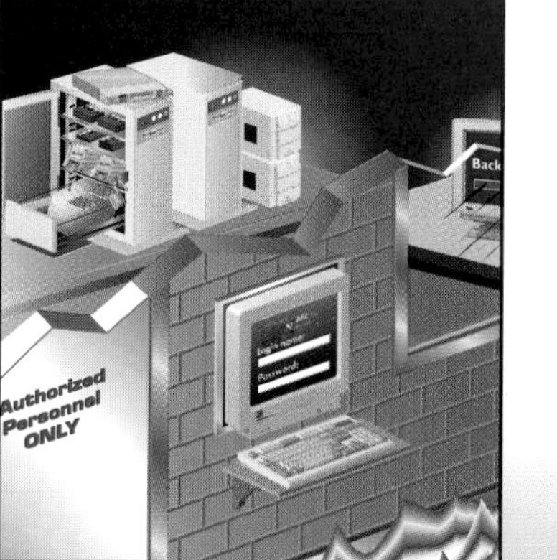

Threats to Network Data 138
Firewalls 142
Passwords 144
File Permissions 145
Back Up Network Data 146
Tape Backup Devices 148
Uninterruptible Power Supplies 150
Fault Tolerance 152

Chapter 10 NETWORK ADMINISTRATION

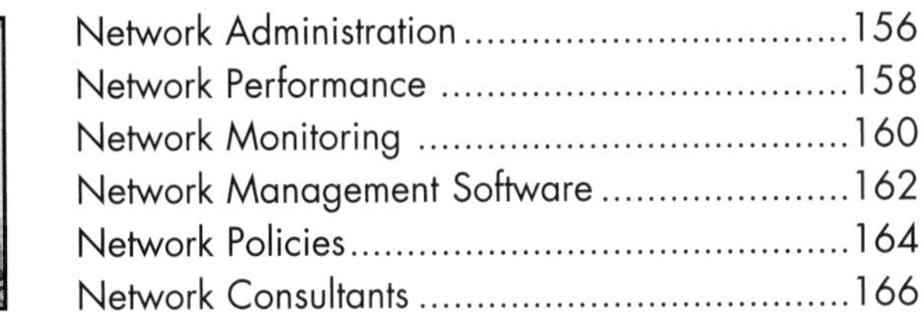

Network Administration 156
Network Performance 158
Network Monitoring 160
Network Management Software 162
Network Policies 164
Network Consultants 166

Chapter 11 NETWORK CERTIFICATIONS

Introduction to Certifications 170
Novell Certification 172
Microsoft Certification 174
Solaris Certification 176
Linux Certification 177
Oracle Certification 178
Manufacturer Certification 179
CompTIA Certification 180

Chapter 12 INSTALLING OR UPGRADING A NETWORK

Planning a Network 184
Upgrading a Network 186
Evaluate Current Network 188
Determine Network Design 190
Upgrading Network Architecture 192
Upgrading Transmission Media 194
Installing Cable 196
Choosing Network Hardware 198
Installing Network Hardware 200
Installing the Network Operating System 202
Configuring Client Computers 204
Testing the Network 206

TABLE OF CONTENTS

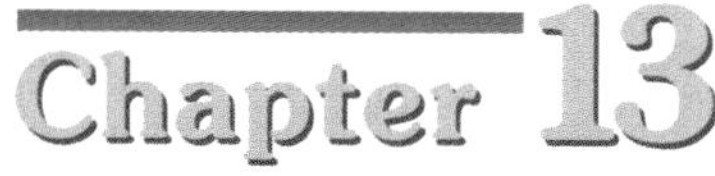

Chapter 13

CONNECTING TO THE INTERNET

Connect a Network to the Internet 210
Considerations for Connecting to the Internet....212
Internet Service Providers................................216
Internet Hardware 218
Internet Software..220
Internet Connection Types 222
Using TCP/IP to Connect to the Internet............224
Troubleshoot Internet Connections....................226

Chapter 14

INTRANETS

Introduction to Intranets 230
Videoconferencing on Intranets.......................232
Scheduling on Intranets 234
Intranet Web Systems 236
E-mail on Intranets..238
Newsgroups on Intranets 240
Chat on Intranets 242
File Transfer on Intranets 244
Intranet Software 246
Groupware 248
Voice Over IP...250

Chapter 15

WIRELESS NETWORKS

Introduction to Wireless Networks...................254
Wireless Applications 256
Wireless Devices 258
Wireless Operating Systems...........................260
Wireless Technologies 262

Chapter 16 — HOME NETWORKS

Introduction to Home Networks 266
Ethernet Network Interface Cards 268
Ethernet Hubs 270
Network Protocols 272
Connect a Home Network to the Internet 274

Chapter 17 — NETWORK PROGRAMMING

Introduction to Network Programming 280
Scripting Languages 282
C and C++ 283
Active Server Pages 284
Perl 285
Java 286
JavaServer Pages 287
XML 288
CORBA 289

Chapter 18 — VISUAL GLOSSARY

Visual Glossary 292

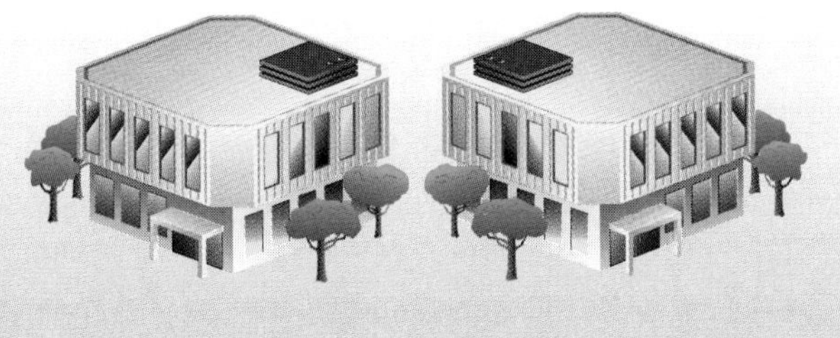

CHAPTER 1

Introduction to Networks

This chapter introduces networking basics, including types of networks and network hardware and software. Network benefits and considerations are also discussed.

What is a Network....4

Types of Networks....6

Network Hardware....8

Network Software....10

Peer-to-Peer Networks....12

Client/Server Networks....16

Network Benefits....20

Network Considerations....22

A network is a group of connected computers that allow people to share information and equipment.

Network Size

A network can be any size. For example, connecting two home computers so they can share data creates a simple network. Companies can have networks consisting of a few dozen computers or hundreds of computers. The Internet is the world's largest network and connects millions of computers all over the world.

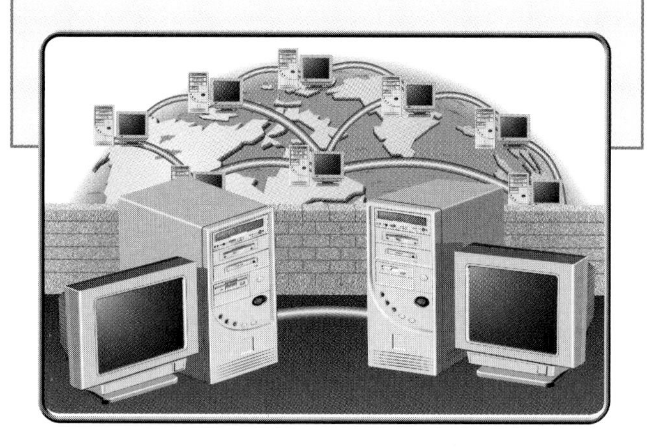

Logging On

Network users are usually required to identify themselves before they can gain access to the information on a network. This is known as logging on. Each user must enter a personalized user name and password to access a network. By keeping this information secret, users can prevent unauthorized people from accessing the network.

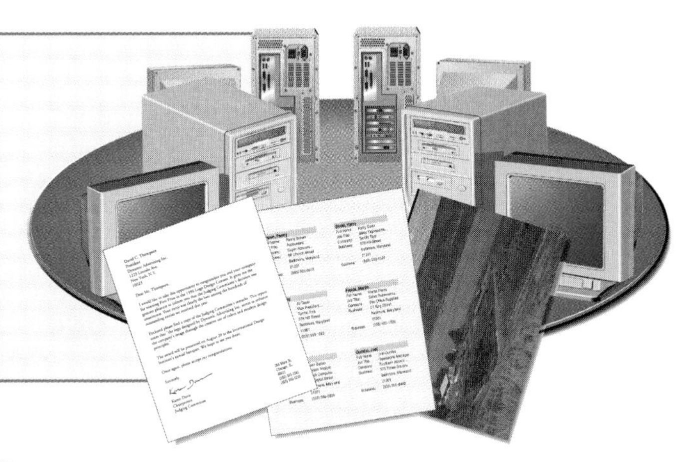

Sharing Information

You can use a network to share information with other people. Information can be any form of data, such as a document created in a word processing program, a picture drawn in an imaging application or information from a database. Before networks, people often used floppy disks to exchange information between computers, which was a slow and unreliable process. With networks, exchanging information between computers is quick and easy.

Sharing Resources

Computers connected to a network can share equipment and devices, called resources. The ability to share resources reduces the cost of buying computer hardware. For example, instead of having to buy a printer for each person on a network, everyone can share one central printer.

Sharing Programs

Networks allow people to access programs stored on a central computer, such as a spreadsheet or word processing program. Individuals can use their own computers to access and work with the programs. By sharing a program, a company can avoid having to install a copy of the program on each person's computer.

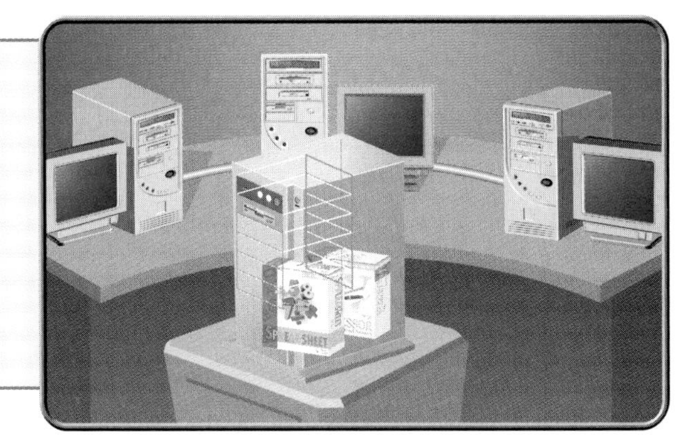

There are many different types of networks used by businesses and organizations. Since each business and organization has its own needs, each network is unique.

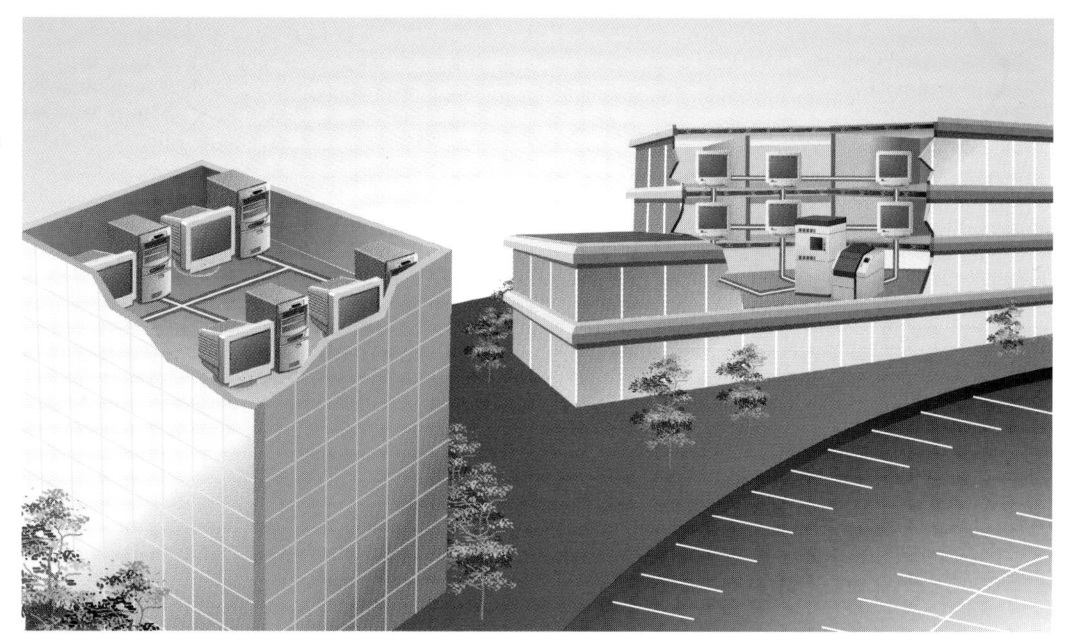

Network Size

The size of a network can often determine which type of network a business or organization should use. Different sized networks transmit data in different ways. For example, a network with over 1,000 users is organized differently and requires a variety of components not found on a network with only five users.

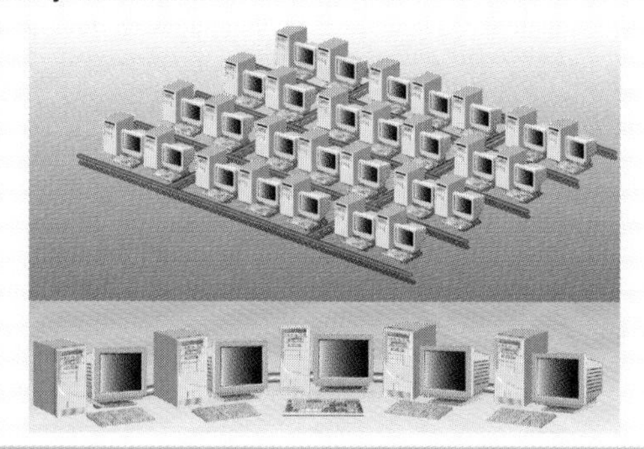

Network Cost

The size and type of a network determine its cost. The larger the network, the more costly the network is to build, set up and maintain. In addition to needing extra hardware and cables, a large network also requires specialized cabling and computers to link users and devices that are far apart.

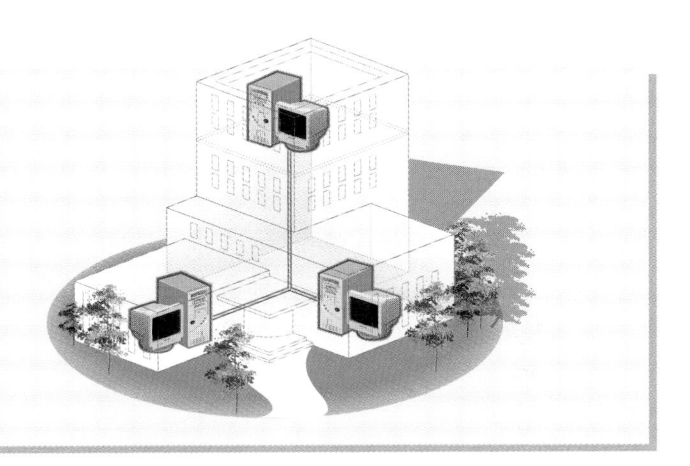

Local Area Networks

A Local Area Network (LAN) is the most common type of network found in businesses. Local area networks connect computers and devices located close to each other, such as in one building. Local area networks connect from as few as two computers to usually no more than 100 computers.

Metropolitan Area Networks

A Metropolitan Area Network (MAN) is a collection of local area networks. Metropolitan area networks connect computers located in the same geographic area, such as a city or town. For example, a college may use a MAN that connects the local area networks on each campus throughout a city.

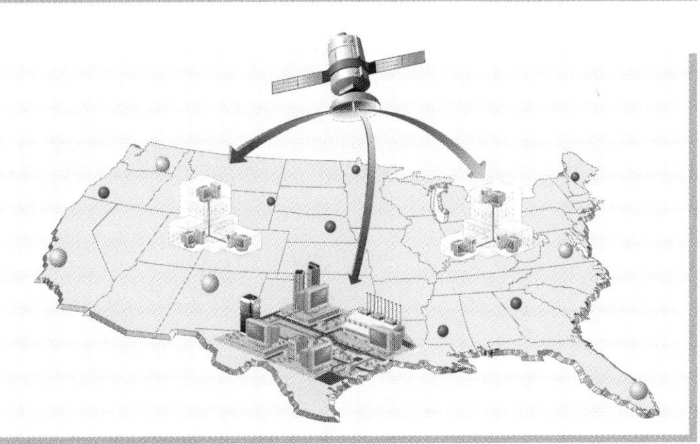

Wide Area Networks

A Wide Area Network (WAN) connects local and metropolitan area networks together. The networks that make up a wide area network may be located throughout a country or even around the world. When a single company owns and controls a wide area network, the WAN is often referred to as an enterprise network. The Internet is the largest wide area network.

Network hardware includes the physical devices used on a network. All networks require network hardware to function.

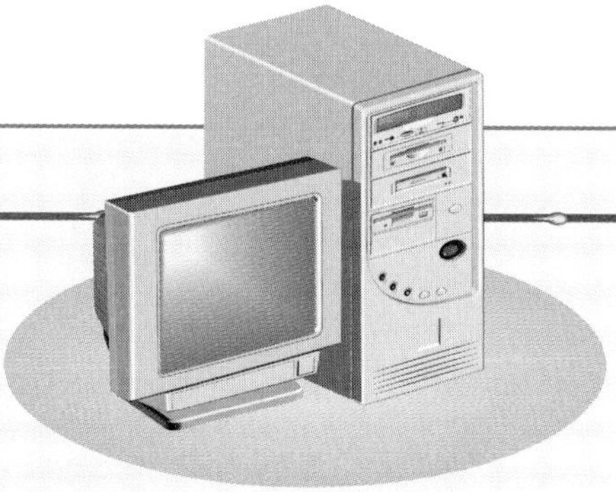

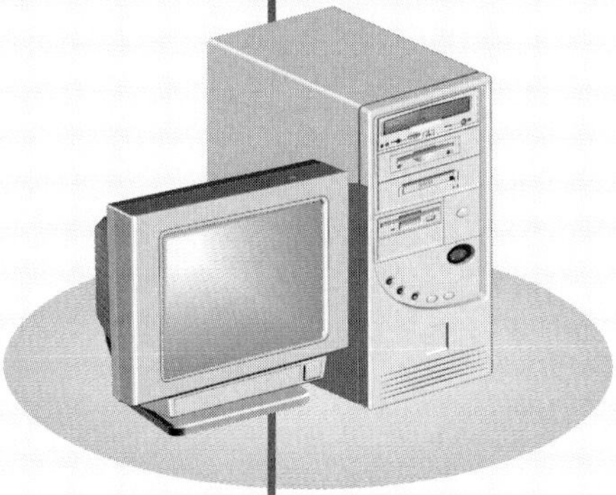

Computers

The most important job of a network is to link computers together. When computers are linked, the people using the computers can work more efficiently. Computers connected to a network do not have to be the same type. For example, a network could contain desktop computers, such as IBM-compatible and Macintosh computers, or portable computers, such as notebooks and Personal Digital Assistants (PDAs).

Resources

A network resource is a device that computers on a network can use. The most common type of network resource is a printer. All of the users on a network can send documents to a printer that is connected to the network. Other examples of network resources include fax machines, tape backup units and file storage devices, such as hard drives.

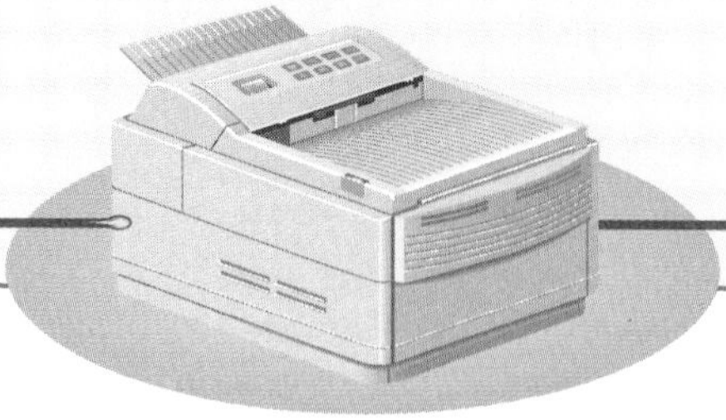

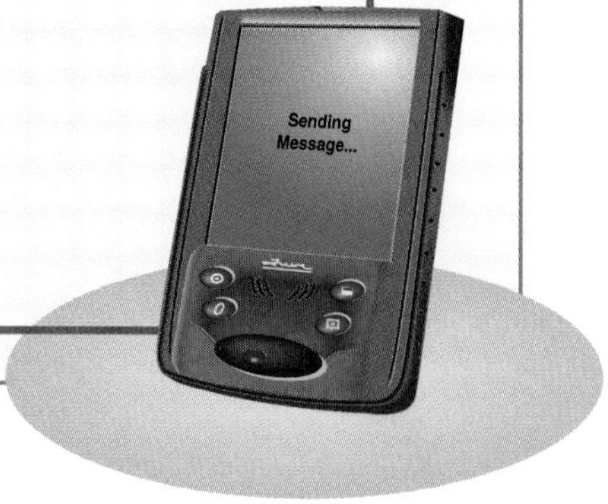

Sending Message...

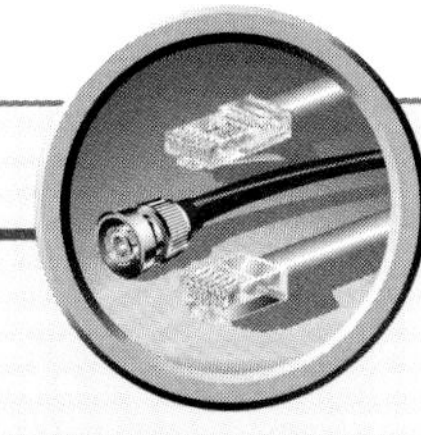

Cables

Cables are the wires that connect computers and resources on a network. Many different kinds of cables can be used, depending on the type and size of a network. The type of cable used often determines how quickly information will transfer through a network. For some large networks, many miles of cable may be required.

Connectors

A connector is a device that joins two networks together. When two networks are connected, all of the computers on both networks can exchange information. The most common types of connectors are bridges and routers.

Network Interface Cards

A Network Interface Card (NIC) is a device that physically connects a computer to a network and controls the flow of information between the network and the computer. NICs are installed inside a computer. The edge of the network interface card can be seen at the back of the computer. A NIC has a port where the network cable plugs in.

NETWORK SOFTWARE

Network software consists of programs that manage the network, provide services and allow computers to communicate and share information on the network.

Network Operating System

The Network Operating System (NOS) is the most important software on a network. The network operating system organizes and manages all the activities on a network. On some networks, one central computer, called a server, is responsible for running the network operating system. NetWare, Windows 2000 Server, Linux and LANtastic are examples of popular network operating systems.

Network Driver

A network driver is the software that allows the network interface card in a computer to communicate with the network. The network driver must be compatible with the network interface card and the operating system on a computer.

Server Software

A server is a computer that makes information and resources available to other computers on a network. Server software enables a server to perform a specific task. For example, e-mail server software allows a server to process and manage e-mail messages. The server software must be compatible with the network operating system.

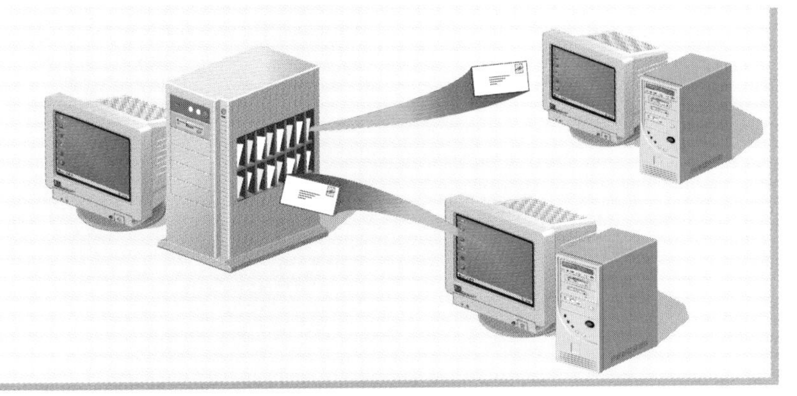

Application Software

Application software consists of the programs that run on computers connected to a network. Application software includes productivity programs, such as word processors, spreadsheet and database programs, and customized software, such as programs used for inventory and accounting purposes. Application software can be stored on each computer connected to the network or on a server used only for storing application software.

Management Software

Networks that connect several computers often use management software, which allows network administrators to organize and manage a network more efficiently. Management software can help maintain network performance and alert the network administrator in case problems or errors occur on a network.

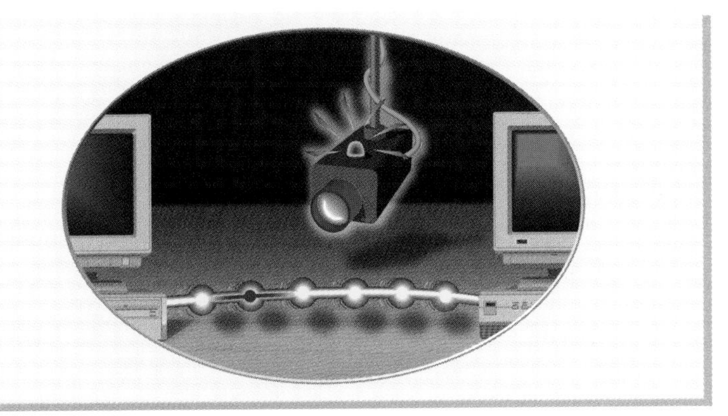

Peer-to-peer networks allow computers on a network to share their data and resources. Each computer on a peer-to-peer network stores its own information and resources. There are no central computers that control the network.

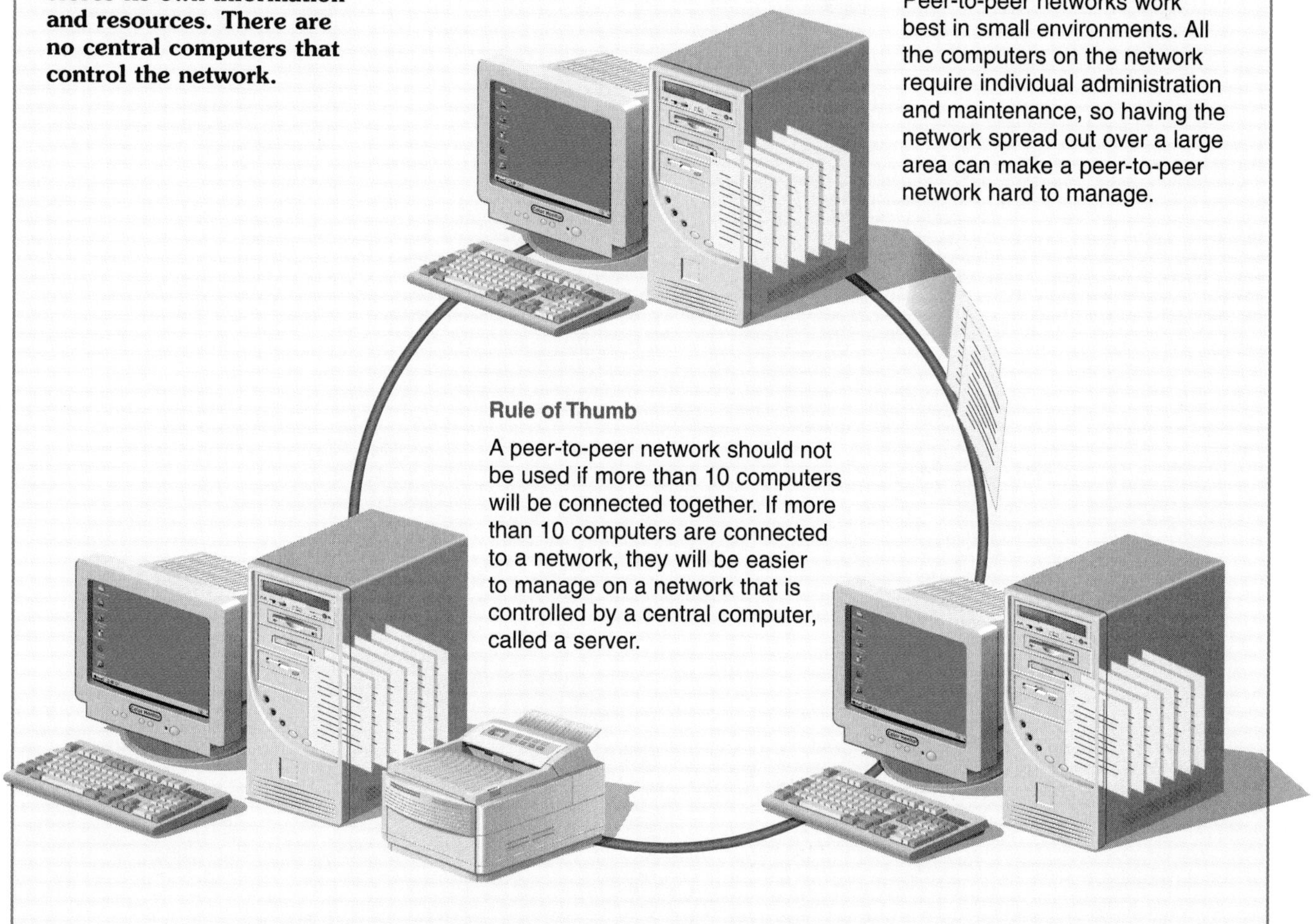

Network Size

Peer-to-peer networks work best in small environments. All the computers on the network require individual administration and maintenance, so having the network spread out over a large area can make a peer-to-peer network hard to manage.

Rule of Thumb

A peer-to-peer network should not be used if more than 10 computers will be connected together. If more than 10 computers are connected to a network, they will be easier to manage on a network that is controlled by a central computer, called a server.

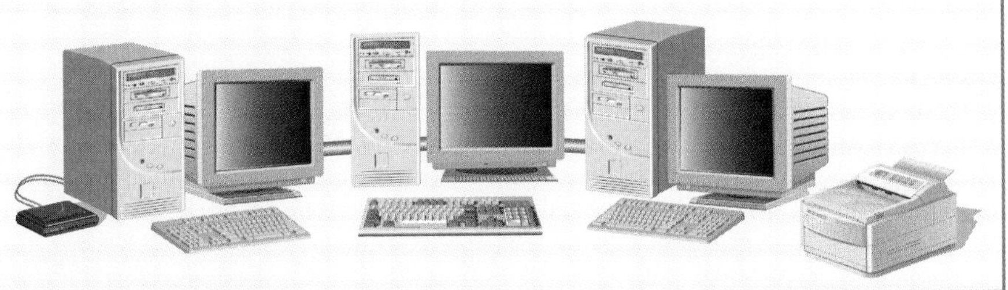

Resources

Resources such as printers and modems are usually connected to one computer on a peer-to-peer network. The computer then shares these resources with other computers on the network.

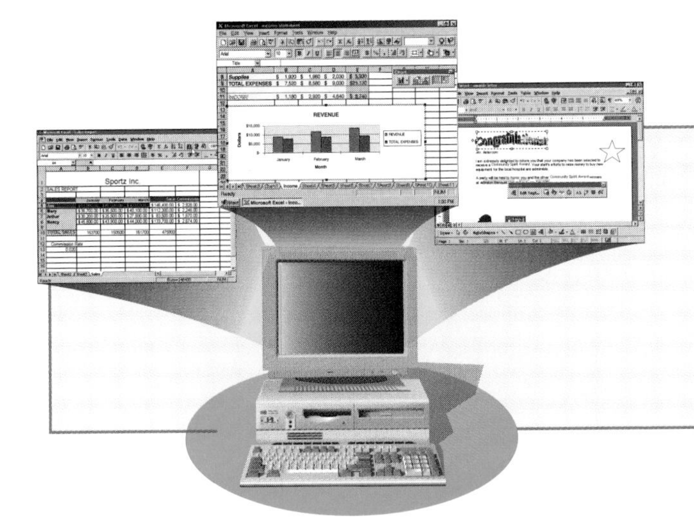

Programs

Most software applications, such as word processors and spreadsheet programs, used on a peer-to-peer network are installed on each computer. Users can use the programs on their computers to view and work with documents created by other users on the network.

Performance

When a computer is being used to provide access to information and resources, the performance of the computer can be affected. For example, if a printer is connected to a computer on a peer-to-peer network, the computer may run slower each time a user on the network prints a document.

Installation

The network operating system and all applications must be installed on each computer on a peer-to-peer network. Each computer must also be set up individually to share and access information and resources on the network.

Administration

Since computers on a peer-to-peer network are configured to share and access information individually, users will have to learn how to administer their own computers. There is usually no dedicated system administrator for a peer-to-peer network.

Access Resources

If a computer on a peer-to-peer network is not turned on or malfunctions, the other computers on the network will not be able to access the computer's files and resources. However, files and resources on other computers on the network will not be affected.

Expansion

Peer-to-peer networks should be used only in situations where the network is not expected to grow in size. Many peer-to-peer networks have to be replaced when they grow to include several more computers.

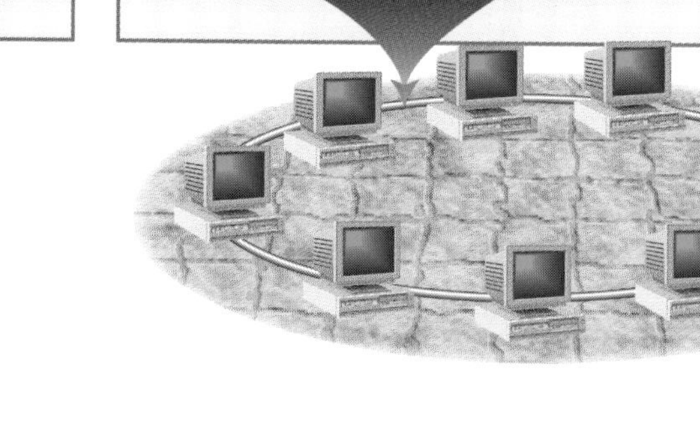

Security

Since users on a peer-to-peer network store files and information on their own computers, anyone may be able to access the information on another user's computer by using that computer. This makes information on a peer-to-peer network less secure than a network where information is stored in a central location.

Cost

The cost of a peer-to-peer network is generally low when only a few computers are being connected. As a peer-to-peer network grows, the system can become quite expensive.

Advanced Features

Peer-to-peer networks are often used to let people share information and resources such as printers and modems. Peer-to-peer networks often do not offer features found in more advanced networks, such as office e-mail and remote access.

Popular Operating Systems

Popular operating systems that provide peer-to-peer networking capabilities include LANtastic, Windows 98 and Windows Me.

CLIENT/SERVER NETWORKS

A client/server network consists of a central computer that serves information and resources to other computers, called clients. A client/server network is often the most efficient way to connect 10 or more computers.

Server

A server is a computer that makes information and resources available to other computers on a network. A server is usually a more powerful computer than the other computers on a client/server network. A common example of a server is a central computer where computers on a client/server network store and retrieve files.

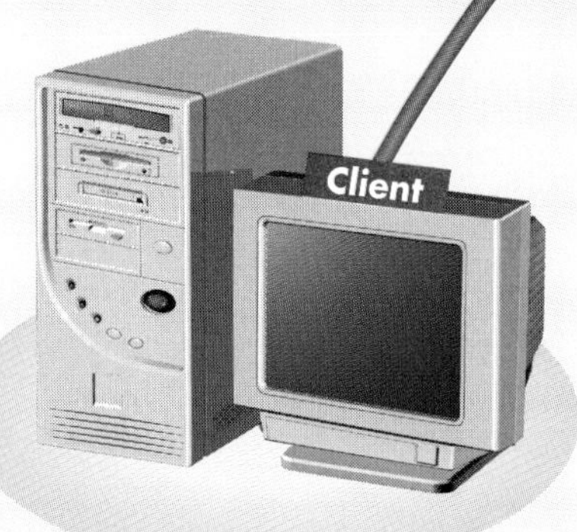

Client

A client is a computer that can request a service or access information stored on a server. People use client computers to enter and display information processed by a server on a network. Each user on a network usually has their own client computer.

Size

Client/server networks can be used with any size of network, but are especially suited for large networks. Client/server networks are easy to set up and can be configured to meet most of the requirements of large companies.

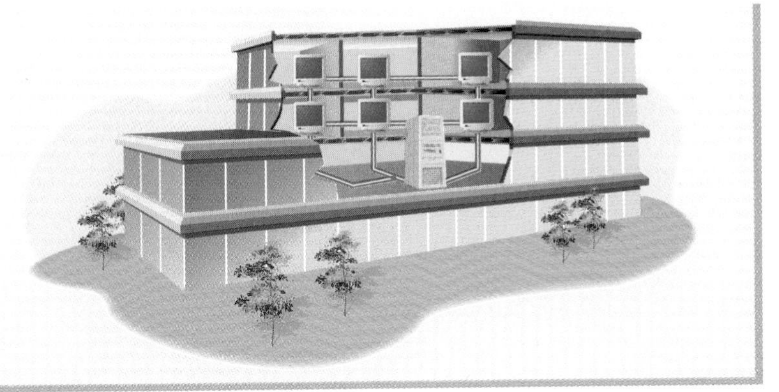

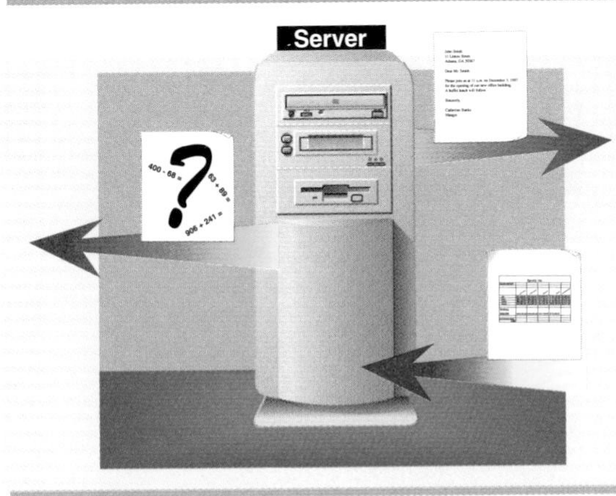

Efficiency

On a client/server network, servers perform most of the processing and resource-intensive tasks. Since servers have more memory and are faster than desktop computers, they are better suited to performing complex tasks than client computers. Servers also have more storage space than client computers, so servers can efficiently store and manage all the files for a network.

Services

A server is usually dedicated to providing one specific service to clients on a network. For example, a print server controls printing for all the clients on a network. An application server stores and runs all the programs on a network. A database server stores and organizes large amounts of information.

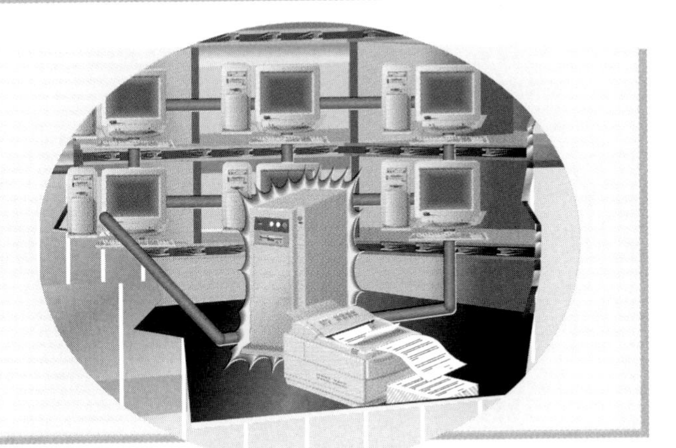

Administration

As with all networks, administrative tasks such as data backups and security monitoring must be performed on a regular basis to ensure that a client/server network runs efficiently. Most client/server networks have a network administrator who manages the network. The servers on a client/server network are usually located in one central area to make administration easier.

Security

If a network server is tampered with or malfunctions, the entire network will be affected. Most companies store network servers in locked rooms that only the network administrator has access to. This prevents unauthorized people from interfering with the server.

Expansion

Expanding a client/server network is relatively easy, since the server uses most of the complicated software and hardware on the network. It is simple to add client computers to the network because clients do not require the installation of complex hardware and software.

Cost

Client/server networks require specialized, dedicated servers that can be very expensive. Although client/server networks may seem expensive to construct, they can be a cost-effective way to provide computer services to a large number of people. Since the servers do most of the work, the client computers on a client/server network can be less powerful and less expensive.

Troubleshooting

It is usually easier to find the source of a problem on a client/server network than on a peer-to-peer network. If many client computers are having problems, the cause is often the server. If only one client computer is having a problem, the client can easily be replaced with another computer.

Popular Operating Systems

Popular operating systems that provide client/server networking capabilities include NetWare and Windows 2000. Many operating systems used on client/server networks are complex and should be installed by the network administrator.

NETWORK BENEFITS

Networks offer companies several benefits. Networks can improve the way companies operate by increasing productivity and lowering expenses.

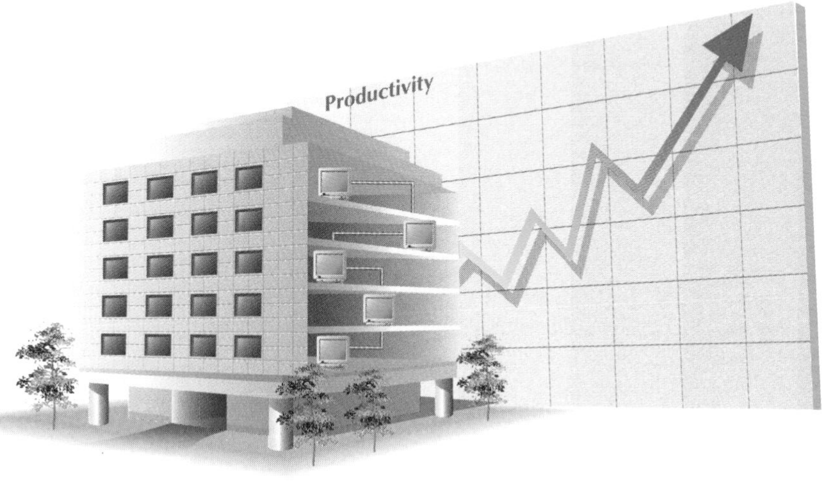

Ease of Access

Many networks make it easier for people to work with and manage their files by storing most information on a central computer. Users are then able to access their information from other computers on the network.

Work from Home

Many networks have dedicated computers that allow people to connect to the company's network using a modem and a computer outside the network. Users can then work with network information from home.

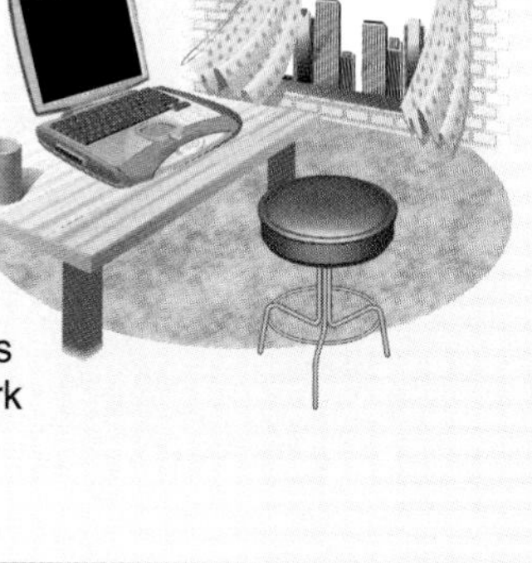

Productivity

Networks can increase productivity by allowing employees to exchange information and communicate more easily. Through a network, people from different offices can work together on the same project.

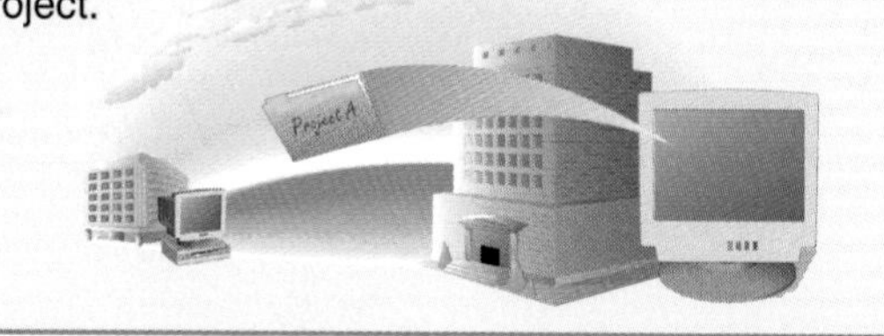

Programs

Many networks make installing programs simple because only one copy of a program needs to be installed on a central computer. All network users can then access and work with an installed program.

Cost

By allowing users to share resources, such as printers and hard drives, networks can help a company reduce the cost of buying computer hardware.

Administration

Many companies have a network administrator, who oversees all administration for the network. The network administrator assigns a user name and password to each person who will access the network. This makes it easy to monitor and control who uses the computers on the network.

Security

Most networks have built-in security programs that can monitor and report any abnormal activity. Many security programs help prevent unauthorized users from accessing information on the network.

Reliability

Most networks are designed to be durable and can operate uninterrupted for long periods of time. Some networks can alert the network administrator if problems or errors occur.

Backup

Many networks back up information on a central computer. When a backup is performed, only the information on the central computer needs to be backed up. This is quicker and more reliable than backing up data on each user's computer.

Protection of Information

Many networks use only a few computers to store all the files and information on the network. Companies can easily protect these computers from fire or theft by keeping them in a secure location.

NETWORK CONSIDERATIONS

Before a company installs a new network or upgrades its existing network, there are many factors to consider.

Planning

When planning a network installation or upgrade, it is important to research different network types by reading network publications and consulting other people who have installed and used networks.

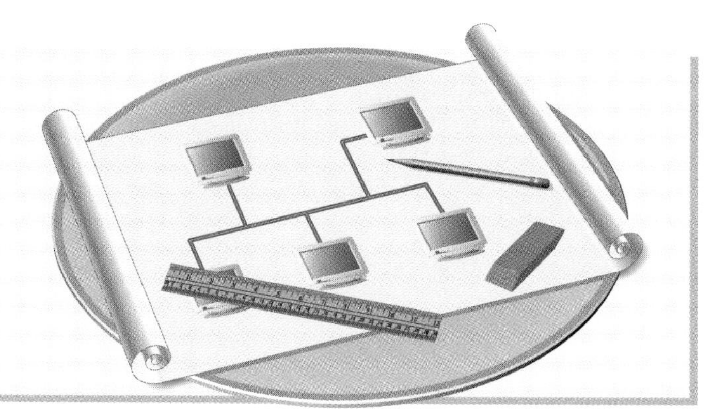

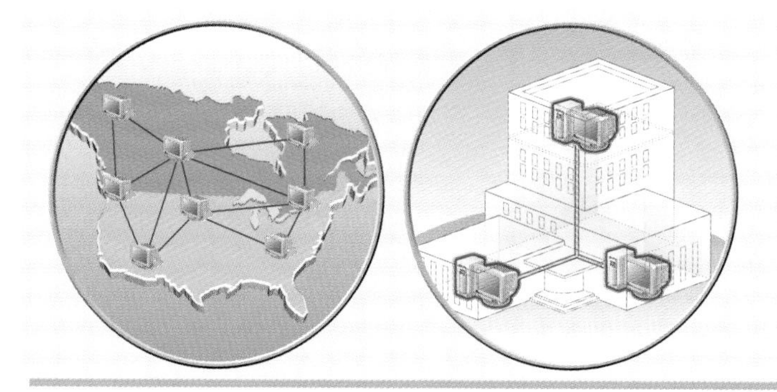

Suitability to Task

Since different types of networks are better suited to different tasks, a company should determine the types of tasks the network will perform. For example, a large company that exchanges files with offices across the country will require a different type of network than a small company that exchanges files between a few computers.

Flexibility

A network must be able to grow and change along with a business or organization. A company that plans to expand should use a network that can easily be upgraded in the future to accommodate new users and equipment.

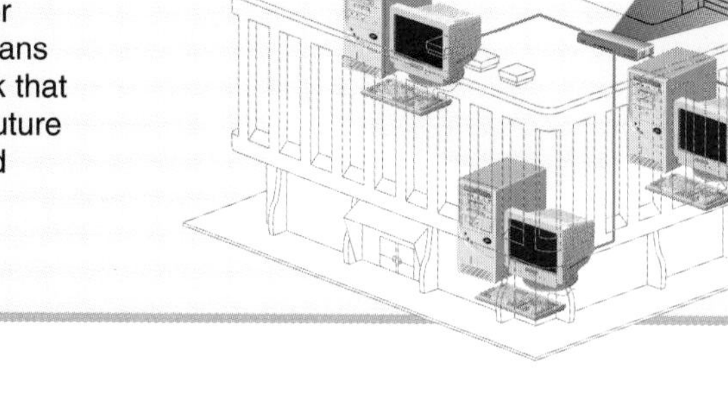

Installation

Networks can be difficult to install and configure. For example, a large network may take weeks to install. Networks should always be installed by qualified technicians.

Save Money

A network should save a company money by making better use of existing resources, such as printers and hard drives. A network should also increase employee productivity by providing better access to company data.

Administration

Most networks require regular administration and maintenance. Complex networks require a highly-skilled administrator, while simpler networks may be maintained by a network user.

Security

Once a computer is connected to a network, the computer can be accessed by other network users. A network should have security features to help prevent unauthorized access to computers.

Service

Problems often occur on networks. Most companies and organizations have employees dedicated to servicing their networks. Some businesses hire people from third-party companies to service their networks.

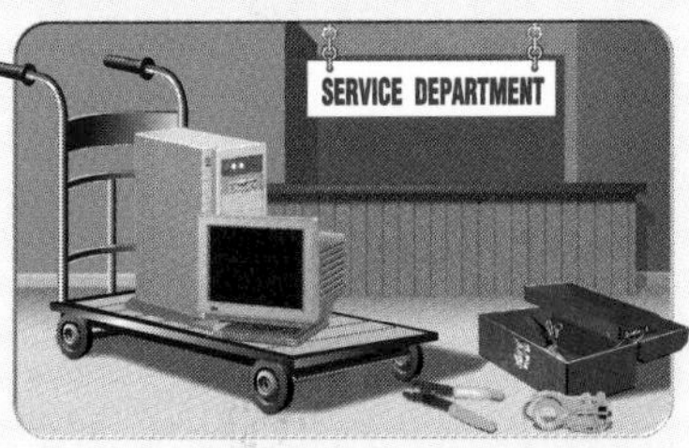

Add-on Features

Add-on features that provide extra capabilities can be purchased for many types of networks. Common add-on features include network administration packages, fax machine servers and CD-ROM servers.

CHAPTER 2

Network Structure

When designing a network, the topology, or structure, of the network must be considered. This chapter discusses the four main network structures used today.

Introduction to Network Structure 26

Star Network Structure 28

Bus Network Structure........................30

Ring Network Structure 32

Hybrid Network Structure 34

Network Layouts 36

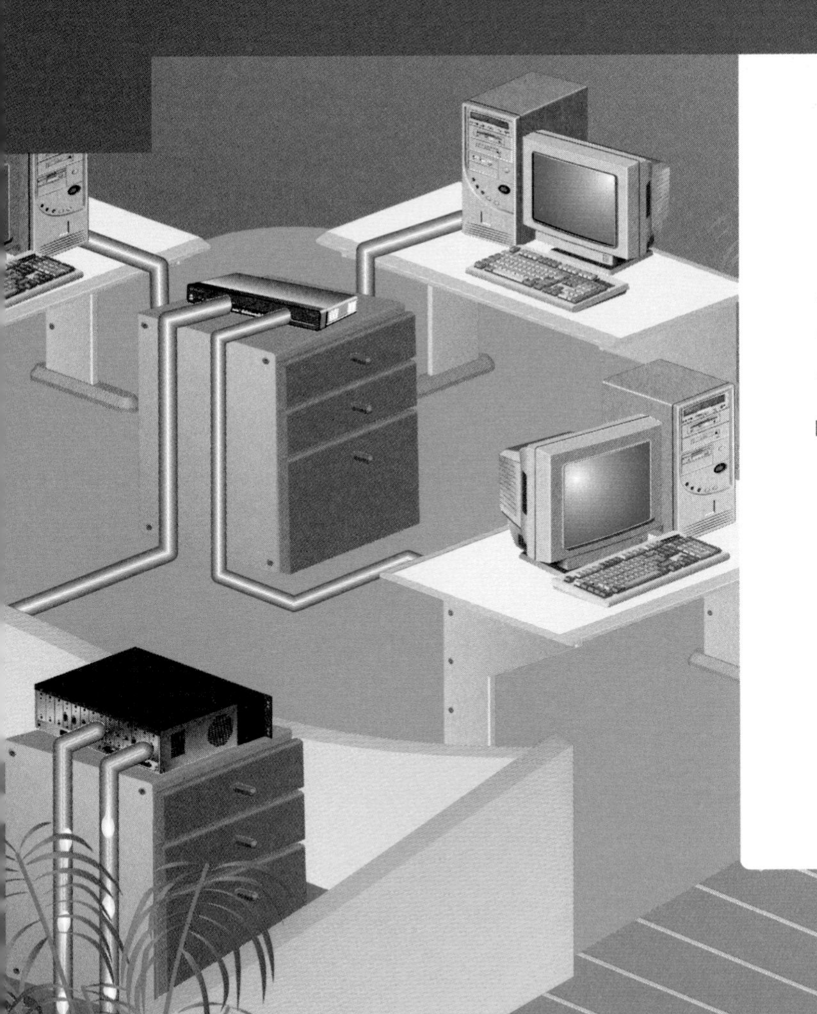

INTRODUCTION TO NETWORK STRUCTURE

Network structure, also called network topology, specifies how a network is designed or laid out. A network structure has both a physical level and a logical level.

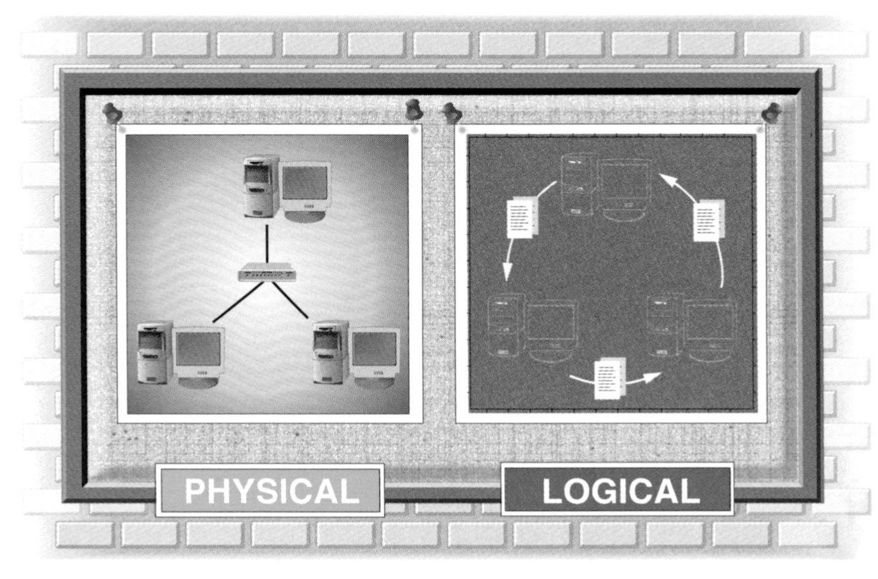

The four main types of network structures are bus, ring, star and hybrid. For information about each network structure, see pages 28 to 35.

PHYSICAL LEVEL

The physical level identifies the parts of a network that physically exist, such as computers, cables and connectors. This level also specifies where the computers on a network are located and how all the parts of the network are connected.

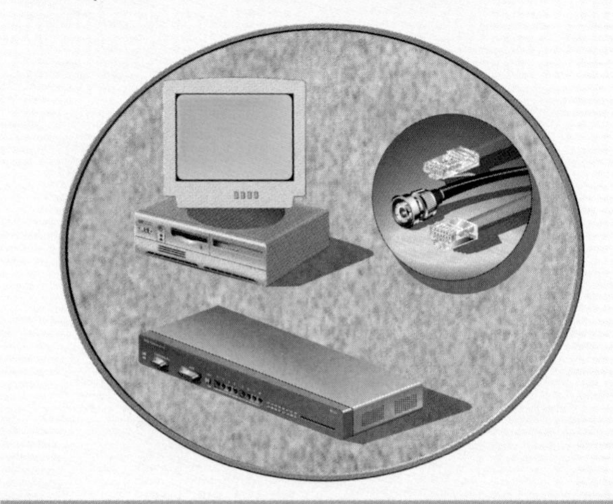

The Physical Transfer of Information

A network must have some form of transmission media to transfer information. Cables are the most popular transmission media, although infrared, radio and microwave systems are also used. The type of transmission medium used may be determined by the network's physical structure.

LOGICAL LEVEL

The logical level determines the path information takes to reach its destination on a network. The logical level of a network is determined by many factors, such as the applications used and the volume of information transferred over the network.

The Logical Transfer of Information

Computers communicate by exchanging electrical signals. Signals are transferred through the transmission medium that connects the computers. Depending on how the network is connected, there may be more than one route for signals to take.

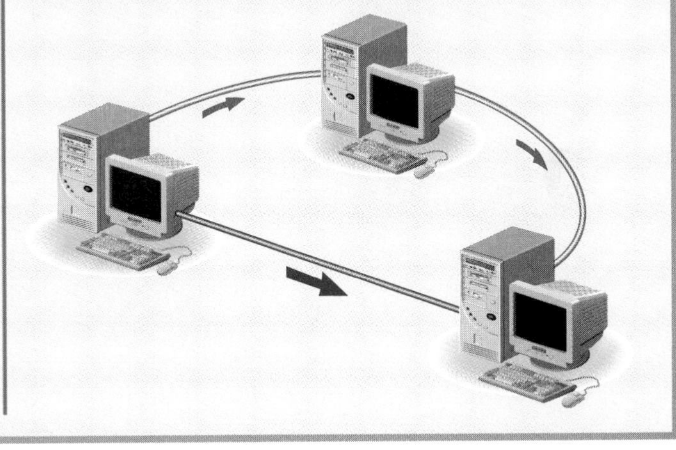

COMBINED NETWORK STRUCTURES

Networks frequently use the same type of network structure for both the physical and logical levels. However, some networks use a different structure for each level. For example, a network may use a physical star network with a logical ring network.

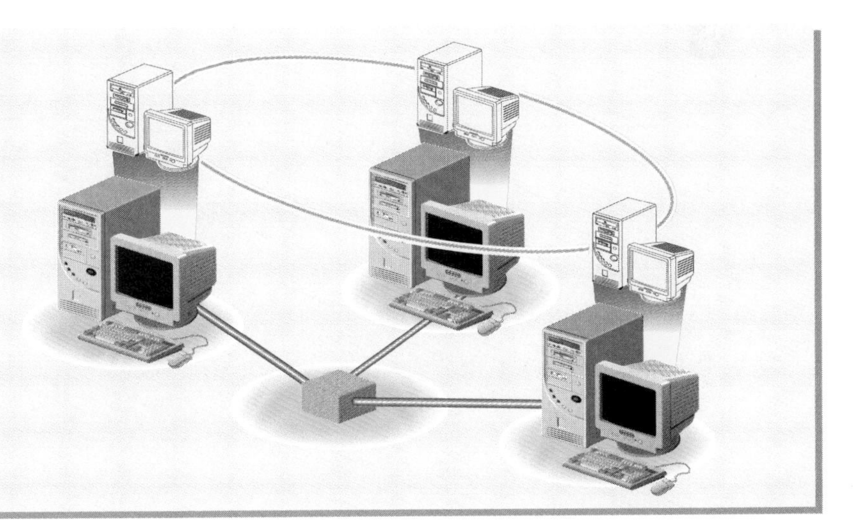

On a star network, each computer is connected by a cable to a central point on the network. Star networks are the most common type of network.

How Information Transfers

A star network consists of computers connected to a central network connector, which is usually a hub or a switch. All information that transfers from one computer to another on the network passes through the hub or switch. For information about hubs, see page 50. For information about switches, see page 52.

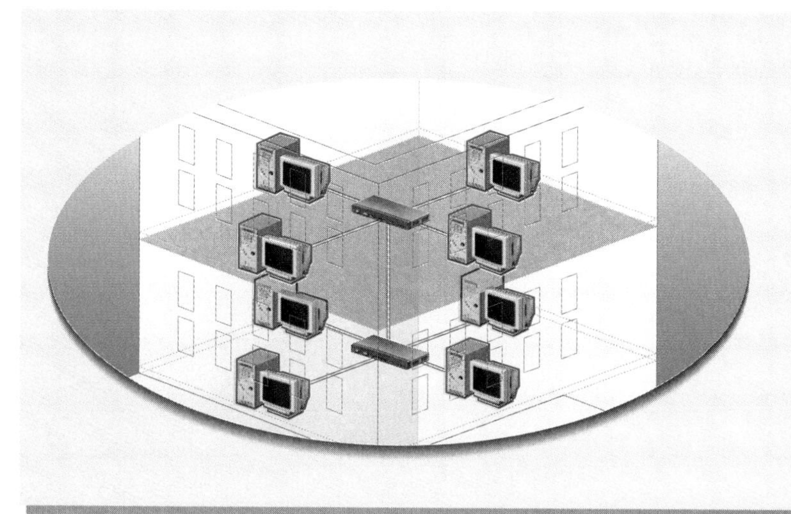

Setup

Each computer on a star network must be located relatively close to the central network connector. Cable lengths between a computer and the connector should be less than 100 meters. Hubs and switches commonly connect up to 24 computers. In a large office building, it is common for each floor of the building to have its own hub or switch. The hubs or switches can then be connected to form one large local area network.

Expansion

As long as there is a free port on the central network connector, only a cable is required to connect another computer to a star network. The network does not need to be shut down when new computers are connected.

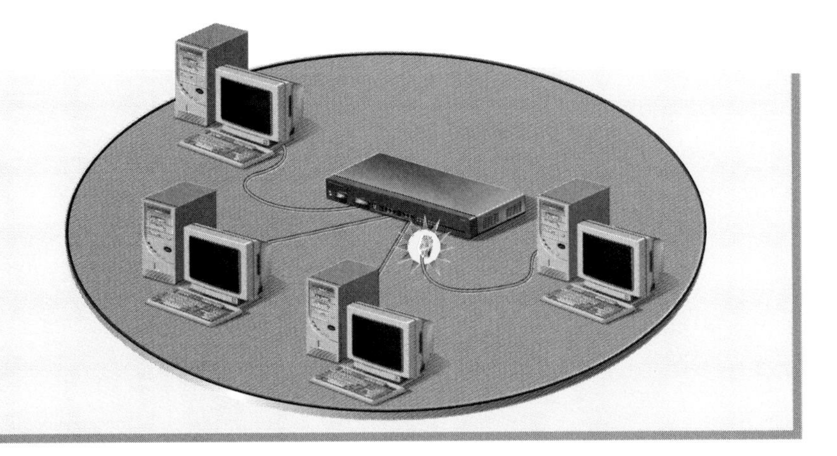

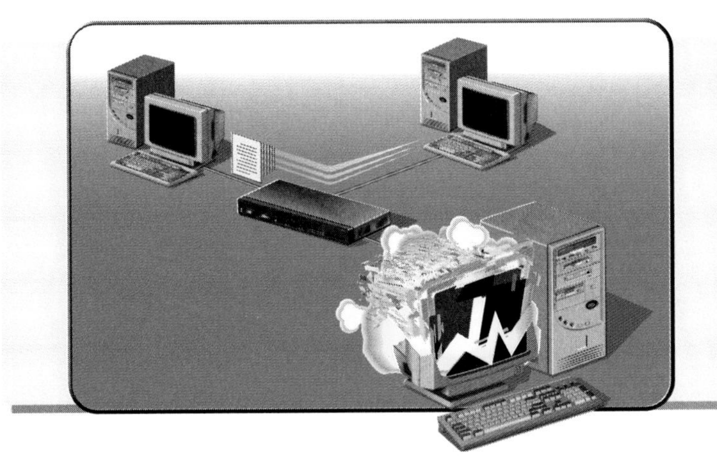

Troubleshooting

When an error occurs on a computer or cable, the rest of the network is unaffected. Many central network connectors are capable of detecting errors and then isolating the problem areas from the rest of the network. When a hub or switch fails, information can no longer be transferred among the computers connected to the hub or switch.

Cost

Star networks cost more to implement than other types of networks. Each computer on a star network must be connected to a network hub or switch, which are relatively expensive devices. Large amounts of cable are also used in star networks because each computer on the network must be independently connected to the hub or switch.

BUS NETWORK STRUCTURE

A bus network consists of a continuous length of cable that connects devices. A bus network is also called a backbone network.

Bus networks are often used on local area networks that contain only two or three computers, such as a home network.

How Information Transfers

On a bus network, only one computer can transfer information at a time. When a computer sends information, the information moves through the entire length of the cable. The destination computer retrieves the information from the cable.

Terminators

A terminator absorbs the signals transmitted on a network cable. Each end of the cable on a bus network must have a terminator. Terminators prevent signals from being bounced back along the cable and causing interference. The type of terminator required depends on the type of cable used on the network.

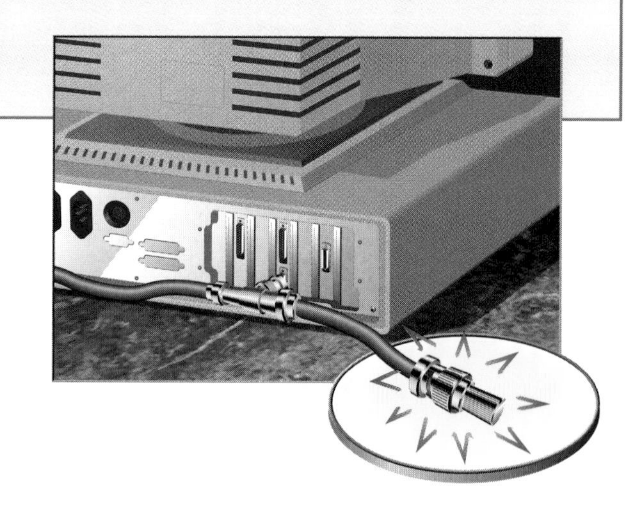

Setup

The setup of a bus network is simple because each computer is connected to a continuous length of cable. Since bus networks are usually used to connect computers located in a small area and no central network connector is required, the length of cable needed to set up a bus network is often fairly short.

Expansion

Expanding an existing bus network can be difficult. When adding a computer to a bus network, the cable must be broken to extend the cable and attach the computer. The other computers on the network cannot exchange information while the cable is broken.

Troubleshooting

If a computer is malfunctioning and disrupting the transfer of information on the cable, the entire network will be affected. This can make the cause of a problem difficult to isolate and repair.

Cost

Bus networks are quite inexpensive. Most bus networks use a continuous piece of copper cable to connect computers together.

RING NETWORK STRUCTURE

A ring network structure consists of computers connected to a single length of cable arranged in a ring. Ring networks are no longer widely used.

How Information Transfers

The information on a ring network travels in one direction only. When a computer transfers information, it sends the information to the computer located next to it. If a computer receives information that is not addressed to it, the computer passes the information to the next computer in the ring. The computers continue to pass the information until it reaches the intended destination.

Setup

Computers connected by a ring network are usually located close together. A ring network is easy to set up because the computers are attached to a single ring of cable and no central connector, such as a hub, is required. There is no beginning or end in a ring network.

Expansion

Expanding a ring network can be difficult. When adding a new computer to a ring network, the cable must be broken to attach the computer. The network will not function properly until the new computer is connected.

Troubleshooting

When a break in the ring occurs, information can still be transferred along the cable to computers before the break, but not to computers after the break. This makes it easy to determine the location of a problem on a ring network. Many ring networks have dual rings that transmit information in different directions to help prevent disruptions in network service.

Cost

Ring networks can be slightly more expensive to set up than other types of networks. Since all the computers on a ring network must be attached to a single ring of cable, the network will require a larger amount of cable if the computers are far apart.

HYBRID NETWORK STRUCTURE

A hybrid network is made up of two or more different network structures.

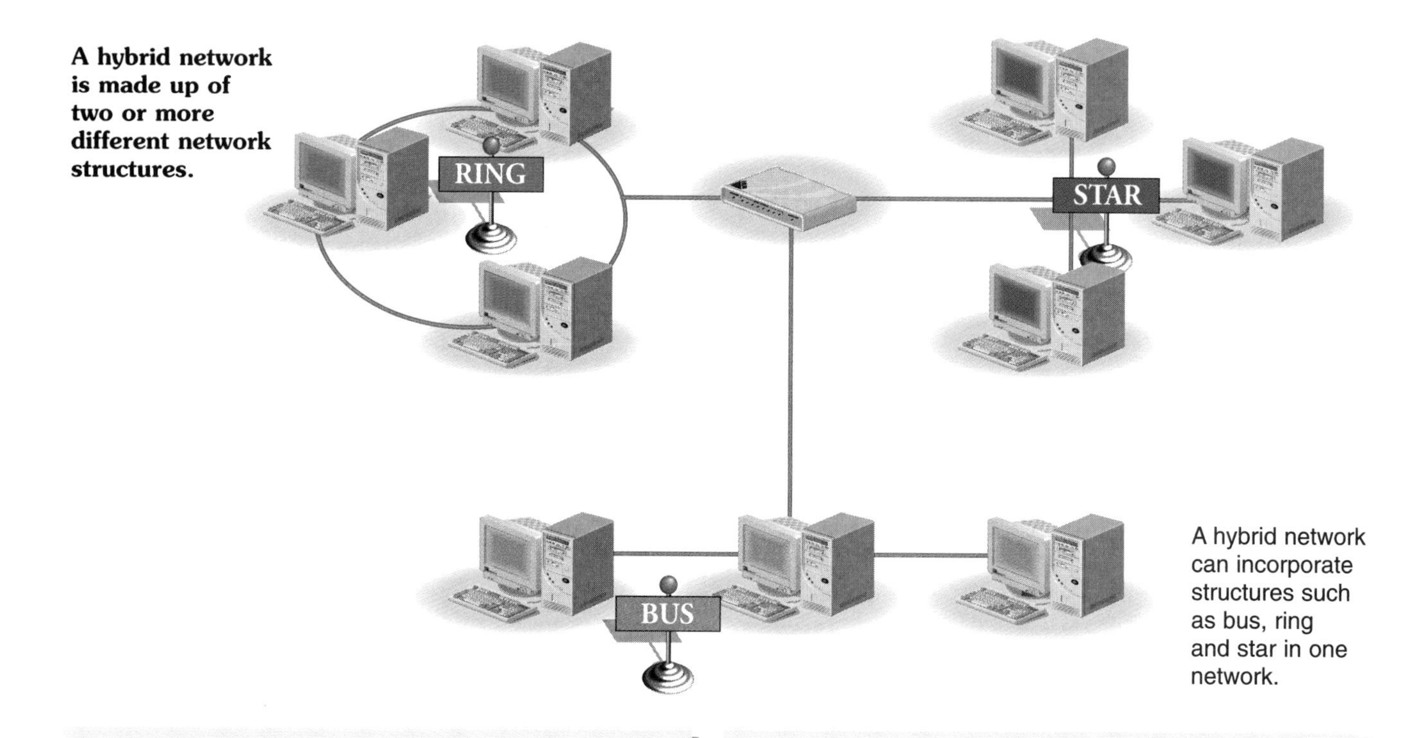

A hybrid network can incorporate structures such as bus, ring and star in one network.

Wide Area Networks

Wide Area Networks (WANs) are commonly hybrid networks. WANs often connect multiple network structures to create one large network. For example, a company could use the star network structure in one office and the bus network structure in another office. The individual networks could then be connected by a microwave or satellite to form a hybrid network.

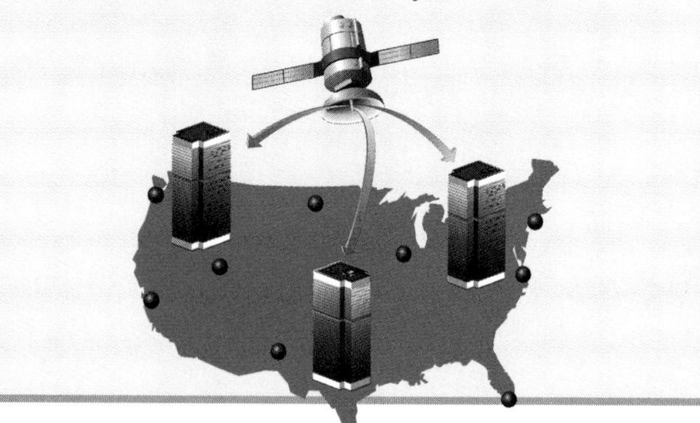

Remote Access

Modems and telephone lines can be used to connect two networks with different structures to create a hybrid network. For example, a person with a home network that uses the bus structure could use a modem to connect to an office network that uses the star structure. When connected, the two networks become one hybrid network.

Setup

A hybrid network is usually created when a network is expanded to accommodate an increase in traffic. Hybrid networks can use a variety of devices, such as hubs, routers and bridges, to join different network structures. A hybrid network is difficult to set up because the devices have to be configured to allow the different network structures to work together.

Troubleshooting

A hybrid network uses many different technologies and therefore can be difficult to manage and troubleshoot. When an error occurs on a hybrid network, the source of the problem can be difficult to locate. A company that uses a large hybrid network usually has its own network support department that is responsible for administrating and maintaining the network.

Cost

Hybrid networks are usually expensive because they are large, complicated networks. Some hybrid networks may need more security features than other networks because they span large distances. A backup network structure may also be required, which can increase the cost of a hybrid network. For example, a company may connect its offices by satellite, but also have a leased telephone line connection in case of satellite failure.

NETWORK LAYOUTS

CENTRALIZED NETWORK LAYOUT

A centralized network layout places important resources, such as file servers, in one central location.

The bus, ring, star and hybrid structures can all be used with a centralized network layout.

Administration

Administration is easier on a centralized network than on a distributed network. On a centralized network, most of the important resources, such as file and database servers, are placed in one secure location that only the network administrator can access. Placing network resources in a secure location can help keep the resources safe from unauthorized tampering, theft and fire.

Cost

Centralized networks require specialized, dedicated servers that can be very expensive. Although centralized networks may seem expensive to construct, they can be a cost-effective way to provide computer services to a large number of people. Since the dedicated servers do most of the work, the desktop computers on a centralized network do not need to be very powerful.

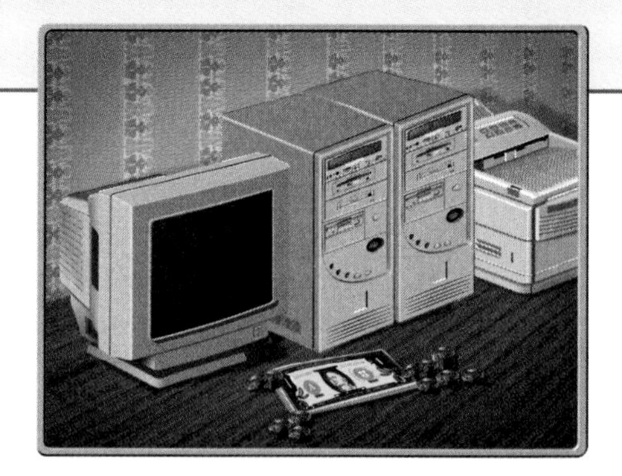

DISTRIBUTED NETWORK LAYOUT

A distributed network layout places the most important functions, such as file and printer sharing, throughout the network. For example, each department in a company may have its own file and print servers.

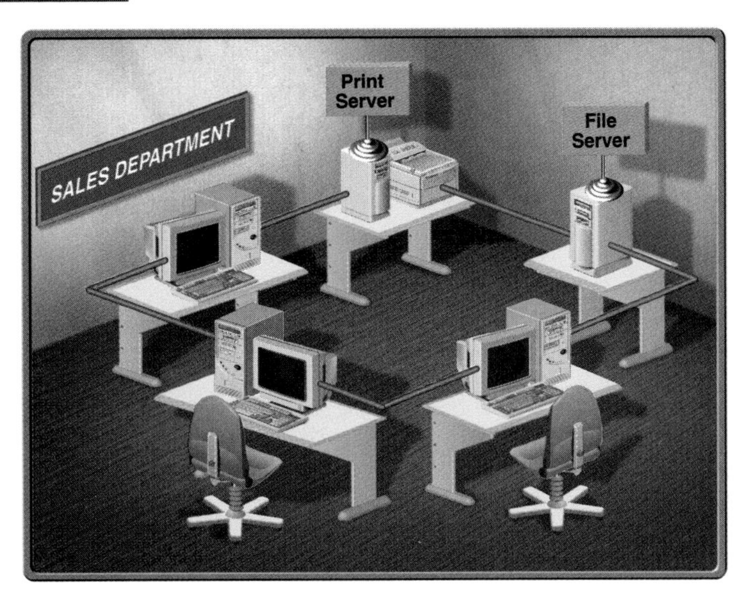

A distributed network layout can be used with any type of network structure.

Administration

Administration on a distributed network can be quite difficult because each user on the network has physical access to network resources. To keep the network running smoothly, users on a distributed network often have to know more about the network operating system than people on a centralized network.

Cost

A distributed network layout usually costs less than a centralized network layout because there is no need for expensive, dedicated servers. Desktop computers used on a distributed network are usually quite powerful.

100
Mbps

CHAPTER 3

Network Hardware

To construct an efficient network, several physical devices are required. Read this chapter to discover the importance of servers, how switches can direct information and the role of network interface cards.

Servers 40

Storage Devices 44

Network Printers..........................46

Network Interface Cards 48

Hubs...50

Switches 52

Repeaters 54

Bridges 55

Routers 56

Brouters.....................................60

Gateways 61

Modems 62

Digital Service and Channel
Service Units 64

Multiplexers................................65

A server is a powerful computer that provides a specific service to users on a network.

Servers commonly found on networks include file servers, print servers and application servers.

Future Needs

Before installing a server, it is important to determine how the server will be used in the future. Many servers have limits on the amount of memory and the processor types that can be installed. Choosing a server that can be modified to meet the changing needs of the network helps to ensure the server will not have to be replaced with a newer model when inexpensive upgrades could be performed.

Speed

The speed of a server is determined by many factors. The two major factors that determine the speed of a server are the amount of memory in the server and the type and number of Central Processing Units (CPUs). Today, servers often contain multiple CPUs.

Memory

Most desktop computers operate with 64 MB of memory. Servers often have at least 256 MB of memory and can have up to 16 GB of memory installed. In most cases, the more memory a server has, the more efficiently the server will run.

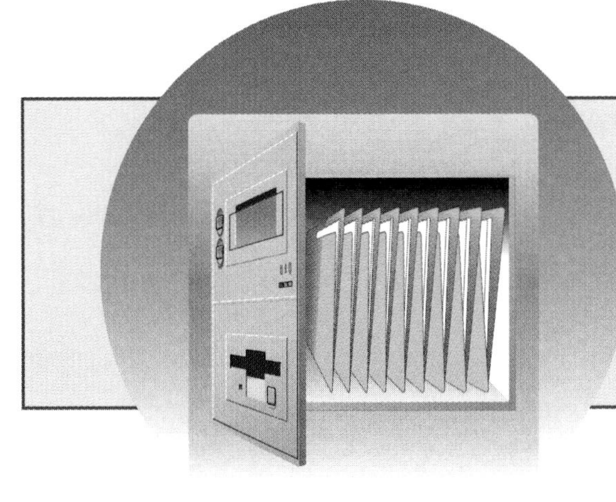

Storage Devices

The storage system is one of the main components of a server. Most servers have access to large storage devices because servers tend to run large programs and store a lot of information. For more information about storage devices, see page 44.

Other Hardware Considerations

Once the network administrator has set up a server, the server will typically run unattended. Since people do not regularly interact with a server, servers usually require only inexpensive monitors, video cards and keyboards. Servers are also often stored in climate controlled rooms that only the network administrator has access to. This prevents accidental or unauthorized tampering with the server.

Operating System

The operating system on a server is often determined by the applications the server runs or the tasks the server performs. Some applications may only be available for one type of operating system. The applications on the server must be compatible with the operating system that runs on the server. For more information about operating systems, see pages 106 to 117.

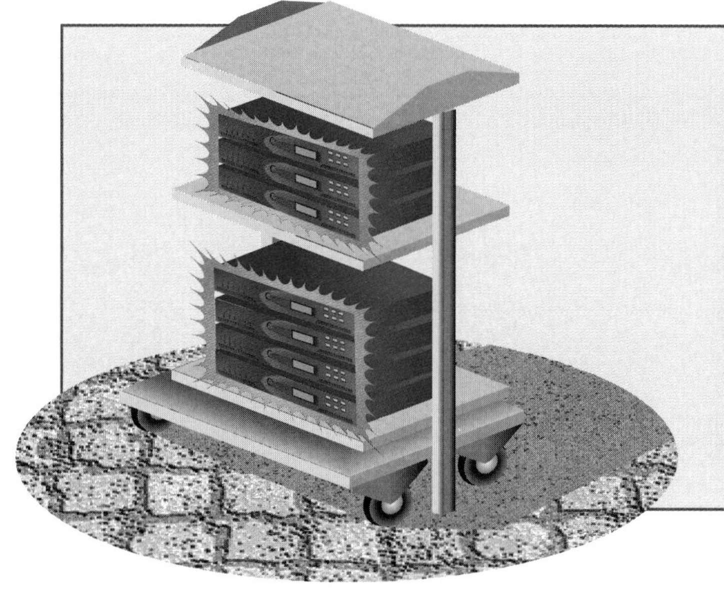

Server Units

There are compact, easy-to-manage servers now available that come with networking hardware and software already installed. These servers are commonly referred to as server units and are most often used as Web servers. Server units can include an operating system, application software, server management software and services, such as an e-mail service. They usually include hardware components such as large storage devices and network interface cards. Cobalt Networks, Inc. is a popular manufacturer of server units. You can visit Cobalt Networks, Inc. on the Web at www.cobalt.com.

RELIABILITY

Fault Tolerance

A network server is accessed by many users. If a problem occurs with the server, it could affect the work of all the users. There are several ways to ensure that the server will not fail or lose power. For example, a server may have two power supplies, so if one breaks down, the other will still be available to supply power to the server. For more information about fault tolerance, see page 152.

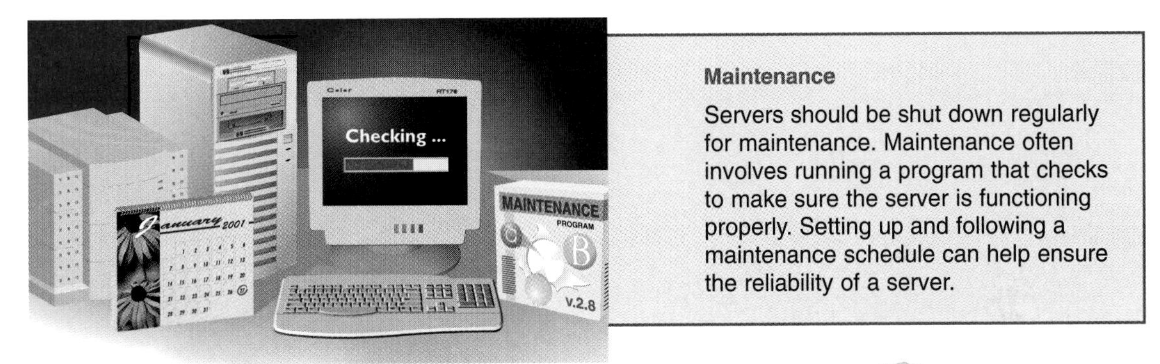

Maintenance

Servers should be shut down regularly for maintenance. Maintenance often involves running a program that checks to make sure the server is functioning properly. Setting up and following a maintenance schedule can help ensure the reliability of a server.

Repair

Just like all computers, there will be a time when a server will need repair. Most servers offer features that make repair simple, such as easy-access panels, which allow fast access to critical areas such as hard drives. Some advanced servers allow components, such as adapter cards, power supplies and memory, to be removed and replaced while the server is still running.

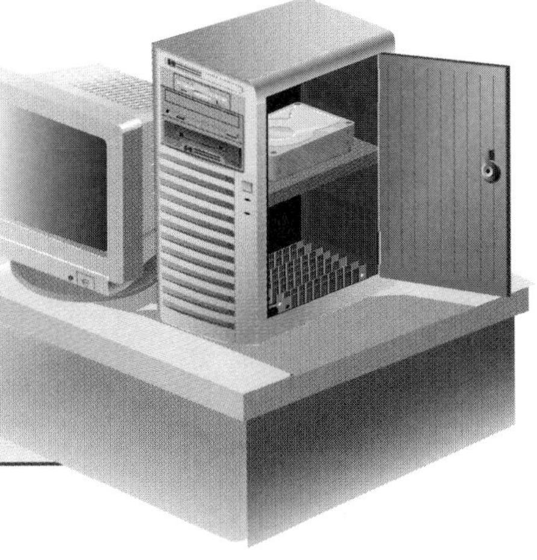

STORAGE DEVICES

Most networks use a file server to store files and other information on the network. All file servers must have a storage device.

The type of storage device used depends on the type and size of data being stored.

Hard Disk Drives

Hard disk drives are the main storage devices on most file servers. Hard disk drives are fast, but they are expensive compared to other storage devices. Because they are accessed more frequently, the hard disk drives on a file server must be larger and more reliable than the hard disk drives on a desktop computer.

Tape Drives

A tape drive is a device that copies information from a file server onto tape cartridges. Tape drives have been used for decades as a reliable way to create backup copies of computer information. The network's system administrator can use a backup program to automatically back up information onto tape cartridges when the file server is not busy, such as at night. A tape cartridge can store more information than any other storage medium.

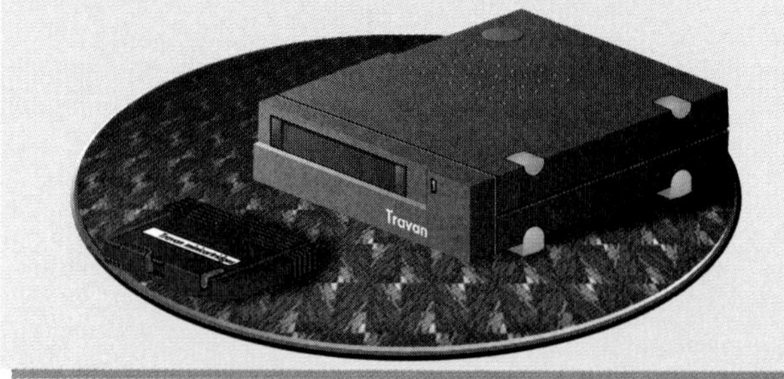

CD-ROM or DVD-ROM Drives

A CD-ROM drive is a device that reads information stored on CD-ROM discs. A DVD-ROM drive is a device that reads information stored on DVD-ROM discs. CD-ROM and DVD-ROM discs can store large amounts of information, but once recorded, the information cannot be modified. CD-ROM and DVD-ROM discs are most often used for retrieving information, such as legal or medical reference material, from a file server.

Optical Drives

Some optical drives record information. Recordable optical drives are often used for archiving rarely used information. Compared to other types of storage devices, optical drives tend to be slow, but have a high storage capacity.

NETWORK ATTACHED STORAGE

A Network Attached Storage (NAS) device attaches directly to the network and is used exclusively for the purpose of storing files. Since NAS devices contain only the elements required for file storage and retrieval, they can help increase the speed at which data is accessed and the overall efficiency of a network.

NETWORK PRINTERS

Companies often connect printers to a network to help reduce printing costs. Without a network printer, each user on the network would require their own printer.

The ability to share printers was one of the original reasons computers were joined together by networks.

Connect to a Network

Most network printers can be attached directly to the network using a network adapter. The network cable plugs into the network adapter at the back of the printer. Most network printers can be attached to several different types of networks.

Print Servers

Print servers are computers used to manage and store print jobs that are going to be printed by a network printer. A print server often manages print jobs for several network printers. Print servers are directly connected to the network.

Features

Network printers have become increasingly sophisticated over the past few years. Many network printers have a sorting feature that organizes printed documents. Some network printers are also capable of stapling print jobs.

Paper Capacity

Before purchasing a network printer, make sure the printer has a large enough paper capacity to meet the demands of the network. Most network printers have a paper capacity of at least 500 pages.

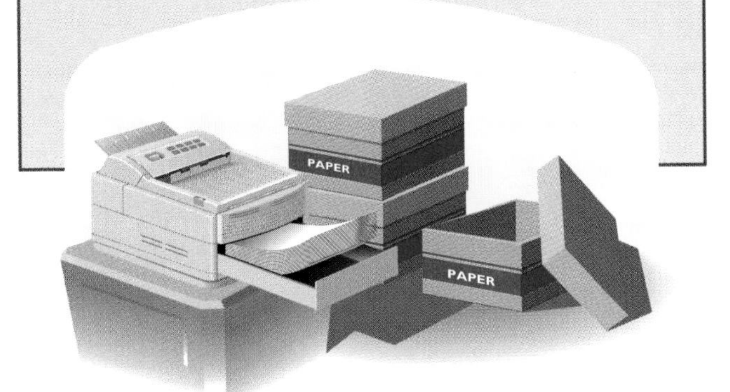

Printer Speed

Network printers have to be very fast if several people use them to print large quantities of documents. A good network laser printer will print at a speed of at least 20 pages per minute (ppm).

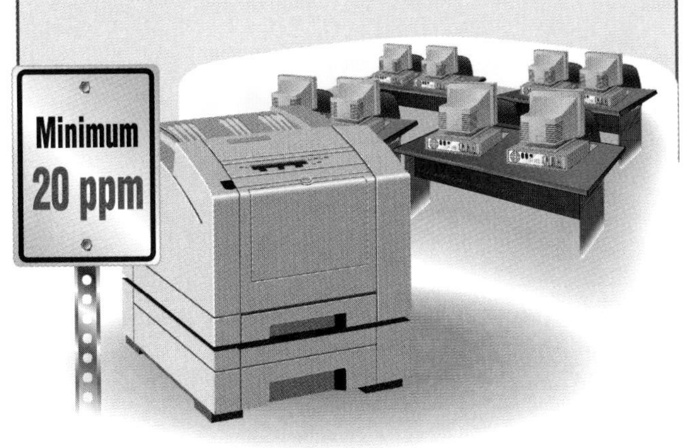

Print Quality

The resolution of a printer determines the quality of the documents it can produce. A higher resolution results in sharper, more detailed documents. Printer resolution is measured in dots per inch (dpi). Generally, a resolution of 600 dpi is acceptable for most office documents.

NETWORK INTERFACE CARDS

A Network Interface Card (NIC) physically connects a computer to the transmission medium used on a network. A network interface card is installed inside a computer and controls the flow of information between the computer and the network.

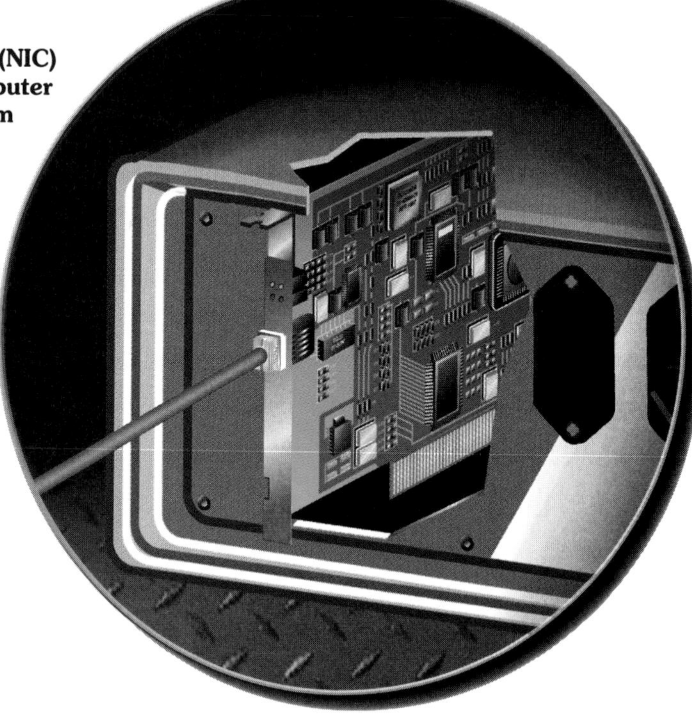

The type of transmission medium used on a network and the amount of information the transmission medium can transfer at once are factors that determine the type of network interface card required.

Servers

Servers are usually the busiest computers on a network. The network interface cards used by servers are often high performance devices that have been specifically designed to transfer large amounts of data.

Ports

A port is used to connect the network interface card to the network. Most new network interface cards have one port that is designed to work with a specific type of network cable. Some network interface cards have two ports, which enables these cards to connect to a network using one of two different cable types. A network interface card can only be used to connect to one network at a time.

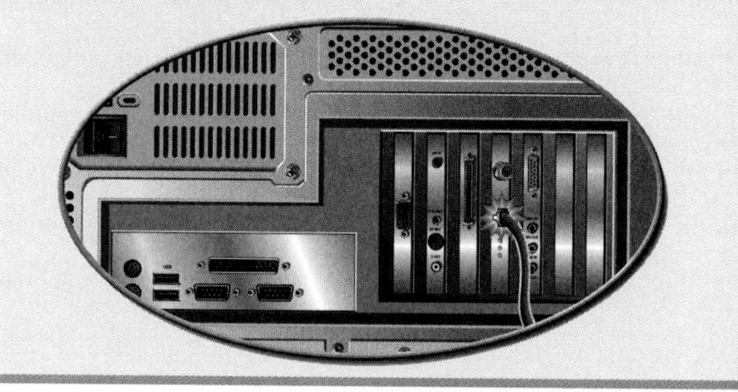

Boot Chips

Some computers connected to a network do not have their own disk drives. These computers boot using information stored on the network. In order to access information on the network, a special computer chip, called a boot chip or boot PROM, must be attached to the network interface card. The boot chip allows the network interface card to connect to the network.

Addressing

When a network interface card is manufactured, the card is given a unique hardware address. The hardware address is used to identify the network interface card when information is being sent or received on a network.

Device Drivers

Network interface cards come with drivers for different types of operating systems. A driver is the software that allows the operating system to communicate with the network interface card. To ensure the network interface card performs optimally, the correct driver must be installed. If the operating system does not automatically install the correct driver after the network interface card has been added to the computer, you will have to install the driver manually.

A hub provides a central location where all the cables on a network come together. Hubs are found on most modern networks.

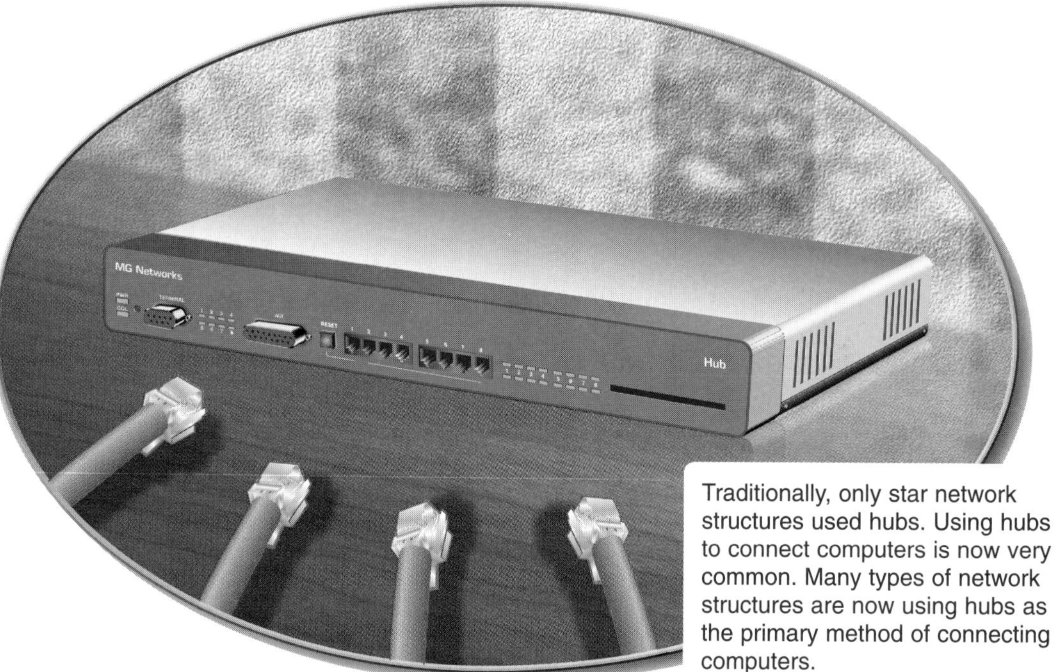

Traditionally, only star network structures used hubs. Using hubs to connect computers is now very common. Many types of network structures are now using hubs as the primary method of connecting computers.

Signal Regeneration

A hub can regenerate a signal as the signal passes through the hub. Signal regeneration helps to eliminate errors on the network that are caused by electrical interference.

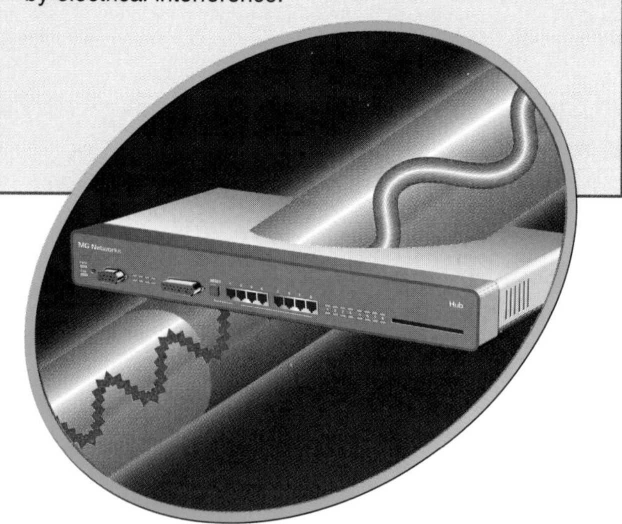

Fault Tolerance

Hubs are an important part of a network, so it is critical that they operate continuously. Many hubs have built-in features that prevent the hub from shutting down when a component in the hub fails. For example, a hub with two power supplies can continue to operate even if one power supply fails.

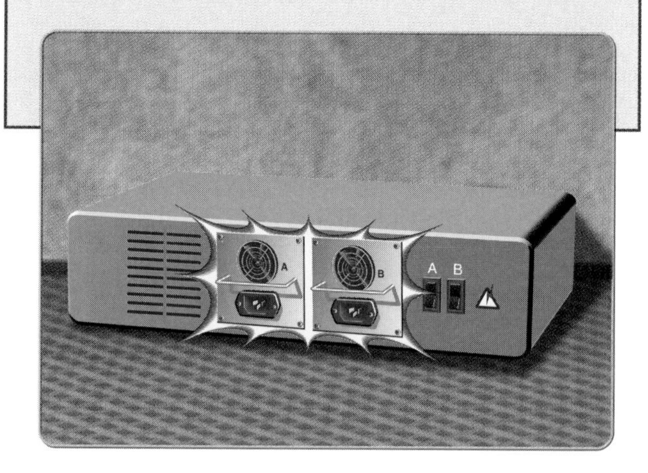

Ports

A hub contains sockets, or ports, where cables from computer devices can be plugged in. Hubs commonly have 4, 8, 16 or 24 ports. Usually each port has an indicator light, called a Light Emitting Diode (LED), which lights up when a computer is attached to the port and turned on. Some LEDs indicate when information is being transferred through the port.

Daisy Chaining

A large hub can attach up to 24 computers. A network that has more than 24 computers can use two or more hubs connected together. Connecting two or more hubs is referred to as daisy chaining.

Easy Reconfiguration

It is simple to add, move or remove a computer from a hub or a series of hubs. A cable can easily be removed from a port on one hub and plugged into a port on another hub. The network does not need to be shut down or disrupted during reconfiguration.

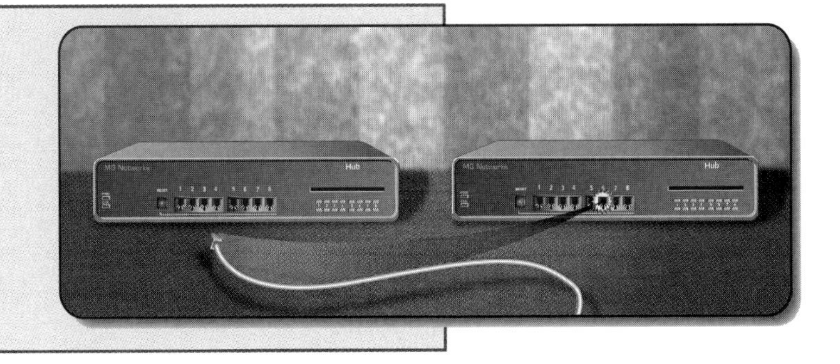

SWITCHES

A switch is a device that connects the cables on a network. Switches can also direct information to a specific destination on a network.

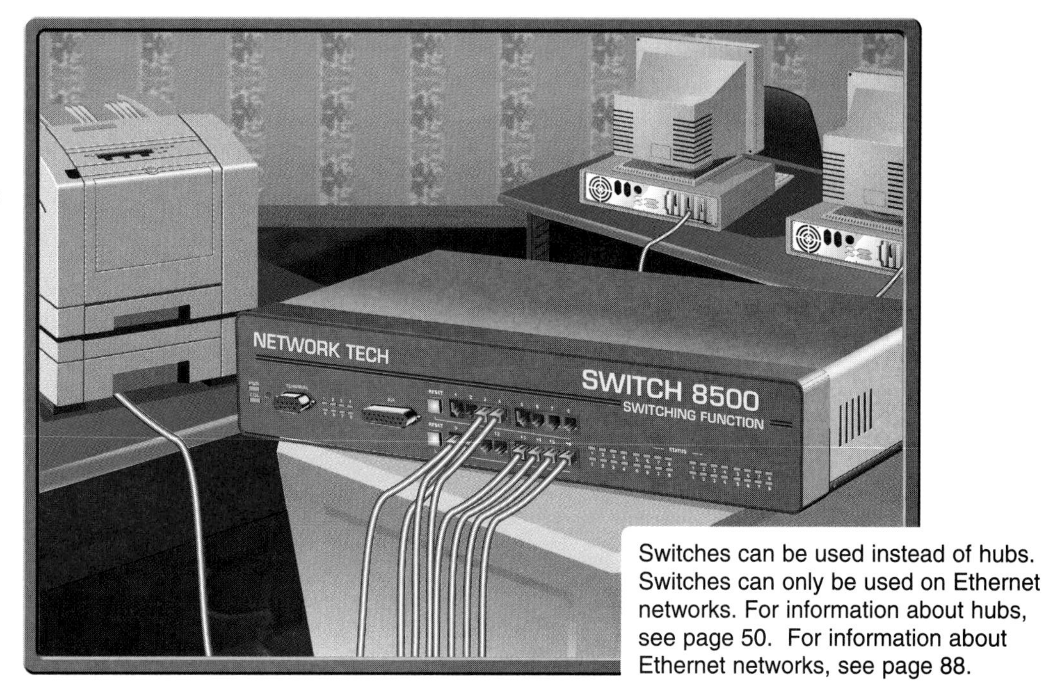

Switches can be used instead of hubs. Switches can only be used on Ethernet networks. For information about hubs, see page 50. For information about Ethernet networks, see page 88.

Congestion

As a network is expanded to accommodate new users and more sophisticated applications, the amount of information being transferred may exceed the amount of information the network was originally designed to handle. This can lead to congestion and a reduction in the performance of the network. Replacing the hubs on an overloaded network with switches can increase the efficiency of the network. You usually do not have to replace other elements of the network, such as the cable system, when you replace hubs with switches.

Speed

Switches can transfer information at the common Ethernet speeds of 10 and 100 Mbps. Some switches can automatically adjust their speed to match the speed of connected devices, while the speed of other switches must be manually configured.

Security

Using switches can help ensure that the information users transfer over a network is secure. Unlike a hub, which sends information to every computer on the network segment, a switch sends data to only the intended recipient.

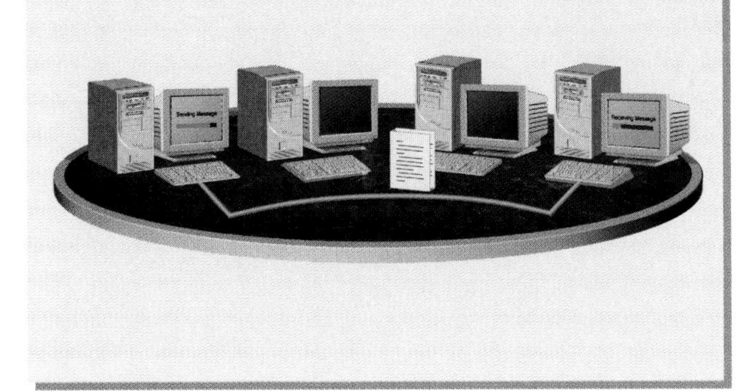

High-speed Backbone

A switch can commonly connect up to 24 computers. If a network has more than 24 computers, two or more switches can be used. Switches should be attached using a high-speed connection called Gigabit Ethernet. Gigabit Ethernet allows switches to transfer information at a rate of 1000 Mbps, providing a high-speed backbone for the network.

Routing Switches

Some switches, called routing switches, have capabilities that are similar to those of a router. For information about routers, see page 56. Routing switches can direct, or route, information to the correct destination on a network. Routing switches may also be able to find the most efficient route for information to travel.

Cisco Systems, Inc.

Cisco Systems, Inc. is a popular manufacturer of networking products, including switches. You can visit the Cisco Systems, Inc. Web site at www.cisco.com to find more information about the switches they offer.

REPEATERS

A repeater is a device that strengthens and then retransmits signals on a network. Repeaters allow signals to travel farther along network cable.

The farther a signal has to travel along a cable, the weaker the signal will become. This is often referred to as attenuation. By strengthening the signal, repeaters prevent problems that might result from weak signals.

Network Extension

Repeaters are used to extend the length of the cables that connect computer devices together on a network. Repeaters are especially useful in areas where long lengths of cable are required to connect computer devices together, such as a network in a large warehouse.

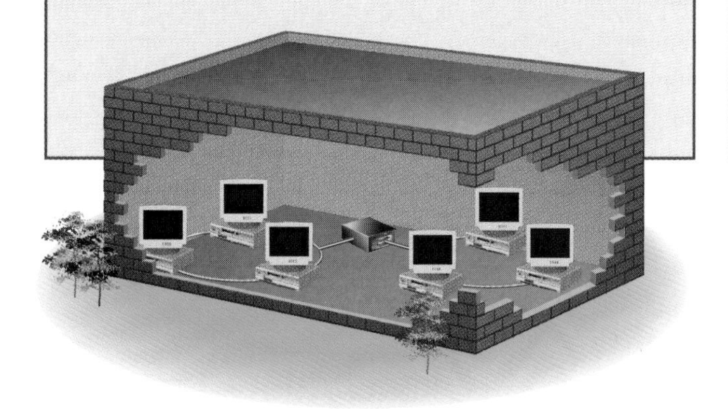

Signal Amplification and Regeneration

A repeater amplifies a signal it receives, so the signal can travel along a longer length of cable. Repeaters can also regenerate a signal by filtering out any interference or distortion before the signal is amplified and retransmitted.

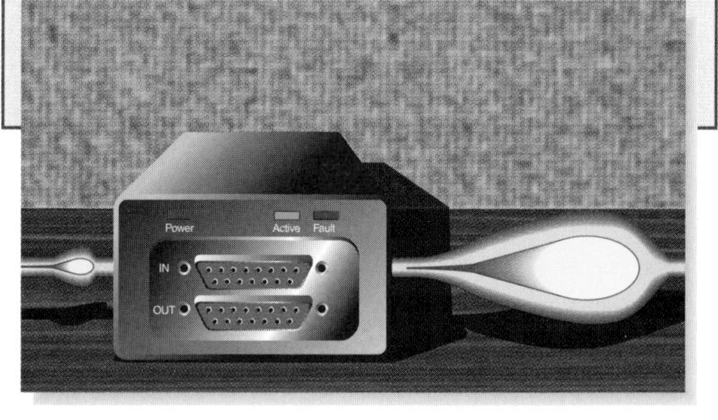

BRIDGES

A bridge is a device that allows computers on different networks or on separate segments of the same network to exchange information.

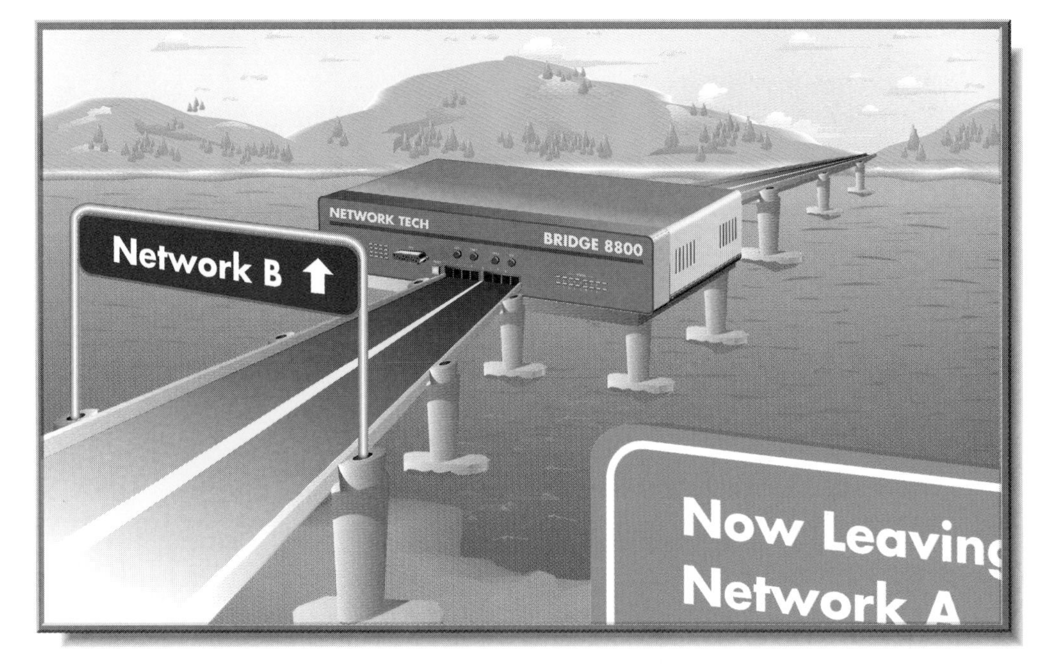

Join or Divide Networks

Bridges can be used to connect a small number of individual networks to make them work together as one large network. A network made up of smaller networks is called an internetwork.

Bridges are also used to split a busy network into smaller segments. Splitting a busy network helps to reduce excess network traffic. For example, if the computers in one department generate a lot of network traffic, a bridge can separate that department from the rest of the network.

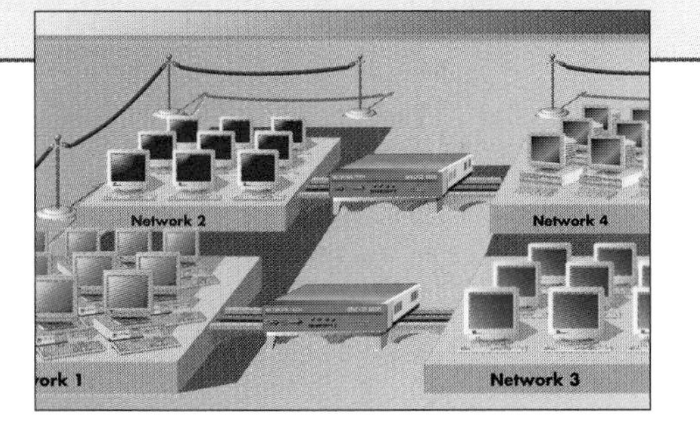

Filtering

Bridges use hardware addresses to determine if information is going to a destination on the same network segment or to the network segment on the other side of the bridge. If the destination is on the other side of the bridge, the bridge forwards the information to that segment. A bridge improves efficiency because information is only forwarded to a different segment when necessary.

Routers are devices that connect network segments and direct, or route, information to the correct destination on a network.

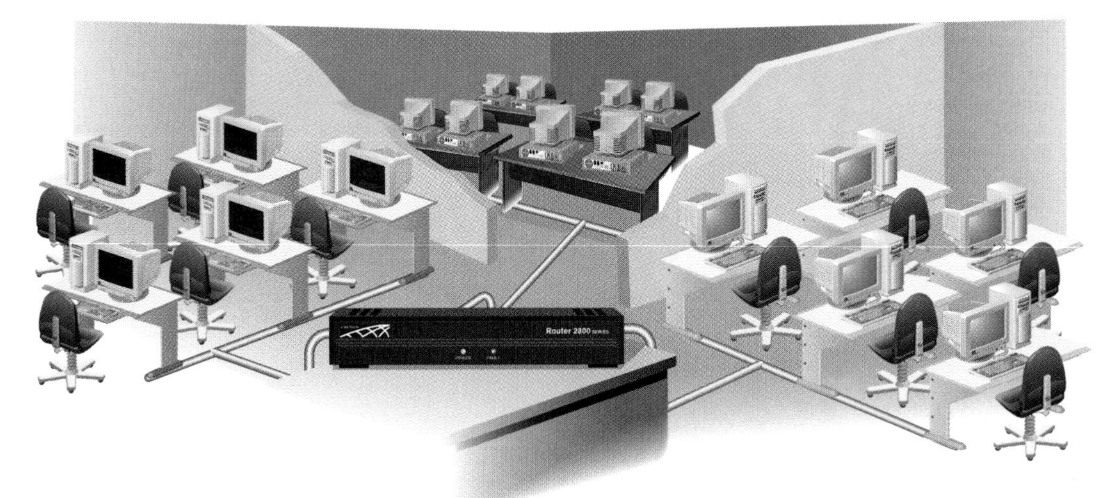

On a large network, there may be more than one route that information can take to get to its destination.

Intelligent

Most routers can automatically detect if a part of the network is not working or is slow. The routers will try to redirect information around the problem area so the impact of the network failure will be minimal. Routers are said to be "intelligent" because they can analyze a network to determine the best route for information to take.

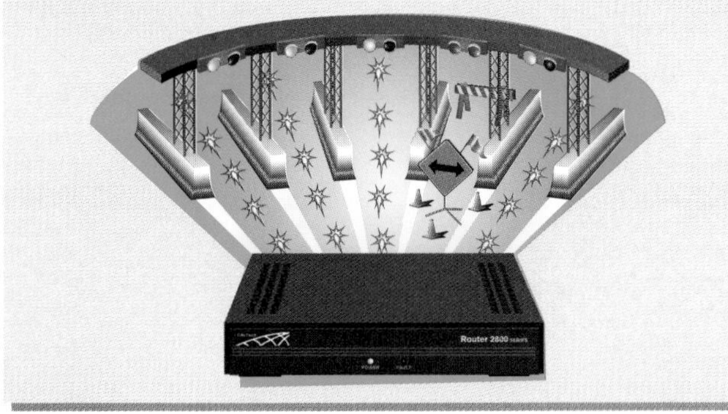

Redundant Paths

Routes that are not normally used to transfer information are called redundant paths. If a section of the network has been shut down for maintenance or is malfunctioning, the redundant paths can be used to transfer information.

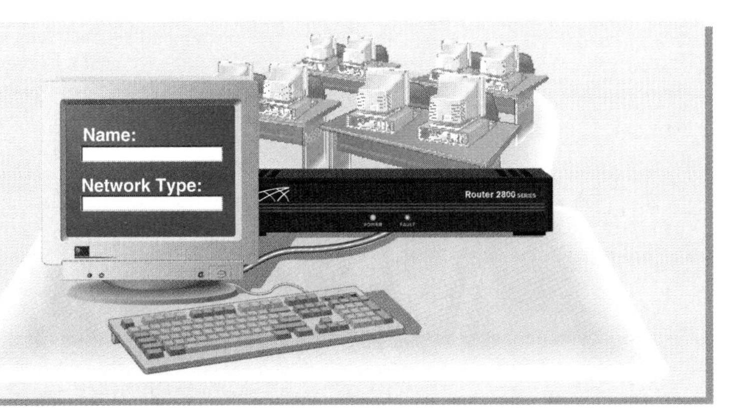

Setting Up Routers

Information such as the name of the router and what types of networks are attached to the router must be entered into the router before it will work. Many routers allow a computer to be attached to them so information can be entered.

Speed

A router must analyze the information passing through it to determine what action should be taken. If the router cannot process the information fast enough, the network will experience a slowdown. Most routers contain very fast processors to help prevent network slowdowns.

Prevent Loops

In a large network, particularly a network that was not planned properly, the same information may continuously transfer, or loop, around the network. Routers prevent looping problems by analyzing the information that is being transferred and directing it to the proper destination.

DETERMINING ROUTES

Router Types

Most routers can automatically determine the best route for information. With older routers, called static routers, a network administrator had to manually configure the router to recognize each route information could take. Newer routers, called dynamic routers, automatically create and maintain a table of the available routes on the network.

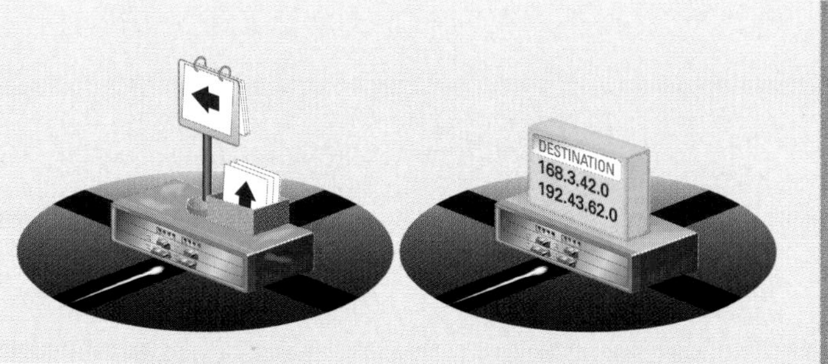

Static Router Dynamic Router

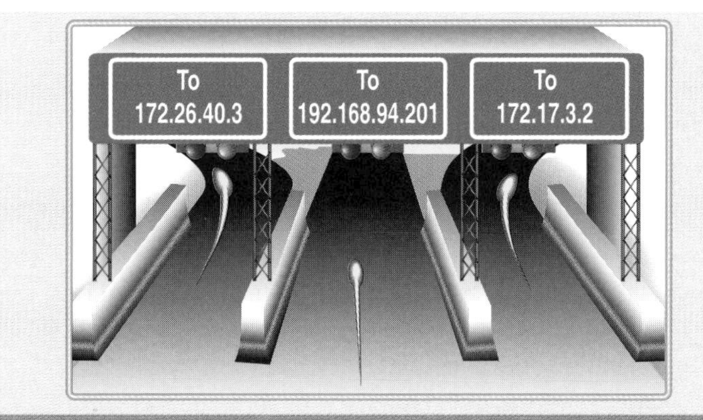

Addresses

Routers map networks and divide them into individual segments. Each segment is assigned a unique address. The network segment address and the address of the destination computer help the router direct information to the correct destination.

Algorithms

Routers use mathematical formulas, called algorithms, to determine the most efficient route for information to take. Routers use many variables, such as distance and the speed of network segments, to determine which path should be used to transfer information.

ROUTERS ON LARGE NETWORKS

Connect Different Network Types

Routers are often used to connect different types of networks, such as a Token Ring network and an Ethernet network. Along with the ability to analyze the information and then determine the best route, routers can also translate the information into a form that can be transmitted on another type of network.

Protocols

A protocol is the language computers and devices use when communicating on a network. A router must understand the protocol being used to transmit information before it can route the information. Most routers understand the TCP/IP, IPX and AppleTalk protocols. Routers cannot work with the NetBEUI or LAT protocols.

Wide Area Networks

Routers are often used to connect local area networks to a wide area network. Routers can also be used to break up a wide area network into segments. This helps reduce the amount of information being transferred over the network and improves the efficiency of the wide area network.

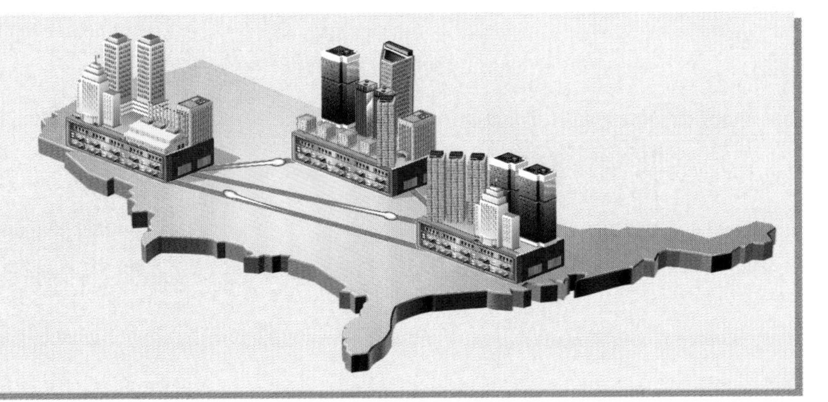

BROUTERS

A brouter is a device that transfers information between networks. A brouter combines some of the characteristics of both a bridge and a router.

For information about bridges, see page 55. For information about routers, see page 56.

Route Information

When information passes through a brouter, the brouter first tries to determine the destination of the information by analyzing the protocol used to transfer the information. If the brouter can determine the destination of the information, the brouter acts like a router and transfers the information along the most efficient route.

Bridge Information

If a brouter cannot determine the destination of the information by analyzing the protocol, the brouter uses the hardware address of the destination computer to determine which network the information should be transferred to. Once the destination network is determined, the brouter acts like a bridge and transfers the information to the network.

GATEWAYS

A gateway is used to connect two different network types. For example, you can use a gateway to link a Mac network and a PC network.

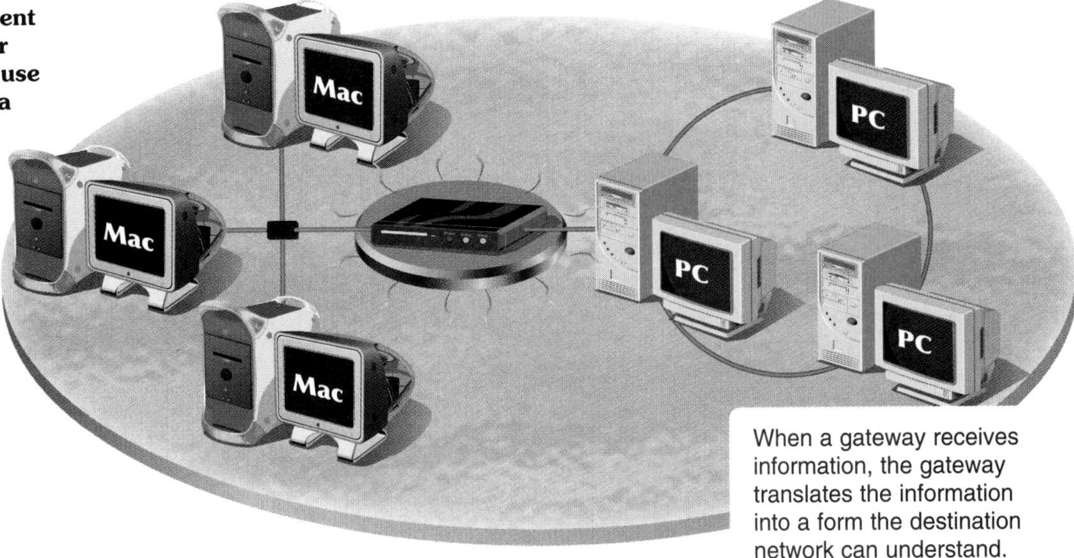

When a gateway receives information, the gateway translates the information into a form the destination network can understand.

Hardware or Software

A gateway allows two different types of networks to exchange information. A gateway can be a hardware device, such as a computer, which is physically connected to the network and transfers information between networks. A gateway can also be software that allows two different protocols to exchange information on the same network.

Default Gateways

Information is forwarded to a default gateway when a network does not recognize the information's destination address. The default gateway then passes the information to the next network. Default gateways are most common on TCP/IP networks, such as the Internet.

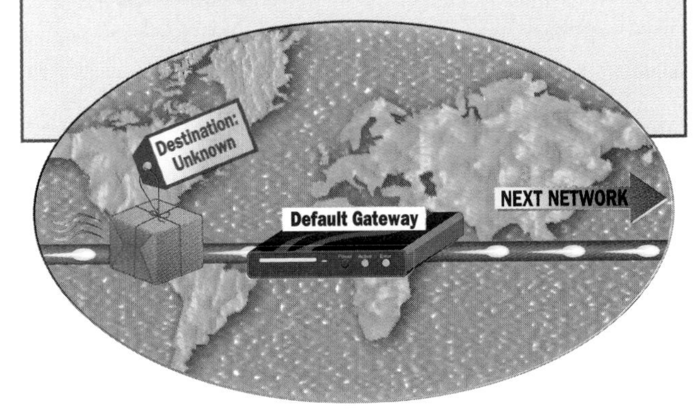

MODEMS

Modems allow computers on a network to exchange information. A modem translates computer information into a form that can transmit over telephone lines. The receiving modem translates the information it receives into a form the computer can understand.

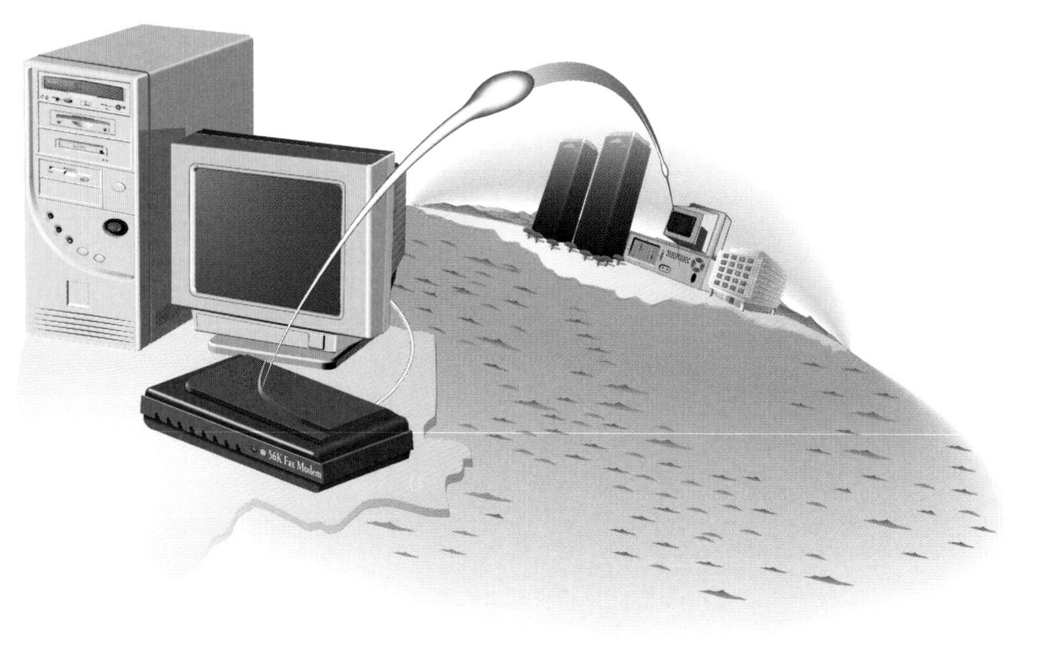

Modems use existing telephone lines to transfer information. By using telephone lines, two computer devices can exchange information across vast distances.

Remote Access

Modems are commonly used to provide people with access to the company network while traveling. By using a modem to connect to the network, a user can exchange messages with colleagues and work with office files from almost anywhere in the world.

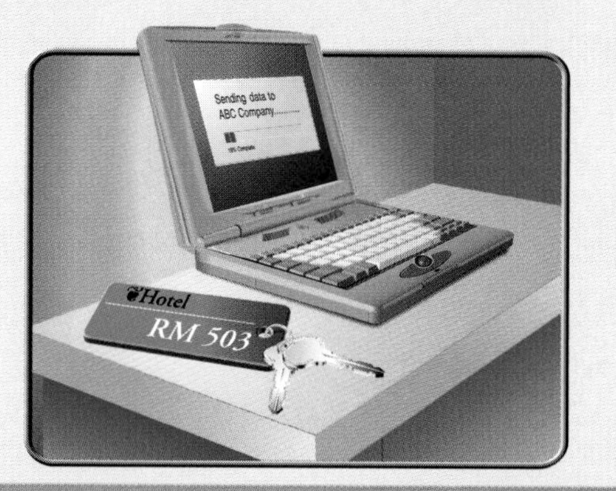

Wide Area Networks

Many companies use telephone lines to establish a permanent link between two modems in a Wide Area Network (WAN). Wide area networks often use modems to connect areas of the network that do not transfer large amounts of information.

Types of Modems

There are two types of modems—internal and external. An internal modem is a circuit board that is installed inside a computer. Internal modems can be difficult to install and set up. An external modem is a device that connects to a port at the back of a computer. External modems are portable and easy to install.

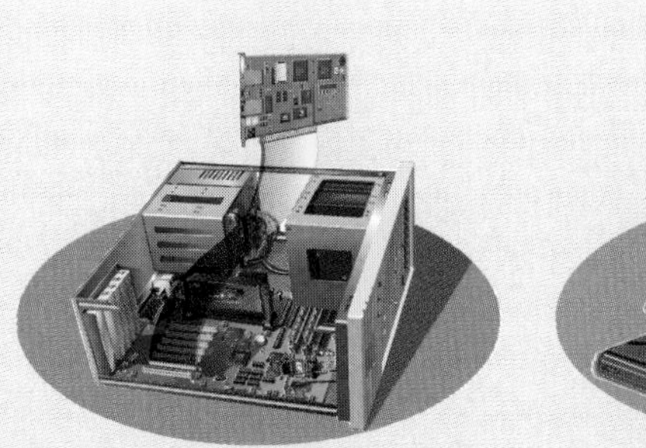

Internal Modem

External Modem

Speed

The speed of a modem is measured in kilobits per second (Kbps) and determines how fast the modem can send and receive information through telephone lines. To enable a user to work efficiently on a network, a modem should have a speed of 56 Kbps. A 56 Kbps modem can receive information at 56 Kbps and send information at 33.6 Kbps. Poor telephone line quality can reduce the speed at which a modem can transfer information.

Cost

Compared to other network devices, modems provide a cost-effective way to communicate on a network. Since modems are inexpensive and use existing telephone lines, a modem is a practical option for companies who want to extend their network or allow employees to access the network while away from the office.

DIGITAL SERVICE AND CHANNEL SERVICE UNITS

A digital service unit and a channel service unit are used to connect a computer network to a public telephone network.

Public Telephone Networks

A public telephone network is similar to the regular telephone system. A public telephone network is usually run by a company that allows businesses to lease a telephone line so they can transfer information from one city to another. This saves businesses from having to construct an expensive wide area network.

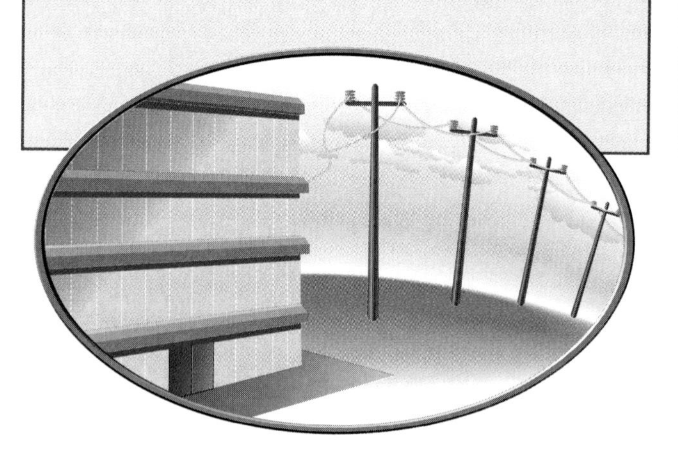

Data Conversion

Before information from a computer network can be transferred on a public telephone network, the computer information has to be converted into a form that will transfer over a telephone line. A Digital Service Unit (DSU) is the device used to convert the information.

When the information reaches the other side of the connection, a Channel Service Unit (CSU) is used to convert the information back into a form that a computer can understand.

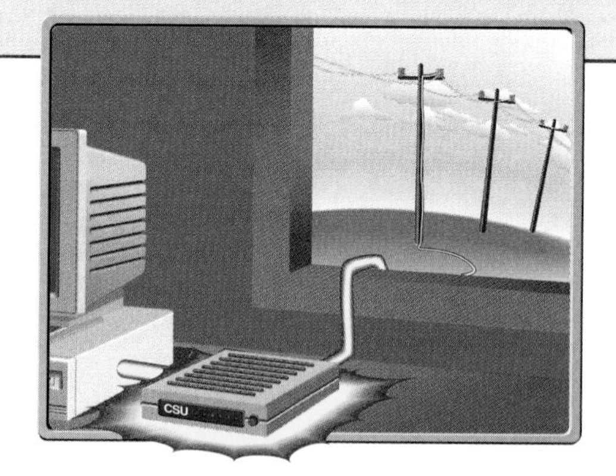

Multiplexers allow different types of information to transfer over a single transmission medium at the same time.

Information Types

Multiplexers are useful when a network has several different types of information to transmit, but only one transmission medium. Multiplexers can transfer several different types of information at once, such as voice, video and computer data.

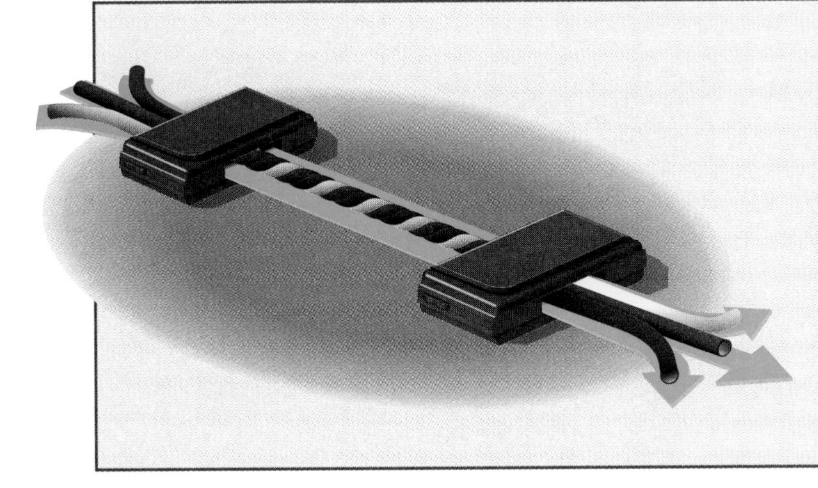

Combining Information

In many wide area networks, a single connection is used to link different segments of the network. To transfer different types of information over the connection at the same time, the information must be combined into a single signal. A multiplexer combines the information into one signal and then transfers the combined signal over the connection. When the combined signal reaches the other side of the connection, a multiplexer separates, or demultiplexes, the information.

Transmission Media

Transmission media are used to transfer information on a network. This chapter examines the different types of cables that can be used to construct a network, as well as wireless transmission media.

Introduction to Transmission Media......68

Transmission Media Considerations 70

Coaxial Cable 72

Unshielded Twisted Pair Cable............74

Shielded Twisted Pair Cable 76

Fiber-optic Cable 78

Infrared Systems................................80

Radio Systems 81

Microwave Systems 82

Satellite Systems................................83

INTRODUCTION TO TRANSMISSION MEDIA

Transmission media are the physical pathways that connect computers and devices on a network.

There are types of transmission media available to suit any size or type of network.

Compatibility

A transmission medium allows two or more computers on a network to communicate. Each transmission medium requires specialized network hardware, such as network interface cards, to transfer information. Network hardware must be compatible with the type of transmission medium being used.

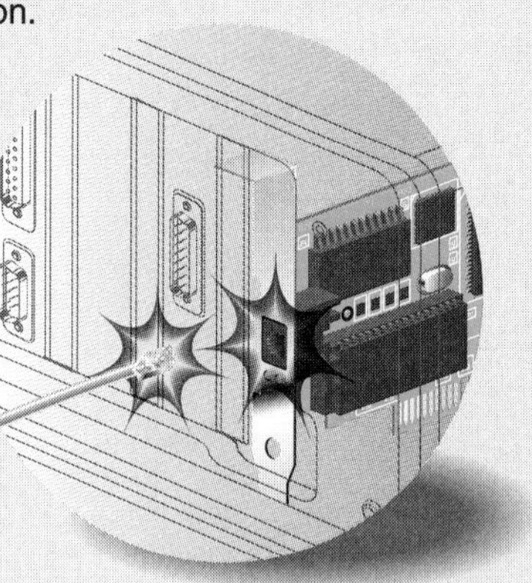

Combined Media

There are many different types of transmission media. Smaller networks are usually constructed using only one type of transmission medium. Larger networks may use different types of transmission media in various parts of the network. Networks using a combination of transmission media are more complex and are often difficult to build and maintain.

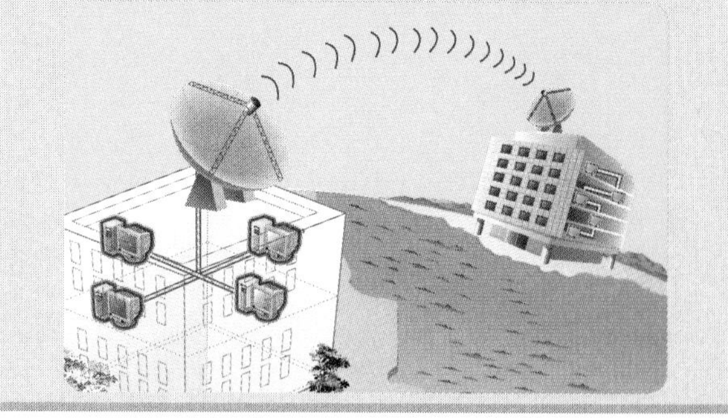

POPULAR TYPES OF TRANSMISSION MEDIA

Cable

Cable is the oldest and most commonly used type of transmission medium. Cable usually consists of copper wires covered with a protective plastic coating. Cable is inexpensive compared to other types of transmission media. The three main types of cables are coaxial, unshielded twisted pair and shielded twisted pair.

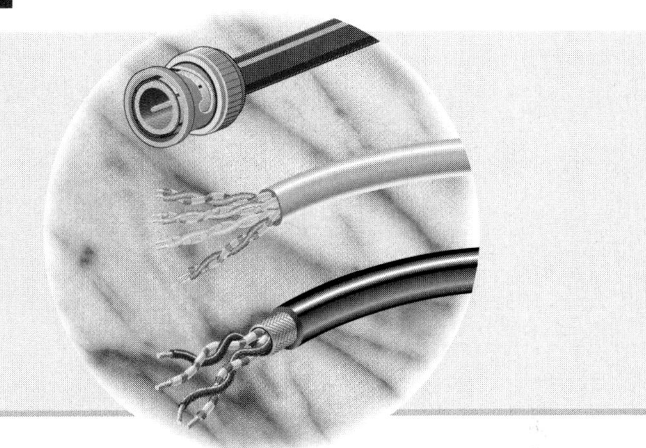

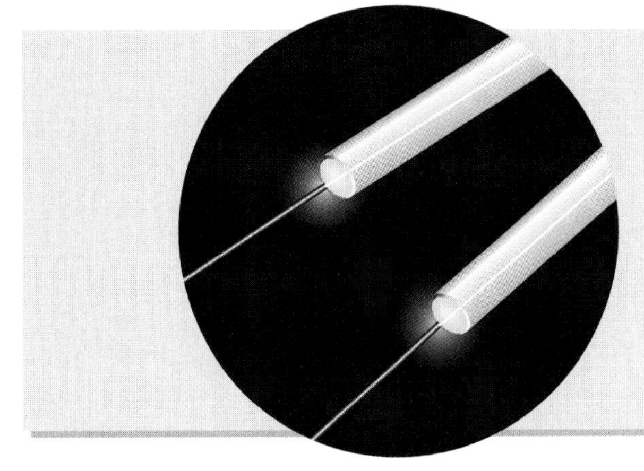

Light

Some networks use light to transfer information. Fiber-optic cable transmits information by sending light signals through a core made of glass or plastic. Networks using fiber-optic cable transfer information quickly, but they are expensive and difficult to install.

Wireless

A wireless transmission medium is often used when parts of a network cannot be physically connected. For example, a company may use a wireless transmission medium to connect office buildings that are on opposite sides of a lake. Examples of wireless transmission media include infrared, radio, microwave and satellite systems.

There are many factors to consider before deciding which type of transmission medium should be used to build or expand a network.

Cost

The price of transmission media plays an important role in determining how much it will cost to build a network. Transmission media range in price from a few cents per foot for cable to billion dollar satellite systems.

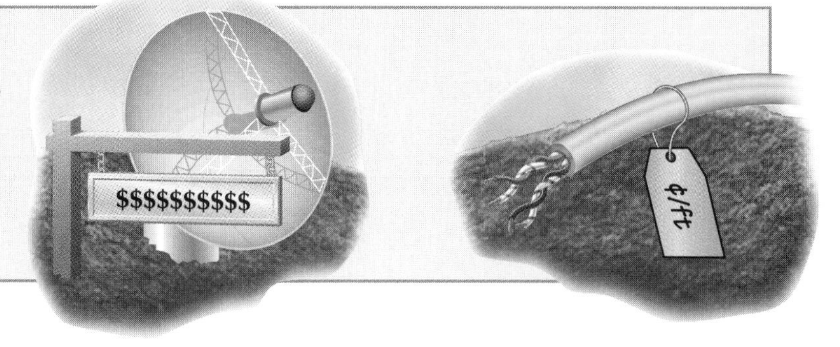

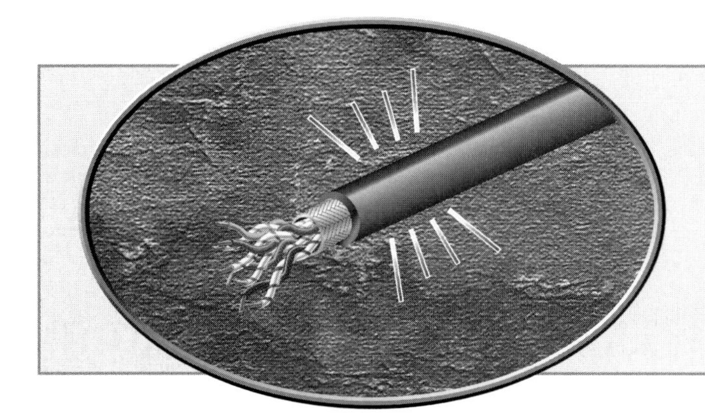

Installation

Some types of transmission media are more difficult to work with than other types of transmission media. For example, shielded twisted pair cable is bulky and inflexible, which can make installation awkward if many cables need to be grouped together in a small space.

Expansion

As the needs of a company grow, the network may need to be expanded to accommodate new equipment or users. Since some types of network transmission media are difficult to alter after installation, it is important to consider the possibility of expansion before beginning to build the network. For example, fiber-optic networks are not easy to change once installed.

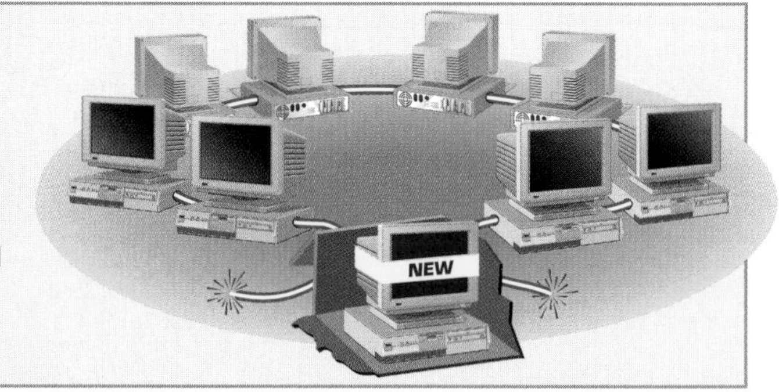

Bandwidth

Bandwidth describes the rate at which information can be transferred using a specific transmission medium or the amount of information that can be transferred at once. Bandwidth is usually measured in megabits per second (Mbps) or gigabits per second (Gbps).

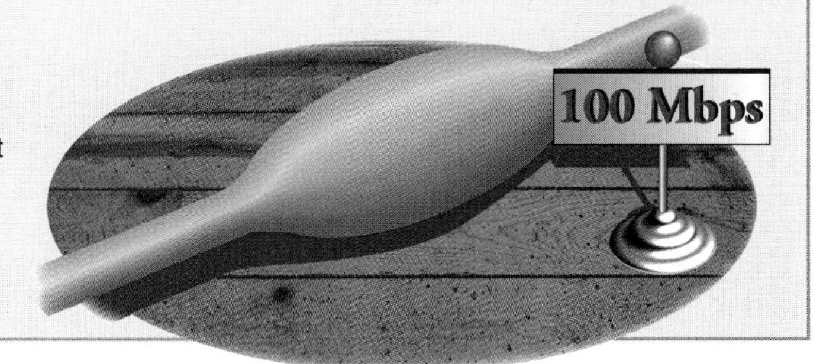

Signal Degradation

The further a signal has to travel along a transmission medium, the weaker the signal will become. The weakening of the signal is referred to as attenuation. Each type of transmission medium can transmit signals a certain distance. The distance signals are required to travel may determine the type of transmission medium to use on a network.

Interference

Modern office buildings include many devices that may interfere with signals traveling along transmission media. Devices such as photocopiers, elevators and fluorescent lights may emit signals that could disrupt the transfer of information. Some types of transmission media are designed to better withstand interference.

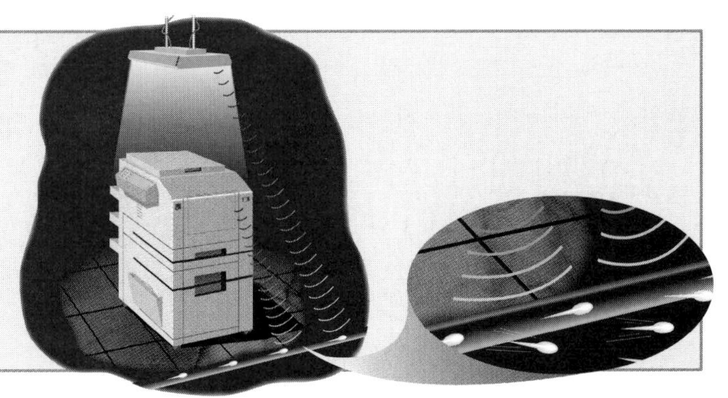

COAXIAL CABLE

Although no longer widely used to create new networks, coaxial cable is commonly found on older networks.

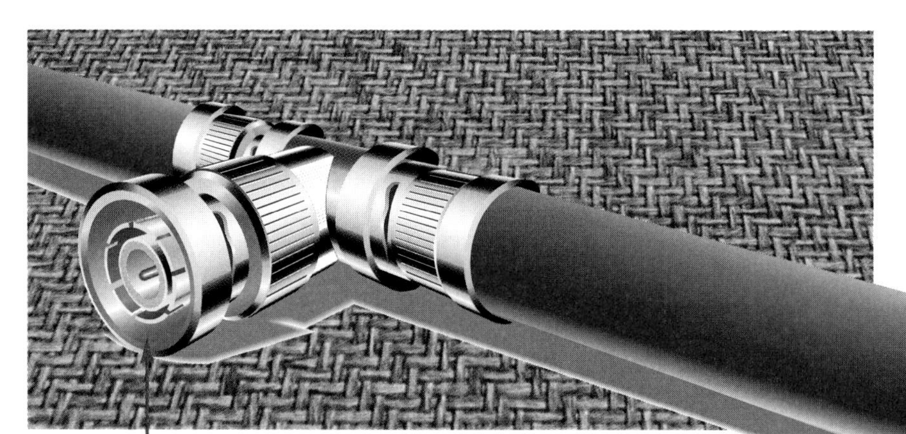

Coaxial cable has a core of solid copper wire surrounded by an insulating layer of plastic. A shield of metal mesh or foil surrounds the plastic layer. The entire cable is covered in a protective jacket.

Coaxial cable must be linked using devices called British Naval Connectors (BNCs). A BNC connector that links a computer or other device to a coaxial cable is called a T-connector.

Coaxial cable is rated using an RG number, such as RG-58 or RG-62.

Interference

Coaxial cable transmits electrical signals through a network and employs features, such as an insulating layer of plastic and a metal or foil shield, to help protect the signals from interference. However, the electrical signals produced by nearby devices can affect the signals being transferred by coaxial cable. It is also possible for coaxial cable signals to interfere with other sensitive electrical devices in the area.

Electrical Resistance

Coaxial cable is rated by the amount of resistance the cable has to the transmission of electrical signals. Electrical resistance is measured in ohms. The most common rating of coaxial cable is 50 ohms.

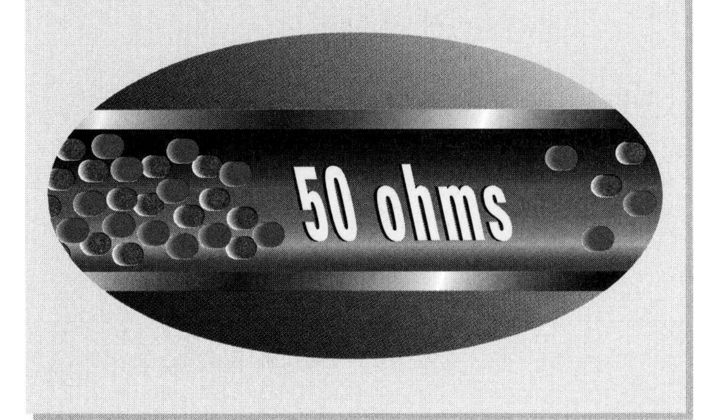

Terminators

When coaxial cable is used on a bus network, there must be a terminator at each end of the cable to absorb the signals and prevent the signals from being bounced back along the cable. A terminator must have the same electrical resistance rating as the cable. For example, a 50 ohm coaxial cable must use a 50 ohm terminator.

Bandwidth

Most coaxial networks transmit information at speeds of up to 10 Mbps. This is considerably slower than other types of cable.

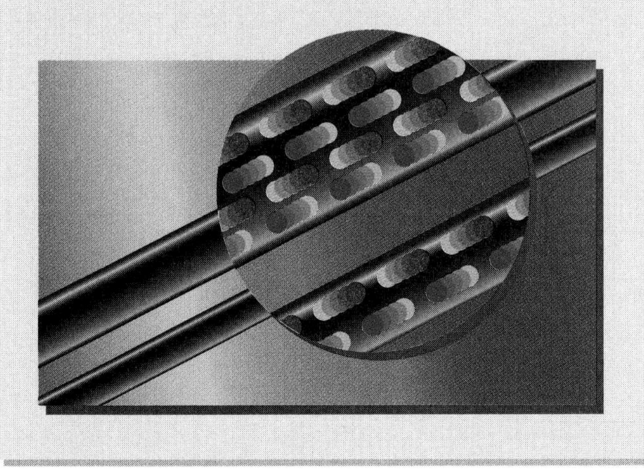

Cost

Coaxial cable is very inexpensive, but is more difficult to work with than other types of cable. Today, coaxial cable is most commonly purchased for use on home networks that connect only a few computers.

UNSHIELDED TWISTED PAIR CABLE

Unshielded Twisted Pair (UTP) cable is the most popular type of cable used to build new networks.

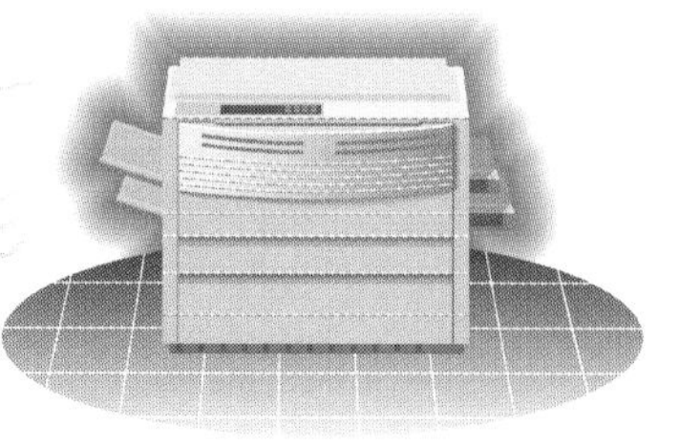

Unshielded twisted pair cable consists of one or more pairs of copper wires. The copper wires in each pair are twisted around each other. By twisting the wires around each other, the cable is less prone to interference from other electrical signals, such as the signals emitted by photocopiers or alarm systems.

There are commonly 1, 2, 3 or 4 pairs of wires in an unshielded twisted pair cable. To distinguish the pairs, the wires are color coded. The entire cable is covered in a protective plastic coating.

Connectors

Unshielded twisted pair cables are attached to computers using connectors that are similar to those found on telephone cable. These connectors are referred to as RJ-45 connectors.

Cost

Unshielded twisted pair cable is the least expensive of all cable types. Using unshielded twisted pair cable can be a cost-effective way to create or expand a network.

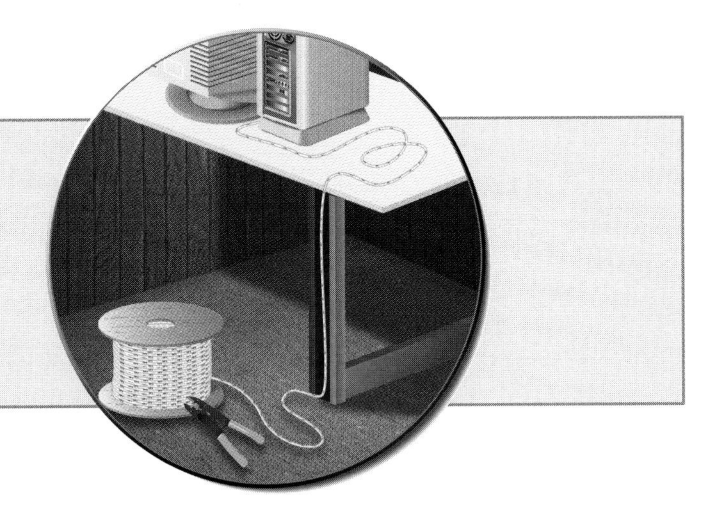

Installation

Unshielded twisted pair cable is very lightweight and flexible compared to other cable types. These characteristics make unshielded twisted pair cable easy to install. Except for very basic installations, qualified cable contractors should install all networking cable.

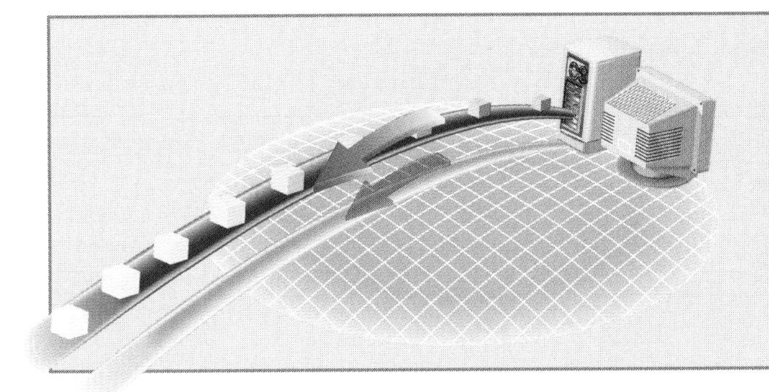

Cable Lengths

Unshielded twisted pair cable is not suitable for connecting devices that are far apart. The farther a signal must travel along a cable, the weaker the signal becomes. Unshielded twisted pair cable can reliably transmit information for up to a few hundred feet, but longer lengths may not transmit information properly.

Bandwidth

There are five main categories of unshielded twisted pair cables. Each category is capable of transmitting different amounts of information at once. Categories 1 and 2 can transfer up to 4 Mbps. Category 3 can transfer up to 16 Mbps and category 4 can transfer up to 20 Mbps. Category 5 can transfer up to 100 Mbps and is also known as 100BaseT.

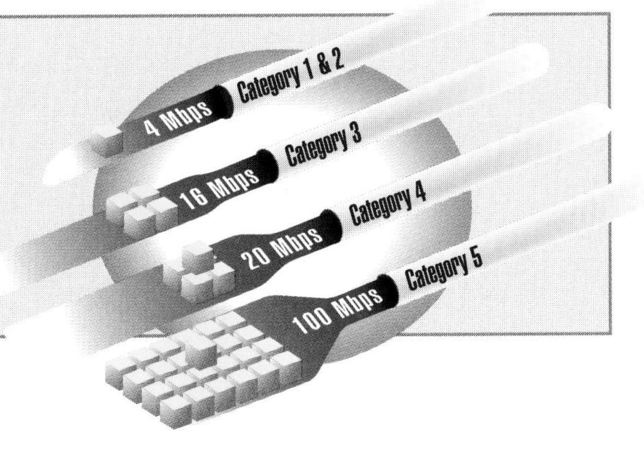

SHIELDED TWISTED PAIR CABLE

Shielded Twisted Pair (STP) cable is similar to unshielded twisted pair cable, except that shielded twisted pair cable includes a protective metal or foil covering.

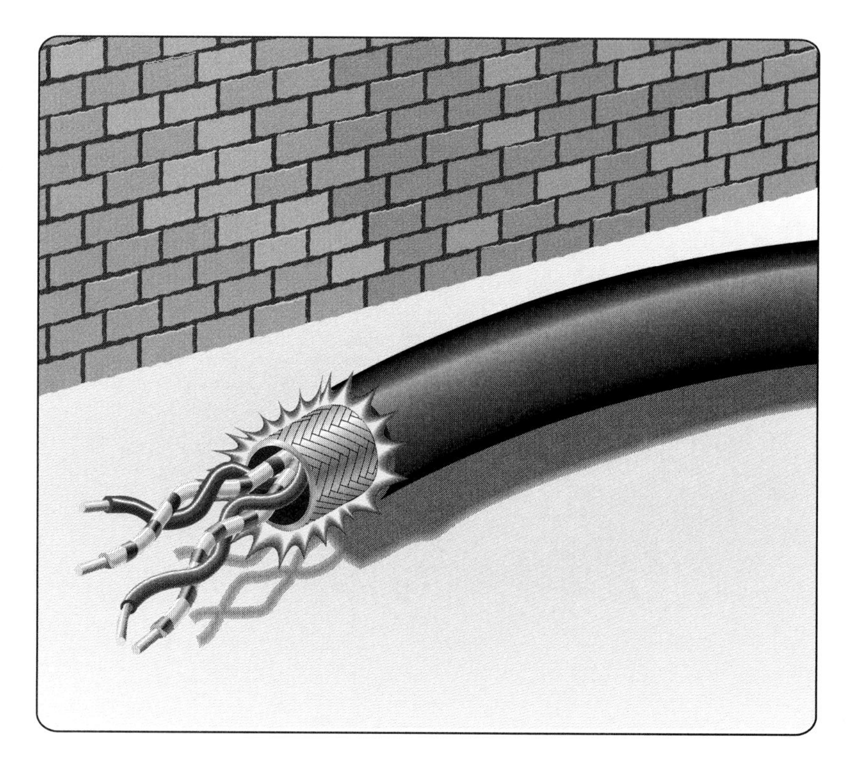

A shielded twisted pair cable can contain a single pair of wires or several pairs of wires.

Interference

Shielded twisted pair cable consists of pairs of twisted copper wires wrapped in a metal mesh or foil cover, called a shield. The copper wires are twisted to help safeguard the cable against interference from outside electrical signals. The metal or foil shield further protects the cable from electrical interference. The shield also prevents the cable from emitting its own electrical interference.

Cost

Shielded twisted pair cable is more expensive than unshielded twisted pair cable, but is considered to be quite inexpensive compared to other types of transmission media, such as fiber-optic cable.

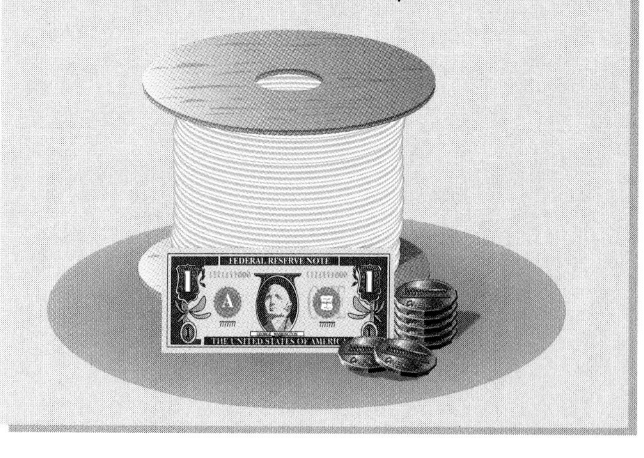

Bandwidth

Shielded twisted pair cable is capable of transmitting data at a very high speed of about 150 Mbps. Most networks constructed with shielded twisted pair cable do not exceed a data transfer speed of 20 Mbps.

Connectors

Shielded twisted pair cable can use two types of connectors, depending on the network type. Apple LocalTalk networks use small pin and socket connectors, while IBM Token-Ring networks use bulky two-way connectors. Both of these connectors are difficult to install. Cable can often be purchased with the connectors already attached.

Installation

It is sometimes difficult to install shielded twisted pair cable because it is bulky and not very flexible. Shielded twisted pair cable can be up to 0.5 inches in diameter, which can make installation awkward if a lot of cables need to be grouped together.

Cable Lengths

Shielded twisted pair cable can reliably transmit information for up to a few hundred feet. Longer cable lengths may require the use of a device, such as a repeater, to transmit information properly.

FIBER-OPTIC CABLE

Fiber-optic cable uses light to transfer information through a network.

Fiber-optic cable transmits light through a core made of glass or plastic. The core is surrounded with gel or plastic to protect it from damage and signal loss. The cable is then covered with a plastic, typically orange, covering.

Computers communicate by exchanging electrical signals. Electrical signals are converted into light signals before being transmitted over fiber-optic cable. The light signals are converted back into electrical signals at the end of the cable.

Cost

Fiber-optic cable and related components are very expensive to purchase and install. Fiber-optic cable is usually used only as the main cable of a network, called the backbone, or where high bandwidth is required.

Installation

Fiber-optic cable can be difficult to work with and should only be installed and serviced by experienced technicians. Particular care should be given to glass core fiber-optic cable, which can break easily. Expensive monitoring equipment may be required to locate a break in a fiber-optic cable.

Interference

Fiber-optic cable does not emit electrical signals and is not susceptible to electrical interference from other devices, such as photocopiers. This makes fiber-optic cable ideal for companies concerned about network security and electronic eavesdropping.

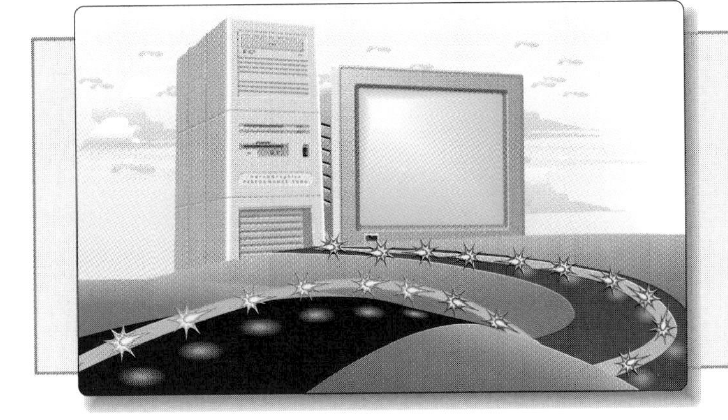

Signal Degradation

With all types of transmission media, the farther a signal travels over the medium, the weaker the signal becomes. Signals transmitted through fiber-optic cable are not greatly affected by attenuation. It is possible to transmit signals for many miles through fiber-optic cable without any detectable degradation in the signal.

Bandwidth

Fiber-optic cable can transfer information at speeds of over 100 Mbps. Some types of fiber-optic cables are capable of transferring information at well over 2 Gbps, but equipment that can utilize such a high rate of speed is not readily available.

INFRARED SYSTEMS

Infrared systems use infrared light to carry information between devices on a network. Infrared systems use the same technology as household remote controls.

On local area networks, infrared systems can typically transfer information at speeds of up to 4 Mbps.

Installation

The installation of an infrared system on a local area network is quite easy. Computers and equipment, such as printers, send infrared signals to a receiver attached to a central point on the ceiling. The receiver then beams the signals back down to all the devices. The devices must be positioned where they can easily send and receive infrared signals.

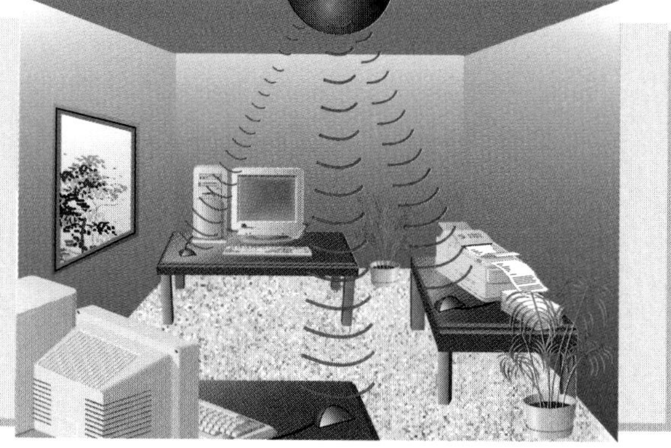

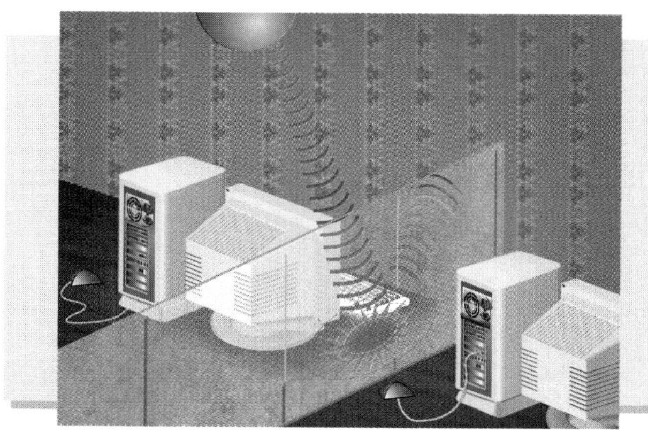

Interference

A physical barrier that obstructs the signals being passed between a device and the receiver is usually the cause of interference on an infrared system. This can be remedied by moving the device to a location where there is a clear line of sight to the receiver.

Cost

Infrared systems are more expensive than cable-based systems. If a high-powered laser-based system is required to transmit signals over a long distance, an infrared system can be particularly costly.

RADIO SYSTEMS

Many companies use radio waves as a wireless transmission medium to connect devices on a network.

Radio systems are most often used to connect devices spread over a wide area, such as a city. Radio systems usually transmit information at speeds of up to 11 Mbps.

Radio Waves

Radio waves are often used as a wireless method of communication between networks. Buildings have special transmitters and receivers positioned where they can easily exchange radio wave signals with networks in other buildings.

Interference

Radio systems transmit signals on radio frequencies. Radio systems are usually capable of detecting which frequencies are clear before starting to transmit information, so interference from other transmissions is usually not a problem.

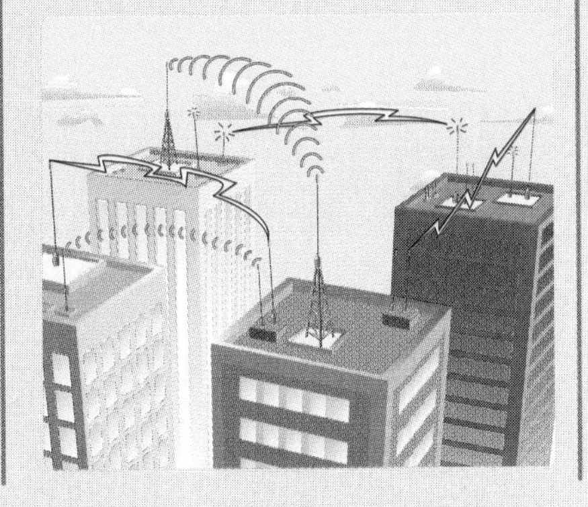

Cost

Radio systems are very expensive when compared to cable-based networks. Some radio systems also require the approval of a local communications authority before they can be used.

MICROWAVE SYSTEMS

Microwave systems can be used to transfer information between networks in a wide area network.

Microwave systems are useful for connecting networks that are separated by a barrier, such as a major highway or a lake.

Microwave systems typically transfer data at speeds of up to 10 Mbps.

Installation

Microwave transmitter and receiver stations must be precisely aligned to efficiently transfer information. Microwave systems must be installed and maintained by properly trained and licensed service technicians. Almost all microwave installations are subject to the regulations of a governing body, such as the Federal Communications Commission (FCC) in the United States.

Interference

Microwave transmitting and receiving stations are designed to function under most environmental conditions. However, some microwave transmissions may be affected by environmental conditions such as smog or rain.

Cost

Microwave systems are costly to install but in many cases they are the only option for creating a connection between two locations that are separated by a barrier or a great distance.

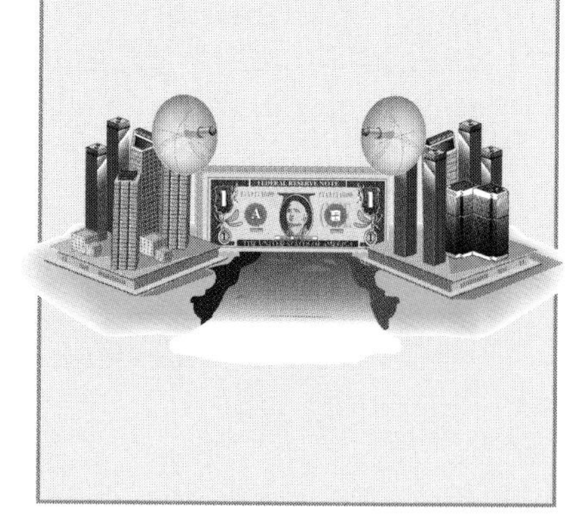

SATELLITE SYSTEMS

Satellite systems use satellites orbiting at approximately 22,300 miles above the Earth to relay signals from one part of a wide area network to another.

Satellite systems are ideal for communicating with remote areas, such as ships at sea.

Installation

The building and launching of a satellite system is extremely expensive. Satellite system installations are completed by firms and service technicians who are governed by a regulatory body, such as the Federal Communications Commission (FCC) in the United States.

Delays

Each time a signal is transferred over a satellite system, the signal travels 22,300 miles up to the satellite and then back down to the receiving system on Earth. This can cause delays in transfer time from 0.5 to 5 seconds. Sending a signal to another part of the state by satellite takes approximately the same amount of time as sending a signal to the other side of the country.

Bandwidth

The total bandwidth available on a satellite system is very high and is typically shared by many companies. Each company would use a bandwidth of between 2 and 10 Mbps.

TOKEN-
RING
ARCNET
ETHERNET
Computer 1
Computer 2
Computer 6
Computer 3
Token
Computer 5
Computer 4
RING
Computer 1
Computer 2
Computer 3
Computer 4
Computer 5
Hub
Computer 6
Computer 7
Computer 8
Computer 9
Computer 10
BUS

CHAPTER 5

Network Architecture

Network architecture defines how information transfers on a network. This chapter discusses the main network architectures used on networks around the world.

Introduction to Network Architecture....86

Ethernet Architecture 88

Token-Ring Architecture 92

ARCnet Architecture 94

AppleTalk Architecture 95

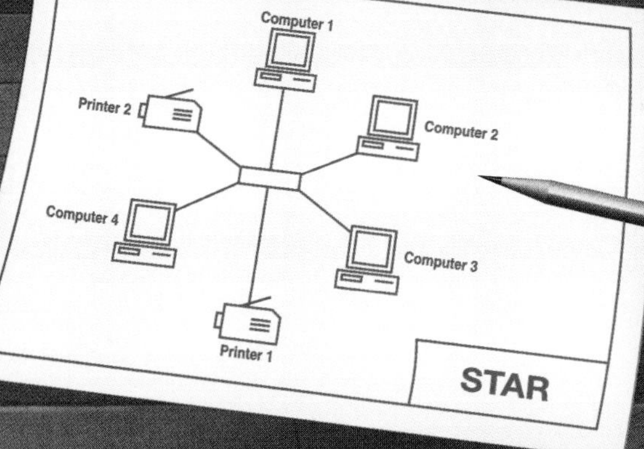

INTRODUCTION TO NETWORK ARCHITECTURE

Network architecture refers to how information transfers on a network.

The most common type of network architecture is Ethernet. Other network architectures include Token-Ring and ARCnet.

Network Architecture

Network architecture defines how computers and devices access a network to transfer information through the transmission medium. Network architecture also determines the network structure used, such as the bus, ring or star structure, and how information transfers through the structure.

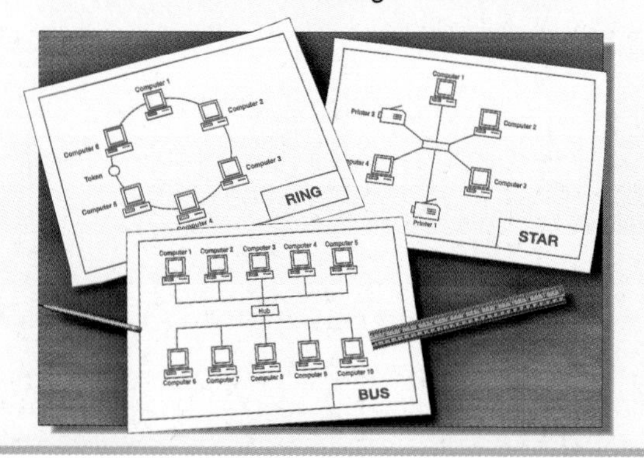

Network Standards

All of the components of a network, such as hardware, software and transmission media, are designed to work with a specific type of network architecture. Network standards ensure that all of a network's components can work together. A device designed for one type of network architecture cannot be used on another type of network.

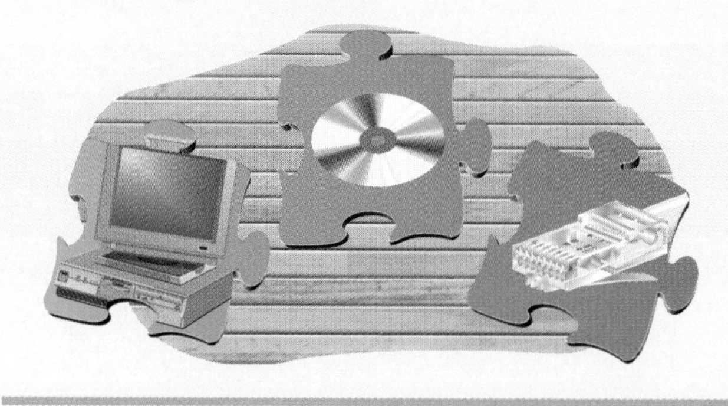

ARCHITECTURE CONSIDERATIONS

Information Transfer

The speed at which information can transfer and the amount of information that can transfer at once, referred to as bandwidth, varies for each network architecture. As the bandwidth increases, the network becomes more complex. The type of information that is transferred is another factor to consider. For example, the Ethernet architecture is well suited to transfer large files, such as videos and images.

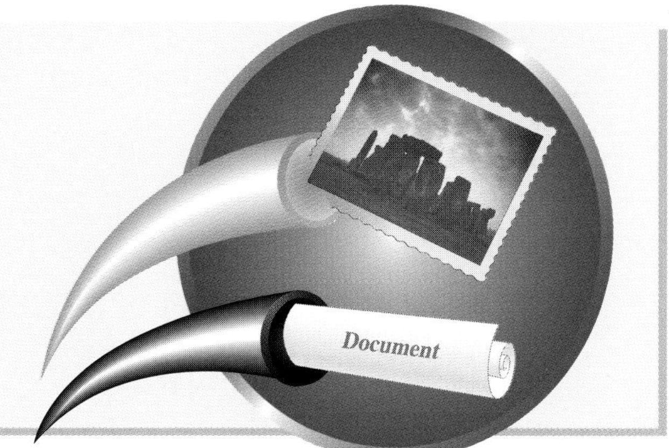

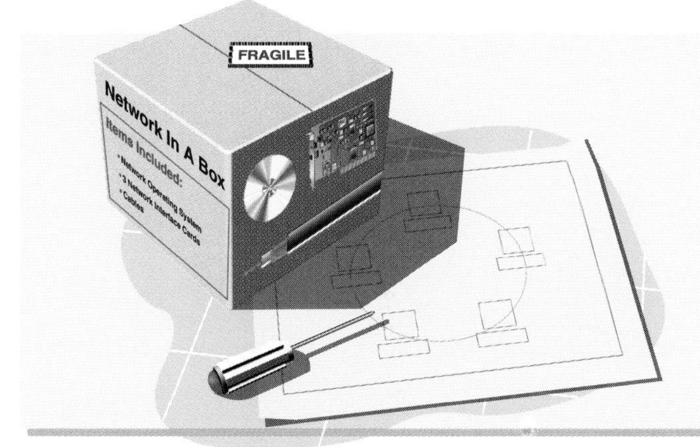

Network Size

Many networks can be purchased as a single kit that will connect a small number of computers. Large networks are often complex and must be installed by trained professionals. Since some architectures restrict the maximum number of computers and devices on a single segment of the network, the size of the network may affect which architecture is used.

Cost

Each architecture has different requirements for installation, maintenance and expansion. These differences affect the overall cost of the network. An efficient, reliable network that can transfer information quickly is usually more expensive.

ETHERNET ARCHITECTURE

Ethernet is the most popular architecture used when building new networks. Ethernet is the least expensive and easiest type of network to set up.

The Ethernet architecture has been widely accepted as a network standard since the early 1980s.

Information Transfer

Unlike other network architectures, Ethernet does not use a token to transfer information on a network. To send information, each computer on an Ethernet network waits for a pause on the network. If two computers send information at the same time, a collision will occur and the computers must try again to send the information.

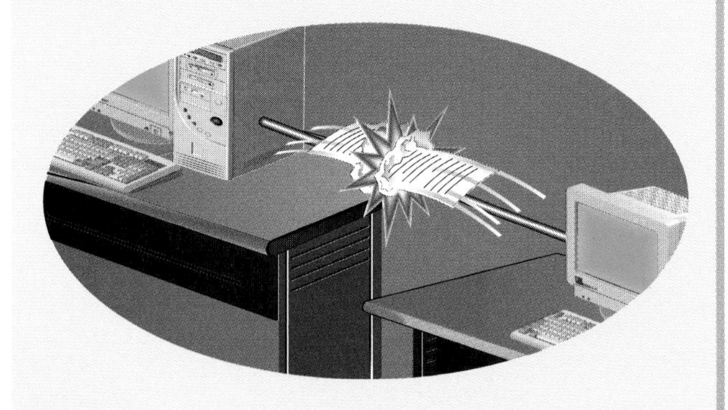

Compatibility

Since Ethernet is so popular and widely accepted, most manufacturers of network software and hardware ensure that their products will work when used on an Ethernet network. The operating standards for Ethernet networks are defined by the Institute of Electrical and Electronics Engineers (IEEE) and are known as IEEE 802.3. For more information about Ethernet operating standards and the IEEE, visit the www.ieee.org Web site.

Bandwidth

Ethernet networks can transfer information at different speeds, depending on the type of Ethernet network and cable used. Category 5 unshielded twisted pair cable, also known as 100BaseT, is commonly used to build new Ethernet networks. These networks, called Fast Ethernet, can transfer information at speeds of up to 100 Mbps. Older Ethernet networks can transfer information at only 10 Mbps.

Gigabit Ethernet

Gigabit Ethernet can transfer information at speeds of up to 1000 Mbps and is typically used as the backbone of a local area network. Gigabit Ethernet commonly uses fiber-optic cable, but Category 5 unshielded twisted pair cable can also be used.

Network Size

One segment of an Ethernet network constructed using category 5 unshielded twisted pair cable can connect 2 computers or network devices. A variety of devices, such as hubs, switches and routers, can be used to join network segments and create a large Ethernet network.

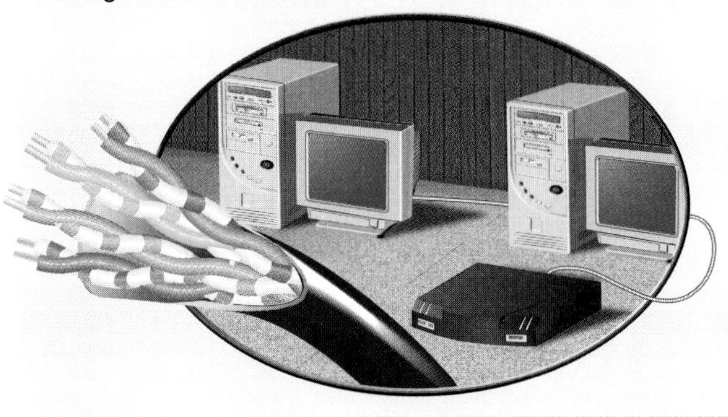

Cost

One of the many reasons Ethernet is the most popular network architecture is because it is relatively inexpensive when compared to other network architectures. The Ethernet cards used in most personal computers can be purchased for less than 20 dollars and can be connected to the network using cable that costs only pennies per foot.

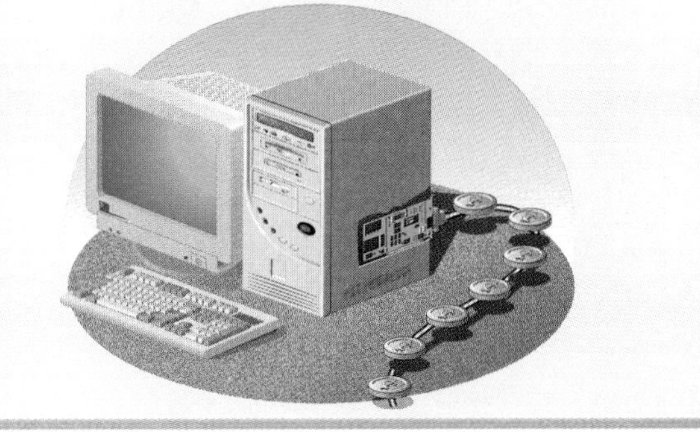

ACCESS METHODS

Ethernet networks have different methods of specifying how devices can access a network to send information.

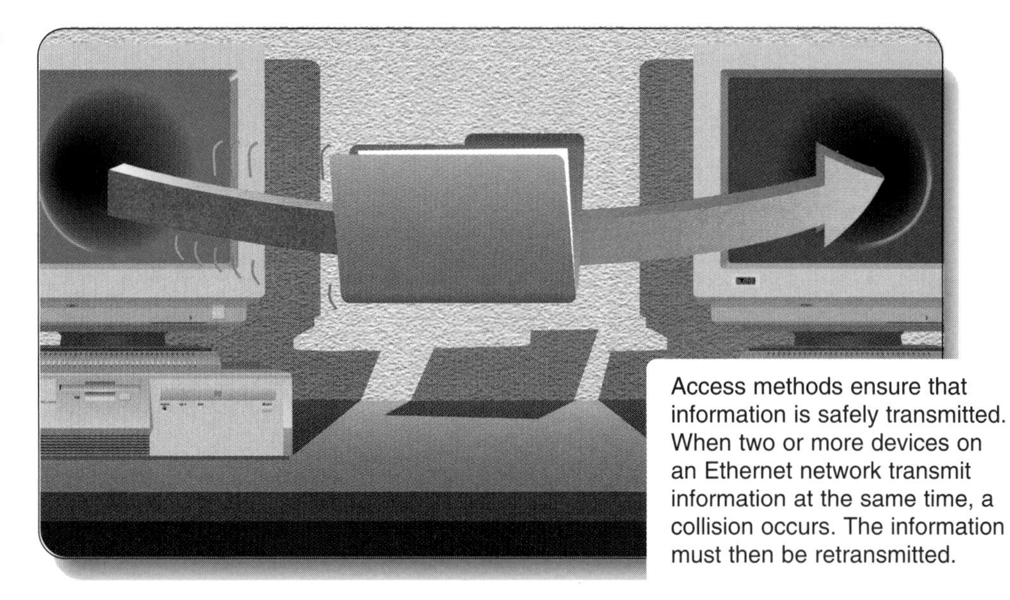

Access methods ensure that information is safely transmitted. When two or more devices on an Ethernet network transmit information at the same time, a collision occurs. The information must then be retransmitted.

CSMA/CD

Carrier Sense Multiple Access with Collision Detection (CSMA/CD) is the most popular method of controlling the transfer of information on an Ethernet network. This method is very effective when used on Ethernet networks that have large numbers of users.

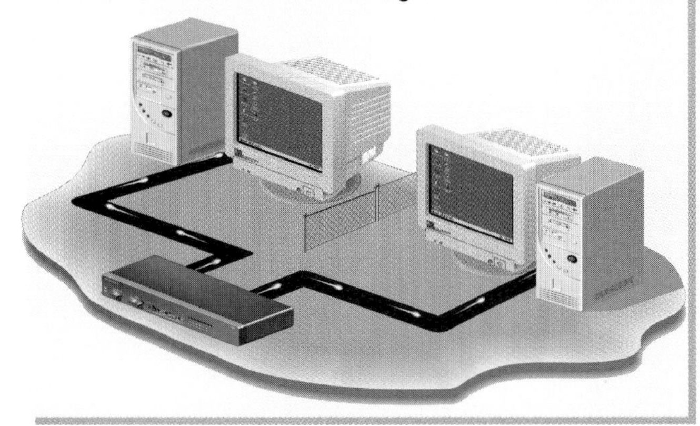

CSMA/CA

Carrier Sense Multiple Access with Collision Avoidance (CSMA/CA) can also be used to control the transfer of information on an Ethernet network. CSMA/CA is the access method used on AppleTalk networks.

Carrier Sense

When a device needs to transmit information on a network, it monitors the network to see if other devices are transmitting information. If the device detects another signal, called a carrier, the device waits until the network is free before beginning to transmit information.

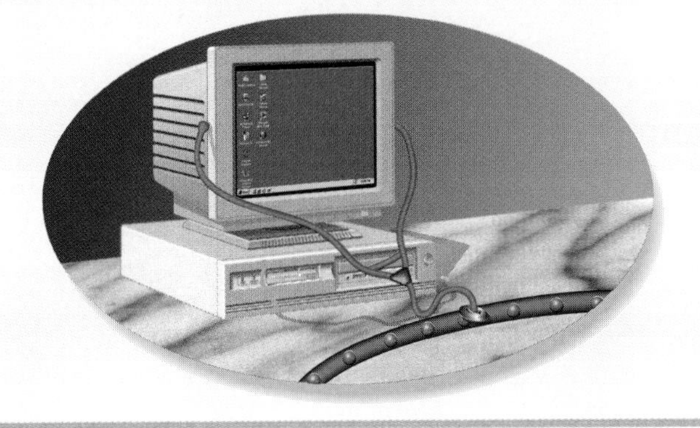

Multiple Access

Multiple access means that many computers and other network devices have access to the network and can attempt to send data.

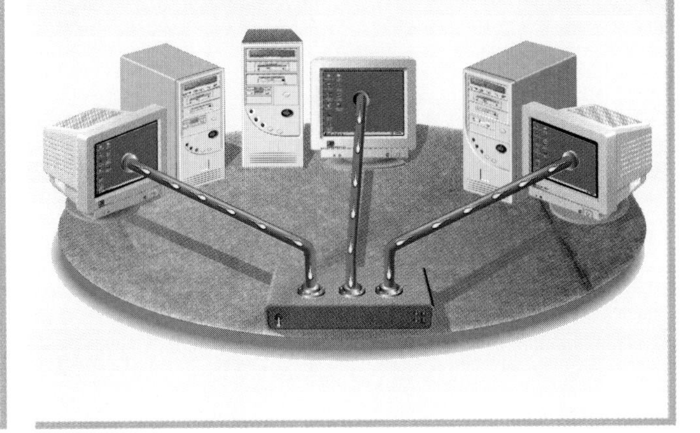

Collision Detection

After a device sends information on an Ethernet network, the device checks the network transmission medium to make sure the information has not collided with any other information. If the device detects a collision, it pauses and then tries to resend the information.

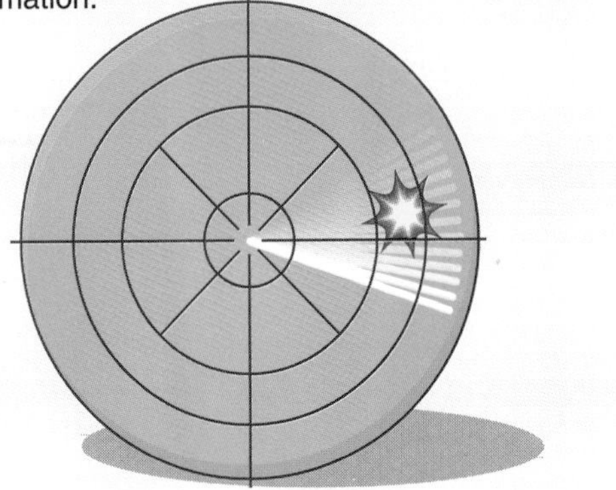

Collision Avoidance

A device on an Ethernet network can avoid collisions by letting other devices know when it is about to transmit information. All the other network devices then refrain from using the network. Since each device is informed about every transmission on the network, this method of access control can be very inefficient.

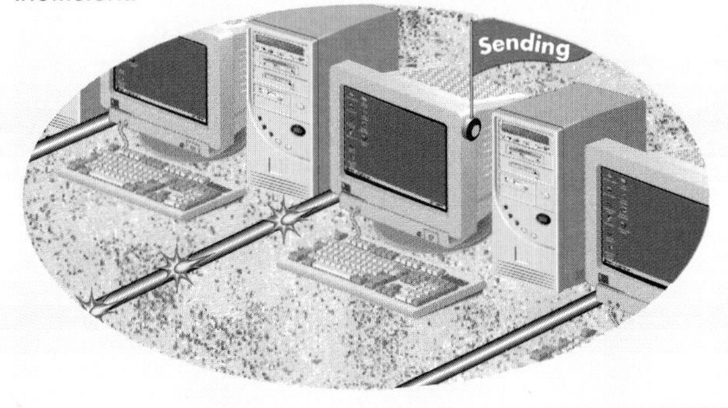

TOKEN-RING ARCHITECTURE

Token-Ring architecture was developed by IBM in 1984. Token-Ring networks are most often found in large organizations, such as banks and insurance companies.

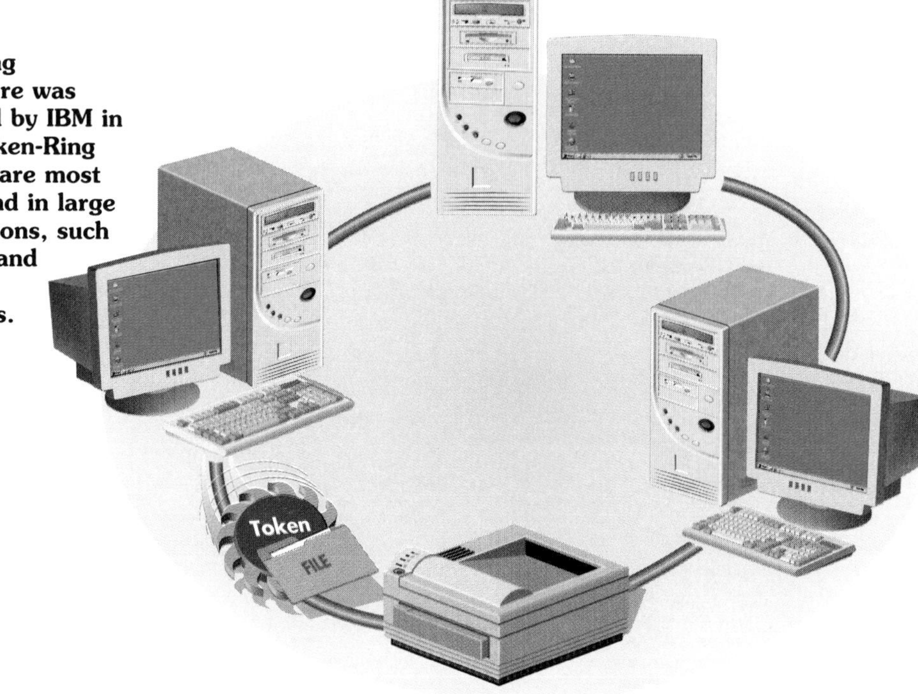

Token-Ring is no longer a popular choice for new network installations.

Token-Ring networks use the logical ring network structure.

Tokens

A token is a signal that regulates the flow of information on a network. Token-Ring networks work by passing a single token from computer to computer. Before a computer can send information, the computer must collect the token. Only one computer can transmit information at a time on a Token-Ring network. This ensures that collisions never occur.

Transmission Media

Unshielded and shielded twisted pair cables are the most common transmission media used in Token-Ring networks. Token-Ring networks can transfer information at 4 Mbps using unshielded twisted pair cable or 16 Mbps using shielded twisted pair cable. Many Token-Ring networks are now using fiber-optic cable. With fiber-optic cable, Token-Ring networks are capable of transferring data at very high speeds.

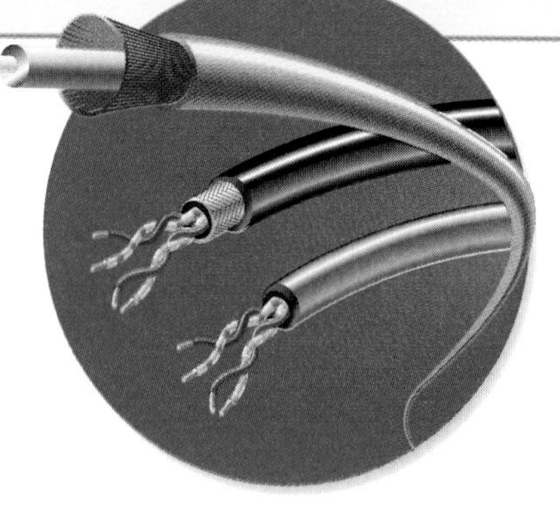

Network Size

One segment of a Token-Ring network constructed using unshielded twisted pair cable can connect up to 72 computers and other network devices. One segment of a Token-Ring network that uses shielded twisted pair cable can connect up to 255 computers and devices.

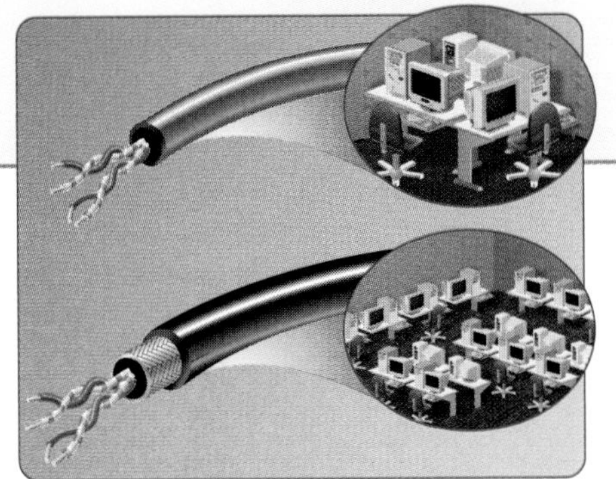

Troubleshooting

The token typically travels in one direction around a Token-Ring network. If the token cannot pass beyond a certain point, the token can travel in the opposite direction until it encounters the error again. This helps to pinpoint the location of an error on the network.

Cost

The components required by a Token-Ring network are more expensive than the components required by other types of cable-based networks. This is one reason the Token-Ring architecture is becoming less popular and is being replaced by the Ethernet architecture.

Compatibility

Since Token-Ring networks are still widely used, most manufacturers of network software and hardware ensure their products will work when used on a Token-Ring network. The operating standards for Token-Ring networks are defined by the Institute of Electrical and Electronics Engineers (IEEE) and are known as IEEE 802.5. For more information about the IEEE and Token-Ring operating standards, visit the www.ieee.org Web site.

ARCnet is one of the oldest types of network architectures used for personal computers. ARCnet networks are often simple, inexpensive and flexible.

Although the ARCnet architecture is not popular in the construction of new networks, there are still many existing ARCnet networks.

Transfer Information

Like the Token-Ring architecture, ARCnet uses a token to control the flow of information on a network. A computer must collect the token before it can transmit information. ARCnet networks can transfer information at speeds of up to 20 Mbps.

ARCnet does little processing of the information that transfers over a network and is often used in networks that gather information, such as networks in manufacturing plants or laboratories.

Hubs

ARCnet networks use the physical star structure where a hub is the center of the network. There are three types of ARCnet hubs. Passive hubs simply connect the cable segments together. Active hubs reproduce signals as they pass from segment to segment, preventing errors and interference. Smart hubs can perform tasks, such as error detection, and allow network administrators to have more control over each network segment.

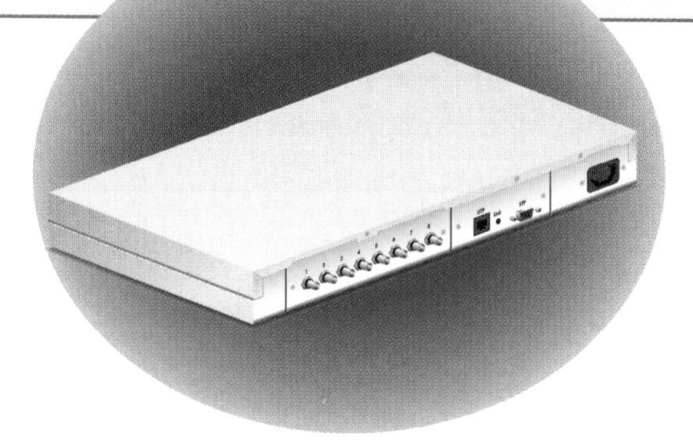

APPLETALK ARCHITECTURE

Apple developed the AppleTalk architecture to control the transfer of information on networks with Apple computers.

The AppleTalk architecture is built into the Macintosh operating system. Each computer using the Macintosh operating system has networking capabilities.

AppleTalk networks are often called LocalTalk networks. LocalTalk refers to the network hardware on an AppleTalk network. Many Macintosh computers have built-in LocalTalk network hardware, such as connectors and interface cards.

Transfer Information

LocalTalk networks usually use shielded twisted pair cable, although standard telephone cable can also be used. LocalTalk networks can only transfer information at speeds of up to 0.22 Mbps. This slow transfer speed often discourages large companies from using LocalTalk networks.

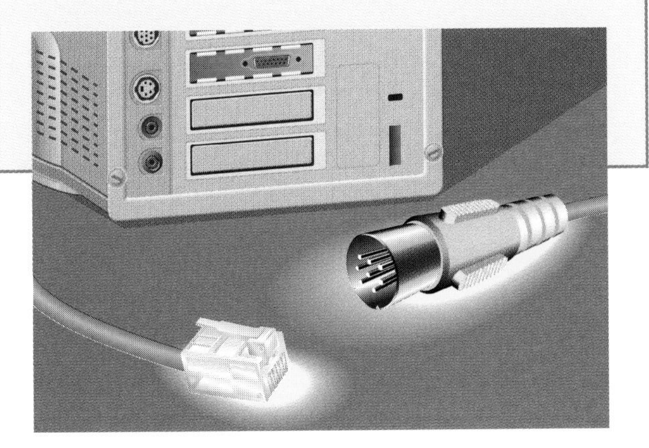

Zones

LocalTalk networks are made up of small networks or workgroups, called zones. Each zone can contain a maximum of 32 computers. Several zones can be connected to form a single, larger network, called an internetwork. Computers on the internetwork can then access resources located in other zones.

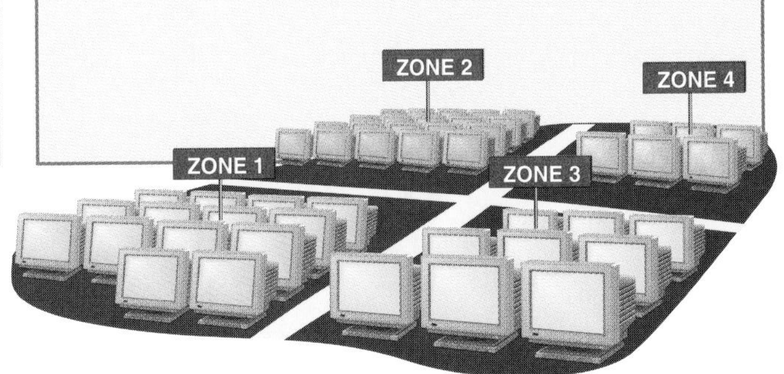

Mail Server
RESET
File Serv
RESET
XLS

CHAPTER 6

Network Services

Network services allow users to perform many different types of tasks on a network. Read this chapter to learn about common network services, including file, print, database, application and message services.

Introduction to Network Services 98

File Services 99

Print Services 100

Database Services 101

Application Services 102

Message Services 103

Network services allow users to share and access information and resources on a network.

The main purpose of computer networks is to provide services and ensure users have access to the services. The use of services on a network reduces equipment costs.

Services

There are many types of services available for networks. Each type of service is responsible for performing a specific task. The most common types of services help users exchange files, use a network printer or access a database. Most network operating systems include several types of services.

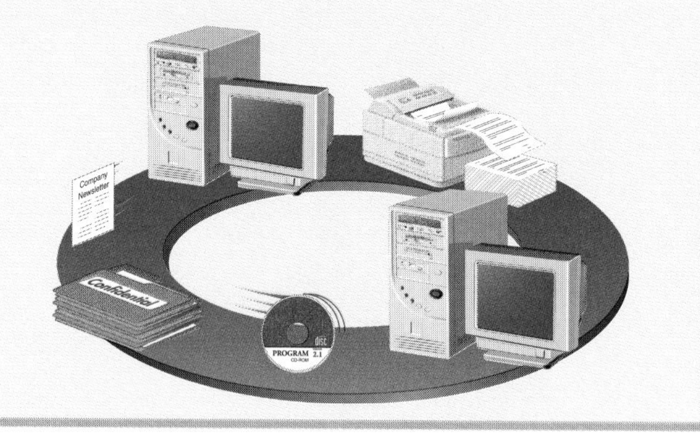

Servers

Network services are usually organized, managed and run on servers. A server may control one service or several services. Servers are powerful computers that have a lot of memory and processing power. Most servers on a network are kept in a central location to help make administration easier. Network servers are very expensive to buy and maintain. Most servers on a network operate continuously.

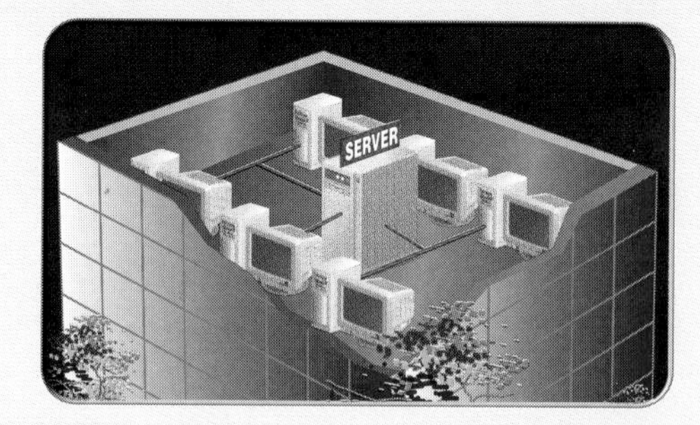

FILE SERVICES

File services allow users to store and share files on a network. File sharing is one of the most important features of a network.

Storage

The primary function of file services is to allow users to access files on a network. File services can let computers connected to a network store and retrieve files on a file server's hard drive or retrieve information from a CD, DVD or optical drive on the server. If a network has a Network Attached Storage (NAS) device, file services can also be used to access information on the device.

Security

File servers have very elaborate security systems to prevent unauthorized access or the accidental destruction of files stored on the network. Individual files on a file server may be restricted to a specific user or group of users.

Backup

Important files used on a network should be stored on a file server. Having important files stored in one location makes it easy to back up the data in case of a system failure. Most backup devices, such as a tape drive, can be connected directly to a file server.

PRINT SERVICES

Print services allow users on a network to share the same printer. Print services also control and manage print jobs.

Cost Effective

Using a print service to share a printer eliminates the need to buy a printer for each user on a network. Print services also make using expensive printing equipment, such as a color laser printer or a plotter, more cost effective since the company only needs to buy one device that all users can share.

Remote Access

Network users may send information to a printer, regardless of the distance between their computers and the printer. For example, a person in the sales department may be able to print an order in the warehouse across the street if the person's computer and the printer are on the same network.

Restrict Access

If everyone on a network uses the same network printer, the printer may take a long time to produce print jobs. A print service can restrict access to a printer so only a specific group of people can use the printer. This is useful if a network is too large to share one printer.

DATABASE SERVICES

Database services allow people on a network to manage and work with large collections of information. Database services are one of the most common types of services found on corporate networks.

Database Servers

Database servers are used to store databases and perform tasks that have been requested by clients, such as finding information in a database. A database server is a very powerful computer that can handle requests from several clients at once.

Clients

A client computer requests information from the database server. Client computers rarely process information from a database and therefore require much less processing power than a database server.

Database Programs

There are several different database programs available for use on networks. Two of the most popular are Oracle and Microsoft SQL Server. For more information about Oracle, you can visit the www.oracle.com Web site. For more information about Microsoft SQL Server, you can visit the www.microsoft.com/sql Web site.

Structured Query Language

Database services use a series of instructions called Structured Query Language (SQL) to access and work with the information in a database. SQL is the industry standard language for managing and manipulating database information.

APPLICATION SERVICES

An application service is dedicated to running a program, or application, which anyone on the network can use.

Application services are often used to run programs that require a lot of processing power, such as Computer Aided Design (CAD) programs.

Application Server

Application servers are very powerful computers that store and run applications for use on a network. The client computers on a network do not need to have a lot of memory or processing power because the application server runs the program.

When applications are stored on an application server, it is easier for the network administrator to set up and update the applications used on the network.

Application Service Provider

An Application Service Provider (ASP) is a company that sets up applications and then rents access to the applications to businesses over the Internet. Using an ASP saves businesses from having to install and manage their own software. ASPs offer a range of software from simple applications, such as invoicing programs, to complex software, such as a suite of applications used to manage information in multinational corporations.

MESSAGE SERVICES

Message services allow people to exchange electronic mail. E-mail is a convenient way to exchange ideas with colleagues and request information.

Electronic Mail

E-mail enables people in a company to exchange information quickly. Many message services allow users to attach information, such as word processing documents, spreadsheets, video files and sound files, to the messages they send. Message services may offer features such as the ability to confirm that a message sent on the network was received and the ability to send messages to people on the Internet. Some message services also allow users to see when their contacts are online and send messages to mobile devices, such as pagers.

Collaboration

Some messaging services allow people within the same organization to form a team to work on a specific project. The members of the team can use the messaging service to schedule meetings, exchange information and track the current status of the project they are working on.

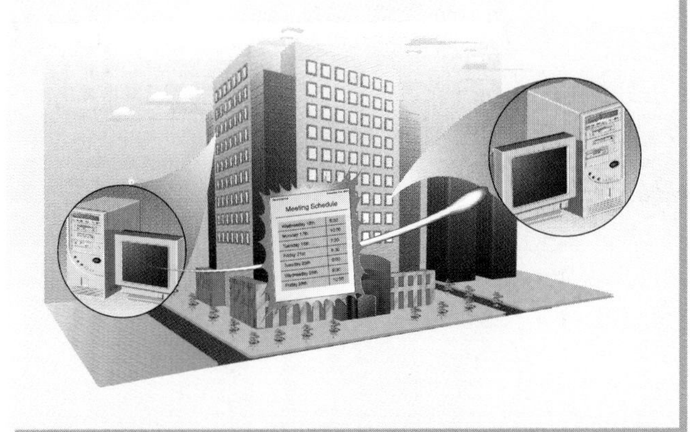

My Documents
My Computer
My Network Places
Recycle Bin
Internet Explorer
Connect to the Internet
Start
12:00 PM
Home directory
File Edit Settings Layout Commands Help
Back Up Forward Rescan Home Icons Brief Detailed Custom
Location: /home/tsmith
Show all files
9000

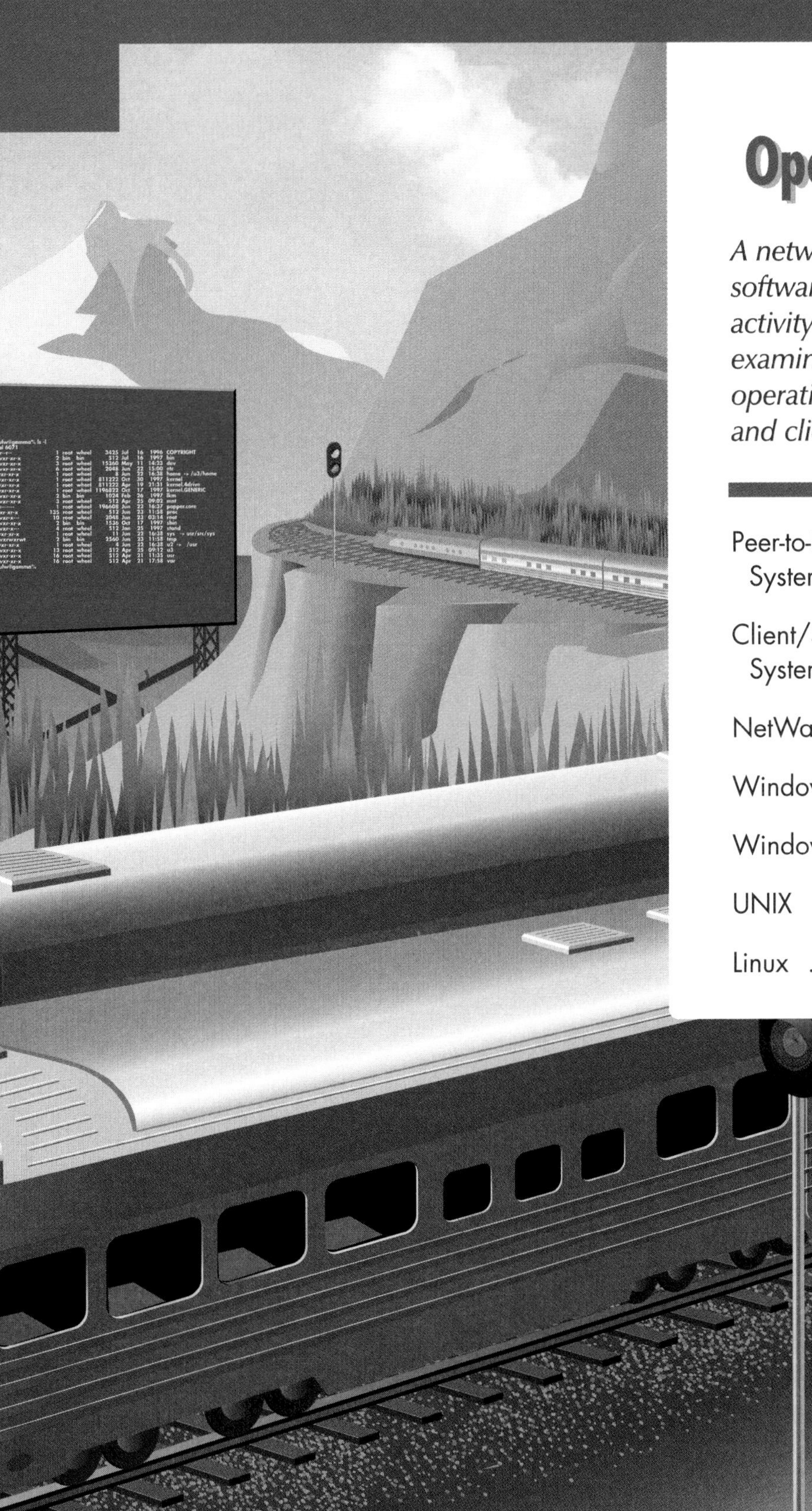

CHAPTER 7

Network Operating Systems

A network operating system is the software used to control the overall activity of a network. This chapter examines the different network operating systems used on peer-to-peer and client/server networks.

Peer-to-Peer Network Operating Systems 106

Client/Server Network Operating Systems 108

NetWare 110

Windows NT 112

Windows 2000 114

UNIX 116

Linux 117

PEER-TO-PEER NETWORK OPERATING SYSTEMS

A network operating system organizes and manages all the activities on a network.

Peer-to-peer network operating systems are used on small networks that usually connect up to 10 computers. Each computer on a peer-to-peer network stores its own information and resources.

Sharing

Peer-to-peer networks allow users to share the information and resources, such as files and printers, stored on their individual computers. After information or resources have been shared, they are accessible to other users on the network.

Security

Most peer-to-peer network operating systems have only basic security features, such as password protection for shared information to prevent unauthorized access. Since each computer on a peer-to-peer network stores its own information, a person may be able to access restricted information by using the computer the information is stored on. Peer-to-peer networks are less secure than client/server networks.

POPULAR PEER-TO-PEER NETWORK OPERATING SYSTEMS

Windows 95, Windows 98 and Windows Me

Although the Windows 95, Windows 98 and Windows Me operating systems were developed for use on a single desktop computer, these operating systems have built-in networking capabilities that allow them to be used on a peer-to-peer network. More information about these operating systems is available at the www.microsoft.com Web site.

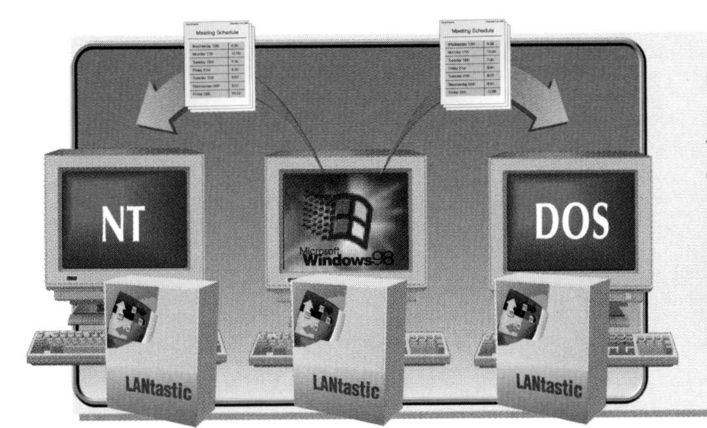

LANtastic

LANtastic is a peer-to-peer operating system that can be used to connect a group of computers that use different operating systems. For example, LANtastic can allow computers using DOS or Windows NT to access information stored on computers using Windows 98. LANtastic also makes it easy to expand a network and add features at a later time. For more information about LANtastic, visit the www.lantastic.com Web site.

PC MACLAN

PC MACLAN is a peer-to-peer network operating system that allows computers using Windows operating systems and computers using the Macintosh OS operating system to share resources, such as drives and printers. PC MACLAN can also convert data, which enables Windows-based computers and Macintosh computers to exchange files. For more information about PC MACLAN, visit the www.miramar.com Web site.

CLIENT/SERVER NETWORK OPERATING SYSTEMS

A network operating system is the software used to control the overall activity of a network. A client/server network connects 10 or more client computers to a server. The server makes information and resources available to the clients.

There are several operating systems available for client/server networks, including NetWare, Windows NT, Windows 2000 Server, UNIX and Linux.

Powerful

Network operating systems are powerful programs that are capable of quickly processing large amounts of information. Many client/server network operating systems are complex and should be installed by qualified professionals.

Servers

Client/server networks use servers to run the network operating system. A network operating system may run on multiple servers, each performing a specific task. For example, one server may be used to control the user names and passwords of each user on the network. Another server may be used to allow users on the network to exchange e-mail messages.

Organize Resources

A network may use many resources, such as fax modems, printers and software applications. A network operating system organizes the resources on a network and ensures that all the parts of the network work together smoothly and efficiently.

Security

Client/server network operating systems generally have sophisticated security features to control access to information and devices on a network. For example, a network operating system can ensure that only authorized people with the correct access rights can use the information stored on the network.

Operating System Drivers

An operating system driver is software that allows the computers on a network to communicate with the network operating system. A computer must have the appropriate drivers to access the network. When a user performs a task, the driver determines whether the user's computer needs to access the network to complete a task.

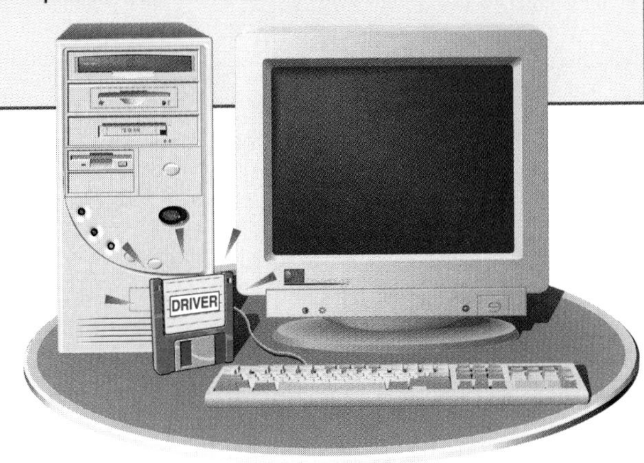

Administration

Client/server network operating systems allow network administrators to perform tasks such as creating user accounts and setting account policies. A client/server network operating system can also be used to monitor network performance and view information about the hardware and software on the network.

NetWare is an operating system developed by Novell for client/server networks. NetWare is one of the most widely used network operating systems in the world.

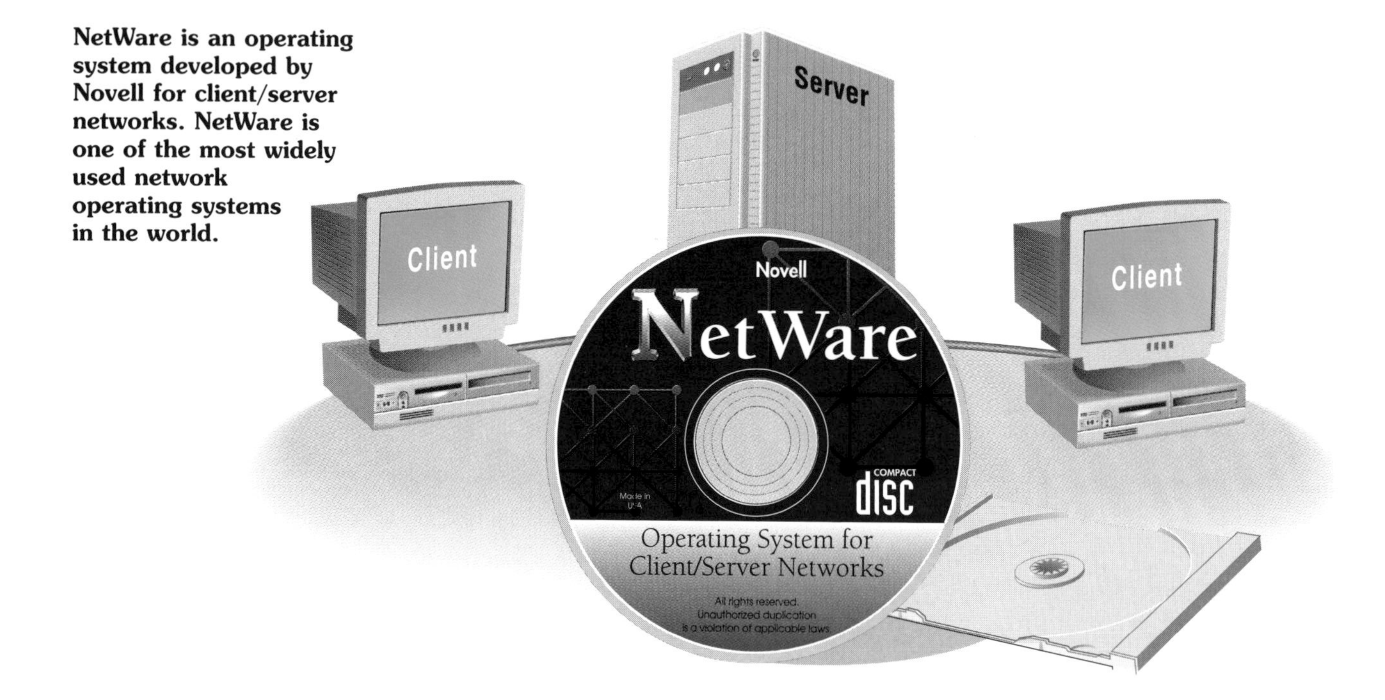

Versions

NetWare is available in different versions. Each version allows a limited number of computers to connect to the NetWare server at one time. The cost of NetWare increases with the number of connections permitted. Before purchasing the NetWare operating system, make sure the version provides the required number of connections.

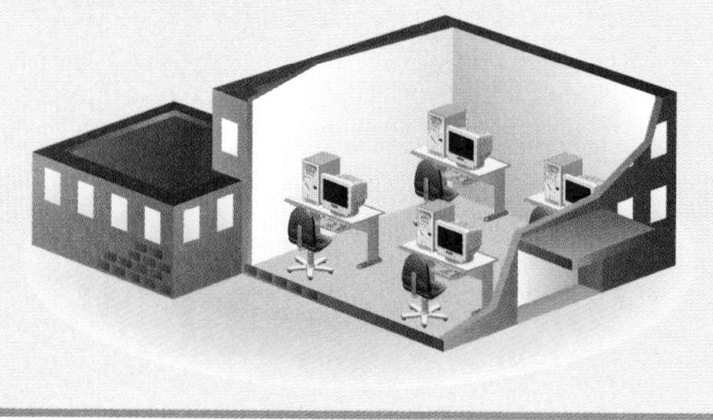

Modules

The capabilities of a NetWare server can be increased by adding modules. Modules are add-on programs that provide additional features and work as part of the network operating system. Popular modules include programs that let the network administrator back up information on the network or monitor an uninterruptible power supply.

Support

Due to its popularity, there is a wide range of support available for the NetWare operating system. Books, software applications and technical support are readily available for NetWare users.

Novell has designed courses for people who plan to use and maintain the NetWare operating system. Novell has also made online support and product updates available on the Web at www.novell.com.

Hardware

Since so many companies use the NetWare operating system, most manufacturers of computer hardware, such as network interface cards and printers, ensure that their products will work efficiently on a network running NetWare.

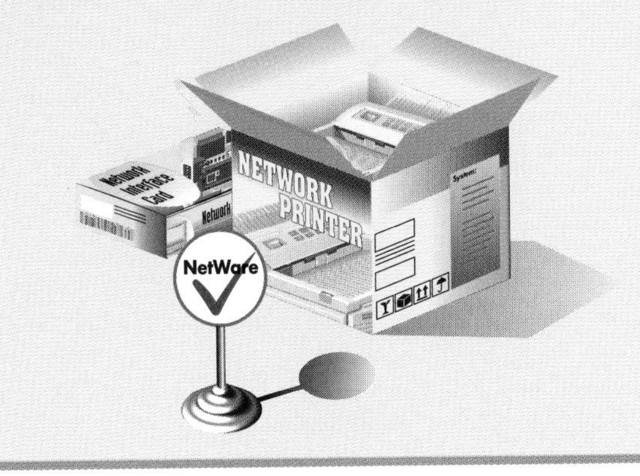

Scalability

The NetWare operating system can be used on a small network consisting of only a few computers or on a large network with hundreds of computers. Since the size, or scale, of a NetWare network can vary greatly, the NetWare operating system is a good choice for networks that may expand in the future. A NetWare network can easily be upgraded to accommodate new users and resources.

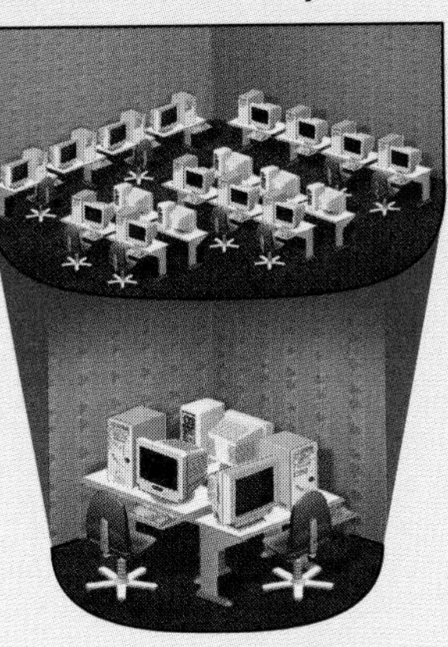

Compatibility

NetWare can connect client computers running different operating systems. Client computers on a NetWare network can use operating systems such as Windows 95, UNIX or DOS.

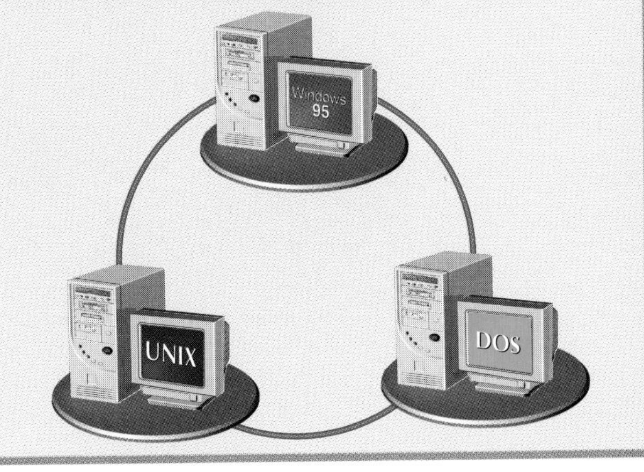

WINDOWS NT

Microsoft Windows NT is a powerful network operating system. Windows NT is available in two main versions—Windows NT Server and Windows NT Workstation.

Windows NT Server

Windows NT Server is used on client/server networks and is designed to support the heavy processing demands of a dedicated network server. The client computers on a network running Windows NT Server can use a variety of operating systems, including Windows NT Workstation, Windows 98 or Linux.

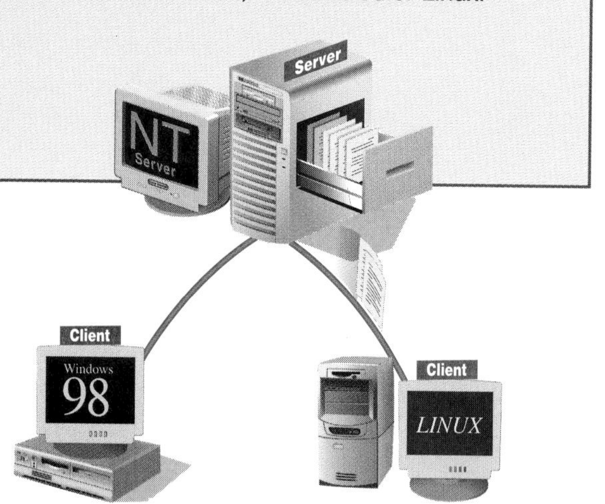

Windows NT Workstation

Windows NT Workstation is a version of the Windows NT operating system that is used on client computers in a client/server network and can also be found on peer-to-peer networks. Many powerful applications, such as 3-D design software, are designed specifically to run on Windows NT Workstation. Many programs designed for other versions of the Windows operating system, such as Windows 95 and Windows 98, will perform better on Windows NT Workstation.

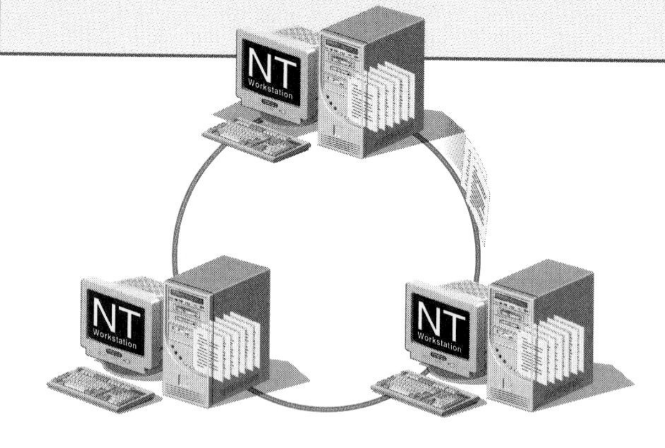

Popular

Windows NT is one of the most popular network operating systems in the world. Although Microsoft has released other client/server network operating systems that offer more features, many people continue to use Windows NT because of its reliability and power.

Ease of Use

The Windows NT operating system is very easy to use. Windows NT uses a Graphical User Interface (GUI, pronounced "gooey") to communicate with users. Administrative tasks are made easier when graphics, instead of plain text, are used to display information. Windows NT has the same look and feel as the Windows 95 and Windows 98 operating systems.

Support

There are many books and software applications, as well as technical support, available for people who use the Windows NT operating system.

Microsoft has made online support and product updates for Windows NT available on the Web at www.microsoft.com. Microsoft has also designed courses to certify people who use and maintain the Windows NT operating system.

WINDOWS 2000

Windows 2000 is the successor to Windows NT and offers improved networking features. There are several versions of Windows 2000 available.

Windows 2000 Professional

Windows 2000 Professional is commonly used on client computers in a client/server network, but can also be found on peer-to-peer networks. Although recommended as a desktop operating system, Windows 2000 Professional may be used as a server for some tasks, such as a Web server for a small intranet. For more information about intranets, see page 230.

Windows 2000 Server and Windows 2000 Advanced Server

Windows 2000 Server and Windows 2000 Advanced Server are usually found on large client/server networks. These operating systems are designed to support heavy network processing demands and can be used to host network services, such as database services and messaging services. Windows 2000 Advanced Server offers more features and can support a larger network than Windows 2000 Server.

Windows 2000 Datacenter Server

Windows 2000 Datacenter Server is typically used on high-traffic networks, such as those found in large multinational companies, and to host large applications, such as high-volume Web sites. Windows 2000 Datacenter Server can be used where network reliability is essential.

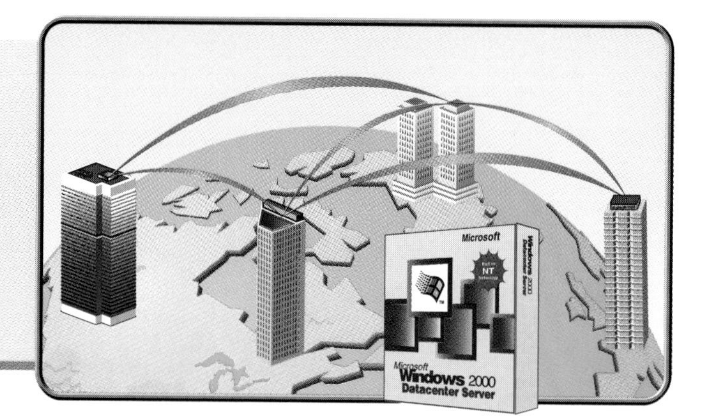

Upgrading

It is easy to upgrade an older Windows operating system, such as Windows NT, to a Windows 2000 operating system. It is usually cheaper to upgrade an existing Windows operating system than it is to install a Windows 2000 operating system on a new network.

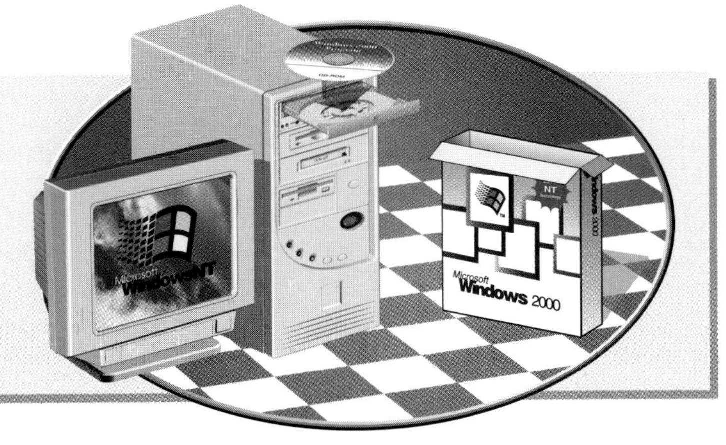

Clustering

Clustering is the term that describes using two or more servers to perform the same task. Operating systems that support clustering can distribute a heavy workload over many servers to increase the performance of a network. Clustering also allows one of the servers to be used as a backup in the event another server performing the same task fails. Both Windows 2000 Advanced Server and Windows 2000 Datacenter Server support clustering.

Internet Ready

The Windows 2000 operating systems include applications and services, such as Web server software and the TCP/IP protocol, which allow users on a network to access and work with information on the Internet. Today, most corporate networks are connected to the Internet.

UNIX

UNIX is an older, powerful operating system that can be used to run an entire network or a single computer.

Many of the first computers used to establish the Internet, the world's largest network, ran the UNIX operating system. Even today, UNIX is the most commonly used operating system for servers on the Internet.

Versions

UNIX is the oldest computer operating system still in widespread use today. Since its development in the late 1960s, many companies have owned the UNIX name. There are several versions of the UNIX operating system available. Hewlett-Packard makes a UNIX operating system called HP-UX. IBM's UNIX operating system is called AIX.

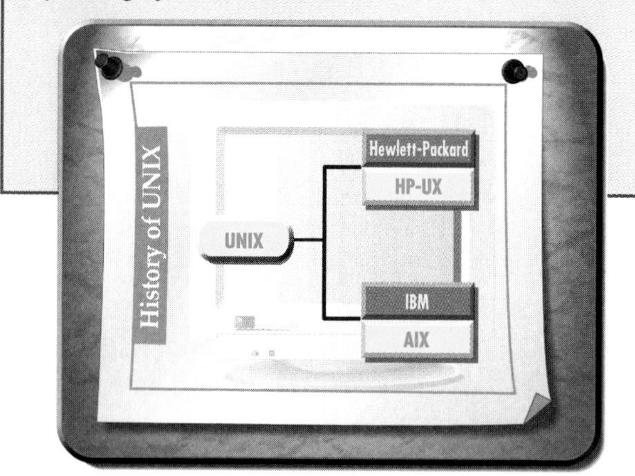

Multitasking

UNIX was originally developed to be the operating system for a single large computer, called a mainframe computer. Since multiple users can access a mainframe computer at the same time, UNIX was developed to run many programs and perform numerous tasks at once, referred to as multitasking. UNIX's multitasking capabilities make it an efficient network operating system.

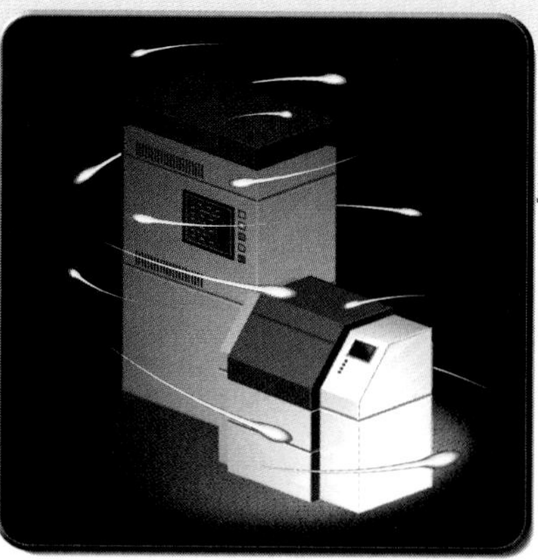

Linux is a UNIX-based operating system that is available free of charge on the World Wide Web.

Linux is a popular operating system due to its availability and flexibility. More information about Linux is available at the www.linux.org Web site.

Distributions

There are several versions, or distributions, of the Linux operating system. Companies that distribute Linux, such as Red Hat, Mandrake and Slackware, often include their own applications and enhancements to distinguish their version from those provided by other manufacturers. The most popular version of Linux is distributed by Red Hat. A free version of Red Hat Linux is available at the www.redhat.com Web site. Linux is also available for purchase at computer stores.

Open Source Code

Linux is an open source code operating system. This means that Linux can be copied, modified and redistributed with few restrictions. Since Linux is open source code, the operating system can be customized to meet the individual needs of different networks. This flexibility is one of the reasons Linux is growing in popularity.

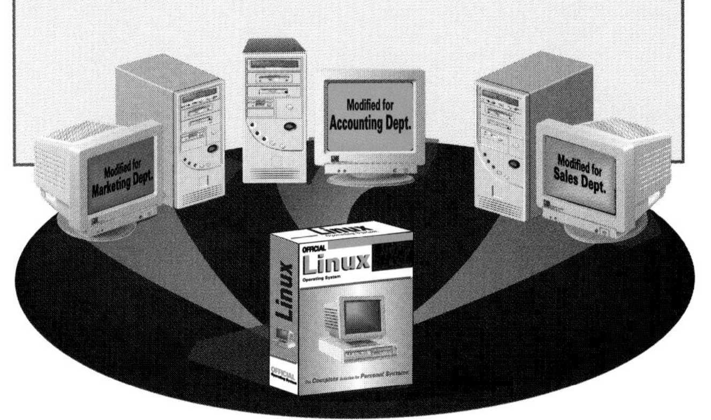

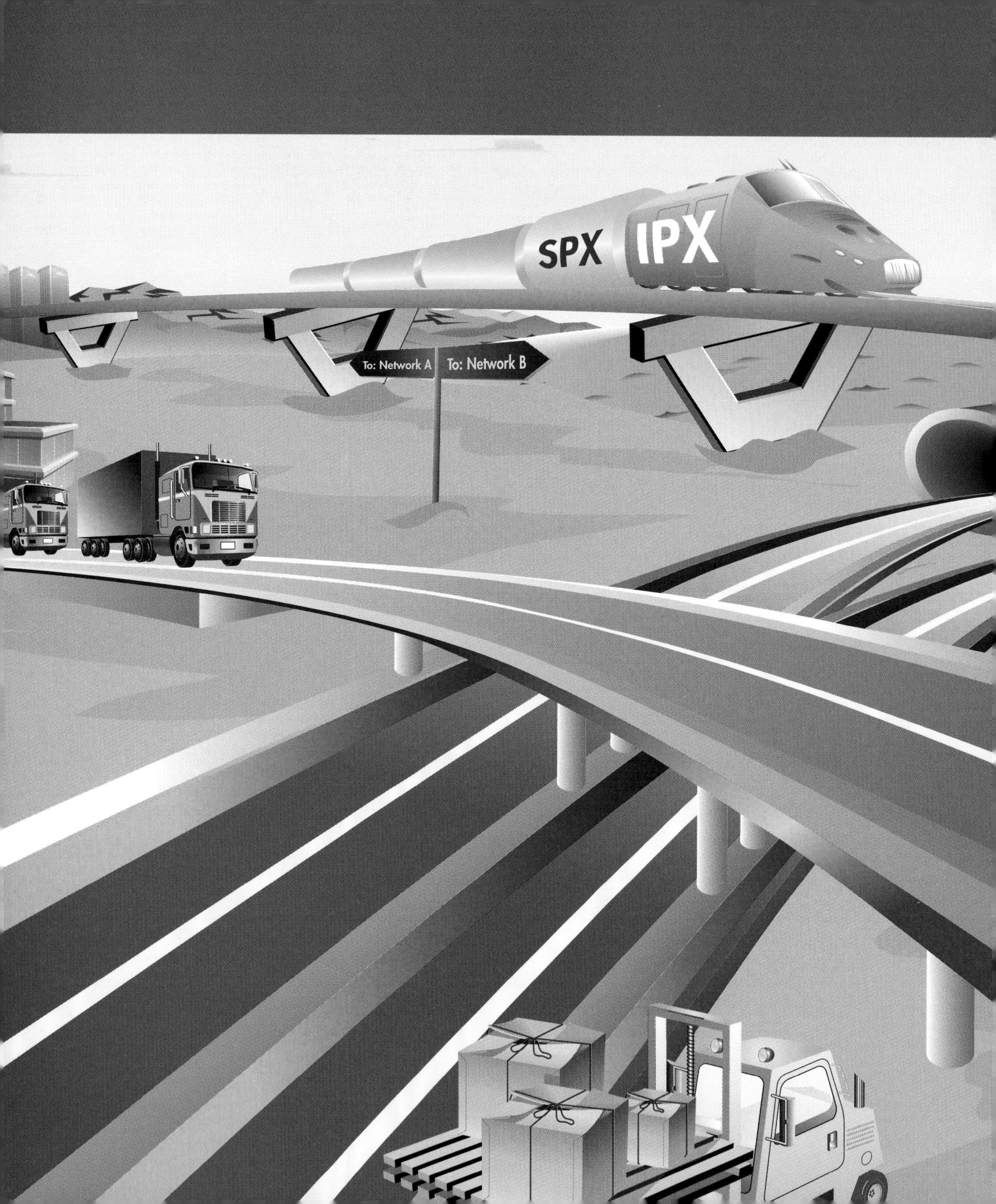
SPX
IPX
To: Network A
To: Network B

CHAPTER 8

The OSI Model and Protocols

The OSI model specifies how communication between computers on a network should occur. This chapter discusses the role of the OSI model, as well as the IPX/SPX, NetBEUI and TCP/IP protocols.

The OSI Model 120

OSI Model Layers............................122

Protocols 124

IPX/SPX Protocols............................126

NetBEUI Protocol 128

TCP/IP Protocols..............................130

Common TCP/IP Protocols...............132

The Open Systems Interconnection (OSI) model specifies how communication between computers on a network should occur.

The Open Systems Interconnection Model

The Open Systems Interconnection (OSI) model is a set of guidelines that describes the process that should take place when two computers communicate on a network. The OSI model is also a standard that specifies how network hardware and software should be designed to ensure they are able to work together on a network.

Layers

There are seven layers in the OSI model–Application, Presentation, Session, Transport, Network, Data Link and Physical. When information is transferred on a network, each layer performs a specific task to help transfer the information. For example, the Transport layer checks for errors in the transmission and the Network layer identifies the computer the information is addressed to. For more information about the OSI model layers, see page 122.

International Organization for Standardization

The International Organization for Standardization (ISO) is an organization that develops product standards for the computer industry and coordinates the activities of other standards organizations. The ISO's main objective is to ensure the reliability of products and services used throughout the world. The ISO developed the OSI model. For more information about the ISO and product standards, visit the www.iso.ch Web site.

Standards

Many products, often manufactured by different companies, are needed to create and maintain a network. Before a network can function properly, all the products on the network must be able to communicate with each other. Before the OSI model was introduced, there was no standardized way to exchange information on a network. Many companies developed their own network devices without considering how the devices would work with or affect other products on a network. Most manufacturers now follow the OSI model so that their products will work with products developed by other companies. When companies follow the OSI model, they ensure that their devices will communicate with other devices on a network.

Company B
Company A
Company C
Company D

The OSI model has seven layers that describe the tasks that must be performed to transfer information on a network.

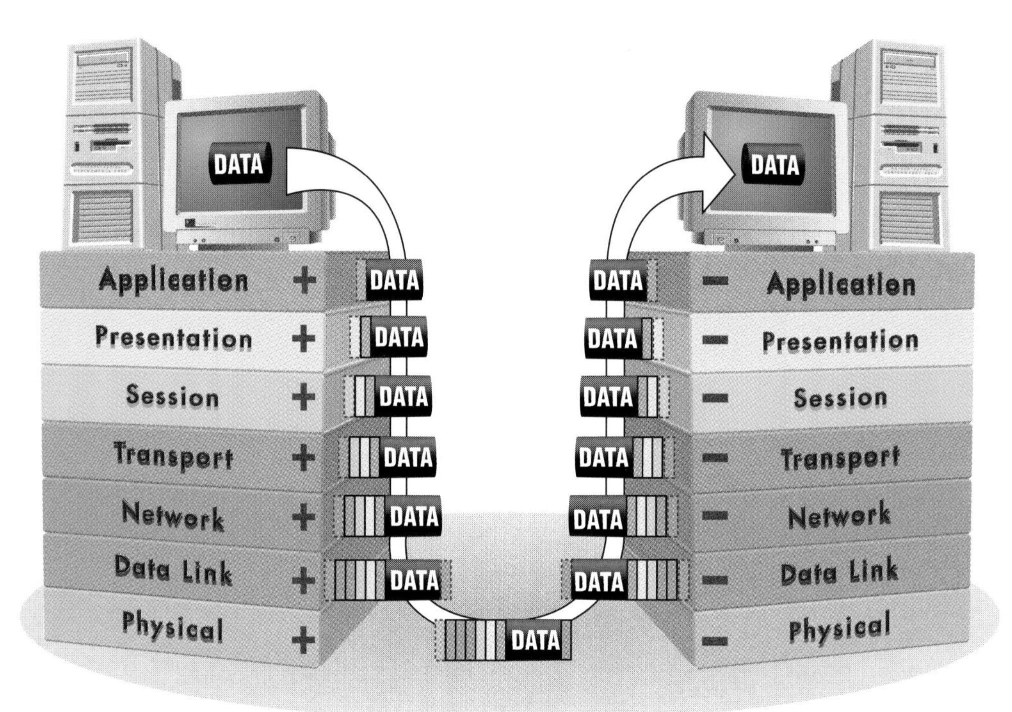

When data is being transferred over a network, it must pass through each layer of the OSI model. As the data passes through each layer, information is added to the data. When the data reaches the destination, the data must again pass through the layers of the OSI model. The additional information is removed at each layer.

Application Layer

The Application layer is responsible for exchanging information between the programs running on a computer and the services running on a network, such as database or print services.

Presentation Layer

The Presentation layer converts information from one format to another.

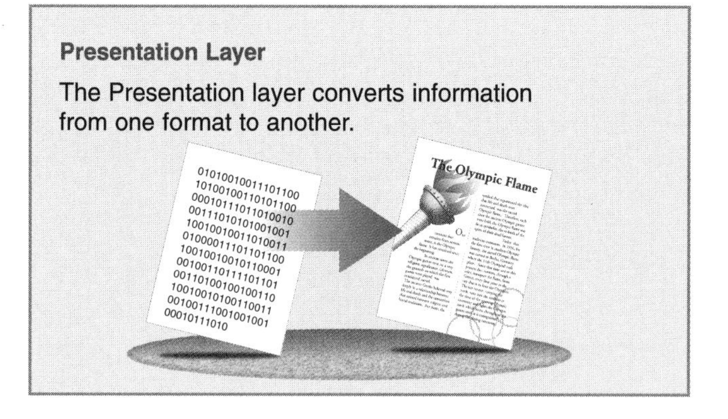

Session Layer

The Session layer determines how two devices communicate. This layer establishes and monitors connections between computers.

Transport Layer

The Transport layer corrects errors in transmission and ensures that information is delivered reliably.

Network Layer

The Network layer identifies computers on a network and determines how to direct information transferring over a network.

Data Link Layer

The Data Link layer groups data into sets to prepare the data for transferring over a network.

Physical Layer

The Physical layer defines how a transmission medium, such as a cable, connects to a computer. This layer also specifies how electrical information transfers on the transmission medium.

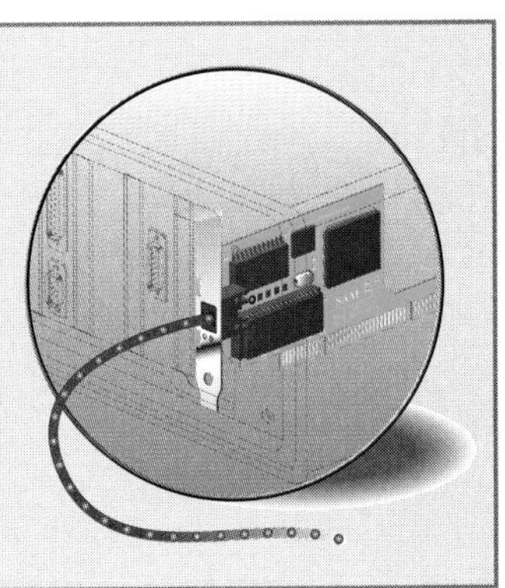

Before computers or other network devices can exchange information, they must establish communication. A protocol is a language, or set of rules, which determines how devices on a network communicate with each other.

Protocols

Protocols are the actual hardware and software components that carry out the OSI model guidelines for transferring information on a network. A network often uses multiple protocols that work together to carry out a task.

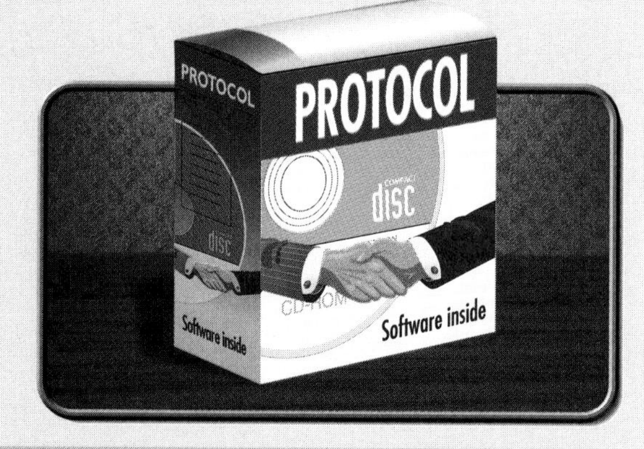

Protocol Stacks

A protocol stack, also called a suite, is made up of multiple protocols that are used to exchange information between computers. Common protocol stacks include IPX/SPX and TCP/IP. In the TCP/IP stack, the TCP protocol is used to transfer information between two devices, while the IP protocol is responsible for addressing information and directing information to its proper destination.

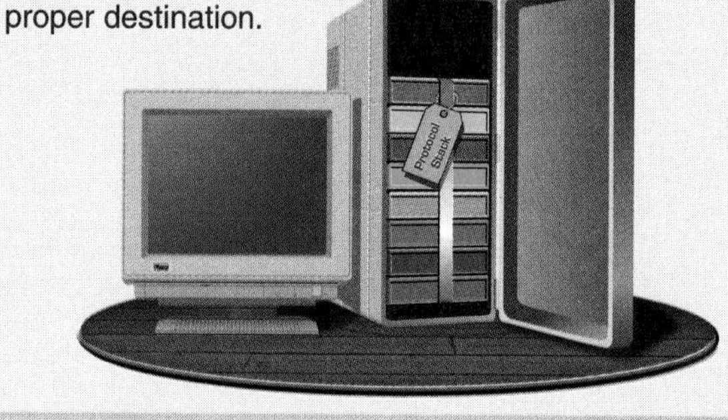

Layers

A layer is a section of a protocol stack that is responsible for performing one particular aspect of information transfer. The OSI model determines which protocols should be used at each layer. Since some protocols are capable of performing more than one function, one layer in a protocol stack may not necessarily correspond to one layer in the OSI model.

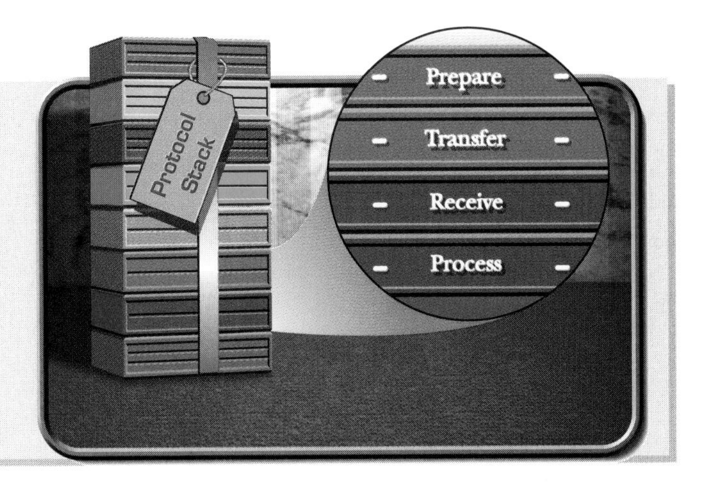

Compatibility

Computers and network devices must use the same protocols to exchange information. For example, a computer and network printer must use the same protocol before the computer can successfully send print jobs to the printer. A layer in a protocol stack on one computer must be able to communicate with the same layer in the protocol stack on another computer or device.

Standards

When a networking device is designed to communicate using an accepted protocol, the device can communicate with any other device that uses the same protocol. The OSI model and protocol standards help ensure networking devices will be able to work together on a network.

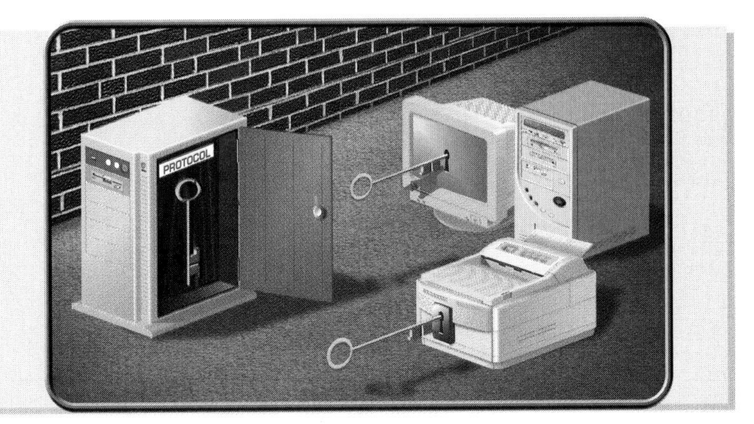

IPX/SPX PROTOCOLS

The IPX/SPX protocols make up the protocol suite that is used to transfer information on networks running the NetWare operating system.

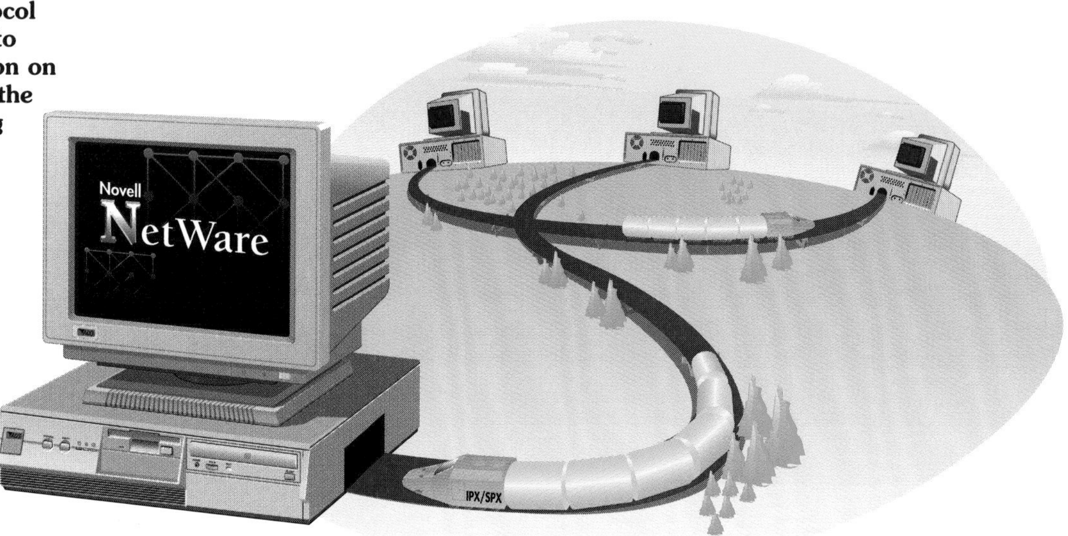

IPX

The Internetwork Packet Exchange (IPX) protocol is derived from a protocol developed by Xerox Corporation called Xerox Network System (XNS). The IPX protocol is most often used to transfer information between devices located on NetWare networks. The IPX protocol uses addresses to keep track of devices located on different networks.

When the IPX protocol transfers data from one device to another, the protocol does not set up a connection between the two devices. The protocol also does not monitor the transmission or check the reliability of the data.

SPX

The Sequenced Packet Exchange (SPX) protocol is an extension of the IPX protocol. Unlike the IPX protocol, the SPX protocol makes a connection between the two network devices that want to exchange data and monitors the transmission. The SPX protocol also ensures the data exchanged has no errors.

Popular

NetWare is an operating system developed by Novell for client/server networks. NetWare is one of the most popular network operating systems available and is often found on large corporate networks. Since many networks use the NetWare operating system, the IPX/SPX protocols are widely used and supported by many manufacturers.

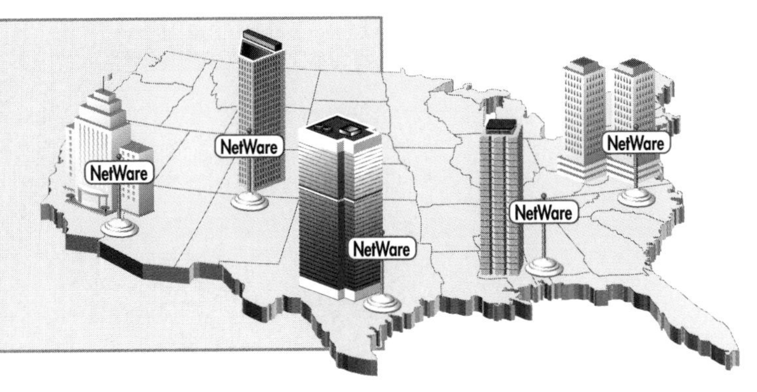

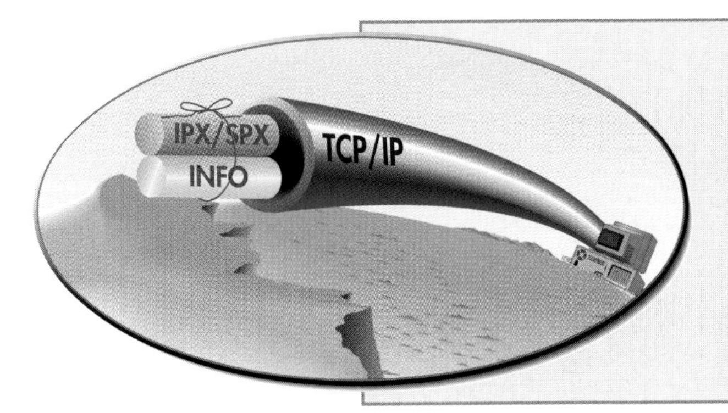

Tunneling

Tunneling describes the process of using a protocol to transfer information through a different type of network. The IPX/SPX protocols support IP tunneling, so information can be transferred between NetWare networks using a TCP/IP network or the Internet. The information and IPX/SPX protocols are bundled within the TCP/IP protocol suite. When the information reaches its destination, the TCP/IP protocols are removed.

Ports

A port is a location in a computer's memory that is used by a program. Ports are virtual locations and exist only when the computer is running. When the IPX/SPX protocols transfer information to a destination computer, the protocols use ports to indicate where the information must be delivered in the computer's memory to reach the appropriate program.

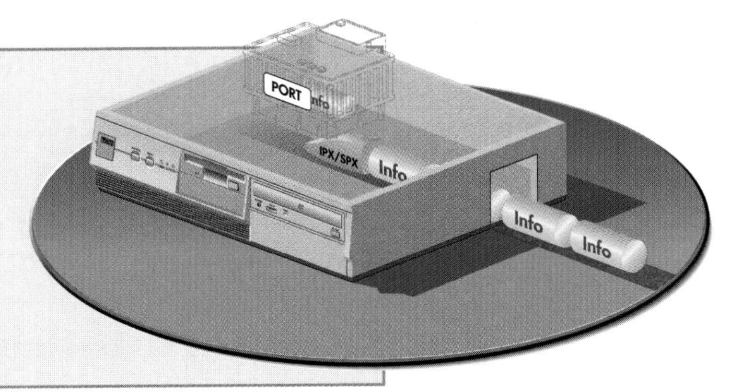

NetBEUI (NetBIOS Extended User Interface) is a network protocol used on small local area networks.

NetBEUI is a popular protocol due to its speed, efficiency and ease of administration. NetBEUI was developed by IBM and has been adopted by the Microsoft Windows family of networking products.

NetBIOS

NetBIOS (Network Basic Input/Output System) was developed by IBM as a way of allowing computers to communicate with each other on a network. The NetBEUI protocol was developed to improve upon NetBIOS and make it more efficient.

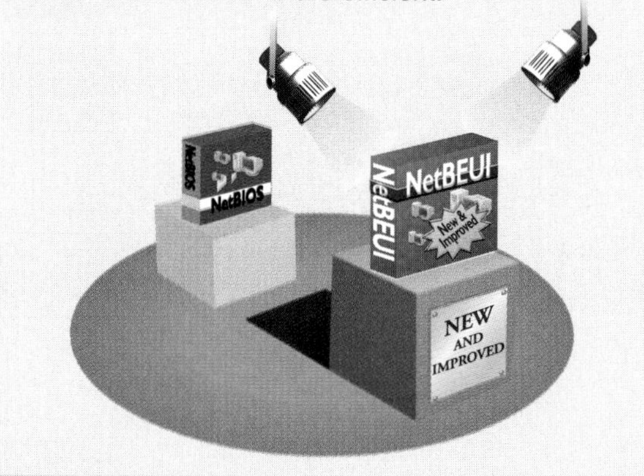

Performance

NetBEUI is a very small and efficient protocol that does not require a lot of computer resources, such as memory or processing power. NetBEUI can transfer information on a network much faster than many other protocols.

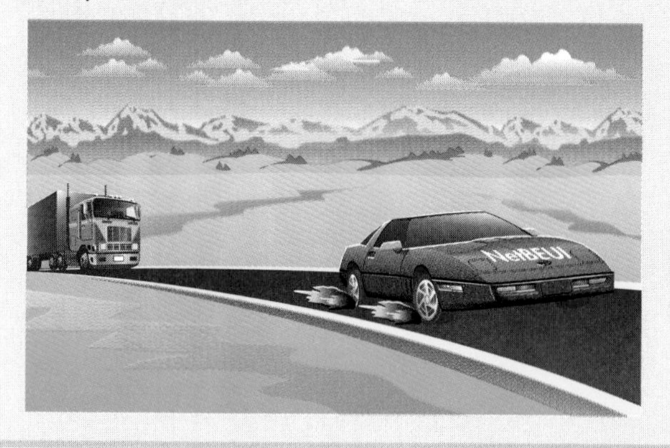

Microsoft

NetBEUI is found almost exclusively on networks that are based on products developed by Microsoft. All Microsoft products that connect to a network can use the NetBEUI protocol.

Configuration

NetBEUI is quite simple to set up. When configuring a network computer using the NetBEUI protocol, the administrator must give the computer a unique name to identify it on the network. The administrator also needs to assign the computer to a workgroup, which allows the computer to access a predetermined set of network resources.

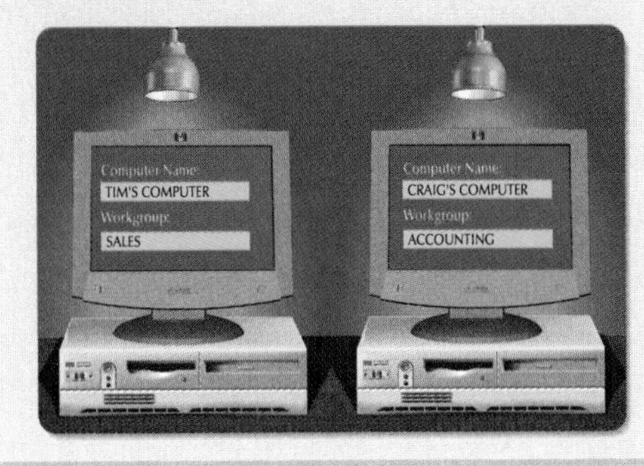

Non-routable Protocol

The major disadvantage of using the NetBEUI protocol is that the protocol cannot be used on a large network. Many large networks use routers to link parts of a network. NetBEUI is a non-routable protocol, which means it cannot pass through network routers.

Internet

The NetBEUI protocol cannot be used to connect to the Internet. Since most businesses are now connected to the Internet, NetBEUI is becoming less popular and is being replaced by the TCP/IP protocol. For more information about the TCP/IP protocol, see page 130.

TCP/IP PROTOCOLS

TCP/IP is a collection, or stack, of protocols used to allow communication between networks with different types of computer systems. TCP/IP is the suite of protocols used on the Internet.

Development

TCP/IP was originally developed in the late 1960s to accommodate the networking needs of the U.S. Department of Defense. The TCP/IP protocol suite has been available for many years and has been repeatedly tested and improved. However, most TCP/IP protocols used to connect today's computers are the original protocols developed over 30 years ago.

Popularity

TCP/IP quickly became a popular suite of protocols because the companies that supplied products to the Department of Defense had to ensure their products supported TCP/IP. As a result, many devices now support TCP/IP and many companies use TCP/IP to transfer information. The rapid growth of the Internet has also been a factor in the widespread popularity of TCP/IP.

Reroute

TCP/IP was designed to ensure that a collection of connected networks would be able to withstand a major disruption, such as war, that could damage several parts of the network. One of the main benefits of TCP/IP is that it can be used to easily reroute information around damaged parts of connected networks.

Network Types

TCP/IP is used on different types of networks including Ethernet, Token-Ring and even networks using modem connections. Almost all networks are capable of supporting TCP/IP.

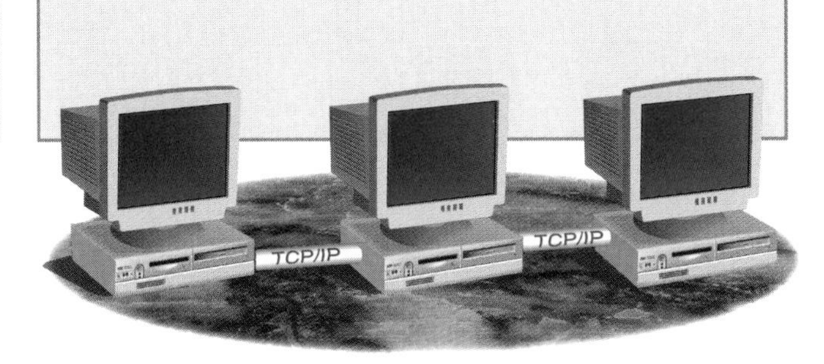

Compatibility

Since TCP/IP is the only protocol suite that can be used to connect to the Internet, other protocols, such as IPX/SPX and NetBEUI, have been adapted to work with TCP/IP.

Open Standard

A major benefit of TCP/IP is that it is an open standard protocol. This means that any company or person can design a device or software program that uses TCP/IP without having to pay a royalty or licensing fee.

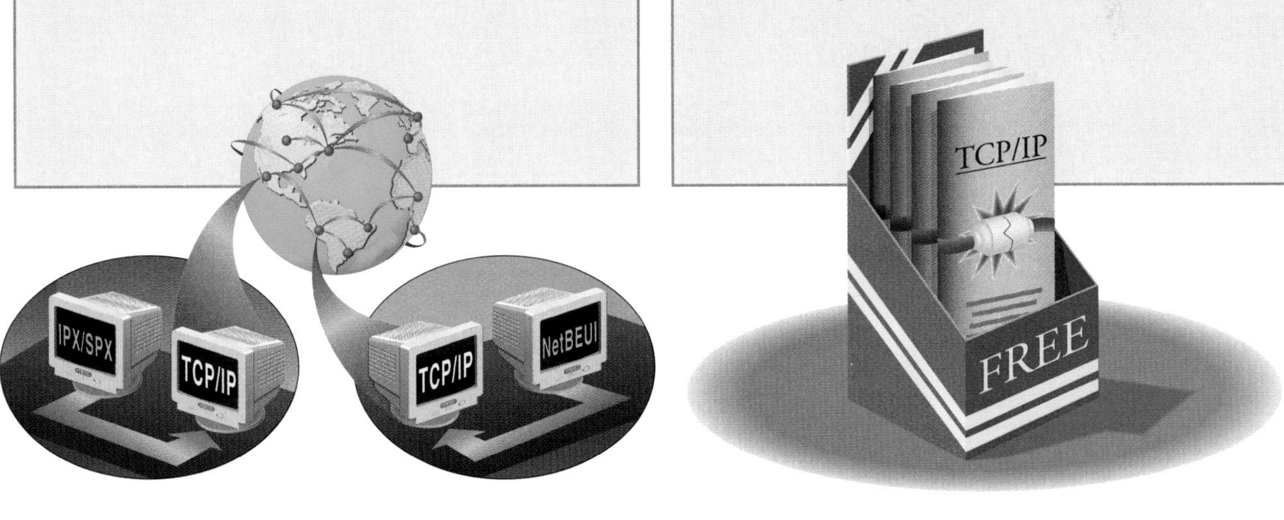

There are many protocols that make up the TCP/IP protocol suite. Each protocol in the suite is responsible for performing a specific task.

TCP

Transmission Control Protocol (TCP) is used to transfer information between two devices on a TCP/IP network. TCP uses virtual ports to make connections between devices and also monitors the transmission of information.

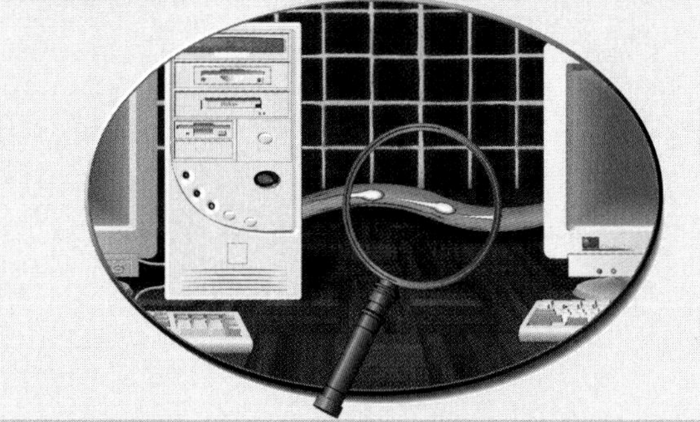

IP

Internet Protocol (IP) is responsible for addressing information and directing information to its proper destination on a TCP/IP network.

FTP

File Transfer Protocol (FTP) is one of the most widely recognized and used TCP/IP protocols. FTP is used to transfer documents between different types of computers on a TCP/IP network.

HTTP

HyperText Transfer Protocol (HTTP) is one of the most widely used protocols for transferring information on the Internet. HTTP is used to transfer information from Web servers to Web browsers.

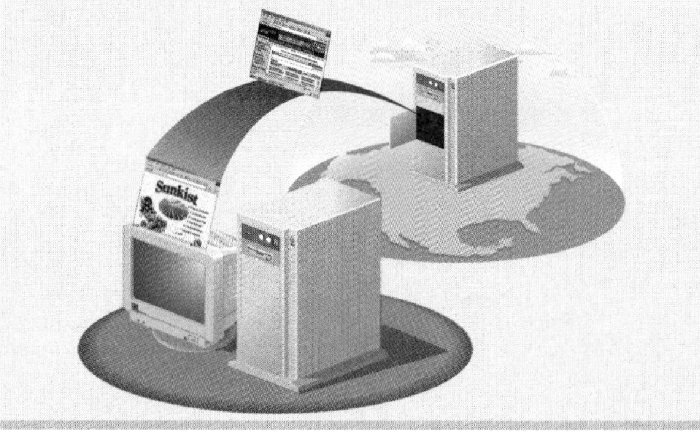

UDP

User Datagram Protocol (UDP) uses virtual ports to transfer information between two applications on a TCP/IP network. UDP is slightly faster than the TCP protocol, but it is not as reliable.

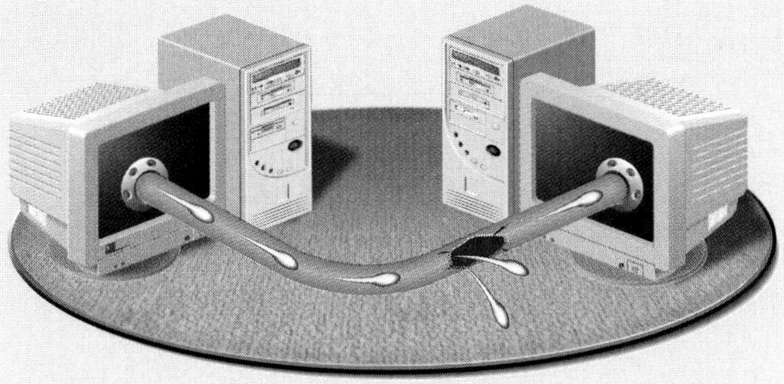

DHCP

Dynamic Host Configuration Protocol (DHCP) is used to allow communication between network devices and a server that administers IP numbers, called a DHCP server.

DHCP Server

172.16.212.12

DNS

Domain Name System (DNS) is used to match Internet computer names to their corresponding IP numbers. DNS allows users to type a computer name, such as www.company.com, instead of an IP number, such as 192.168.53.3, to access a computer.

www.company.com

DNS Server

192.168.53.3

WINS

Windows Internet Naming Service (WINS) is a protocol used on Microsoft-based TCP/IP networks. A server running WINS can match Microsoft network computer names to IP numbers. This allows computers on the Microsoft network to communicate with other networks and computers that use the TCP/IP suite.

Paul's Computer

WINS

192.168.42.28

HTTPS

Secure HyperText Transfer Protocol (HTTPS) is used to securely transfer information on the Internet. HTTPS encrypts and decrypts the information exchanged between a Web server and a Web browser using a system called Secure Sockets Layer (SSL).

SMTP

Simple Mail Transfer Protocol (SMTP) can be used to send and receive e-mail messages. SMTP is generally used only to send e-mail messages, while another protocol, such as POP3, is used to receive e-mail messages.

POP3

Post Office Protocol 3 (POP3) is responsible for receiving e-mail messages and storing the messages on a server, often referred to as a POP server.

ICMP

Internet Control Message Protocol (ICMP) controls messages and reports errors on a TCP/IP network. The PING command uses the ICMP protocol to test if a network device is available.

SLIP

Serial Line Internet Protocol (SLIP) is an older and simpler protocol used to connect computers over serial lines. SLIP is being replaced by PPP, which offers improved error control and security.

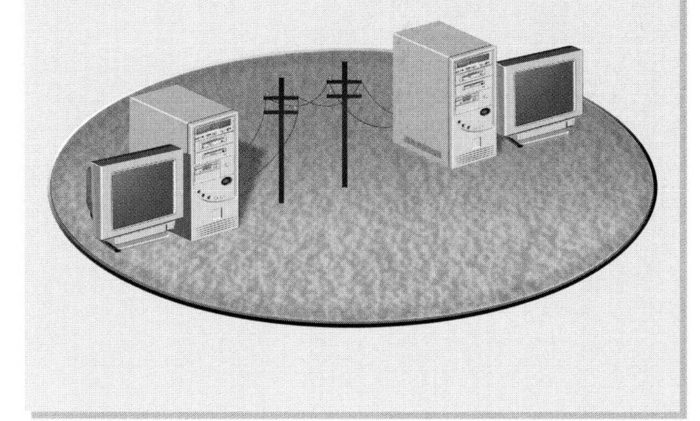

PPP

Point-to-Point Protocol (PPP) allows two computers to communicate over serial lines. Some high-speed connections, such as ISDN, can use PPP to connect computers.

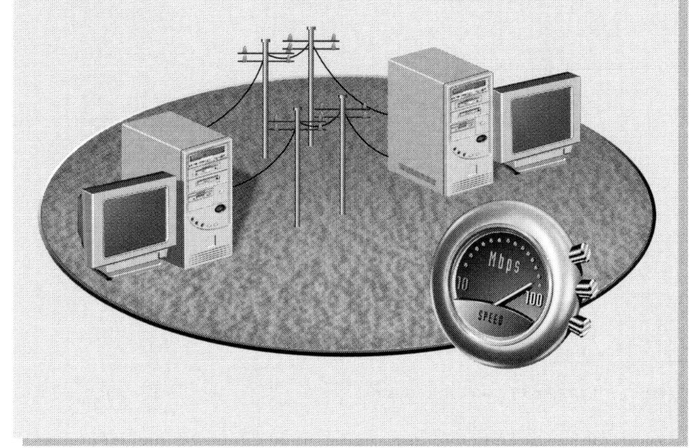

IGP/EGP

Interior Gateway Protocol (IGP) and Exterior Gateway Protocol (EGP) allow networks to exchange routing information. Routing information is used to determine the best path for information to travel across multiple networks.

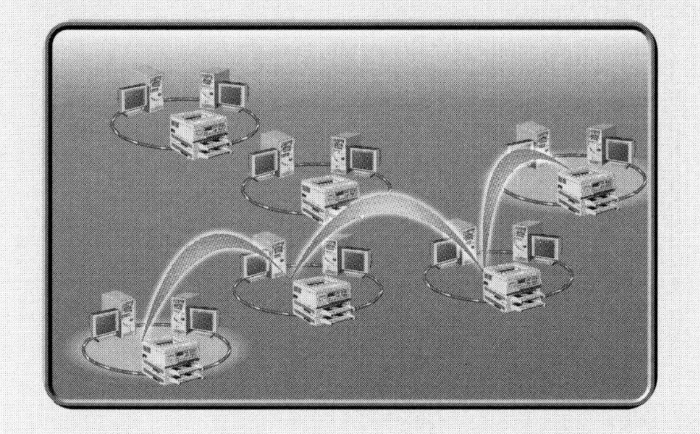

RIP/OSPF

Routing Information Protocol (RIP) is used to specify how routers on small to medium sized networks exchange routing information. Open Shortest Path First (OSPF) is used on large networks to specify how routers exchange routing information.

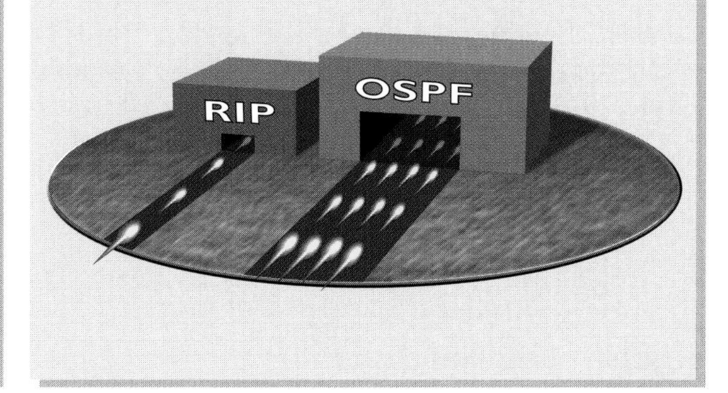

DAT2
Backup
Backup
Welcome to ABC Inc.
Network
Login name:
Password:
Authorized
Personnel
ONLY

CHAPTER 9

Protecting Network Data

It is important for every company to protect its network data. This chapter examines the major threats to network data and how companies can protect their information.

Threats to Network Data 138

Firewalls 142

Passwords 144

File Permissions 145

Back Up Network Data.....................146

Tape Backup Devices 148

Uninterruptible Power Supplies..........150

Fault Tolerance 152

There are many ways that data can be lost, damaged or destroyed. Protecting important data is one of the primary responsibilities of a network administrator.

If data on a network is destroyed, a company could experience serious financial losses and reductions in employee productivity.

Computer Failure

The main cause of lost information is computer failure. Most storage devices, such as hard drives, are mechanical devices, which can become worn out and prone to failure. A storage device is often the first component to malfunction in a computer. When a storage device fails, all the data stored on the device may be lost.

Accidents

Accidents are a common and frustrating way to lose data. A service technician performing maintenance or repairs on a computer may inadvertently erase the contents of a hard drive.

Computer users may also mistakenly erase information they think is unimportant, only to discover later that the information was needed.

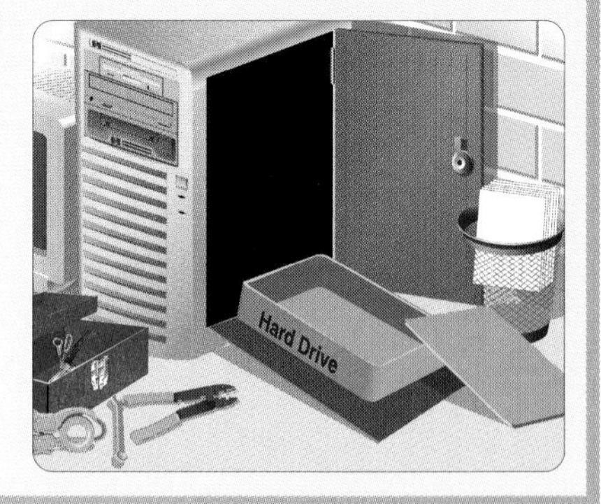

Lack of Training

Network users who are not properly trained in how to access network data and use network equipment are likely to damage the data or equipment. Users who have not been trained to recognize suspicious changes in their computer systems are also a threat to network data because they are unable to alert the system administrator to possible security breaches.

Fire

Fires may be started by faulty wiring, carelessness or even arson. If a building catches fire, computers and the information stored on a network are at risk of being destroyed.

Natural Disasters

Natural disasters can be devastating to a business. Disasters such as earthquakes, floods and tornadoes can destroy all the information on a network in a matter of moments. Most large organizations have disaster recovery programs in place that outline how these types of disasters are handled.

COMPUTER CRIME

Criminal acts, such as vandalism and theft, can compromise the security of network data.

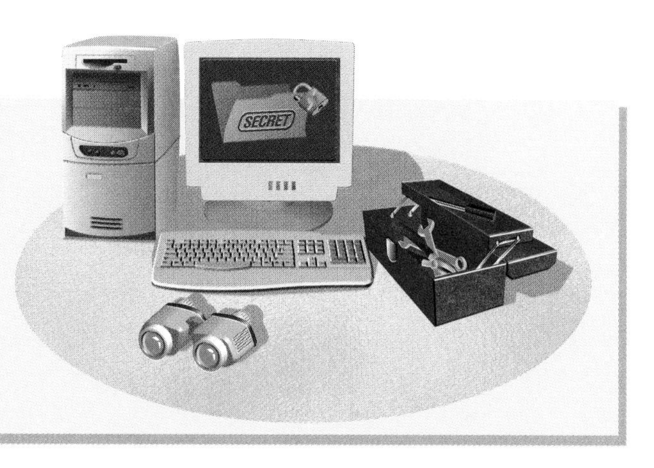

Crackers

Crackers are people who enjoy the challenge of illegally breaking into computer systems and breaching network security. Crackers usually do not cause any damage to the networks they successfully break into, but they may be able to view private or confidential information stored on the network.

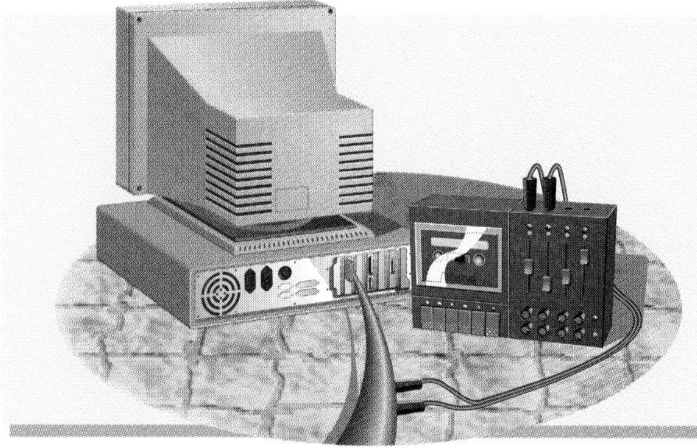

Electronic Eavesdropping

Sophisticated monitoring equipment can be used to record and decipher the electrical signals that are transmitted on network cables. If a network is used to transfer confidential information, the network administrator should ensure that steps are taken to prevent electronic eavesdropping, such as using fiber-optic cable. Fiber-optic cable does not emit electrical signals that can be monitored.

Theft

Almost every company is vulnerable to computer theft. Most computer systems are easily transported and can be very profitable for thieves. Most computer thieves are very knowledgeable about computers and often strip the computers and sell the parts.

VIRUSES

A virus is a program that can cause a variety of problems, including the destruction of information on a computer system.

Infection

Networks can become infected with viruses through files, such as files received on floppy disks, files downloaded from the Internet or files received as e-mail attachments. These types of files should not be used on a computer connected to a network until an anti-virus program has scanned the files.

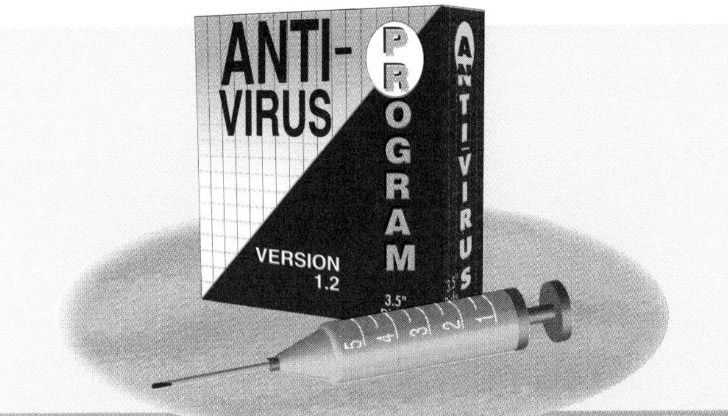

Detection

There are many anti-virus software programs available that will scan information stored on a computer to try and detect if there are any viruses on the computer. Many anti-virus programs can also remove viruses once they are detected. Some viruses cannot be removed without deleting the infected information.

Backups

When a virus is discovered on a computer that is regularly backed up, it is important to determine when the computer became infected with the virus. If a backup was performed while the virus existed on the computer, the computer may be reinfected if the backup copy is restored.

FIREWALLS

Firewalls protect network data by controlling the information that passes between a private network and the Internet. Without a firewall, a private network could be susceptible to a variety of attacks, including unauthorized remote log on attempts, viruses and electronic junk mail, called spam.

Firewalls

Most buildings are constructed with special walls designed to stop or slow the spread of fire through a building. A network firewall follows the same principle. A network firewall is designed to prevent or inhibit unauthorized individuals from accessing a private network.

Hardware and Software

Firewalls can be hardware devices, software programs or a combination of hardware and software. Some companies use expensive commercial firewall systems to provide increased security to their network data. Firewalls are usually designed for easy upgrading and reconfiguration to protect against new methods of attack.

Filters

A firewall can be configured to filter information sent to a network. If the information does not originate from an approved source, then the information is discarded. This is the simplest form of a firewall.

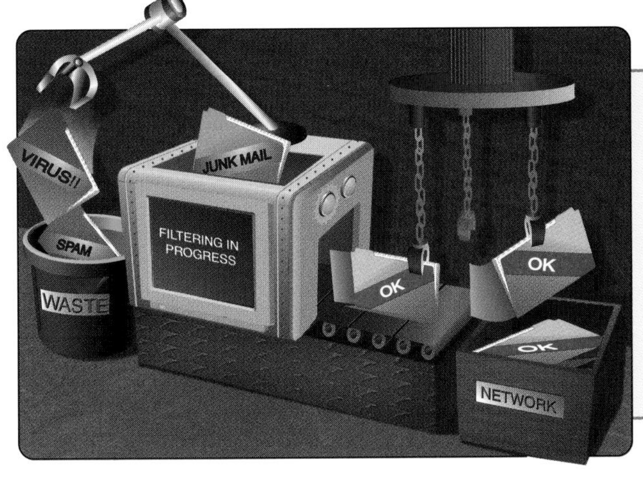

Sophisticated Filters

Some firewalls check the characteristics of each piece of information sent from a network. When information is returned to the network, the firewall compares the characteristics of the incoming information to the characteristics of the information that was sent. If a match is found, the incoming information can pass through to the network. If no match is found, the incoming information is discarded.

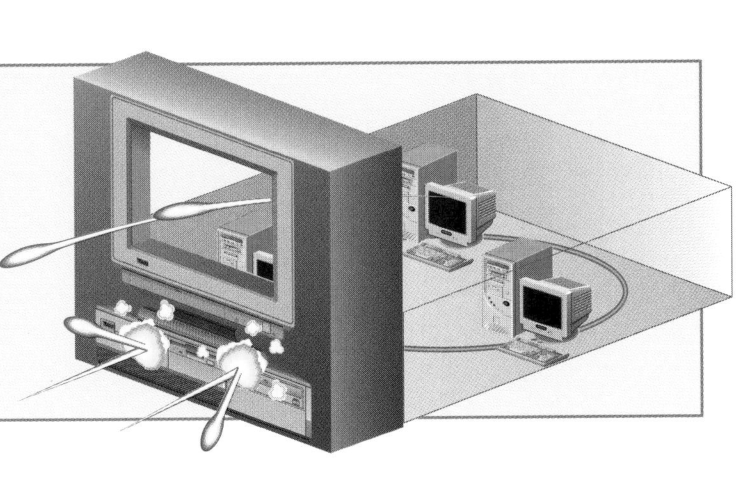

Gateways

A gateway is usually a computer that acts as a connector between a private, internal network and another network, such as the Internet. Gateways used as firewalls can transmit information from an internal network to the Internet. Gateways can also examine incoming information to determine if the information should be allowed entry to the network.

PASSWORDS

Passwords protect network data from unauthorized access. Passwords are the first line of defense in securing information and resources attached to a network.

As a general rule, users are assigned a password along with their user name. User names and passwords should always be kept secret to ensure network security.

Group Passwords

A group password allows members of a specific group to access certain resources and data on a network. Most operating systems allow a user to be assigned to more than one group. This gives the network administrator more flexibility when assigning access to various network resources.

Resource Passwords

Some network operating systems allow a network administrator to assign a password to a specific resource connected to the network, such as a modem or printer. Users will need to enter the appropriate password before gaining access to the resource. This is an effective way of regulating the use of busy network resources.

FILE PERMISSIONS

Permissions, also referred to as privileges, can be used to control access to specific files, directories or storage devices attached to a network. Permissions are an important part of network security and provide better protection for network data than passwords alone.

Common Permissions

Depending on the network operating system, a network administrator may be able to assign individual permissions for each file, directory or storage device on the network. The most common permissions include the following:

Read	Allows users to read or copy the file.
Execute	Allows users to run the program.
Write	Allows users to modify the contents of the file.
Delete	Allows users to delete the file.
No Access	Does not allow users to access the file.

File Activity Logs

One of the most useful network features is the ability to monitor file activity. Many network operating systems allow network administrators to examine who accessed certain files and when the files were accessed. By examining file activity, network administrators can adjust the permissions to better suit the requirements of the users.

FILE ACTIVITY LOG

FILE NAME	ACCESSED BY	TIME
2000 Sales Report	James Garrett	9:35 AM
Technical Guidelines	Rose Henry	9:56 AM
June 2000 Budget	Marcie Bush	11:00 AM
Ongoing Projects	Hal Morrison	2:19 PM
Current Assignments	Alex Greene	3:08 PM
Marketing Proposal	Anna Stelleck	3:45 PM

BACK UP NETWORK DATA

Network data should be backed up on a regular basis. Backing up data creates an extra copy in case the original files are lost or damaged.

It is important to carefully schedule network backups to ensure that all valuable data is protected.

Backup Programs

A backup program copies the files stored on a computer to a storage device, such as a tape drive. Most storage devices come with a backup program specifically designed for use with the storage device. Most backup programs compress the data being backed up to save space on storage media, such as tape cartridges.

Internet Backups

Many organizations offer backup services over the Internet. If a network is connected to the Internet, network data can be backed up by sending the data to another organization for safekeeping. Information can be restored by downloading the data back to the network. Internet backups are most effective when using a high-speed Internet connection to back up small amounts of information.

Backup Strategies

When developing a backup strategy, a company must consider the amount of work it cannot afford to lose. If the company cannot afford to lose a day's work, backups should be performed on a daily basis. If data does not change much during a week, a backup could be performed once a week.

Scheduled Backups

A company should create and then strictly follow a backup schedule. Most backup programs can be set to run automatically. Backups should be scheduled during times when the network is not busy, such as lunchtime or the middle of the night.

Types of Backups

There are different ways of backing up information. For example, a full backup backs up all the files on a network computer. This type of backup requires the most time and media space. A selective backup backs up files that have been selected and is useful when media space is limited. An incremental backup only backs up the files that have changed since the last backup. This type of backup requires less time and media space than a full backup.

TAPE BACKUP DEVICES

Tape drives are the most common devices used for backing up data on networks. Tape backup devices copy the files stored on a computer onto a tape backup medium.

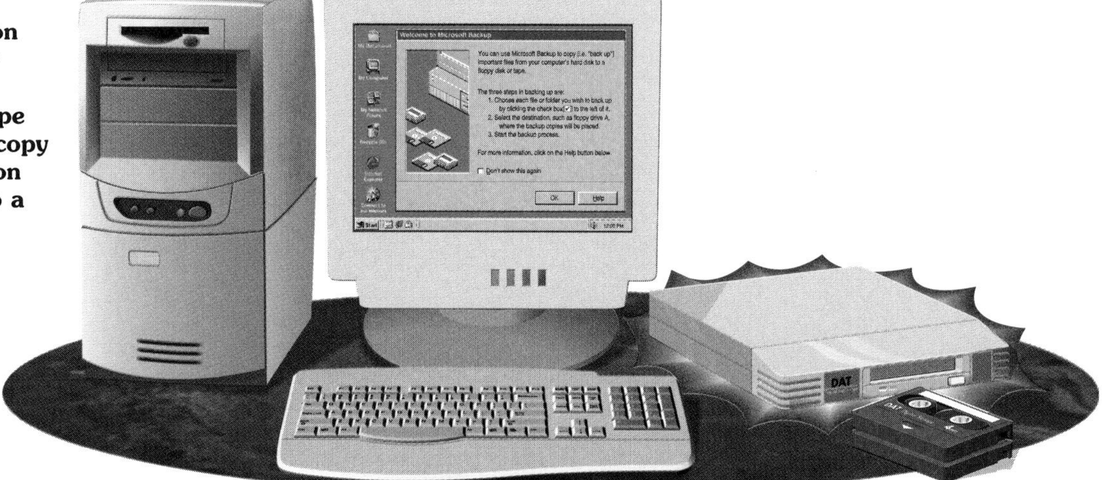

A tape drive can be installed inside a computer or connected externally using a cable. External tape drives are more expensive than internal tape drives.

Tape Backup Media

Tape backup media are commonly cartridges. Inside a tape cartridge, there is a thin strip of plastic tape coated with a magnetic material, similar to the tape found in audio and video cassettes.

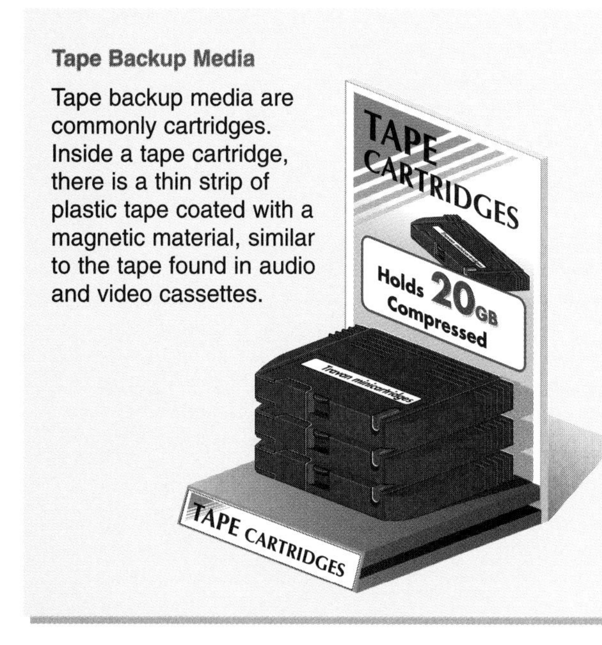

Care of Tape Backup Media

If taken care of properly, tape cartridges can reliably store data for many years. Tape backup cartridges should never be exposed to extremely hot, cold, dry or humid environments. They should also be kept away from devices that generate magnetic fields, such as speakers or monitors. If cartridges are stored for a long period of time, they should be rotated regularly to prevent the tape from stretching or sagging.

TYPES OF TAPE BACKUP DEVICES

Travan Drives

Travan drives are relatively inexpensive, but are not as fast as other types of tape backup devices. Travan cartridges can store up to 20 GB of data and are commonly used to back up information on home computers and small networks.

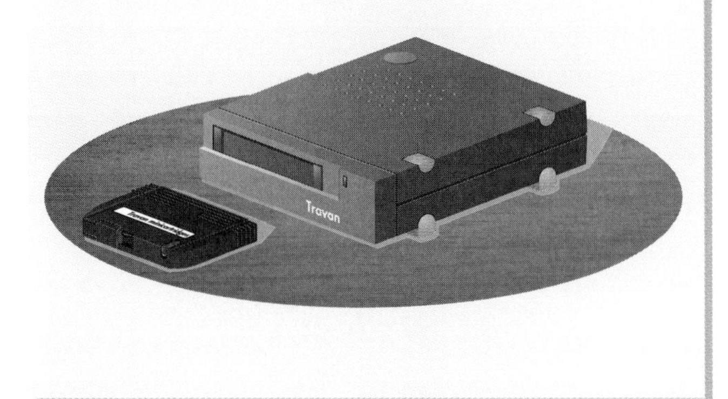

DAT Drives

Digital Audio Tape (DAT) drives use technology originally developed for audio and video products. DAT cartridges are available in 4 millimeter (mm) and 8 mm versions. DAT cartridges can store up to 40 GB of data. DAT drives are expensive, but the cartridges are inexpensive.

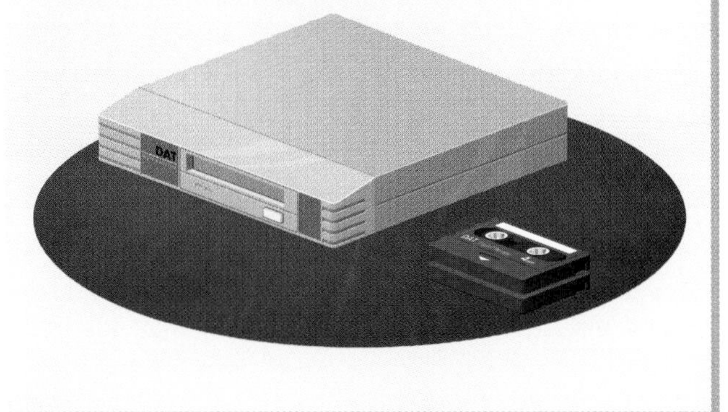

DLT Drives

Digital Linear Tape (DLT) drives are very expensive, but are able to store large amounts of information on one cartridge. DLT cartridges can store up to 80 GB of data and are used to back up information on medium to large sized networks.

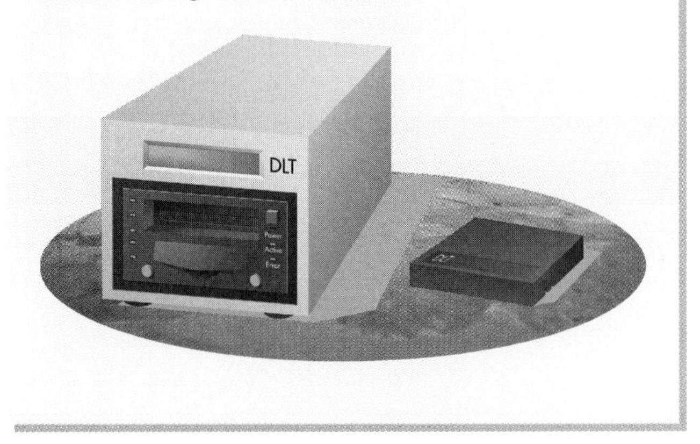

LTO Drives

Linear Tape-Open (LTO) drives are a new type of tape backup devices. LTO cartridges are able to store up to 200 GB of data and are ideal for networks that need to back up very large amounts of information.

UNINTERRUPTIBLE POWER SUPPLIES

An Uninterruptible Power Supply (UPS) is a device that can provide temporary power to a computer in the event of a power failure.

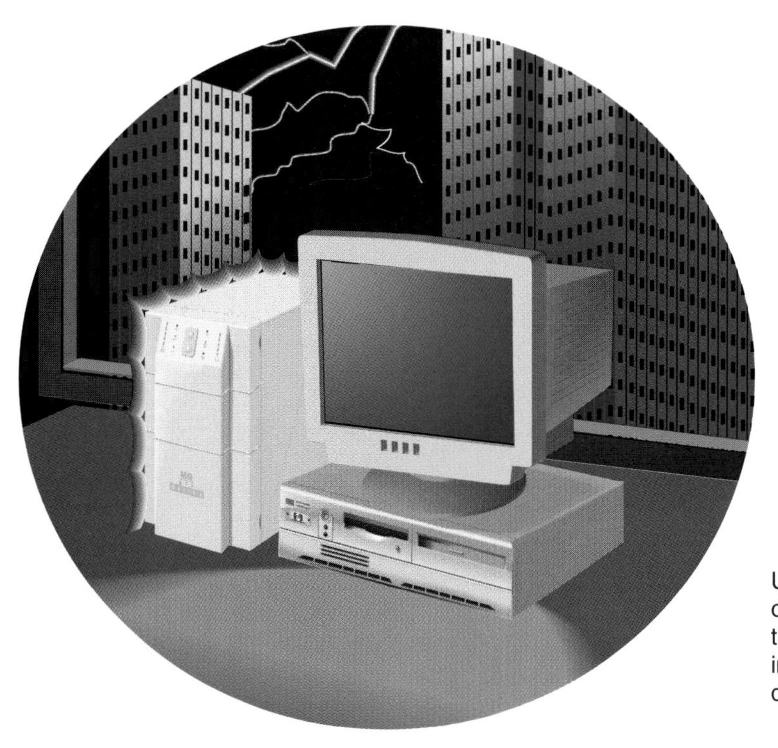

UPSs are often used on networks to ensure that servers do not lose important information due to power failures.

Batteries

Most UPSs use rechargeable batteries to store power. The documentation provided with a UPS can be consulted for information about charging the battery. The amount of power the battery can store determines how long the UPS can supply power in the event of a power failure. Since the amount of power a battery can store diminishes over time, most new UPSs have replaceable batteries.

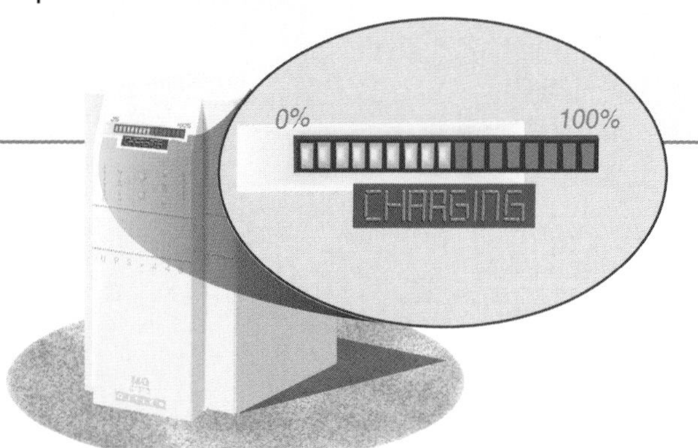

Types of UPSs

There are three common types of UPSs—standby, line-interactive and online. A standby UPS switches to battery power when it detects a power failure. There is usually a brief delay before the battery begins supplying power. A line-interactive UPS contains a transformer that continuously conditions the incoming power. This type of UPS switches to battery power only when a power failure occurs. An online UPS constantly uses the battery to condition the incoming power and therefore does not have to switch in the event of a power failure.

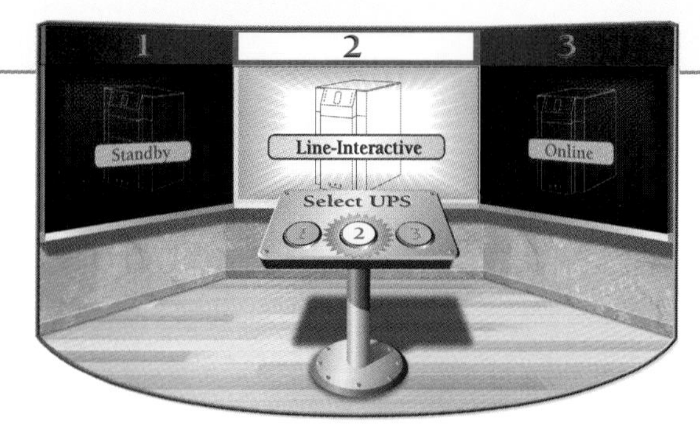

Power Backup

Most UPSs can detect a power failure and switch to battery power within a fraction of a second. A UPS enables users to finish their tasks and safely shut down their computers, but it is not intended to supply power for an extended period of time. In the event of a power loss, most UPSs will provide power for only 5 to 20 minutes.

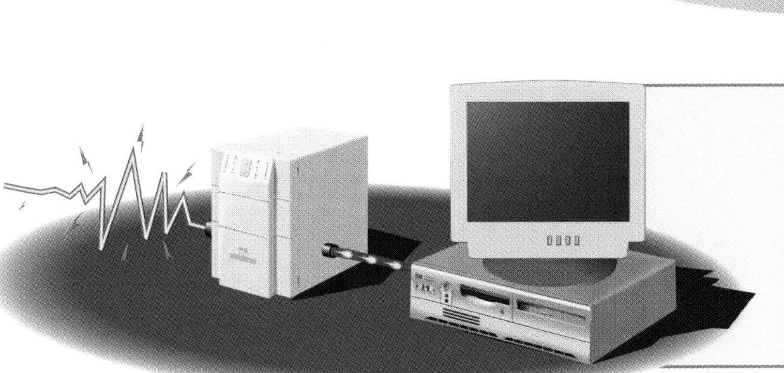

Surge Protection

A surge, or spike, is a fluctuation in electrical power that can damage computer equipment and result in the loss of network data. Many UPSs have a built-in surge protection feature to prevent computers from being damaged by power surges.

Automatic Shutdown

You may be able to install software on a computer attached to a UPS to monitor and control the operation of the UPS. When the power does fail, the software program instructs the UPS to automatically close applications, shut down the operating system and shut off the attached computer. This is useful if the computer is unattended when the power fails.

Fault tolerance systems are designed to protect network data by storing data on several devices in different locations. This helps ensure users will be able to access important information even if one storage device fails.

Server Protection

The servers on a network are often critical to the operation of a company. Companies cannot afford to have their servers fail or have information destroyed. Fault tolerance is an effective method of protecting data on network servers.

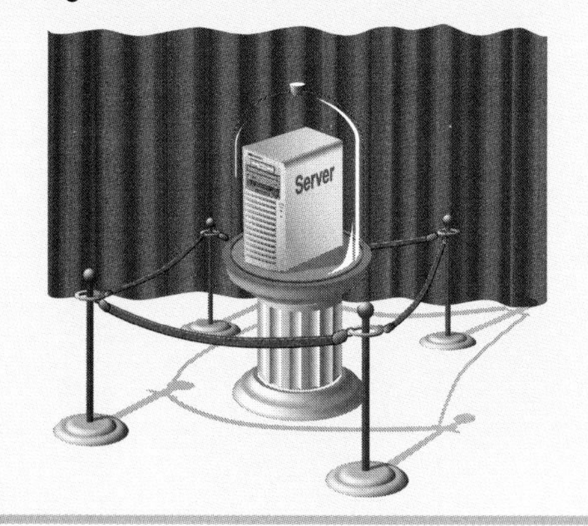

RAID

The most common type of fault tolerance system found in large companies is called a Redundant Array of Inexpensive Disks (RAID) system. RAID systems often consist of several hard drives that are used to store duplicate data. There are seven accepted levels of RAID, each specifying a different method for storing data. A higher RAID level does not indicate a higher level of protection.

FAULT TOLERANCE METHODS

Each RAID level uses one or more fault tolerance methods to prevent data loss.

Striping

Striping involves breaking data into small pieces and distributing the data evenly over all the hard drives in the system. Striping is not the best method for protecting data because if one drive fails, all the data will be lost.

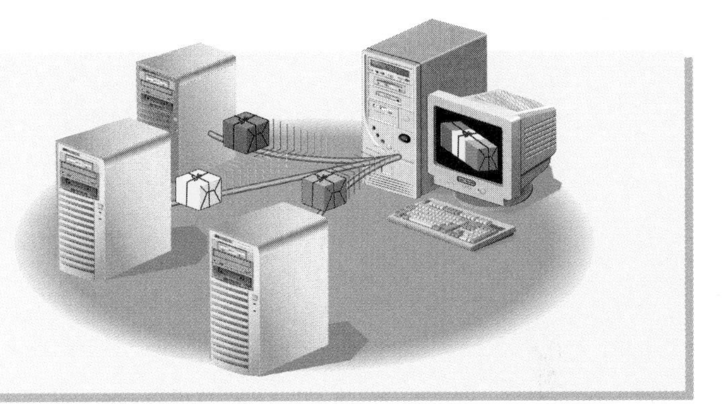

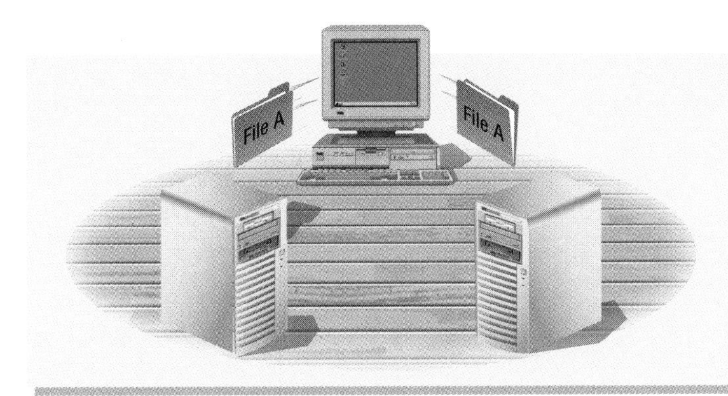

Mirroring

Mirroring occurs when all the data on a drive is duplicated onto another drive. For example, each time a user saves a change to a document, the change is saved in both locations. Mirroring provides effective protection because if one drive fails, the mirrored drive can be used to store and access the same information.

Error Checking

Parity is a method of checking whether data has been lost or written over when the data is moved from one storage device to another. Parity is the most common form of error checking. Data is always stored as a series of 1s and 0s. Parity ensures that errors have not occurred by verifying that the number of 1s in a series is consistently odd or even.

Certificate
A+
This is to certify that Treena Lees
has successfully completed the A+ Certification
program sponsored by CompTIA.
Dated this 21st of February, 1998
9:50 am
Testing ...
maranGraphics
PERFORMANCE 9000
Manual
Manual
Network Update
Time
Status
09:15 am
OK
09:30 am
OK
09:45 am
OK
10:00 am
10:15 am
10:30 am

Network Administration

Proper administration is necessary to keep a network running efficiently. Read this chapter to learn about the importance of monitoring network performance, setting network policies and more.

Network Administration....................156

Network Performance 158

Network Monitoring 160

Network Management Software........162

Network Policies 164

Network Consultants.......................166

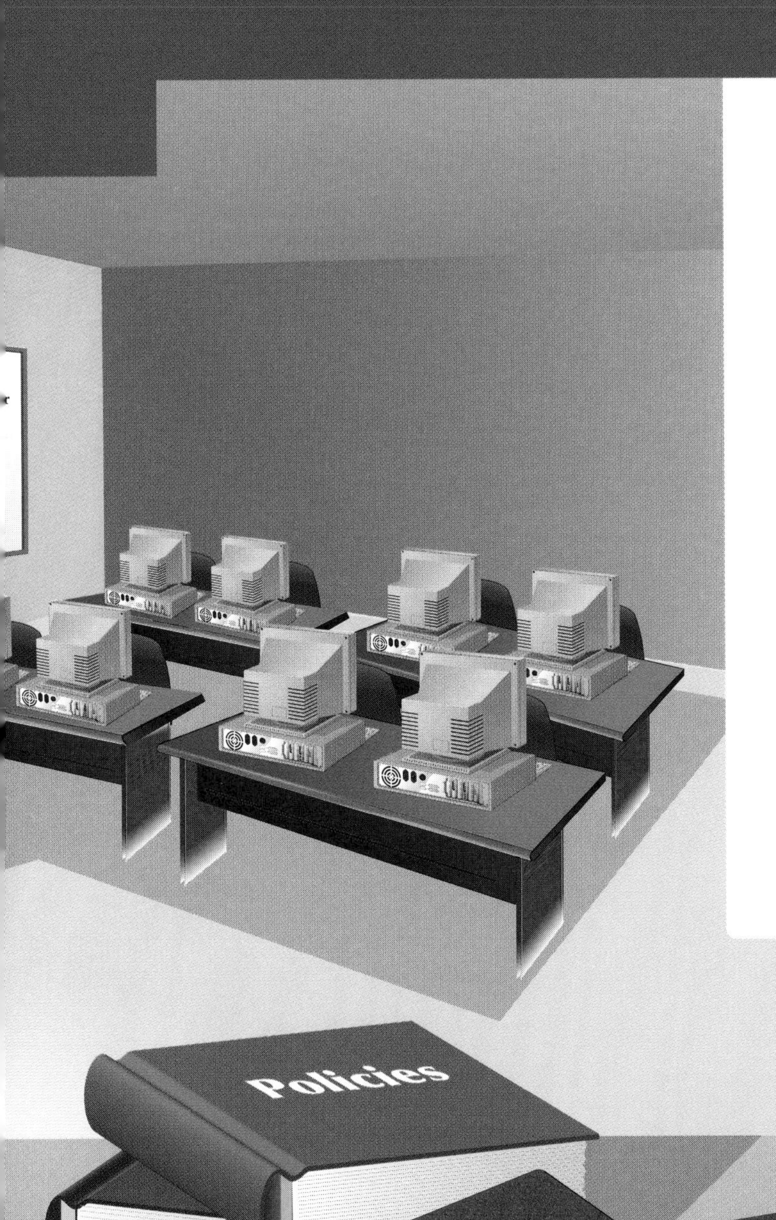

Administering a network can be a complex and demanding job. There are many responsibilities in ensuring a network runs efficiently, including the administration of individual user activities, network security and backups.

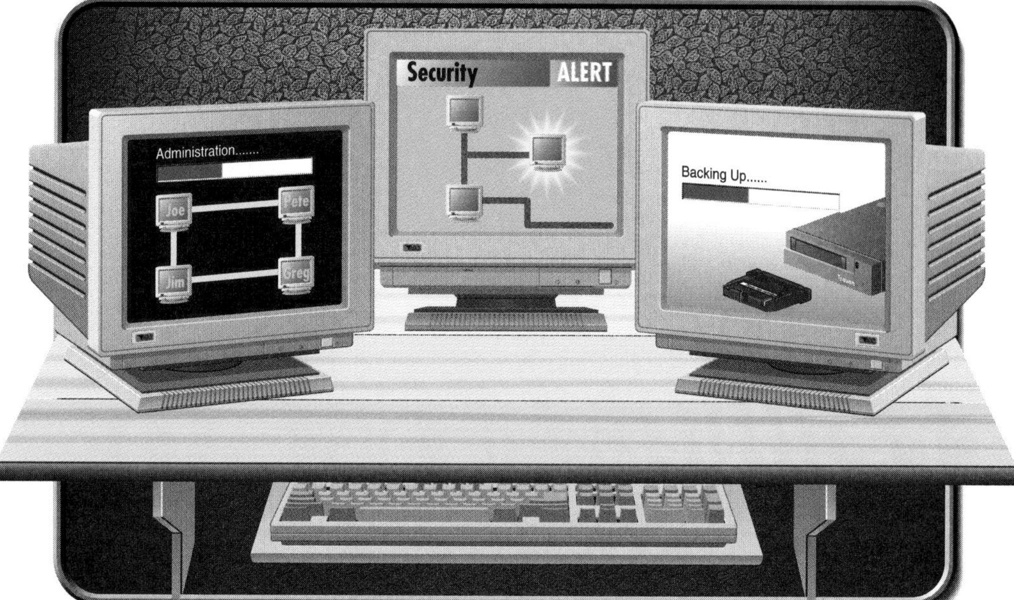

Responsibility

The main responsibility of the network administrator is to keep the network functioning at a level that accommodates the needs of all its users. Having the network functioning properly at all times is critical to a business. For this reason, the network administrator is often on call 24 hours a day.

Teams

Although small peer-to-peer networks can usually be administered by only one person, a single network administrator is often not enough to manage larger networks effectively. Many companies have administration teams with different people responsible for different parts of the network. In some large corporations, there are entire departments dedicated to administering the network.

Training

It is important for network administrators to keep up-to-date with all current technologies. Network administrators should constantly be anticipating the future growth and maintenance of the networks they administer. Network administrators also need to be aware of the technologies they can use to make their networks function more efficiently or troubleshoot any future problems.

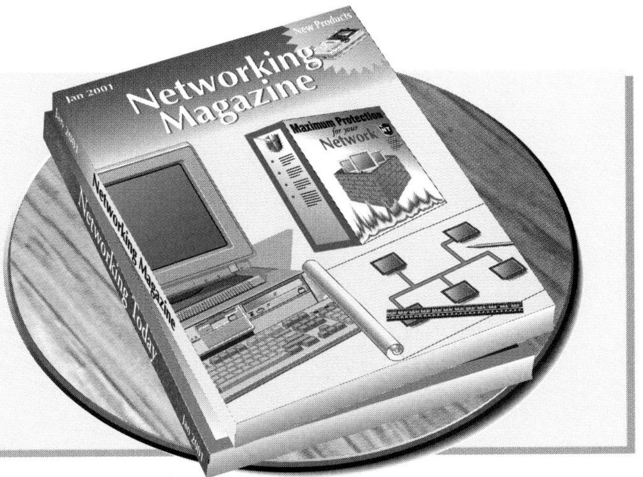

Records

Network administrators should keep very detailed records concerning all aspects of the network. The original plans for the network and any documents recording changes made to the network should all be kept in a safe place. Detailed records make it easier to plan the future growth of the network and are invaluable in helping troubleshoot network problems.

Constraints

Network administrators must take into account many factors when performing their jobs. Monetary budgets and time constraints are the two most common factors that determine how network administrators perform their work.

NETWORK PERFORMANCE

The performance of a network determines how efficiently the network can transfer information.

Maximize Performance

Like most computer systems, a network should be fine-tuned on a regular basis to achieve maximum performance. For example, replacing network components and updating software applications can help a network run more efficiently. A network that is continually upgraded and optimized will be better suited to handle the present and future requirements of its users.

Performance Monitoring

All networks should be monitored for signs of poor performance. Continually monitoring a network's performance gives the administrator a good indication of how the network runs under normal circumstances. This makes it easier to detect problems when they first occur. Monitoring and recording network performance can also help the administrator predict the future needs of the network.

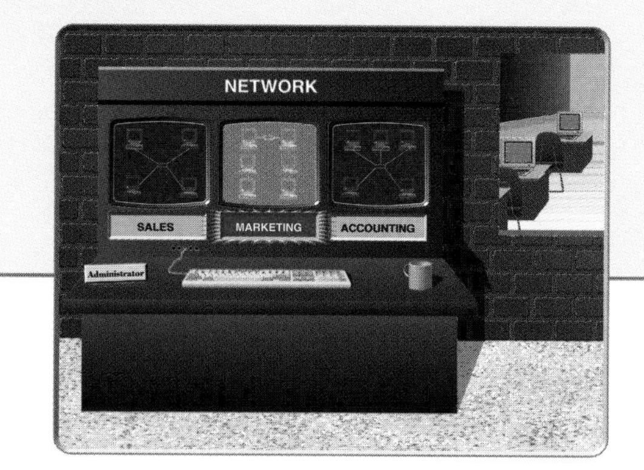

Throughput

Throughput is the measurement of how fast data is transferred through different parts of a network. Throughput should be measured at various points in the network to help forecast where future transmission problems may occur.

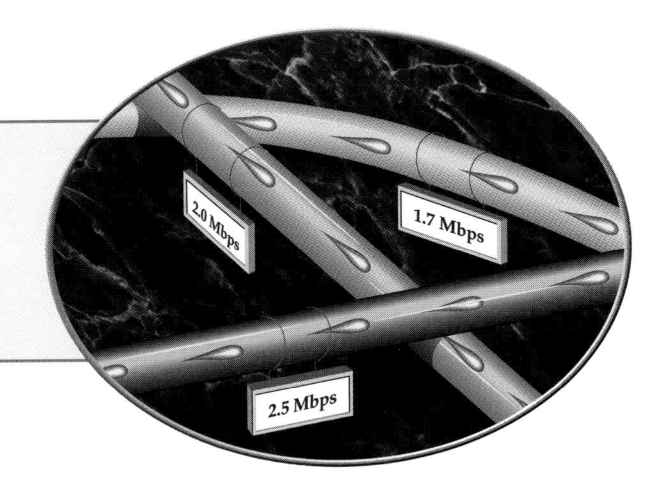

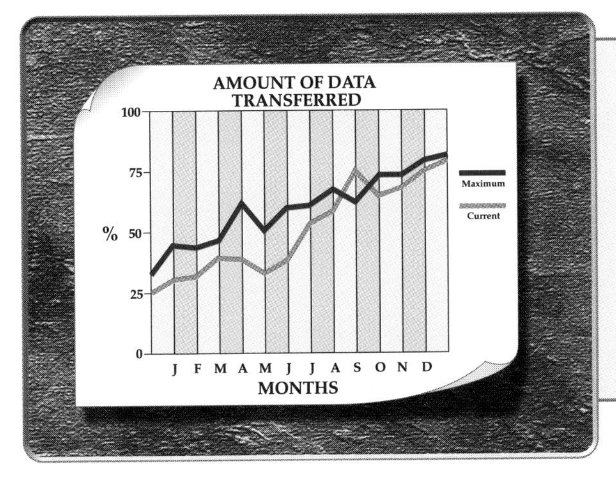

Utilization Level

The utilization level is the amount of information currently being transferred on a network. The network administrator can compare the current utilization level to previously recorded levels and to the maximum amount of information the network is capable of transferring. If the utilization level is becoming too high, the network may need to be upgraded to prevent network performance from being seriously affected.

Errors

Errors commonly occur when data is transferred on a network. The more errors there are, the more network performance is affected. Software and hardware devices have been developed to detect many types of network errors, such as data loss. Errors must be carefully monitored so measures can be taken to avoid a serious decrease in network performance levels.

Network monitoring tools can be software or hardware that are used to monitor faults and activity on a network. The information collected by the monitoring tools is used by the network administrator to help manage and control the network.

Monitoring Network Devices

Monitoring tools are used to communicate with the devices connected to a network. Each network device, such as a hub, router or network printer, can communicate with the network monitoring tool and inform the tool of its current status.

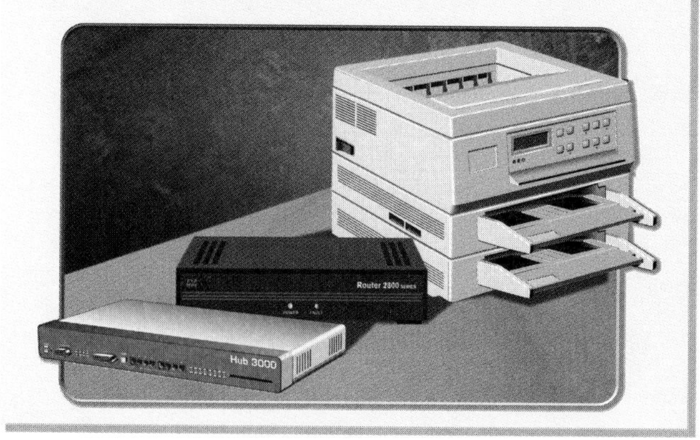

Compatibility

Network devices and monitoring tools must be compatible and must use the same method of communication before they can exchange information. Simple Network Management Protocol (SNMP) is the most common communication protocol used by network devices and monitoring tools. SNMP was developed by companies that manufacture networking products to ensure products created by different companies would be able to communicate.

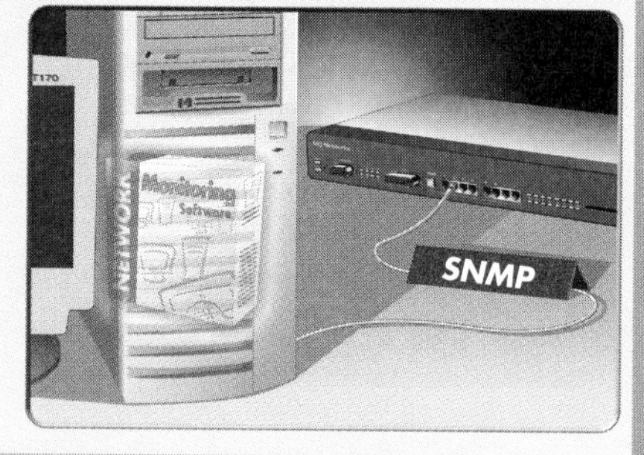

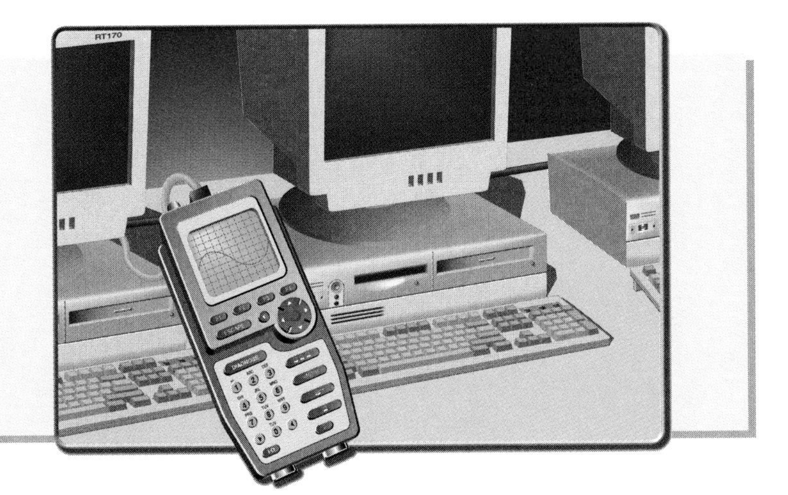

Network Monitoring Hardware

Some network monitoring tools are special hardware devices that are physically connected to a network. Network monitoring hardware can be handheld devices or customized laptop computers.

Network Monitoring Software

Some network monitoring tools can be software that runs on a computer attached to a network. Network monitoring software uses the processing power of a computer to collect and analyze information gathered from the network. Most network operating systems also include a monitoring utility that can help a network administrator keep track of a network server's performance.

Constant Updates

Devices on a network can be configured to send status information to a network monitoring tool at regular intervals. Constant updates on the status of the devices on a network can give the network administrator an overview of how the network is currently operating. The administrator can configure devices to report their status at intervals of minutes or hours.

NETWORK MANAGEMENT SOFTWARE

Network management software can save companies time and money by making it easier for network administrators to control and configure computer networks.

Network management software can be difficult to set up and maintain. Network administrators may require specialized training before they can effectively use complex network management software.

Administration

Network administrators use network management software to control an entire network from a central location. The software can be used to activate or shut down network devices, such as hubs or servers. Network management software may also be used to control user access to a network. For example, the software could be used to prevent unauthorized users from accessing specific information on a network.

Performance

Network management software can be used to increase the performance of a network. Most network management software can direct network traffic around slower sections of the network. The software can also be used to direct traffic around malfunctioning network components that may cause information loss.

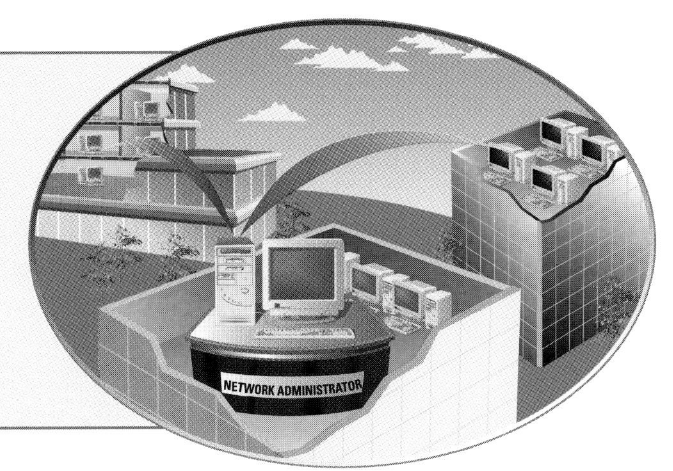

Remote Access

Most network management software allows network administrators to connect to the software from a remote location. Remote access allows a network to be controlled by several administrators who work in different locations. Remote access is also useful for companies that have many offices scattered across a city, but have only one network administrator. The network administrator could manage the network at each location without having to waste time traveling.

Alerts

Network management software can be used to alert the system administrator or team of administrators when errors or problems occur on a network, such as a hard drive failing or a router malfunctioning. Alerts can be sent in many forms, including e-mail or pager messages.

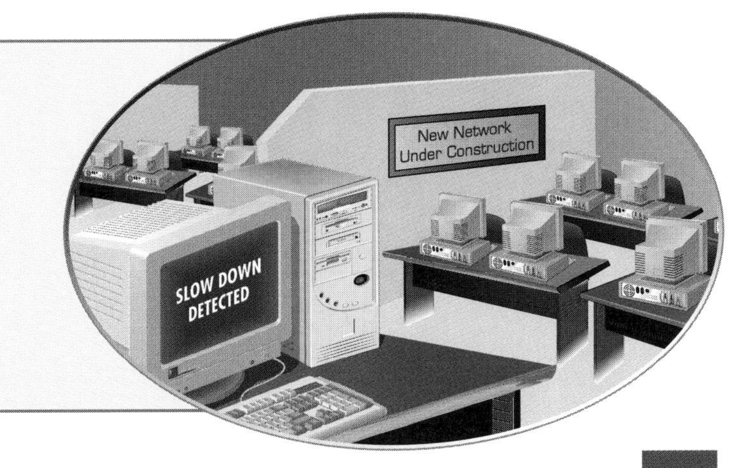

Expansion

Network management software is often used to determine when a network should be expanded. Most network management software have reporting features that can indicate when a network is becoming too busy and can no longer efficiently handle the amount of activity on the network. This information allows the network administrator to take the necessary steps to prevent a major reduction in network performance.

NETWORK POLICIES

All network administrators should have a set of policies determining how users access and use the network. When network policies are followed, many network problems can be avoided.

POLICIES
■ Files from the Internet must be scanned for viruses.
■ All new programs must be approved before they are installed.
■ Documents longer than 5 pages must be printed after 4 PM.
■ Secure procedures must be used when dialing into the network from home.
Administrator

To ensure that everyone who uses the network is familiar with the network policies, the administrator can create manuals describing network guidelines and provide informative training sessions.

Network Guidelines

Each network policy should contain detailed guidelines describing how users should interact with the network. For example, network guidelines may be used to determine what actions users should take if they encounter a virus. The network administrator is usually responsible for developing and implementing network guidelines.

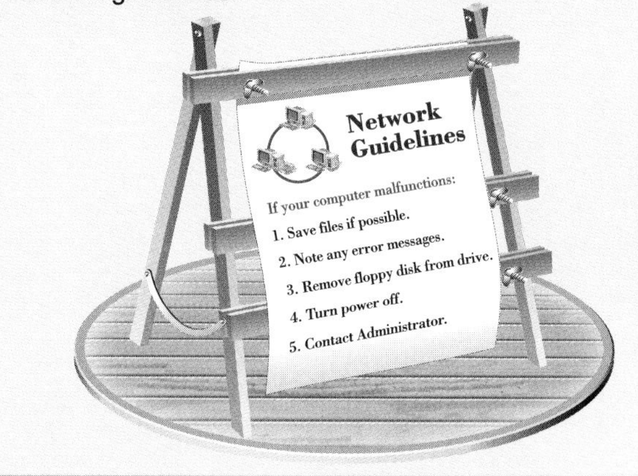

Network Guidelines
If your computer malfunctions:
1. Save files if possible.
2. Note any error messages.
3. Remove floppy disk from drive.
4. Turn power off.
5. Contact Administrator.

Security Guidelines

Network policies should always include guidelines regarding the use of passwords and other security procedures. When users do not follow security guidelines, network security may be compromised. To ensure network security, the network administrator should constantly work with users and company management to create and enforce security guidelines.

GUIDELINES
• Use at least 8 characters for passwords.
• Do not leave work areas unattended.
• Keep passwords secret.
• Use only company disks.
• Log off nightly.
SECURITY

Training

Many policies concerning networks include instructions about technical procedures, such as properly shutting down a malfunctioning computer. The network administrator should ensure that users are trained to perform any procedures that may be required of them.

Updating Policies

Networks can change considerably as they grow. Small peer-to-peer networks can change into large client/server networks in a matter of months. As a network grows, it is important to update policies and guidelines to accommodate the new system.

Policy Enforcement

Network guidelines contain instructions that may be vital to the continued and optimal operation of a network. If these guidelines are not followed, a network disaster, such as a server failure or the destruction of important information, may occur. It is important for companies to implement appropriate disciplinary procedures for users who do not follow network policies.

NETWORK CONSULTANTS

An independent network consultant or a consulting firm is often contracted when a company is installing a new network or planning a major upgrade to an existing network.

Computer Stores

Companies with small networks may be able to install and upgrade their networks with only minimal assistance. Many computer stores provide network planning and installation services as well as troubleshooting advice for customers who purchase their network hardware and software components at the store.

Consultants

Only the largest corporations have the necessary staff and resources to competently complete work on large computer networks. Whenever a company is planning to install a large network or perform a major upgrade, the company should consider retaining the services of a consultant or consulting firm for assistance. A company's network administrator may want to confer with other people in the industry to find a good network consultant or consulting firm.

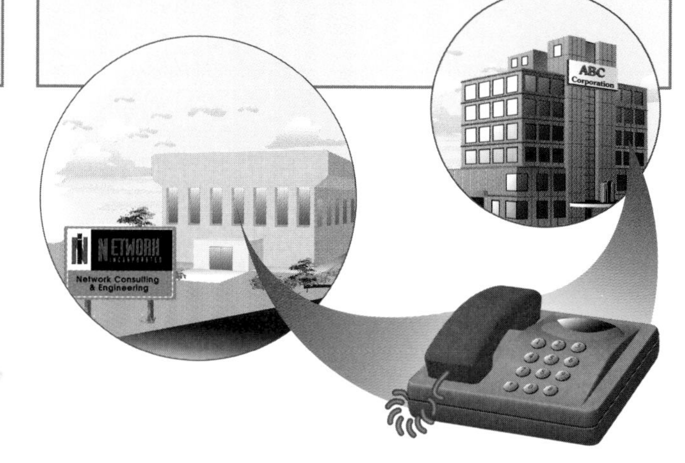

Experience

The network administrator should verify whether potential consultants have previously worked on similar projects. For example, while some consultants may be experts with one particular network operating system, they may have no experience with the operating system required for this project. A competent consultant will always be able to supply a list of previous customers that may be contacted by the network administrator to help evaluate the consultant.

Project Constraints

The consultant often completes the planning stage of a network installation or upgrade. The network administrator should ensure that the consultant is aware of any resource or time constraints that may affect the outcome of the project. This can help ensure that the project will be completed within the time frame required by the company.

Contracts

A company should always have a written contract with any consultants that are hired. Most consultants also have their own service contracts. Situations often arise where it is difficult to determine who is responsible for correcting a problem. A written contract can help resolve these types of issues.

Lesson Plan
- Introduction To Network Operating Systems
- Network Communications
- How Protocols Work
- Troubleshooting Networks

CHAPTER 11

Network Certifications

Many hardware and software manufacturers provide certifications for individuals in computing professions. This chapter discusses the various certifications available and how they are obtained.

Introduction to Certifications 170

Novell Certification..........................172

Microsoft Certification 174

Solaris Certification 176

Linux Certification 177

Oracle Certification 178

Manufacturer Certification 179

CompTIA Certification......................180

Certification confirms a level of knowledge and expertise that is recognized throughout the computer industry. Certifications are offered by many hardware and software manufacturers.

Classroom Instruction

Most certification programs are taught in a classroom setting. Classroom instruction has many benefits, including easy access to an instructor and a structured environment. The main drawbacks of classroom-based training are that the classes are very time-consuming and are often conducted during business hours. Classroom-based training can also be very expensive.

Computer-based Training

Computer-based training is becoming more widely used as a means of enabling people to receive technical certification. In computer-based training, a software program guides the student through the training material. Some programs even adjust the training content according to the student's level of knowledge. Computer-based training allows people to work at their own pace on their own computers.

Testing

Certification is achieved by passing one or more exams. Exams are usually taken in a registered testing center. Most exams are performed on a computer and consist of multiple-choice questions. Students can usually find out if they passed shortly after completing the exam.

Types of Tests

There are two types of certification exams—traditional and adaptive. A traditional exam asks the same questions to each student, regardless of how well each student is doing. An adaptive test customizes the questions for each student based on performance. For example, if a student answers a question correctly, the next question is more difficult. If a student answers a question incorrectly, the next question is easier. Answering more difficult questions earns a higher score.

Experience

While a certificate is a valuable asset, it is equally important to have hands-on experience. A network professional who is certified and has hands-on experience is considered the most qualified individual in the field.

NOVELL CERTIFICATION

Novell popularized computer networking and manufactures NetWare, one of the most widely used network operating systems in the world. Novell provides certifications for people who want to set up and maintain networks using Novell products.

Skill Levels

Novell offers certification programs for people of all skill levels, from the user who wants to administer a small network with only a few computers to the support professional who wishes to administer a wide area network with thousands of users. Novell also offers certifications for people who wish to sell Novell products or teach Novell certification courses.

Certifications

Novell offers a wide assortment of certification programs. To successfully complete a certification program, an individual must pass one or more exams as specified by Novell. Novell's current certifications include Certified Novell Administrator (CNA), Certified Novell Engineer (CNE), Master Certified Novell Engineer (MCNE), Certified Directory Engineer (CDE), Certified Internet Professional (CIP), Certified Novell Salesperson (CNS) and Certified Novell Instructor (CNI).

Training

Training is available in a variety of formats. Novell was one of the first network operating system manufacturers to offer comprehensive training. Classroom-based training is offered at many locations. For people who prefer to learn at their own pace, training books, self-study kits and CD-ROM discs are available. Online training through Novell-authorized companies is also available for individuals who do not have time to attend classroom-based courses, but need more structure than a self-paced program offers.

Novell Press

Novell publishes its own line of books that contain information about its courses and products. Novell books allow people to study at home before a certification exam. These books also serve as excellent reference manuals for individuals who have already earned their certifications.

Certification Benefits

Since networking products form the core of the Novell product line, Novell's certification training covers many aspects of computer networking. As a result, people with Novell certification tend to be competent not only with Novell products, but in other areas of networking as well. Professionals with Novell certifications have a competitive edge in the computer industry.

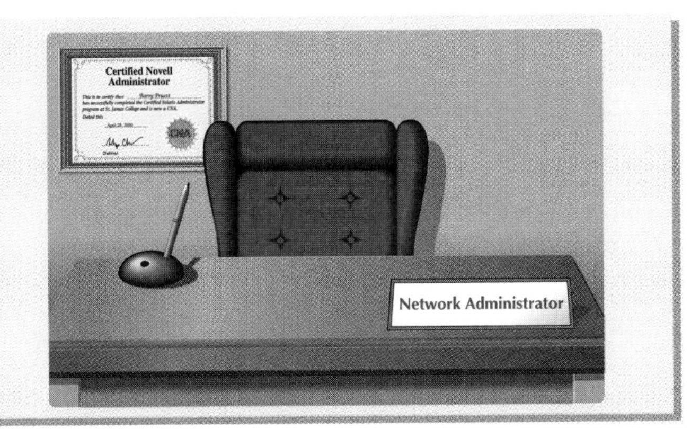

Microsoft certifications are some of the most widely recognized certifications in the computing industry.

Microsoft certifications help businesses identify individuals who have advanced Microsoft product knowledge and technical skills. Service professionals who work with Microsoft products should have Microsoft certification.

Certifications

There are currently five Microsoft certifications available. Certifications include Microsoft Certified Professional (MCP), Microsoft Certified Systems Engineer (MCSE), Microsoft Certified Trainer (MCT), Microsoft Certified Solution Developer (MCSD) and Microsoft Certified Database Administrator (MCDBA). The computing industry recognizes all Microsoft certifications.

Certification Benefits

Microsoft certification provides individuals with benefits such as industry recognized technical skills and a level of expertise with specific Microsoft products. Businesses that use Microsoft products may experience benefits, such as fewer serious technical problems and increased productivity, by hiring network administrators and consultants that have Microsoft certifications. Since there are a variety of certifications available, businesses should ensure that their employees have the appropriate Microsoft certifications.

Training

There are many ways to train for Microsoft certifications. Many schools offer classes over the Internet and in classrooms. Microsoft provides online seminars and practice exams at the www.microsoft.com/trainingandservices Web site. There are also many books available that can assist people in preparing for Microsoft certification exams on their own.

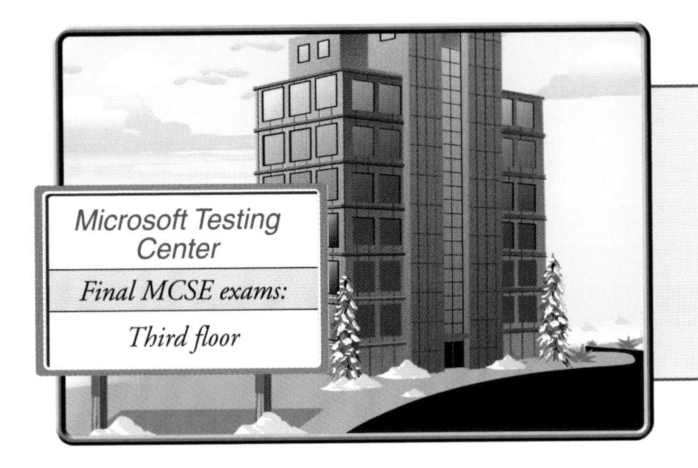

Testing

Each certification is acquired by passing a number of exams specified by Microsoft. The exams must be written at a Microsoft-approved testing center, where the exams can be supervised. Microsoft has many testing and training centers throughout the world.

Up-to-date Certifications

Microsoft is constantly updating the courses required to achieve certification. As new Microsoft products become available and older products become obsolete, Microsoft adds and removes courses to ensure that people are certified to support the most current products.

Sun Microsystems offers certification programs for people who want to administer networks running the Solaris operating system.

Solaris is a UNIX-based operating system that is found in many companies and organizations whose networks are connected to the Internet.

Certifications

Sun Microsystems offers two certification programs for the Solaris operating system. The Sun Certified System Administrator designation indicates that a person has the skills necessary to administer a network running the Solaris operating system. The Sun Certified Network Administrator designation certifies that a person can administer more complex networks and has an expert knowledge of network protocols. Solaris certifications are recognized worldwide. Many people acquire Solaris certifications as a step toward improving their career opportunities.

Certification Benefits

Because Solaris is a UNIX-based operating system, the skills learned by individuals with Solaris certifications can be applied to other UNIX operating systems. People who have a Solaris certification are usually capable of administering networks running other UNIX operating systems.

The most popular version of the Linux operating system is distributed by Red Hat. Red Hat's certification program can be completed by Linux users of all skill levels.

Red Hat Certified Engineer

The Red Hat Certified Engineer (RHCE) certification is awarded to individuals who have completed all the required training and passed the Certification Lab Exam. The exam must be taken at an authorized testing center and is composed of a multiple-choice test and two practical tests that present real-world problems. The RHCE certification is available for different versions of Red Hat Linux.

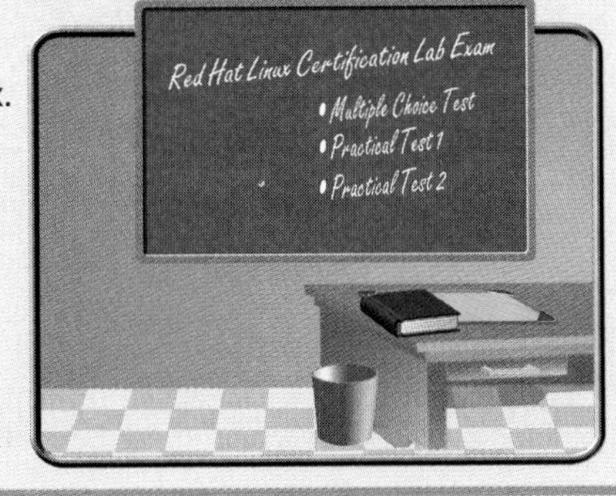

Curriculum Tracks

Red Hat offers two curriculum tracks—Standard and Rapid. The Standard Track curriculum is designed for beginners who are not familiar with the Linux operating system. The Rapid Track curriculum is intended for individuals who already have experience administering a network running a UNIX-based or Linux operating system. People who choose the Rapid Track curriculum do not have to take the more basic parts of the training program.

Oracle distributes the most popular database software in the world. Many large companies use Oracle products to store and organize data. Oracle certifications ensure individuals are able to administer, operate or develop Oracle databases.

Certifications

Oracle offers a range of certifications. The most popular certifications are for database administrators and operators. More advanced certifications are also available for Java and Oracle application developers. People with Oracle certifications are referred to as Oracle Certified Professionals (OCPs).

Oracle Certified Professional

This is to certify that Craig Dearing has successfully completed the Oracle Certified Professional program and is now an OCP.

Dated this April 28, 2000

Chairman

OCP

Training

There are several ways to train for Oracle certifications. Oracle University is an online educational tool that provides course material, discussion groups and practice exams. Oracle University is available at the www.oracle.com Web site. Oracle also offers classroom-based training for individuals and can provide onsite training for companies. Books and CD-ROM discs are also available. When individuals have finished preparing, they can register for certification exams at the Oracle Web site.

MANUFACTURER CERTIFICATION

Most hardware and software manufacturers provide their own certifications. The certifications ensure individuals who sell or service their products have the appropriate knowledge or technical skills.

Certifications

Most manufacturers train and certify the personnel of companies that sell or service their products. For example, a manufacturer may teach employees of a retail computer store how to maintain and repair servers produced by the manufacturer. Manufacturer certifications can help companies become more technically self-sufficient and increase customer satisfaction, which benefits both the manufacturer and the individual companies.

Manufacturer Requirements

Most manufacturers that offer certifications require companies to meet certain certification standards. For example, manufacturers may require companies to have a specific number of employees with certifications and ensure that the certifications are kept up to date. This could mean that employees will have to take additional certification courses as new products become available. Manufacturers may also require companies to employ people with different certification levels to ensure that customers get the best service possible.

Computing Technology Industry Association (CompTIA) is an association that represents thousands of computer hardware and software manufacturers. CompTIA offers certification programs that are not specific to any one manufacturer, but set standards for various segments of the computer industry.

Classroom-based training, self-study materials and online instruction are available for CompTIA certifications.

Certification Benefits

CompTIA certifications provide a level of credibility and give a competitive edge to people who become certified. Employers can be assured that CompTIA-certified individuals possess the technical knowledge required to work in a variety of computer-related positions. As a result, people with CompTIA certifications have better job opportunities and increased salaries.

Testing

A CompTIA certification exam is administered on a computer at an authorized testing center. Certification exams use a multiple-choice format. Most questions have only one correct response, but there could be some questions with multiple correct responses. A score report is provided at the testing center and indicates whether or not the certification was achieved.

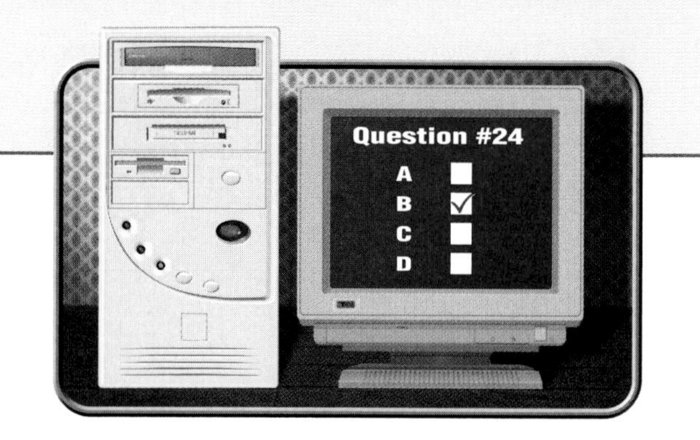

CERTIFICATIONS

A+

A+ certification ensures that an individual has the customer relations skills and basic knowledge needed to be a computer service technician.

A+ certification requires the successful completion of two exams—the A+ Core module and the A+ DOS/Windows specialty module. The A+ Core exam tests a person's knowledge of computer hardware. The A+ DOS/Windows exam tests a person's knowledge of the DOS and Windows operating systems.

i-Net+

CompTIA's i-Net+ certification is intended for Internet and e-commerce professionals who want to demonstrate their technical knowledge concerning Internet and intranet topics. Some of the concepts covered in the i-Net+ certification exam include Internet basics, Web site development, networking and security.

Network+

Network+ certification shows that an individual has a thorough understanding of networking practices and the knowledge needed to work with a variety of networking technologies. Network+ certification is recognized by most manufacturers of networking products and may serve as a prerequisite for some manufacturer certifications.

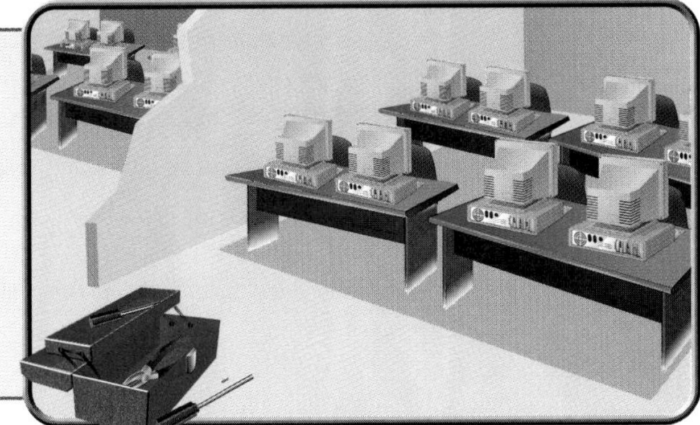

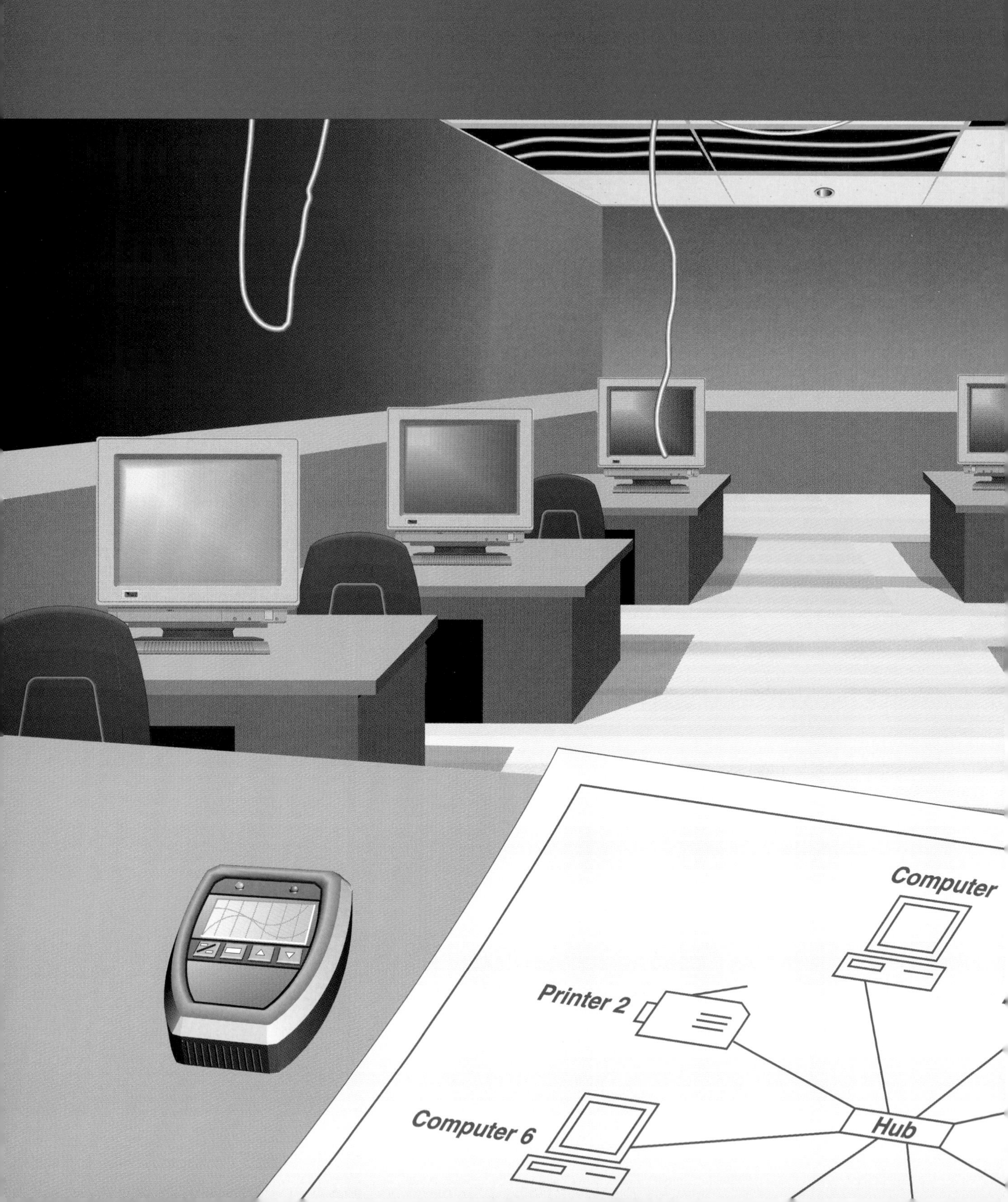
Computer
Printer 2
Computer 6
Hub

CHAPTER 12

Installing or Upgrading a Network

When installing or upgrading a network, many factors should be considered. This chapter explains how to evaluate the current network, install cable, choose network hardware and much more.

Planning a Network 184
Upgrading a Network.......................186
Evaluate Current Network 188
Determine Network Design 190
Upgrading Network Architecture 192
Upgrading Transmission Media 194
Installing Cable 196
Choosing Network Hardware 198
Installing Network Hardware............200
Installing the Network Operating System 202
Configuring Client Computers 204
Testing the Network 206

PLANNING A NETWORK

Planning is one of the most important aspects of installing a new computer network.

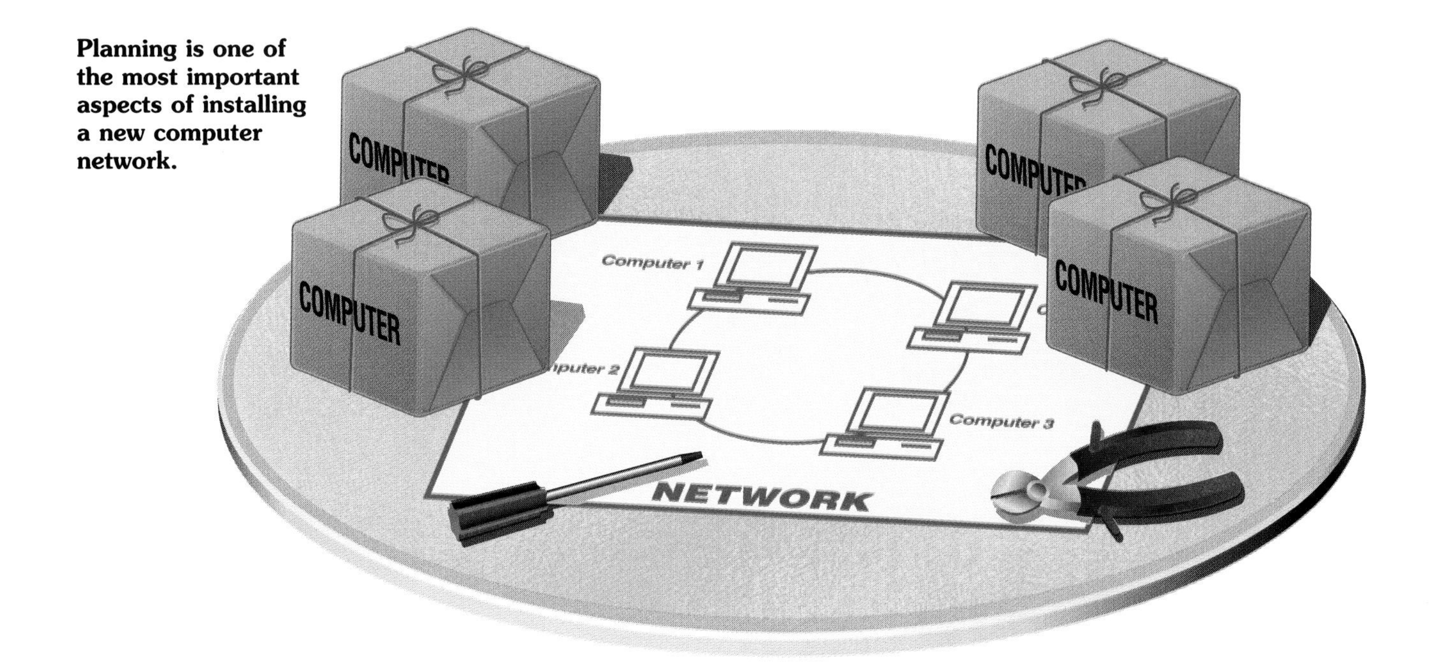

Network Size

When planning a new network, the size of the network must be considered first. Some network operating systems and architectures are optimized for certain network sizes. For example, a peer-to-peer network operating system is adequate for a small network of 10 users, but would be unsuitable for a network of a thousand users.

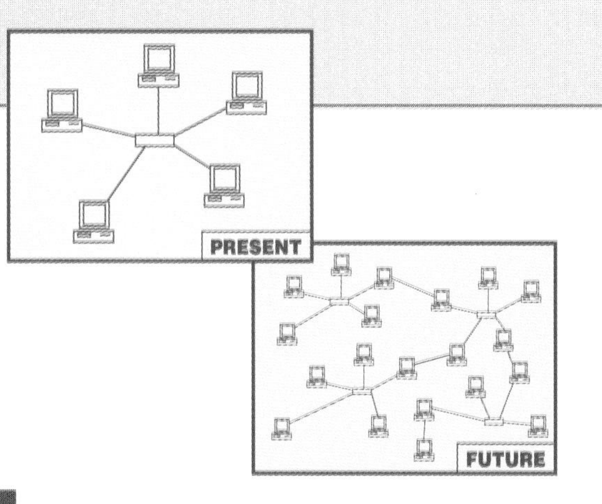

Bandwidth

The amount of information the network will be required to transfer at once helps determine the type of network a company requires. For example, a graphics company that transfers many large files may want to construct a network using fiber-optic cable. A network used primarily for exchanging e-mail messages could be a wire-cable network or a wireless network.

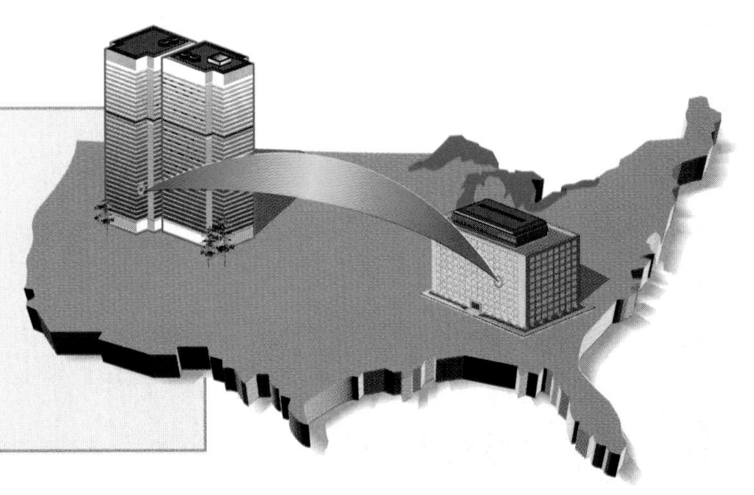

Computer Location

The location of the computers on a network should be considered before choosing hardware or software for the network. For example, a network made up of computers located in one office building may have different protocol and security requirements than a network made up of computers located in two branch offices connected by the Internet.

Logs

Network administrators should keep records concerning any decisions made or procedures performed while planning a network. Problems encountered while planning the network, as well as any steps taken to resolve the problems, should also be recorded. If another person has to work on the network or if the network planning process needs to be re-evaluated, accurate records can be useful.

Consultants

While simple networks can often be installed by someone with only an intermediate knowledge of computers, any network connecting more than a few computers should be planned and installed by a network consultant or a consulting firm. For more information about network consultants, see page 166.

COMPUTER
CONSULTANTS
Specializing in Network
Planning and Installation

UPGRADING A NETWORK

There are many reasons why a network administrator may need to upgrade a network. Most networks will have to be upgraded at some point in time.

A network administrator should continually monitor a network to determine when upgrades need to be performed.

Company Growth

Networks originally designed to be used by only a small number of people often need to be expanded. As companies grow, networks may need to be upgraded and enhanced to accommodate increasing numbers of employees and the use of more advanced software applications.

Obsolete Equipment

Some networks use networking devices that are old and obsolete. Older network devices may no longer be manufactured, making them difficult to find. When older network devices fail, replacing the outdated devices with modern ones may force the network administrator to upgrade the entire network.

Protection

For many companies, a network is crucial for conducting day-to-day business operations. If the network is unavailable, a company may suffer serious financial losses and reductions in employee productivity. Upgrading important systems, such as backup and security systems, can help protect companies against network failures.

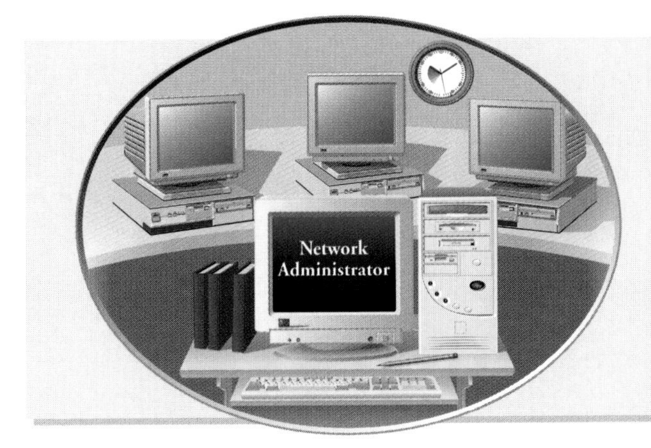

Administration

The administration of older networks is usually done manually and can be very time consuming. Many newer networks and network devices can be administered from one computer using network management software. In some cases, upgrading a network and the network devices can reduce the time and effort required for administering the network.

Software Upgrades

New versions of software applications, such as database programs, are constantly becoming available. A network administrator may need to upgrade a network so it operates efficiently with the newest version of a software application.

EVALUATE CURRENT NETWORK

A network administrator should examine the current status of a network before performing an upgrade. Evaluating the network helps the administrator determine what parts of the network will be affected by the upgrade.

Logs

Every network administrator should keep a log to record any changes made to the network. An up-to-date log can be used to determine what types of hardware and software are currently used on the network. Reviewing the log can help the administrator determine which areas of the network need to be upgraded.

Inventory

The network administrator should take a complete inventory of all the components of the network. When choosing new hardware or software, the network administrator will need a complete list of all the current network devices to ensure the new devices will be compatible with the existing network setup.

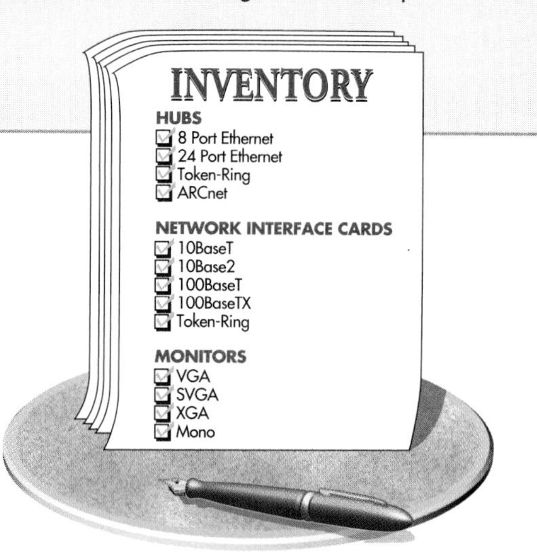

INVENTORY
HUBS
8 Port Ethernet
24 Port Ethernet
Token-Ring
ARCnet
NETWORK INTERFACE CARDS
10BaseT
10Base2
100BaseT
100BaseTX
Token-Ring
MONITORS
VGA
SVGA
XGA
Mono

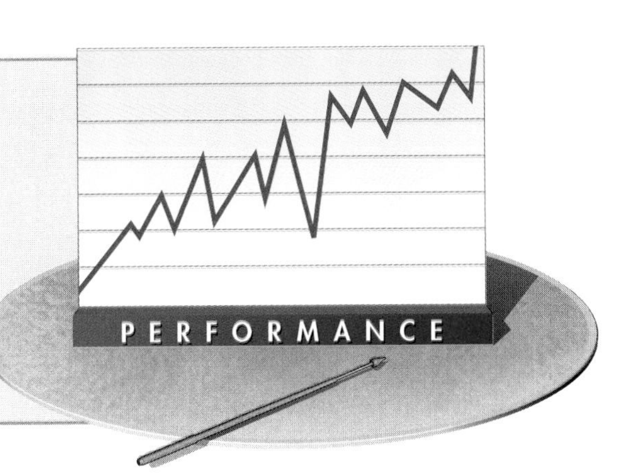

Performance

A network should be evaluated to determine how the performance of individual devices affects the overall performance of the network. Devices causing problems, such as information bottlenecks, should be identified before an upgrade is performed. Many monitoring tools are available that can pinpoint the cause of problems on a network. For more information about network monitoring tools, see page 160.

Technical Support

The network administrator should review the technical support requirements of the current network and determine how the upgraded network will be supported. A new or upgraded network often requires staff training or obtaining the services of a company that can provide onsite support for the network.

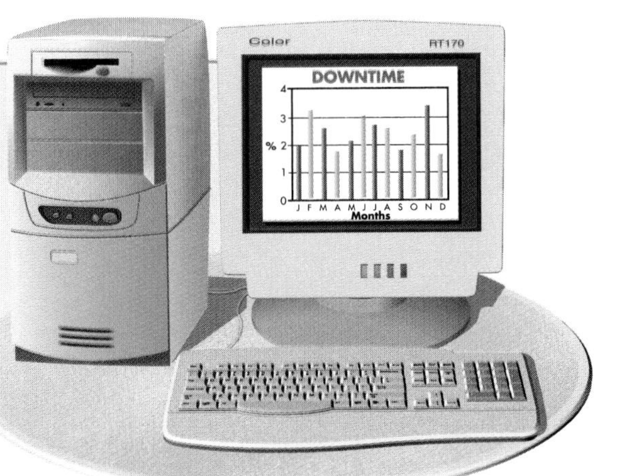

Downtime

Every network has periods, called downtime, when the network does not function due to server failure or other factors. The goal of every network administrator is to prevent downtime from occurring when access to the network is required. A network administrator should evaluate current downtime levels and try to determine how downtime can be reduced or eliminated.

Before installing a new network or upgrading an existing network, a network administrator should determine the design of the network. Establishing a network design provides an outline of the entire network.

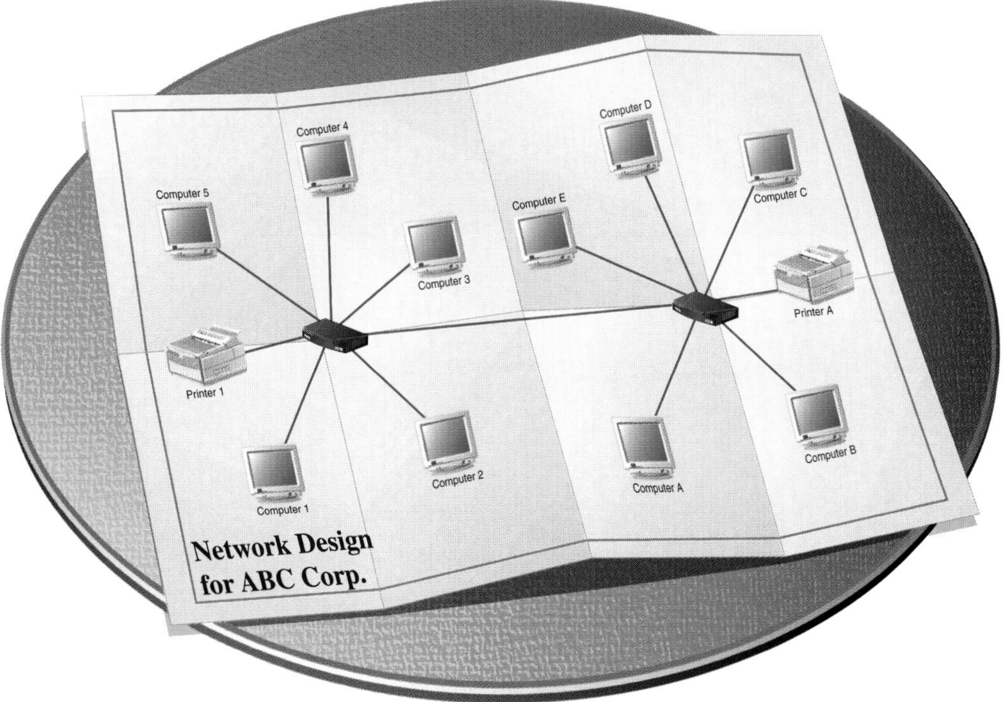

Network Structure

The star structure is the simplest and most widely used network structure. On a star network, each computer is connected by a cable to a central network connector. Unless there are specific reasons for using another structure, such as ring or bus, network administrators should use the star structure since it is easy to administer and expand. For more information about network structures, see pages 26 to 37.

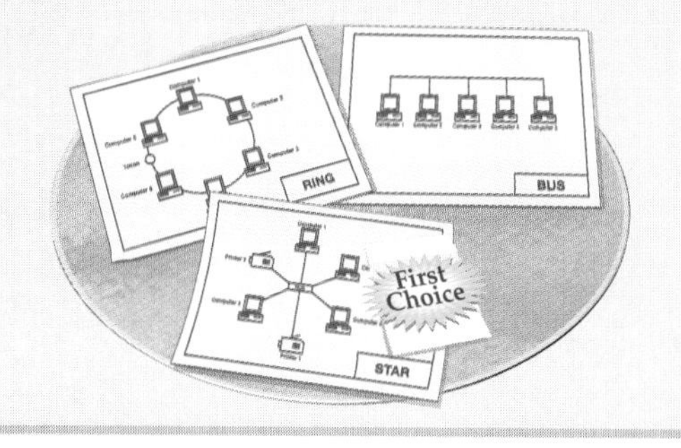

Network Operating System

A network operating system organizes and manages all the activities on a network. Many small networks use a peer-to-peer network operating system, such as Windows 98. If a network connects more than 10 computers, the network administrator should use a client/server network operating system, such as Novell NetWare or Windows 2000. For more information about network operating systems, see pages 106 to 117.

Network Architecture

Most new networks use the Ethernet architecture. Ethernet is popular because it is relatively inexpensive and easy to install. However, upgrading to Ethernet may not be feasible if the current network must be compatible with other network architectures, such as Token-Ring or ARCnet. For more information about network architectures, see pages 86 to 95.

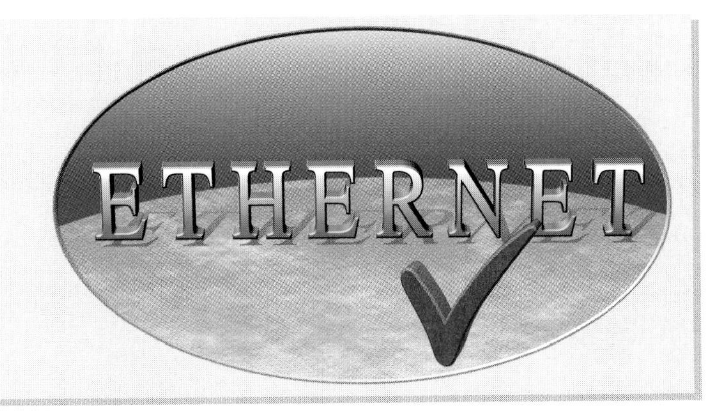

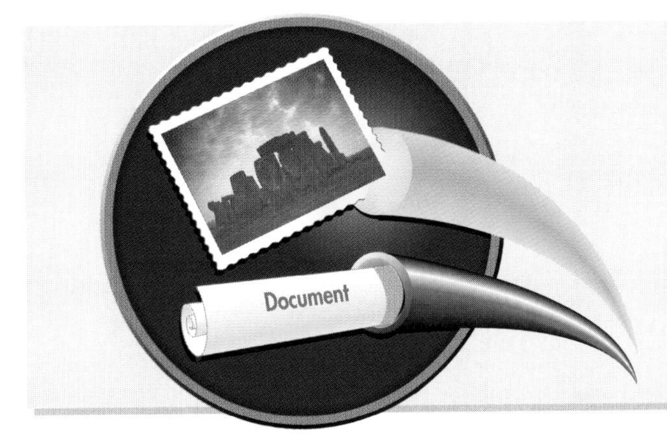

Files and Applications

Some network structures and architectures are better suited for transferring large files created using powerful applications, such as files created in 3-D design programs. Network administrators must make sure the network is capable of efficiently handling all files and applications required by users.

Future Needs

A network administrator should design a network with the future needs of the network in mind. A network administrator will almost certainly have to expand or modify the network in the future, regardless of the size or type of network. Considering future expansion when designing a network will make network modifications easier.

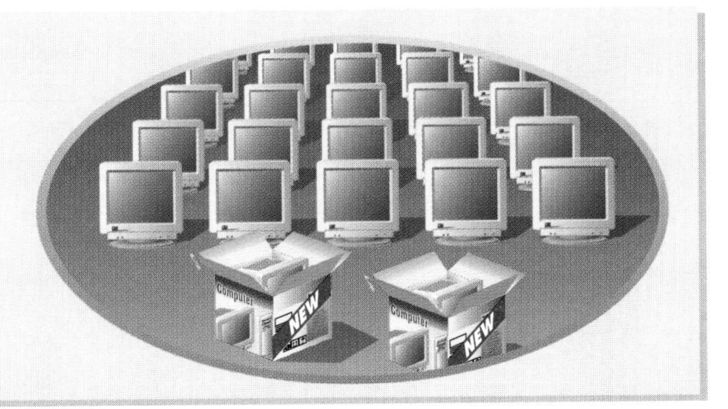

There are several standards of Ethernet architecture that can be considered for new or upgraded networks.

Ethernet

Most new networks should use one of the Ethernet standards available. Ethernet is the most popular and widely supported of all architectures and should be compatible with any future developments in networking, such as wireless local area networks. A company that invests in Ethernet technology today should be able to easily upgrade its network in the future.

Switched Ethernet

On a traditional Ethernet network, all the devices must share the available bandwidth. On a switched Ethernet network, each device can use the full bandwidth to communicate. A conventional Ethernet network can be transformed into a switched Ethernet network by replacing existing hubs with switches. It is also possible to have a hybrid Ethernet network that uses hubs and switches.

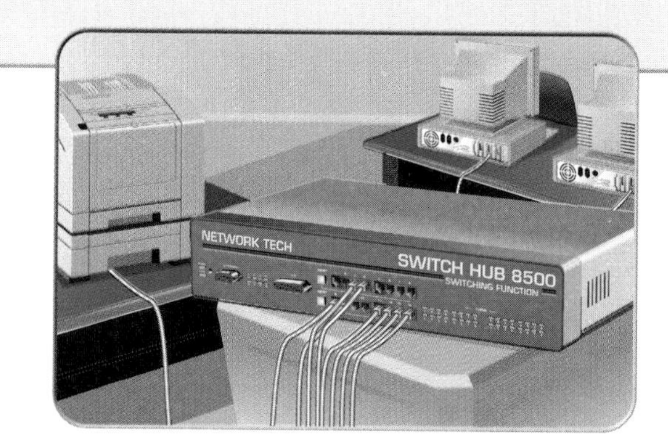

Fast Ethernet

Fast Ethernet is able to transfer data at speeds of up to 100 Mbps and is often referred to as 100BaseT. There are several types of 100BaseT available. 100BaseTX is Fast Ethernet that uses two pairs of Category 5 unshielded twisted pair cable to transfer information. 100BaseT4 is another type of Fast Ethernet that uses four pairs of Category 3 unshielded twisted pair cable. 100BaseFX is a type of Fast Ethernet that uses fiber-optic cable to transfer information.

Gigabit Ethernet

Gigabit Ethernet can transmit data at a rate of up to 1000 Mbps or 1 Gbps. Gigabit Ethernet is most often used for network backbones. There are several types of Gigabit Ethernet available. 1000BaseSX and 1000BaseLX use fiber-optic cable to transfer data. 1000BaseT uses four pairs of Category 5 unshielded twisted pair cable.

100VG-AnyLAN

100VG-AnyLAN is a version of Ethernet that transmits information at speeds of up to 100 Mbps. 100VG-AnyLAN can be configured to give priority to certain types of information, such as audio and video. 100VG-AnyLAN is often found on networks that use videoconferencing.

UPGRADING TRANSMISSION MEDIA

When upgrading a network, the transmission media is one of the most important aspects to consider. If a greater transfer speed is required or a new network architecture is being used, the transmission media may have to be replaced.

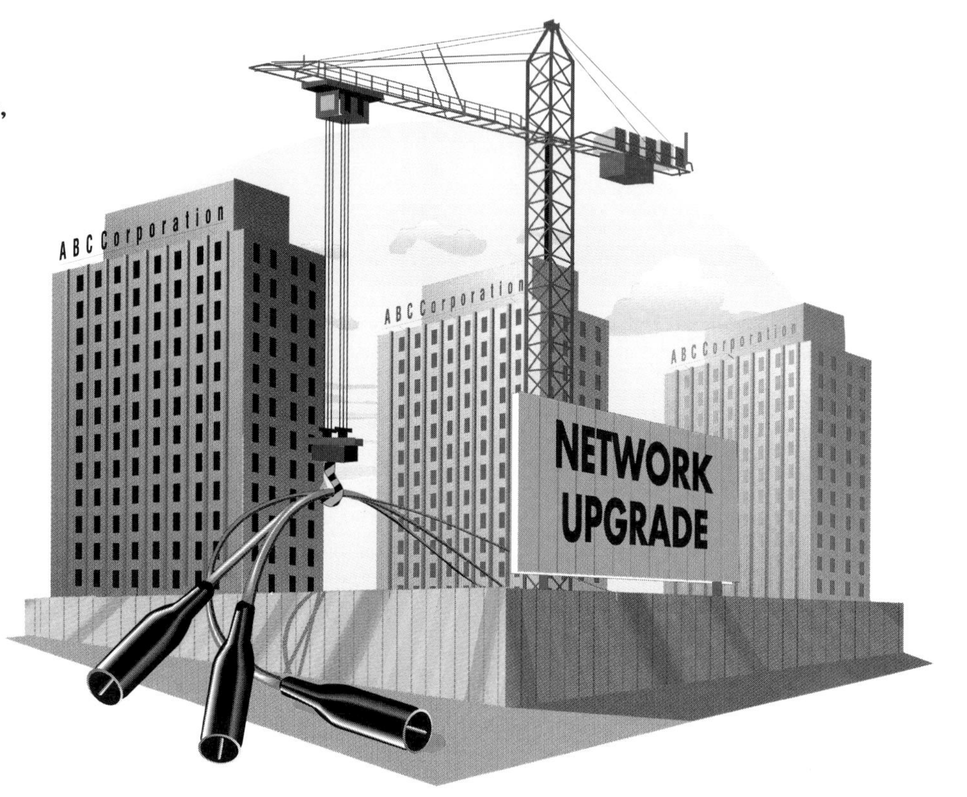

Speed

Older types of network cable may not be able to transfer information fast enough for today's applications. Most new networks are capable of transferring information at speeds of up to 100 Mbps, while older networks may only be able to transfer information at a fraction of that speed.

Network Hardware

Inexpensive network devices are now available that allow easy connection to popular transmission media, such as unshielded or shielded twisted pair cable. Networks that use older cable types, such as coaxial cable, may not be able to take advantage of current, inexpensive network hardware.

Coaxial Cable

Coaxial cable is commonly found on older networks. Although it is inexpensive, coaxial cable has many limitations that could hinder the future expansion of a network. For more information about coaxial cable, see page 72.

Fiber-optic Cable

Fiber-optic cable uses light to transfer information. Fiber-optic cable is a very fast, but expensive, transmission medium. Fiber-optic cable is often used to link busy network devices, such as hubs and routers. For more information about fiber-optic cable, see page 78.

Twisted Pair Cable

Unshielded twisted pair cable and shielded twisted pair cable are the most common transmission media used in new networks. Twisted pair cable is popular because it is relatively inexpensive. For more information about twisted pair cable, see pages 74 to 77.

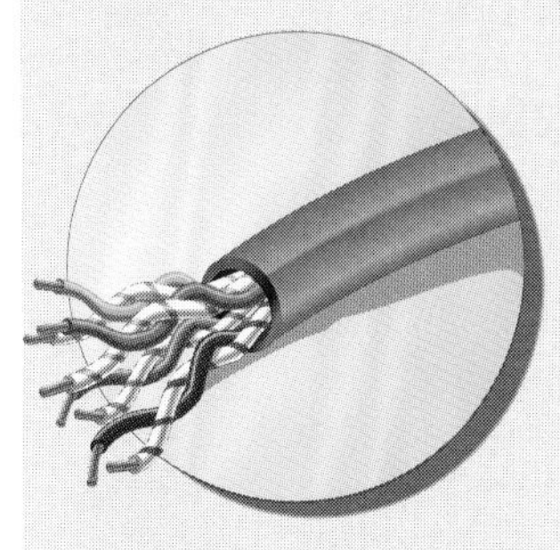

Unshielded Twisted Pair

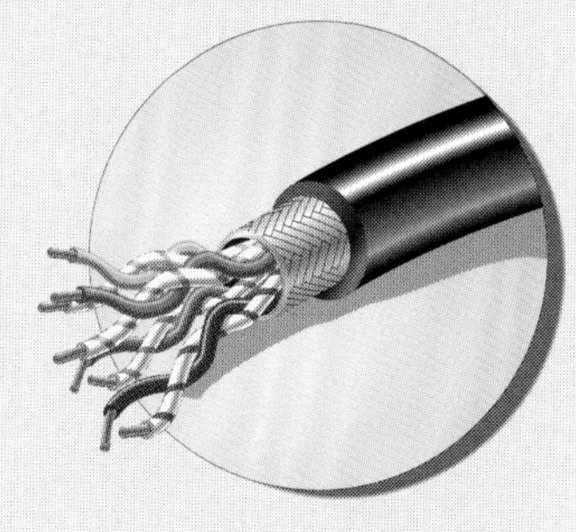

Shielded Twisted Pair

Wireless

A wireless transmission medium may be used when a network expands and parts of the network cannot be physically connected. For example, a company may use a wireless transmission medium to connect office buildings that are on opposite sides of a lake. Examples of wireless transmission media include infrared, radio, microwave and satellite systems. For more information about wireless transmission media, see pages 80 to 83.

Network cable is used to connect all devices on a computer network. It is essential that network cable be installed correctly.

Professional Installation

There are many steps that must be taken to ensure that network cable is installed correctly. If a network is going to connect any more than a few computers, a professional cable installer should be hired to install the cable. Professional cable installers use sophisticated testing equipment to ensure that cables function properly. Most professional installers also guarantee their work, which is useful if problems occur in the future.

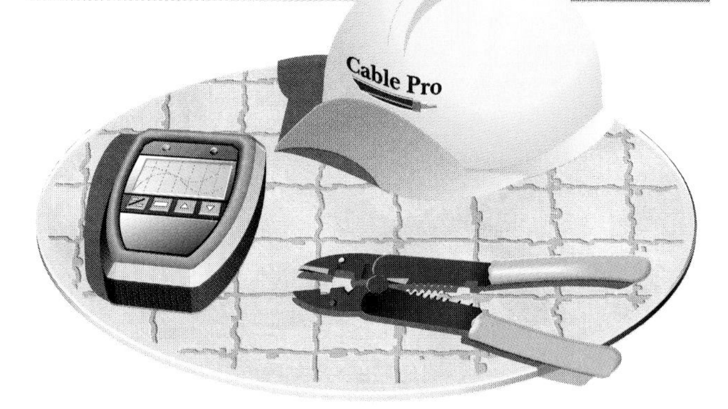

Jacks

Most cable is accessed through jacks that are installed in the walls of a building. Before a jack is installed, the network administrator should determine where the office furniture will be located. Since a length of cable will have to connect the computer to the jack, jacks should be placed in convenient locations.

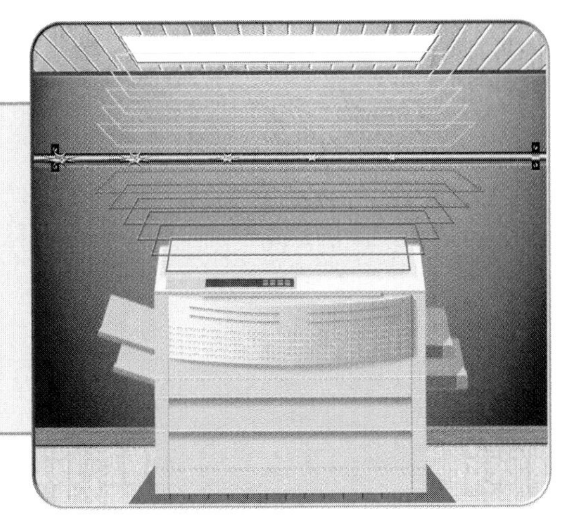

Interference

Modern offices contain electrical devices, such as photocopiers, fluorescent lighting and air conditioners, that can cause interference on network cable. Power cables and electrical wiring are also common sources of interference. To prevent interference, network cable should be installed at least two feet away from any source of electrical signals.

Conduits

When installing new cable, the use of cable conduits should be considered. Conduits are tube-like structures that help protect the cables they house from outside electrical interference. Conduits also make it easier to install additional cable in the future.

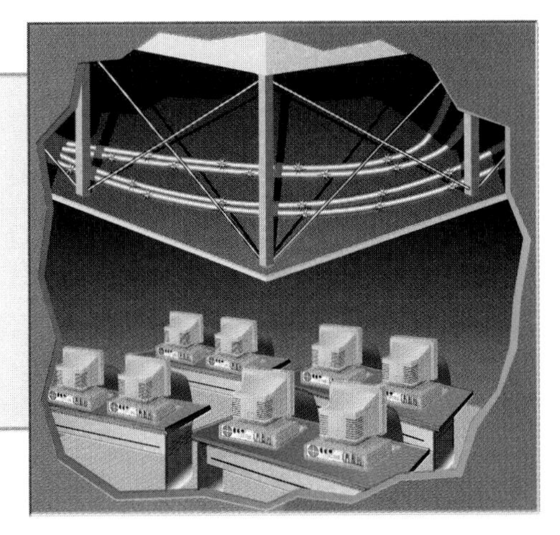

Fire Hazards

Cable is often installed in the space above a dropped ceiling, which is used to distribute air throughout a building. Some types of cable are constructed of material that, if exposed to fire, will emit poisonous fumes that can spread quickly throughout a building. To avoid this type of hazard, many local authorities require a special type of cable be used in areas such as dropped ceilings.

Network hardware are the physical devices used on a network. It is important to choose the correct hardware when installing or upgrading a network.

Purchasing Hardware

There are many locations where computer hardware can be purchased. If expert technical support is required, products should be purchased from a company that specializes in computer networks. Network devices can also be purchased from local computer stores or on the Internet.

Cost

The buying decisions of most network administrators are influenced by the amount of money their company budgets for network hardware. When purchasing network hardware, network administrators should keep in mind that price is often an indicator of product quality. Expensive network devices often perform better and are easier to manage than inexpensive devices.

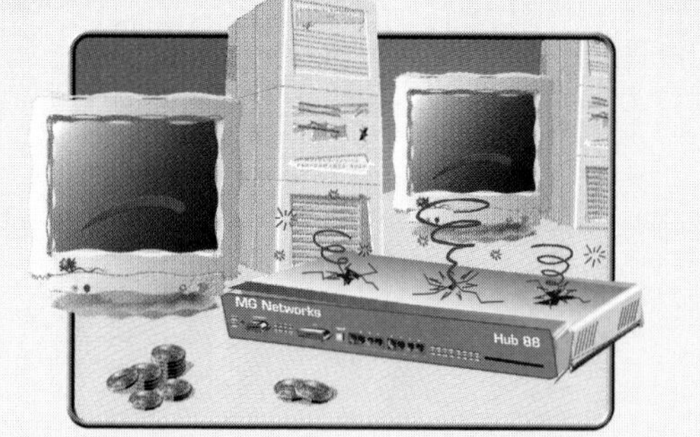

Hardware Functions

There are several types of network devices that perform similar functions. This can make choosing a hardware device difficult. For example, hubs and switches are both devices that provide a central location where the cables on a network come together. However, switches are more efficient than hubs at directing information to a specific destination on a large network. The tasks that the device will need to perform efficiently should be considered when choosing hardware.

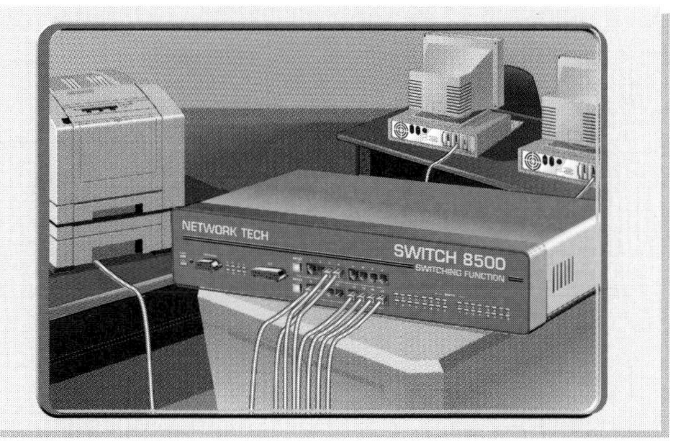

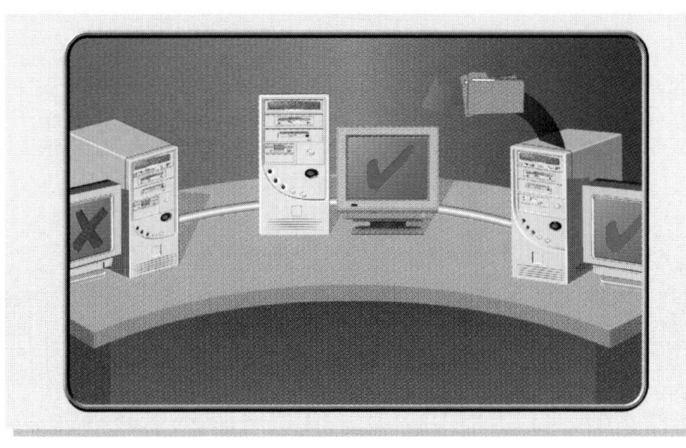

Compatibility

Hardware devices must be compatible with other aspects of the network, including architecture and transmission media, to ensure information can be transferred. For example, each transmission medium requires specialized network hardware, such as network interface cards, to transfer information between computers on a network.

Computer Location

The location of the computers on a network could be a factor that determines what hardware devices the network requires. For example, a network made up of computers located in different cities may require modems to transfer information, while a network connecting computers in a warehouse with computers in a front office may require repeaters.

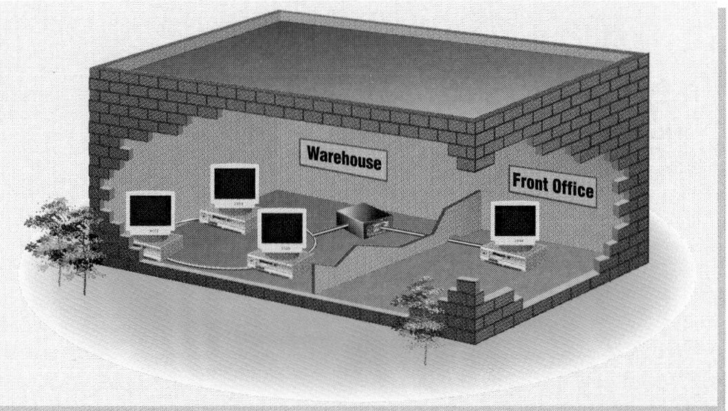

There are several factors to consider when installing network hardware. The network administrator should ensure that the hardware is functional and stored in a secure location, so it will continue to work properly.

Hardware Testing

Most network hardware components include a self-testing system. The network administrator should check new network hardware immediately after it has been purchased to ensure that it functions properly. The installation or upgrade of a network could be delayed if faulty hardware is installed before adequate testing.

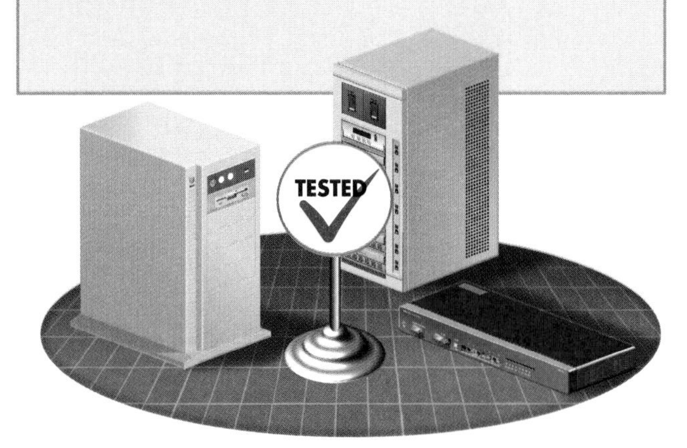

Consultants

A network consultant can be hired to evaluate network design plans and make recommendations about the installation of specific hardware devices. When installing a network that connects more than a few computers, the network administrator may want to consider having a consultant install the entire network. For more information about network consultants, see page 166.

Computer Rooms

Since network hardware is usually very expensive and is important to the operation of the entire network, hardware should be kept in a secure location that can be locked. It is also easier for an administrator to maintain a network when all of the important hardware components are located in one area. Many companies now have computer rooms that are used strictly for the storage of network equipment. This gives the administrator easy access to the network hardware while protecting the hardware from accidental or unauthorized tampering.

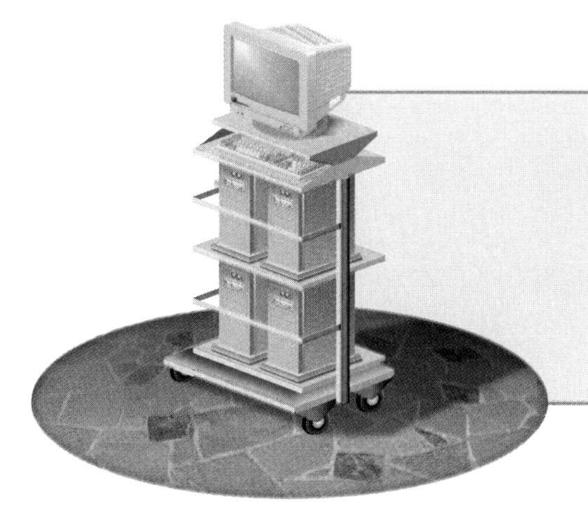

Racks

Many network administrators use racks to organize the network hardware components, such as hubs and servers, stored in computer rooms. Almost all network hardware can be placed on a rack. This allows easy access to the devices while keeping them organized and tidy.

Client Computers

Client computers are usually the easiest network hardware to setup, since they only require a network interface card to connect to the network. Network interface cards usually take only a few minutes to install. Many computers now have built-in network interface cards.

INSTALLING THE NETWORK OPERATING SYSTEM

A network operating system controls the overall activity of a network. To ensure the network runs smoothly, several factors should be considered before and after the installation of the network operating system.

Installation Process

Installing a network operating system is often the most complex part of upgrading an existing network or installing a new network. Several hours may be required to perform even a basic network operating system installation. Since complications may arise during the installation process, only experienced network administrators or qualified third-party professionals should install a network operating system.

Connect Devices

The network administrator should make sure that all network devices are connected and functioning properly before the network operating system is installed. The operating system may need to communicate with network hardware, such as hubs, storage devices or printers, during the installation.

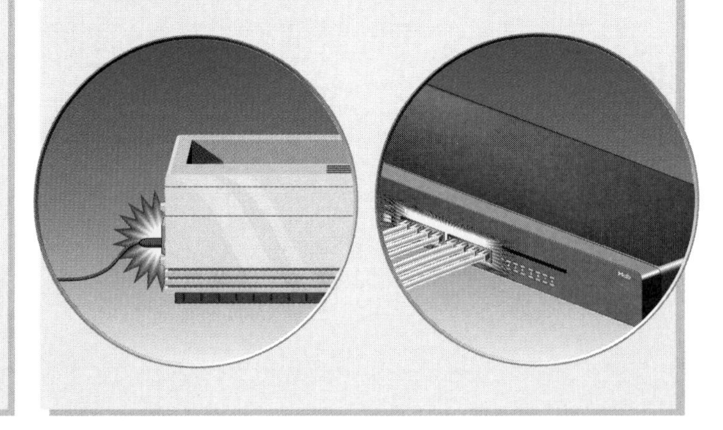

Transfer Information

Once the network operating system has been set up on a client/server network, information will need to be transferred to the servers. The network administrator should carefully plan what information will be stored on the network and on which server. For example, data files accessed by network users should be stored on a file server.

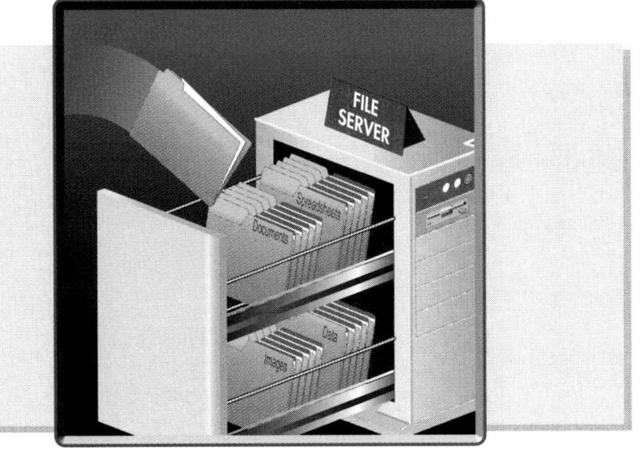

Security

After installing the network operating system, all the security settings should be thoroughly reviewed. One approach to security is to restrict access to all network resources and information. The network administrator can then grant users access to certain resources and information as the need arises.

Manage Users

Once the network is functioning, the network administrator will have to set up user accounts and assign passwords. The administrator can set up workgroups for users who need to access the same sets of resources. If many users need to be set up, the network operating system may allow the network administrator to automate the task.

CONFIGURING CLIENT COMPUTERS

Each user on a network usually has their own client computer. A client computer must be set up before it can be used on the network.

Configuration

The configuration of a client computer depends on the type of network the computer is connected to. Configuring a client may be as simple as assigning the computer a name or as complex as installing protocols and altering the hardware settings on the computer.

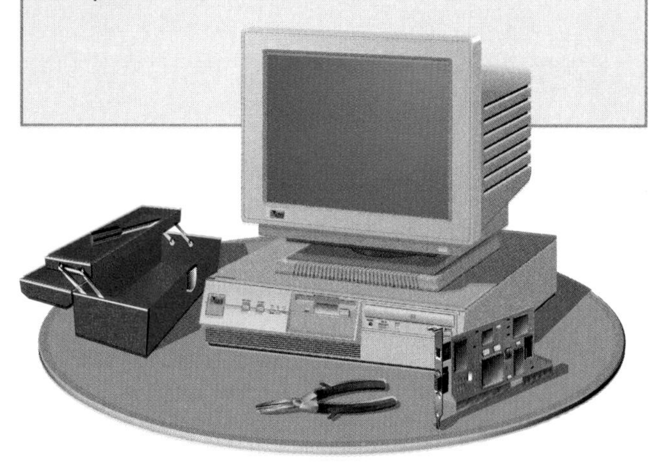

Drivers

A network interface card is the only hardware that is required to connect a client computer to a network. Software, called a driver, must be installed on the client computer before the network interface card can communicate with other devices on the network. Most network interface cards come with multiple drivers that enable the cards to communicate with many different types of networks.

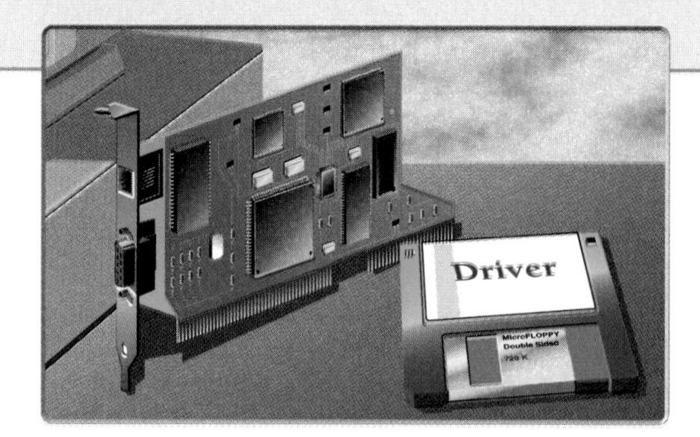

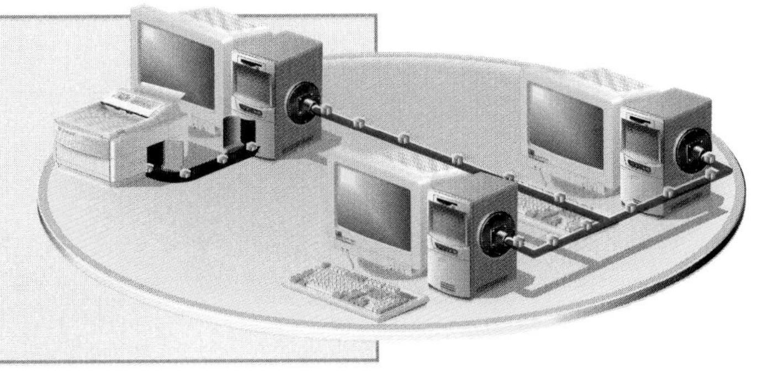

Resources

Other computers attached to a network may use resources, such as printers and modems, attached to a client computer. Before other computers can access a resource, the client computer must be configured to share the resource. The client computer must also be turned on and logged on to the network before the resource can be accessed.

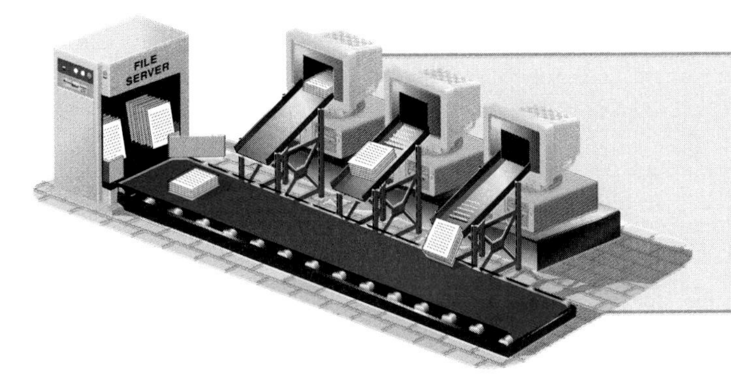

Information

Instead of saving information on its own hard drive, a client computer can save information on a file server on the network. Most client computers on a network will need to be configured before they can access a file server.

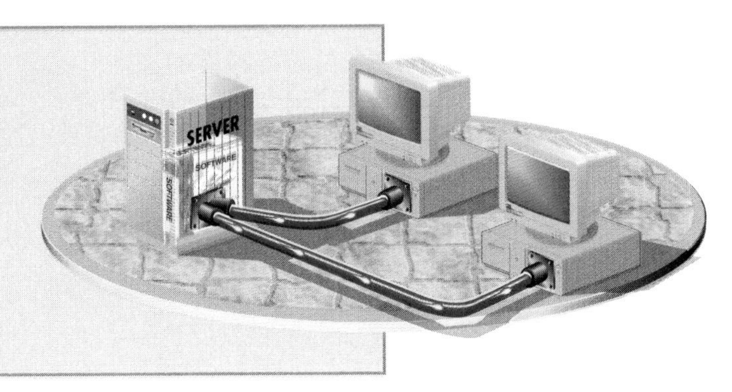

Applications

A program required by network users, such as a word processor, only needs to be installed on an application server. The client computers on the network can then access the application server to use the program. However, the network administrator must configure each client computer to save the user's settings for the application, such as the fonts and color schemes.

Once the entire network is installed and configured, the network should be thoroughly tested to ensure that all the devices are functioning and information is transferring properly.

Notes

When trying to resolve a problem, the network administrator should always keep detailed notes for future reference. Accurate notes will make it easier to repair recurring network problems. The notes could also reveal trends in network performance. By analyzing performance trends, the network administrator may be able to predict when problems will occur.

Professionals

While many network problems can be resolved with basic testing by the network administrator, hiring trained and qualified professionals to handle more complex problems is always a good idea. Most professionals can eliminate a network problem in a matter of minutes, while it may take a less experienced administrator days to fix the problem. If the problem is affecting the entire network, a timely solution is very important.

Cable Testers

Problems with cable, such as breaks, can be very difficult to locate once the cable is installed. There are devices available that can be used to test installed cable. Some devices check the continuity of cable to determine if there is a break, while other devices help pinpoint the location of a break. If there is a break, a cable tracer can be used to locate cable hidden within a floor, wall or ceiling.

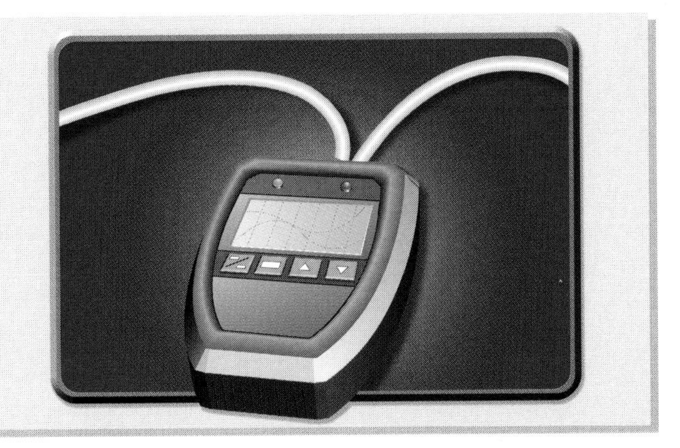

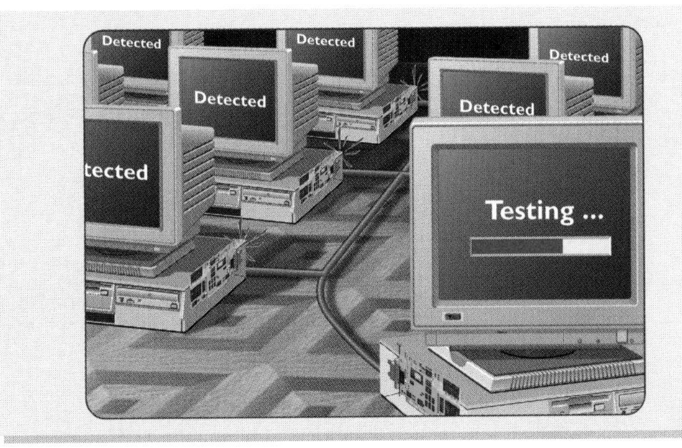

Broadcasts

Many network interface cards come equipped with testing software. The software allows the network administrator to broadcast information that can be detected by similar network interface cards on the network. Broadcasts are a good way to test connections on a network.

Traffic Simulators

Many network problems do not show up until the network is transferring a significant amount of information. Special devices and software programs are available that simulate traffic on a network that is similar to the amount generated when the network is in full use. A network administrator can preview how the network will perform under heavy traffic conditions and identify problems before they occur.

ISP
Internet Service Provider

Connecting to the Internet

The Internet can be an invaluable addition to any network. This chapter discusses how to connect a network to the Internet.

Connect a Network to the Internet 210

Considerations for Connecting to the Internet....212

Internet Service Providers 216

Internet Hardware 218

Internet Software 220

Internet Connection Types 222

Using TCP/IP to Connect to the Internet....224

Troubleshoot Internet Connections......226

CONNECT A NETWORK TO THE INTERNET

Many companies are connecting their existing networks to the Internet. The Internet has proven to be an invaluable tool for businesses and organizations of all sizes.

Purpose

Before connecting a network to the Internet, a company should determine what purpose the connection will serve. Some companies only want to have a Web site that promotes the company and provides information. In this case, a network connection to the Internet is unnecessary since a Web site can be created and maintained by a company that specializes in Web site development.

Planning

A company should develop a detailed plan before connecting a network to the Internet. It is often necessary to purchase or lease costly equipment for an Internet connection. Long-term contracts will also have to be signed with companies, such as the local telephone company and an Internet service provider. Proper planning helps ensure that all necessary equipment and services are in place.

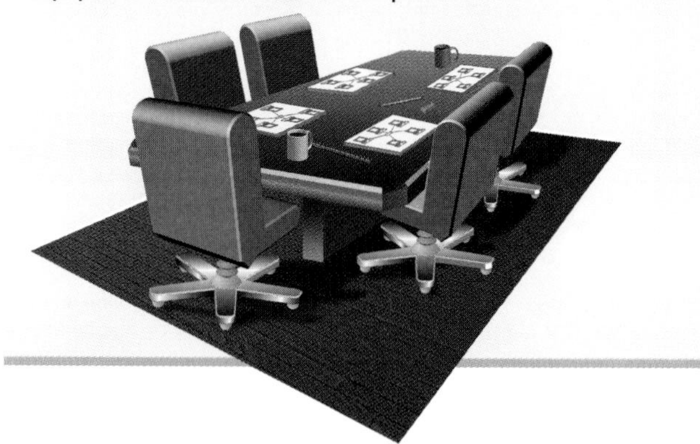

REASONS FOR CONNECTING TO THE INTERNET

Provide Information

Companies use the Internet as a cost-effective method of providing information about their products and services to the public. For example, a Web site can be used to inform the public about product specifications and warranty information.

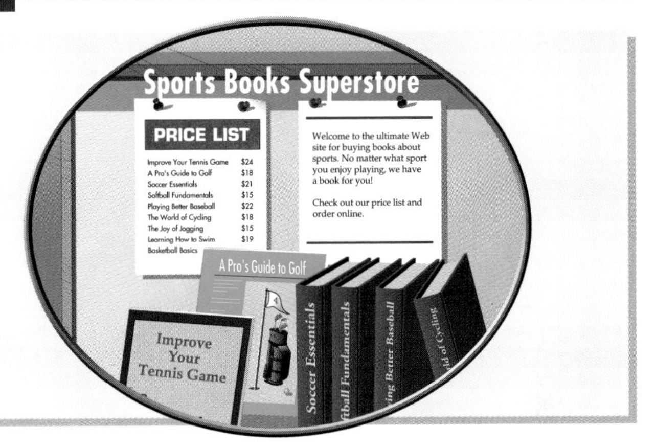

Access Information

The information available on the Internet is becoming better organized and easier to find. Many companies allow their employees to access the Internet because it can be a valuable research and information-gathering tool. There are many databases and news services available, although a fee may be required to access some information.

Communication

With the Internet, employees can communicate using a variety of methods, such as e-mail or videoconferencing. The Internet is an inexpensive method of communication between individuals in different locations because telephone charges and postage fees do not apply. The Internet also provides a quick and easy way for a company to communicate with its clients.

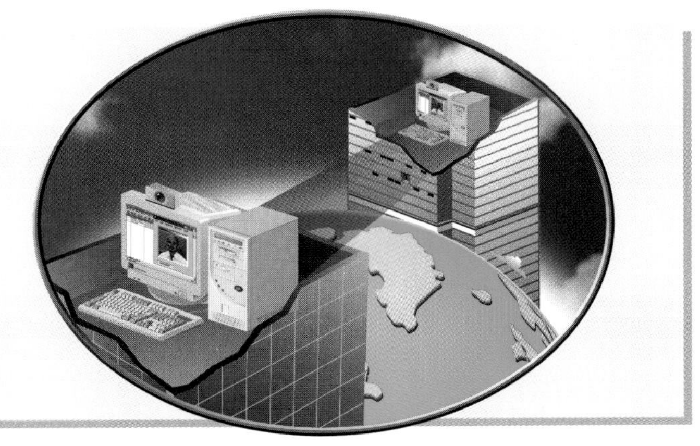

CONSIDERATIONS FOR CONNECTING TO THE INTERNET

There are many important factors to consider when establishing and maintaining a connection between a company network and the Internet.

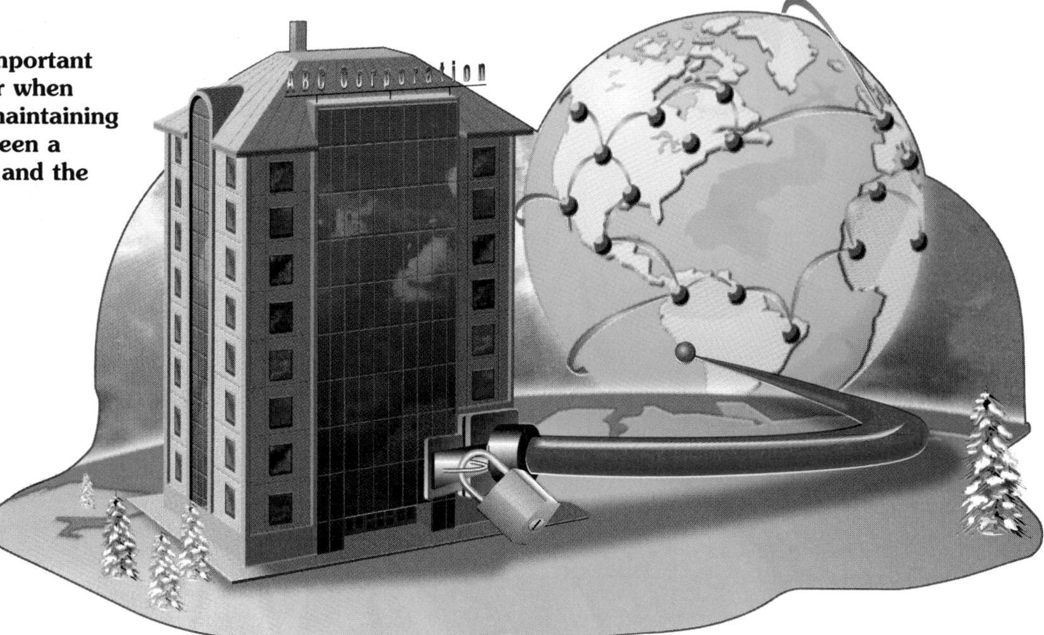

Training

When an existing network is connected to the Internet, many network users will need to be trained to work with the applications used to access Internet information. Applications such as e-mail programs, Web browsers and file transfer programs can be very complex and users should know how to use them properly.

Support

Networks connected to the Internet require more support than other networks. For example, if a company has a Web site, someone will need to create and maintain the Web pages stored on the Web site. Personnel will also be required to support any new Internet-related hardware and software installed on the network.

Network Operating Systems

Many network operating system manufacturers, such as Novell, make products that can simplify the process of connecting a network to the Internet. When planning a connection to the Internet, the network administrator or Internet service provider should determine if there are any products available that may help.

Backup Connection

Companies that connect their networks to the Internet may rely heavily on the information and services available to them, such as e-mail. Some companies find it beneficial to have a second connection to the Internet using a different Internet service provider. The second connection provides a backup system should the first connection fail.

Security

Security concerns are an ongoing issue for network administrators. Security products and techniques are constantly evolving. Network administrators who do not stay up to date with the latest security technologies risk a network attack from better-educated crackers.

CONSIDERATIONS FOR CONNECTING TO THE INTERNET (CONTINUED)

COST CONSIDERATIONS

Budget

Planning, setting up and maintaining a connection between a network and the Internet can be very expensive. Before a network administrator connects a network to the Internet, the necessary budget for supporting a long-term connection should be determined.

Employee Productivity

A connection to the Internet may reduce employee productivity if employees use the Internet for non-work related tasks, such as personal Web browsing. To save a company from this type of financial loss, the network administrator should set and enforce rigid guidelines dictating how employees may use the Internet.

Save Money

Connecting a network to the Internet can save a company money in areas of the business that are not directly related to the use of the network. For example, many companies reduce costs in areas such as long-distance telephone charges and research time by connecting their networks to the Internet.

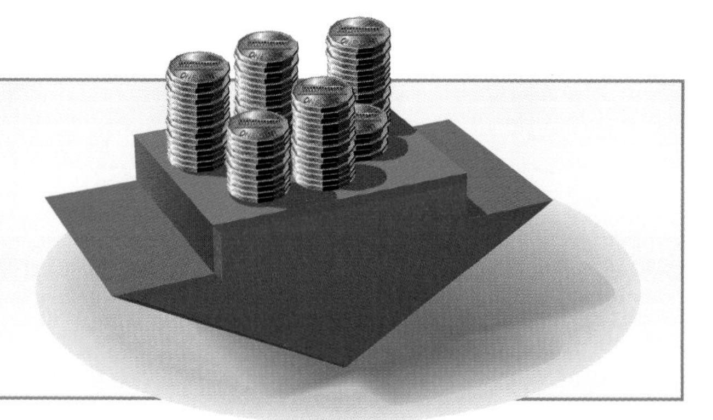

HARDWARE CONSIDERATIONS

Future Needs

When connecting a network to the Internet, the network administrator should keep the future needs of the company in mind. Some types of Internet connections are easier to upgrade than others. If a company is likely to demand higher performance from an Internet connection in the future, the network administrator should choose a connection that can later be upgraded to provide a higher bandwidth.

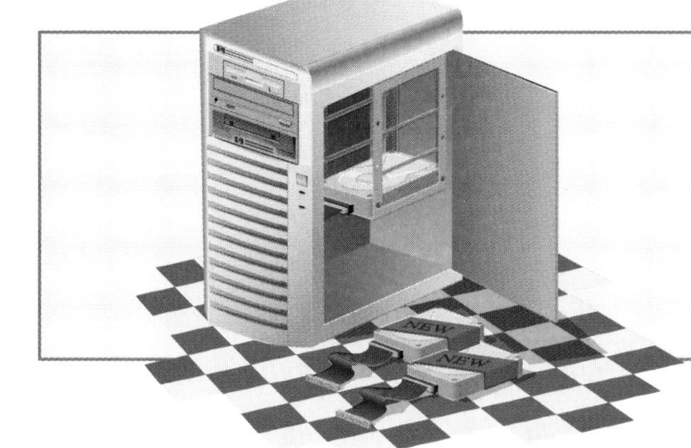

Scalable Hardware

Scalable hardware can be easily upgraded to use new technologies. Since Internet technologies are constantly evolving, hardware that is purchased to connect a network to the Internet should be scalable. This can help avoid the need to frequently replace out-of-date hardware devices.

Connection Analysis

Once a network has been connected to the Internet for a period of time, the network administrator should conduct a review of all the hardware and software components used for the connection. A thorough review can help the administrator determine the effectiveness of the connection.

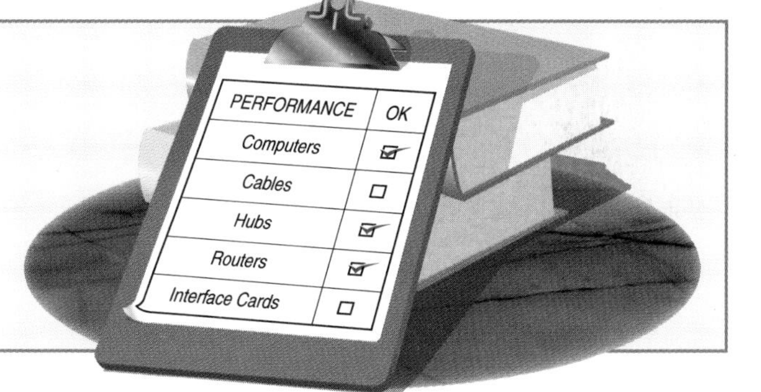

INTERNET SERVICE PROVIDERS

An Internet Service Provider (ISP) is a company that provides access to the Internet for a fee. A network must connect to an Internet service provider in order to access the Internet.

Services

There are many Internet service providers offering a broad range of services. Besides access to the Internet, some ISPs may also offer Web site creation and hosting services, online support and instant messaging. A company should carefully evaluate all aspects of an ISP they are considering.

Contracts

Before using the services of an ISP, a company typically has to enter into a contract, usually for a minimum of one year. Every detail of the expected service should be written into the contract. This may help prevent unnecessary complications, such as the ISP failing to provide acceptable levels of service. As with all contracts, a company should seek legal advice before committing to a long-term contract with an Internet service provider.

Size

An ISP can be a relatively small business that provides Internet access to small companies and individuals using dial-up connections. Large ISPs often connect businesses and organizations to the Internet using dedicated, high-speed connections. Larger ISPs usually provide more efficient service than smaller Internet service providers. For more information about connection types, see page 222.

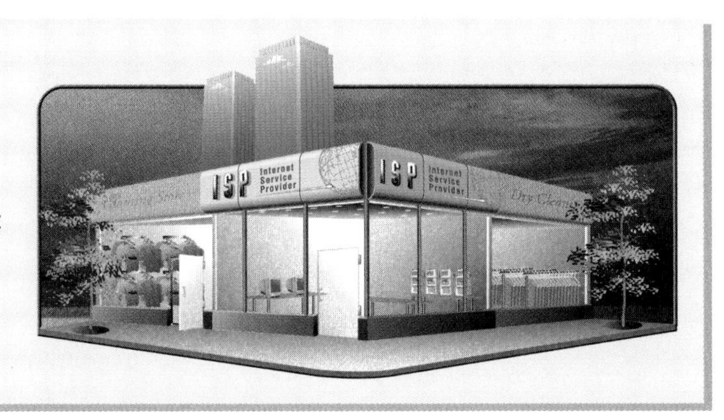

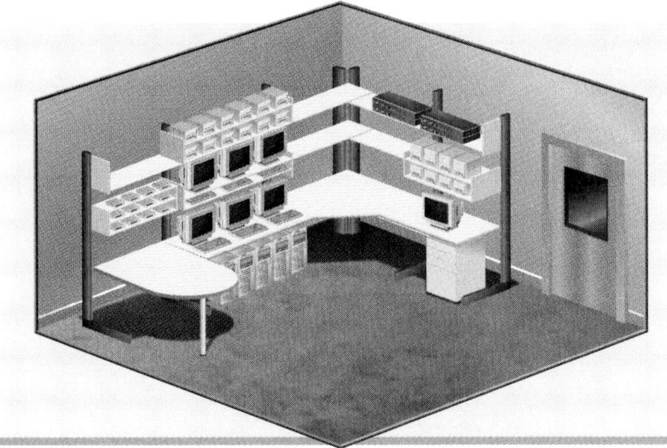

Support and Equipment

Connecting a network to the Internet and maintaining a good quality connection requires trained technicians. The equipment used by an ISP can determine the quality of a connection. Companies should ensure an ISP has the necessary personnel and equipment to properly support a connection to the Internet.

Network Access Points

Internet service providers exchange information with other ISPs at locations called Network Access Points (NAPs). Internet service providers connect to NAPs using high-speed connections. The faster a service provider's connection to a NAP, the faster a company's network connection to the Internet will be. ISPs should be able to provide detailed information about their network speeds and traffic.

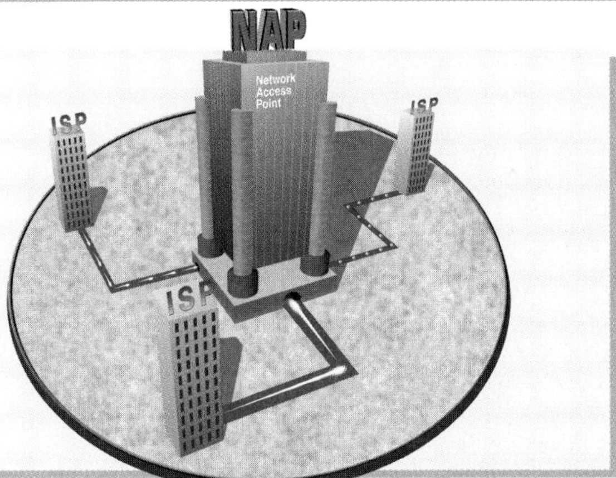

INTERNET HARDWARE

Hardware devices connect a network to the Internet. Depending on the connection, more than one type of device may be required.

Routers

In many cases, routers connect a network to the Internet. One router is connected to the network while another router is connected to the Internet service provider. The two routers are joined by a dedicated connection. When connected to the Internet by routers, network users can access Internet information immediately.

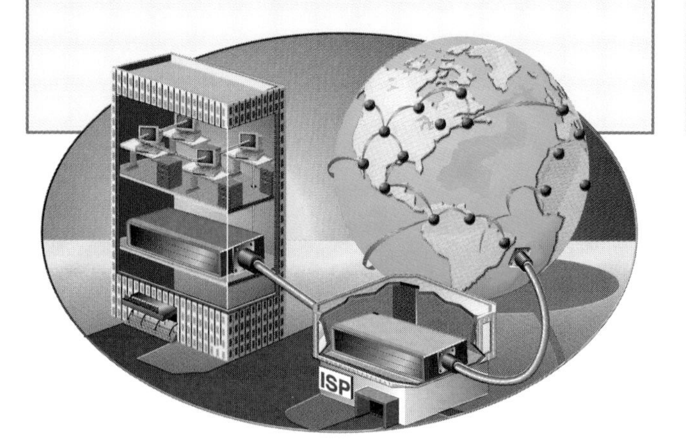

Modems

Modems can be used to connect a network to the Internet. A specialized software application is often required for a network to access the Internet using a modem. Modems are slow and allow a limited number of users access to the Internet at one time. Modem access should only be considered if a minimal amount of information will be transferred.

Firewalls

Security is a major consideration when connecting a network to the Internet. Firewalls are often used to protect network data by controlling the information that passes between a private network and the Internet. Some devices that are used to connect networks to the Internet, such as routers, have basic firewall capabilities but may not provide enough protection for networks that contain confidential information.

Servers

Servers can be used to provide a network with services from the Internet, such as Web browsing, file access and e-mail. Since many Internet service providers offer these services, these types of servers may not be required on a network.

Remote Access Servers

A company can use a remote access server to allow employees to connect to the Internet when away from the office. For example, an employee can connect to the remote access server and then access the Internet through the company network. A remote access server typically consists of a computer connected to one or more modems.

As well as hardware devices, a network may require software when connecting to the Internet. For example, a company may install software to provide information on the Internet or safeguard its own network information.

Built-in Applications

Establishing and maintaining a connection between a network and the Internet requires very little software. Most hardware devices that connect a network to the Internet have built-in applications that allow the hardware to operate without the use of additional software.

Server Software

If a company wishes to set up and maintain servers that provide information on the Internet, such as a Web server, the network administrator will need to install the software required to run the Internet application. There are many server software programs available free of charge on the Internet. Network administrators can also purchase server software at computer stores.

Security Software

Before a company connects its network to the Internet, the administrator may need to install software to prevent unauthorized access to the network by users on the Internet. Some types of security software can be installed on each network computer that accesses the Internet. Other types of security software can be installed on only one computer that will monitor and process all the information exchanged with the Internet.

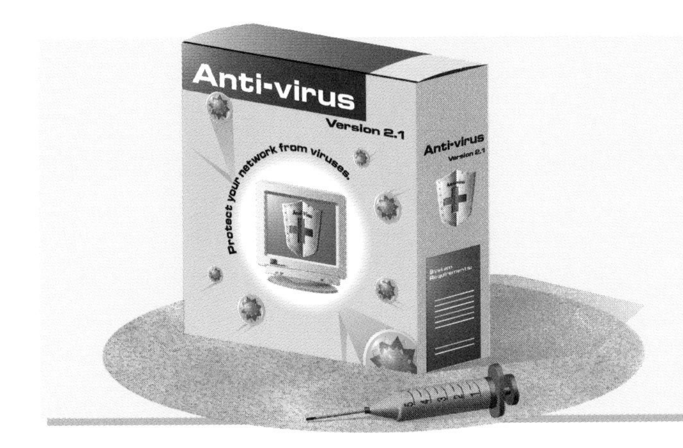

Anti-virus Software

Many programs on the Internet contain viruses that may damage the information stored on a computer network. Anti-virus software should be installed on all computers that receive information from the Internet. Some anti-virus software only needs to be installed on one computer that will examine all the information received from the Internet for viruses.

Application Software

Many networks connected to the Internet run applications that have been developed specifically for use on the Internet. Applications that make databases available on the Internet are popular, as are applications that support credit card purchases.

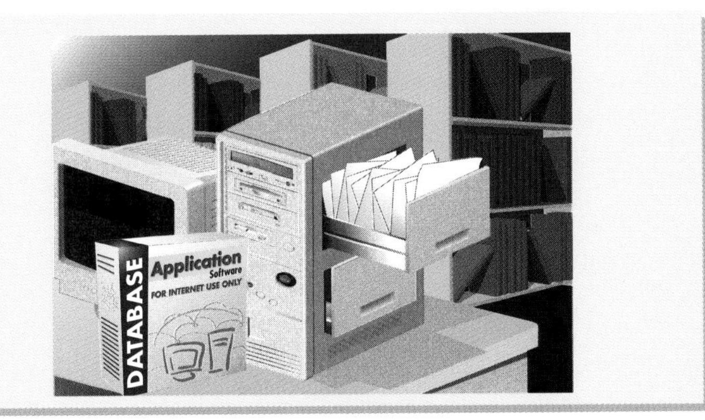

A high-speed connection is used to link a network to an Internet service provider.

The more bandwidth a company requires, the more expensive the connection to the Internet will be.

Installation

Proper planning is required to connect a network to the Internet, since most connection types must be ordered weeks in advance of the required date. Most connection types require the local telephone company to install the connection.

Telephone Lines

Networks that do not exchange a lot of information on the Internet can use phone lines and modems to connect to the Internet. Some modems are capable of receiving information from the Internet at speeds of up to 56 Kbps, but can only send information at 33.6 Kbps.

HIGH-SPEED CONNECTIONS

ISDN

Integrated Services Digital Network (ISDN) can be configured to exchange information at various speeds. The most common speed for connecting networks to the Internet using ISDN is 128 Kbps.

DSL

Digital Subscriber Line (DSL) uses existing phone lines to connect to the Internet. DSL can transfer information at speeds from 1 Mbps to 9 Mbps. DSL is growing in popularity since it is relatively inexpensive.

T1

A T1 connection is capable of transmitting information at 1.544 Mbps. Many small Internet service providers use a T1 connection to connect to the Internet. If a company does not wish to pay for a full T1 line, the company may be able to use only part of the line. This type of connection is referred to as a fractional T1.

T3

A T3 connection can transmit information over fiber-optic cable at speeds of up to 44.73 Mbps. T3 connections are often used to connect large Internet service providers to the Internet. Only large companies that exchange a lot of information on the Internet use T3 connections.

USING TCP/IP TO CONNECT TO THE INTERNET

Any computer or network that exchanges information on the Internet must use the TCP/IP protocol suite. Setting up a network connection to an Internet service provider using TCP/IP protocols can be a very complex and time-consuming operation.

For more information about the TCP/IP protocol suite, see pages 130 to 131.

IP Addresses

Before using TCP/IP to connect a network to the Internet, each computer that accesses the Internet must be assigned a unique IP address. IP addresses are written as four numbers separated by dots, such as 192.168.67.54. This is known as dotted-decimal notation.

Getting an IP Address

An Internet service provider typically obtains the required IP addresses from a central organization called the Internet Network Information Center (InterNIC). Because each IP address must be unique, the Internet is running out of IP addresses. A new system of IP addressing, called IPv6, will provide more IP numbers in the future.

Assigning IP Addresses

There are two ways to assign IP addresses to computers on a network. One way is to configure each computer separately so it will always use the same IP address. Another way is to set up a BOOTP or DHCP server to assign IP addresses to computers each time they connect to the Internet. The type of server a network requires depends on the TCP/IP protocol used to assign the IP addresses.

Domain Name Servers

Domain Name Servers (DNSs) are used to convert IP addresses into readable names, such as www.company.com. Networks often use the domain name servers provided by their Internet service providers. If many computers on a network access the Internet, the network may have its own domain name server.

Drivers

Before a computer can access the Internet, it must have the TCP/IP protocol suite and the appropriate TCP/IP drivers installed. The TCP/IP drivers convert information from the computer into information that can be transferred on a TCP/IP network.

TROUBLESHOOT INTERNET CONNECTIONS

There are many problems that can occur when a network is connected to the Internet. For most companies, it is essential that the network administrator be able to quickly detect and fix Internet connection problems.

Notes

It is important for the network administrator to keep detailed notes and logs concerning Internet connection problems. It is possible that an Internet connection problem is simply a symptom of larger network problems. Detailed notes and diagrams can help network administrators and service personnel quickly track down the source of a problem and fix it.

Hardware

There are many hardware products available that can alert the network administrator when a connection problem is detected. Advanced network components often use methods such as e-mail or paging to alert the network administrator when an error occurs, such as a broken connection. Some simpler hardware devices use colored status lights to indicate that an error has occurred.

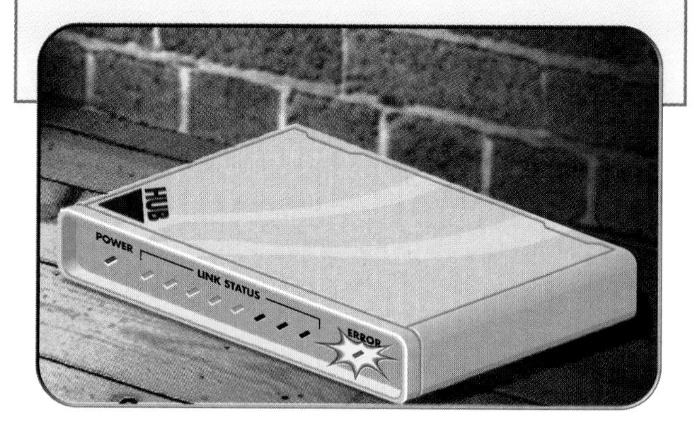

PING

PING is a simple utility that is available on most computers using the TCP/IP protocol suite. The PING utility sends information to a computer on a network and then waits for a reply from the destination computer. PING is a very useful tool for establishing whether or not a connection exists between two computers.

Protocol Analyzers

If there are any difficulties with an Internet connection, a protocol analyzer can be used to check the connection and help pinpoint the problem. For example, a protocol analyzer can be used to examine each piece of data transferred over the connection and determine whether the data contains any errors.

Technical Support

Most Internet service providers offer very good technical support. Some Internet service providers offer 24-hour support over the phone. The Internet service provider's support team should be able to help the network administrator troubleshoot an Internet connection problem.

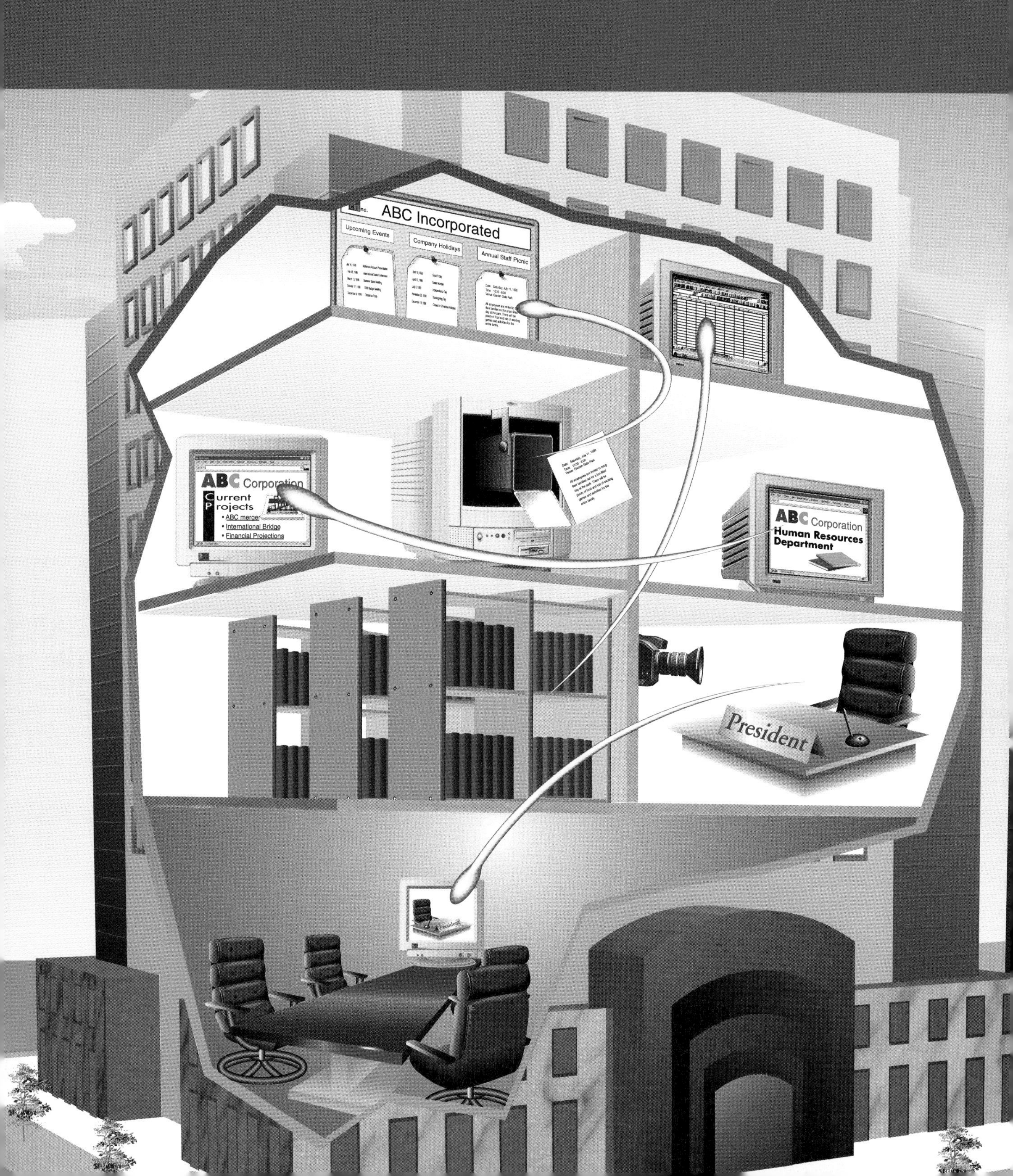
ABC Incorporated
Upcoming Events
Company Holidays
Annual Staff Picnic
ABC Corporation
Current Projects
• ABC merger
• International Bridge
• Financial Projections
ABC Corporation
Human Resources Department
President

Intranets

An intranet is a network, similar to the Internet, within a company. This chapter examines some of the features available on intranets, including videoconferencing, e-mail and newsgroups.

Introduction to Intranets 230
Videoconferencing on Intranets 232
Scheduling on Intranets 234
Intranet Web Systems 236
E-mail on Intranets 238
Newsgroups on Intranets..................240
Chat on Intranets 242
File Transfer on Intranets 244
Intranet Software 246
Groupware 248
Voice Over IP 250

An intranet is a network, similar to the Internet, within a company or organization. Intranets offer many of the features and services available on the Internet, such as a Web system, e-mail, newsgroups and chat.

Intranets allow company information and resources to be shared among employees. Intranets are particularly useful for companies that have offices in multiple locations or whose employees often work in groups.

Internet Technology

Intranets transfer information on a network using the same technology that is used to transfer information on the Internet. This allows intranets to exchange information quickly and easily over different types of networks, without having to consider the network operating systems used on each network.

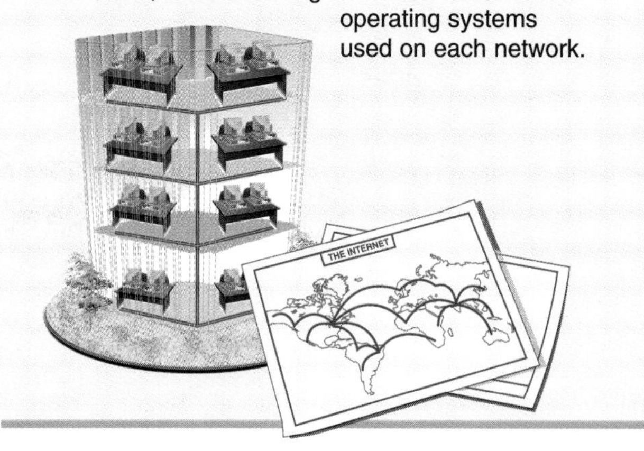

Efficiency

Intranets allow employees to access internal company information quickly and efficiently. When company information is easy to access, employee productivity often increases. Companies can use intranets to distribute information such as phone directories, product listings and job openings. A company could also use their intranet to inform employees of a new project or client.

Servers

Intranets use high-performance computers, called servers, to control the distribution of information on an intranet. On most intranets, each intranet feature is stored on its own server. Many intranet servers are similar to the servers used on the Internet.

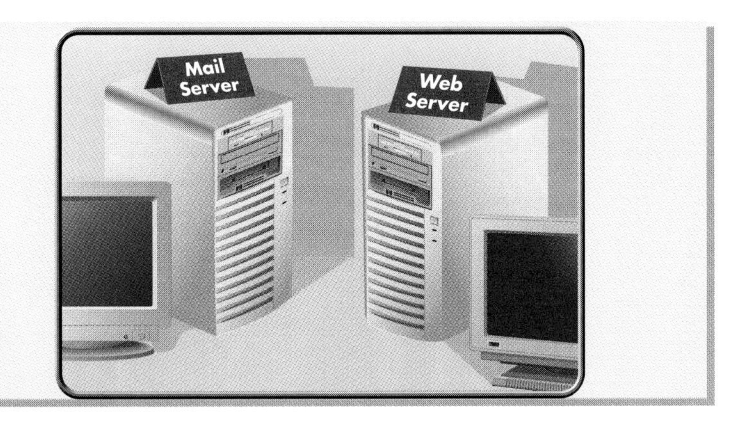

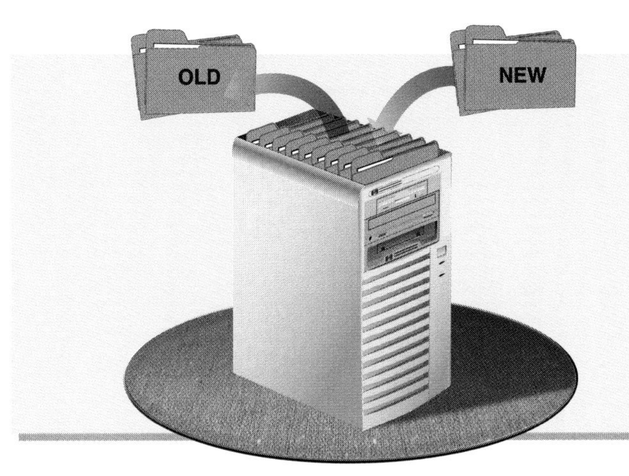

Content

To get the most value from an intranet, companies should ensure that intranet content is relevant and kept up-to-date. Companies should also make sure that information is easy to access. An intranet will not be widely used if it contains outdated information or information that is difficult to obtain.

Extranets

Many companies are now making parts of their private intranet available on the Internet, creating an extranet. An extranet allows users outside the company, such as customers and other businesses, to access specific company information. Extranets are not for the general public and security features, such as firewalls and encryption software, are often used to protect extranet information from unauthorized access.

VIDEOCONFERENCING ON INTRANETS

Videoconferencing can make communication more efficient by allowing users on an intranet to see and hear each other. Videoconferencing is just starting to become feasible on intranets.

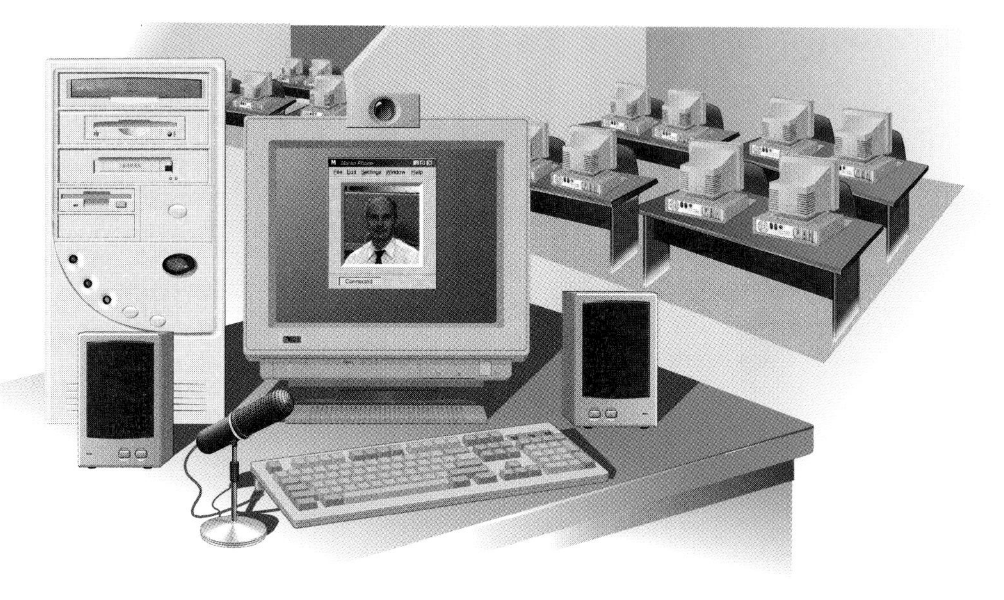

Face to Face

Videoconferencing allows people to have face-to-face conversations with other users on an intranet, whether they are around the corner or on the other side of the city. For example, videoconferencing can be a useful tool for providing training to a new employee located in another office. Using videoconferencing, a member of the training team can provide audio and visual guidance to another person without actually being at the same location. Videoconferencing may substantially reduce travel and training costs for a company.

Multiple Participants

One of the most useful aspects of videoconferencing on intranets is the ability to have several people participate in a videoconference at once. Although videoconferencing is still not feasible for large groups, it is possible to effectively videoconference with up to three other people.

Time-consuming tasks, such as meetings in person, may eventually be replaced by videoconferencing.

Bandwidth

Videoconferencing transmits audio and video signals over the intranet, which allows users to communicate with each other. Videoconferencing requires a lot of information to transfer between computers. Many existing networks are not capable of transmitting information fast enough to support videoconferencing computers. If the bandwidth on a network is not sufficient to host a videoconference, all users of the network may be affected.

Equipment

Specific equipment is required for videoconferencing. All the computers participating in a videoconference must have sound capabilities, speakers and a microphone to transmit and receive sound. A computer must also have video capabilities and an attached video camera to transmit video images.

Programs

There are many software programs available that can be used to facilitate videoconferencing. Many videoconferencing programs allow users to exchange files, share programs and collaborate on group projects.

Scheduling software can be used on an intranet to schedule meetings and organize projects. Scheduling is one of the most important services available on an intranet.

Employee Schedules

Employees can use scheduling software to make their personal schedules, including their daily calendars, appointments and to-do lists, available on the company intranet. This allows other people on the intranet to see their activities and when they are available.

Schedule Meetings

Planning and organizing meetings can be a time-consuming task since everyone in a company usually has a different agenda. Scheduling meetings for large groups of people on an intranet can be made much easier by using scheduling software. Scheduling software can be used to check employee availability and to schedule meetings at a time and place convenient for everyone. Scheduling software also makes it easy to make last minute changes to a meeting and then notify everyone invited to the meeting.

Schedule Resources

A resource can be a device, such as a printer, a person, such as a consultant, needed for the completion of a project. Scheduling software can be used to manage and schedule the use of resources to ensure they are available when required. The time and expense of a project can be better managed by properly scheduling the use of resources.

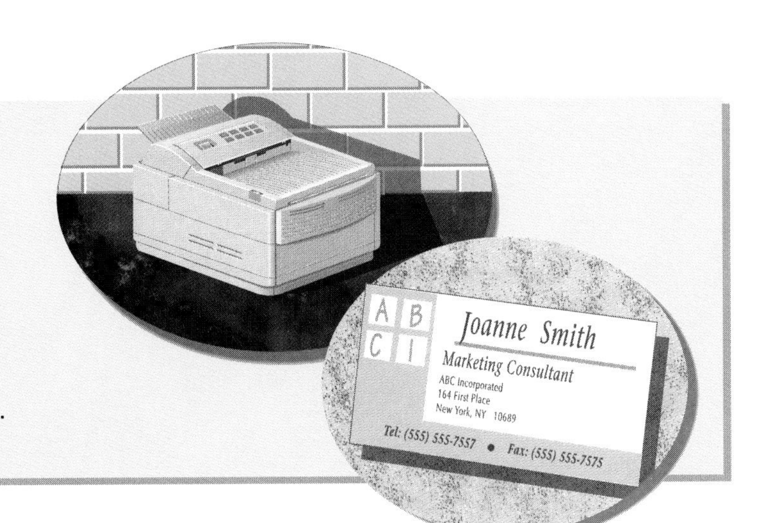

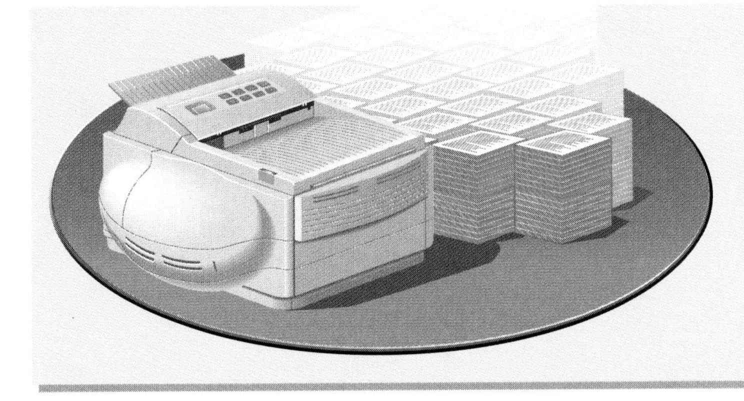

Monitor Resources

One of the benefits of using scheduling software is that users can monitor how a company's resources are used over time. Since users can track how often a given resource is used, problems, such as the inability to access a resource, can be avoided.

Automatic Scheduling

Some scheduling software can automatically perform tasks, such as booking a boardroom, when a user requests a meeting. The scheduling software can also send an automatic invitation to everyone who needs to attend the meeting. The time and place of the meeting will be added to each person's schedule.

INTRANET WEB SYSTEMS

Web sites on an intranet Web system are similar to Web sites found on the World Wide Web.

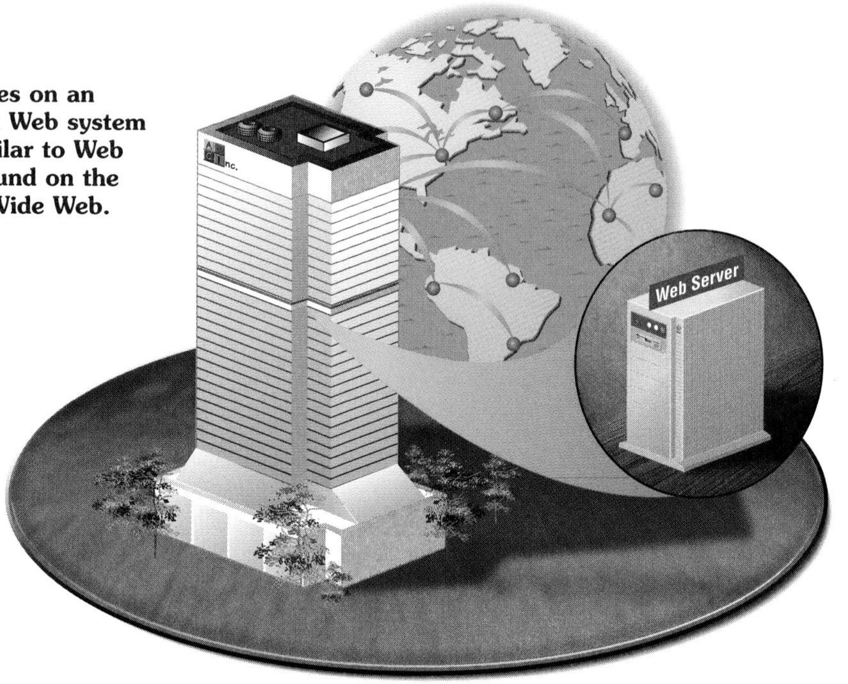

A Web site is a collection of Web pages. A Web page is a document that can include text, pictures, sound, video and animation. A Web server stores Web sites and manages the intranet Web system.

Compatibility

The major benefit of using an intranet Web system is that Web pages can be displayed on any computer that has a Web browser installed, including computers running a Windows, Macintosh or Unix operating system.

Privacy

Many documents found on an intranet Web system, such as company policies or sales reports, are not made available to the general public. A company's intranet Web server is different from the Web server the company uses to provide information on the Internet. This ensures that information on the intranet Web system is not accessible to the public through the Internet.

Create Web Pages

HyperText Markup Language (HTML) is used to create Web pages. HTML uses instructions, called tags, to display text and images on a Web page. There are many programs available that help users construct Web pages even if they are not familiar with HTML. Many applications, such as word processors, spreadsheets and database programs, are capable of saving files in the HTML format. The files can then be transferred to a Web server for display on a company intranet.

Employee Web Pages

If employees are connected to an intranet, they can easily publish their own intranet Web pages. Web pages can contain information such as office telephone numbers, current projects or any other information that might be important to fellow employees.

Department Web Pages

If a company has an intranet Web system, each department in the company can display information on its own Web site. For example, the human resources department may display Web pages concerning company policies and schedules, while the sales department could publish Web pages providing the latest sales figures.

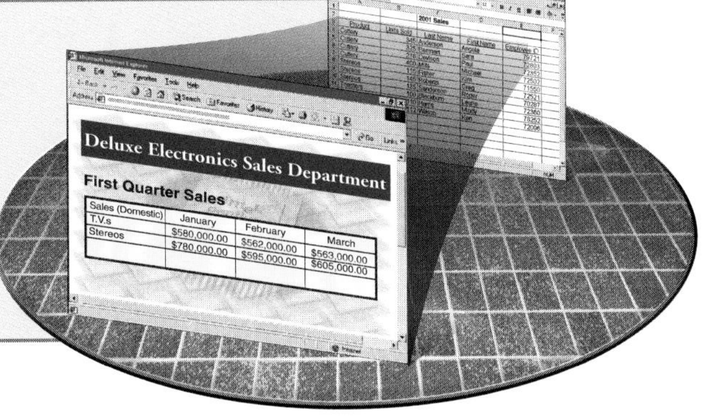

E-MAIL ON INTRANETS

Intranets allow users to exchange messages using the same type of e-mail systems found on the Internet.

A mail server is a computer responsible for distributing e-mail messages to users on an intranet.

Each intranet user has an e-mail program, which is software that sends, receives and manages e-mail messages.

E-mail Benefits

E-mail was one of the first Internet technologies to become widely used on intranets. E-mail provides a fast and convenient way for intranet users to communicate. E-mail messages can travel between computers in seconds. Unlike telephone calls, e-mail messages do not require the recipient to be at their computer when the message arrives.

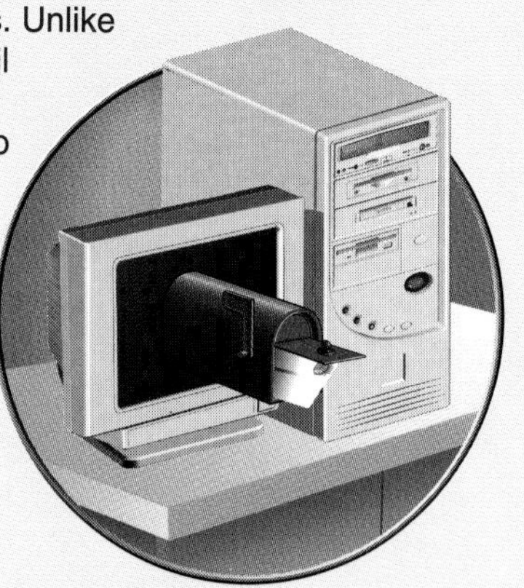

Address Book

Many companies store the intranet e-mail addresses of every user in a single address book. This allows users to quickly find the address of anyone on the intranet.

Attachments

People can use e-mail to send a wide variety of information on an intranet. Almost any type of file can be attached to an e-mail message, making e-mail systems an efficient way of distributing files such as images, word processing documents or spreadsheets.

Multiple Recipients

Intranet users can send an e-mail message to multiple recipients without having to compose a separate message for each person. Sending the same e-mail message to several people at once is a quick and effective method of distributing information on an intranet.

Message Filters

Intranet users may receive a large number of e-mail messages each day. To help users organize their messages, most intranet e-mail programs include filters. Filters sort incoming e-mail messages according to various criteria, such as the sender or subject of the message.

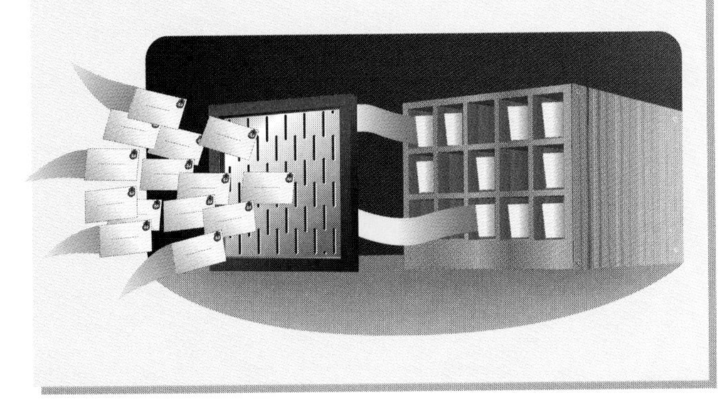

Internet Access

If a company network is connected to the Internet, employees can usually use their intranet e-mail program to exchange messages with people on the Internet.

NEWSGROUPS ON INTRANETS

A newsgroup allows people with common interests to communicate with each other. An intranet newsgroup allows employees to post and read messages, called articles, concerning a specific topic.

Project Newsgroups

Within large organizations there are usually teams of people who work together on different projects. If a company provides newsgroups on its intranet, a newsgroup can be created for each project. This will allow members of a team working on the same project to conveniently exchange ideas and information.

Technical Support Newsgroups

Most large companies have a technical support department dedicated to installing and maintaining their computer systems. A company may want to have a technical support newsgroup where users can post questions or problems and read answers or suggestions from the support department.

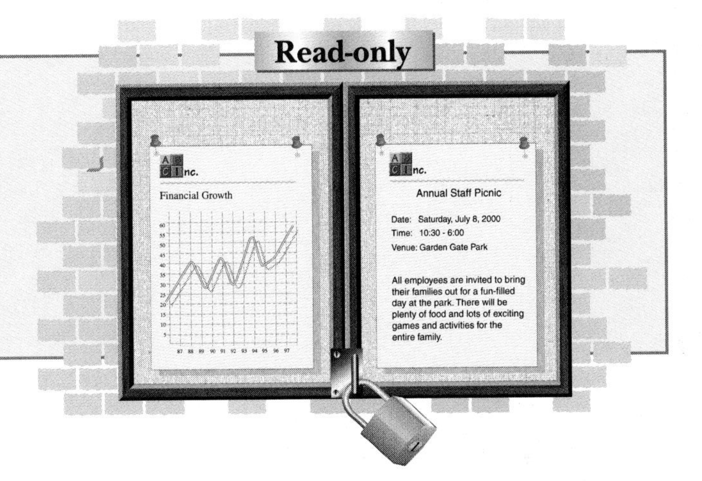

Read-only Newsgroups

Many companies use newsgroups to provide information such as announcements, sales figures or general company information. Employees can access these newsgroups and read the posted information. Employees are usually not allowed to post messages to these types of newsgroups.

Purchased Articles

In addition to creating their own newsgroups, companies can also purchase newsgroup articles. For example, a stock brokerage may purchase the latest news from stock markets around the world to display on its intranet.

Customer Access

Many companies are now making their private intranet newsgroups available to their customers and clients on the Internet. Providing Internet access to a company's intranet news server allows people to ask questions about a product or service, provide feedback to the company and communicate with other customers. A news server is a computer that stores newsgroup articles.

A company can set up chat channels on an intranet. An intranet chat system is a fast and efficient way for users to share information.

Chatting

People using an intranet chat system can instantly communicate with one or more users on the intranet. When a user types text, the text appears almost instantly on the screen of each person involved in the conversation. The name of the person who typed the text appears in front of the text.

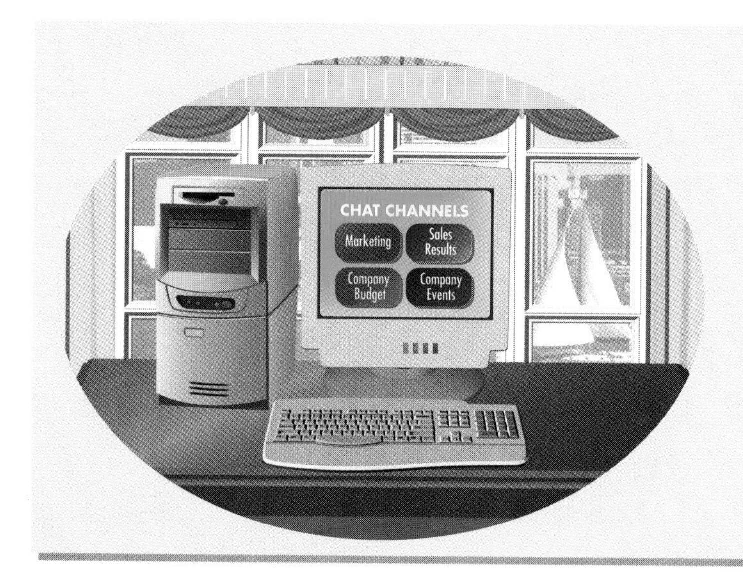

Channels

An intranet chat system may have multiple channels, with each channel dedicated to the discussion of a single topic. Chat channels are often used to allow employees in different locations to hold meetings or conduct training sessions. The name of a channel usually indicates the topic of discussion. For example, a channel called Marketing may discuss current marketing strategies and projects.

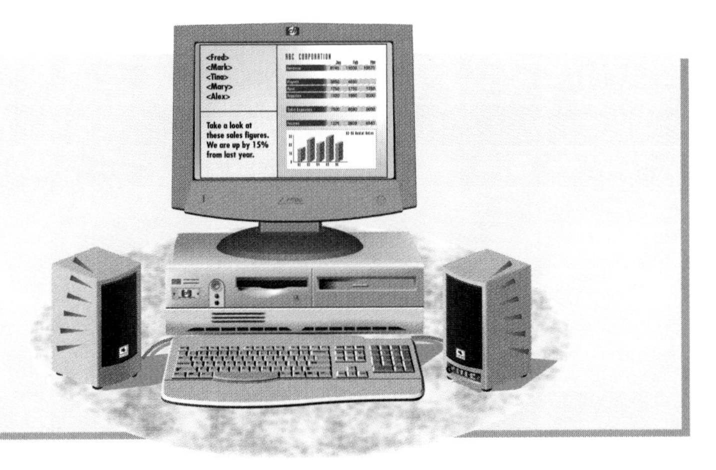

File Transfer

Most intranet chat systems let people send and receive files with others who are in the same chat channel. Besides text files, many intranet chat systems allow users to exchange image and sound files. Users can continue to chat while a file is being transferred.

Technical Support

Many companies use chat systems to provide technical support to their employees. Employees can contact technical support personnel through the chat system to ask questions. The technical support personnel can then instantly provide answers and solutions to technical problems.

Logs

A user can save the text displayed in a chat channel as a file, called a log. Chat logs can be useful if the chat channel is being used to exchange technical or detailed information. This lets users keep a record of the information that is being discussed. Chat logs can also be used to save any information that may have been displayed while a user was away from the computer.

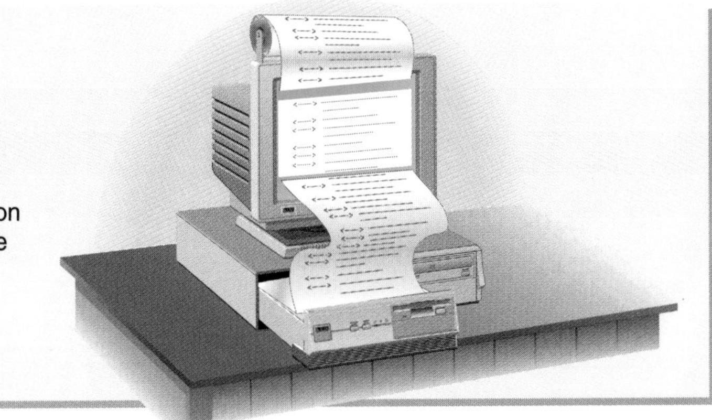

FILE TRANSFER ON INTRANETS

File sharing is one of the main reasons for a company to set up an intranet. The File Transfer Protocol (FTP) allows intranet users to efficiently transfer files between computers.

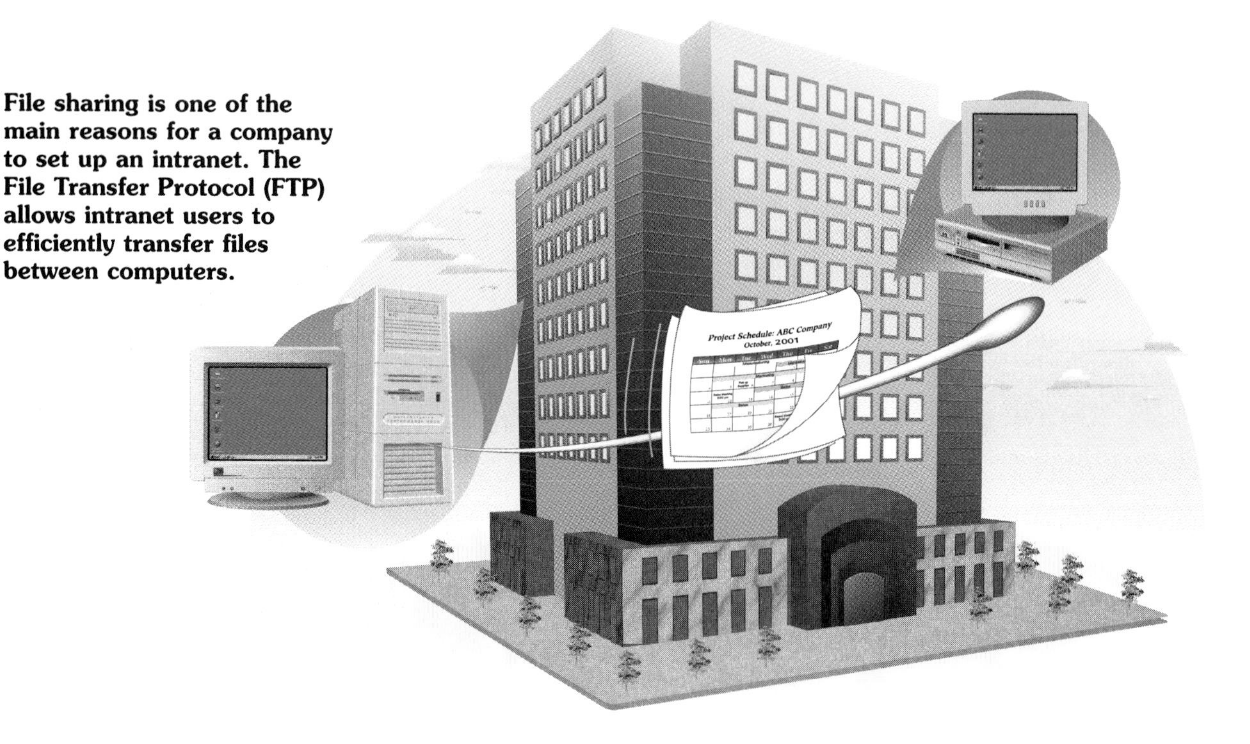

FTP Server

Companies can store frequently accessed documents on an FTP server on their intranet. This allows users to quickly access the files. Many types of files, such as word-processing, spreadsheet and graphics files, can be stored on an FTP server.

FTP Client

The computers on an intranet can connect to the FTP server to access files stored on the server. FTP allows client computers running different operating systems, such as Macintosh and Windows, to access the same files. A Web browser is often the only program a client computer requires to access files using FTP.

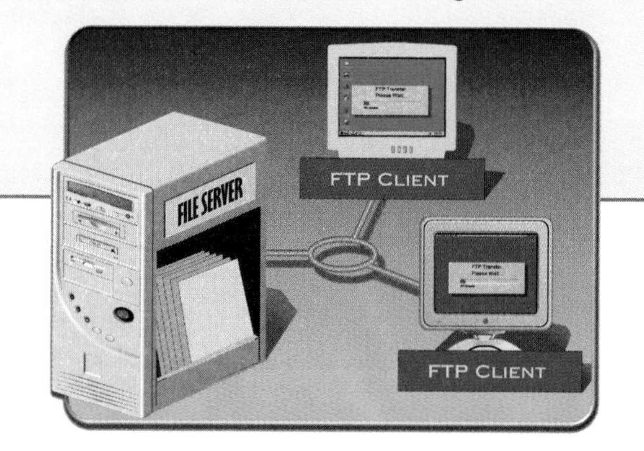

Private FTP

Many companies use private FTP systems that require users to enter a password before accessing any files. This helps protect sensitive files from unauthorized access.

Anonymous FTP

Anonymous FTP systems let users access files without having to enter a password. This is useful for files a company wants to distribute to all employees, such as product information.

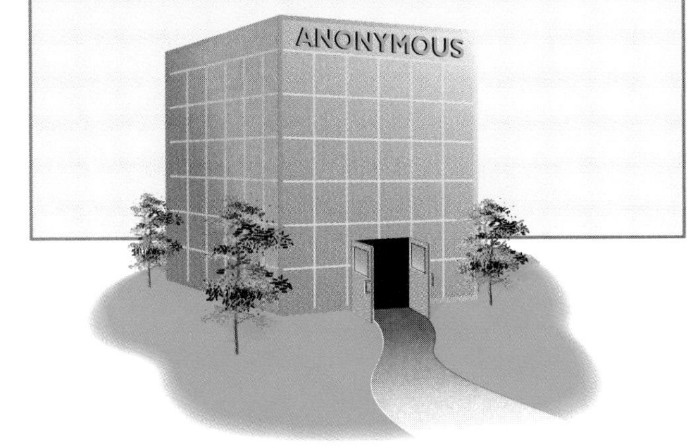

Transfer Speed

Local area network technology is capable of transferring information at much higher speeds than the Internet. Since intranets use a company's existing network, intranets are also able to transfer information at these high speeds. The fast transfer speed of an intranet makes it an effective way to transfer large files, such as program files.

Internet Access

If a company network is connected to the Internet, the company's intranet can be used to transfer files to a destination on the Internet. For example, instead of storing files on floppy disks and using a delivery service to send files to a professional printer, a company can use FTP to transfer the files to the printer over the Internet.

INTRANET SOFTWARE

A company must have intranet software to set up an intranet. There are many types of intranet software available.

The most popular intranet software is developed by IBM, Microsoft and Novell. Intranet software is available at computer stores or on the Internet.

Free Software

Software available for the Internet, such as Web browsers, e-mail and news readers, FTP programs and chat software, can also be used on a corporate intranet. Many of these software programs are available on the Internet for a minimal fee or free of charge.

Intranet Suites

An intranet suite is a collection of several different applications sold together in one package. Intranet suites usually consist of e-mail, Web publishing, database and security applications.

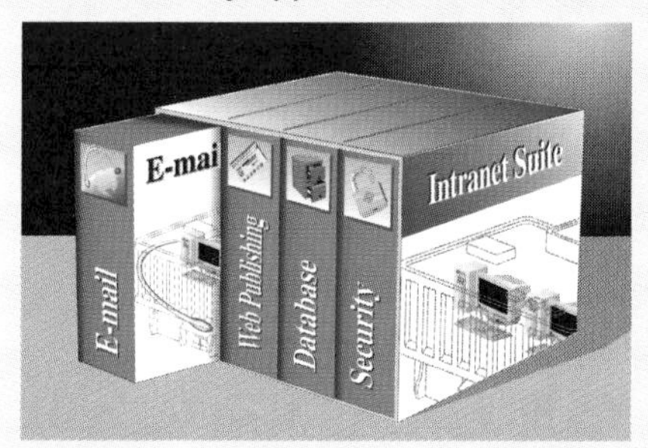

When installing an intranet suite, a network administrator can decide which applications users require and install only the necessary applications.

POPULAR INTRANET SUITES

Lotus Domino

IBM developed the Lotus Domino intranet software suite to meet the needs of both large and small organizations. This software suite can be used to provide Internet and intranet services and includes features such as Web applications and large database support.

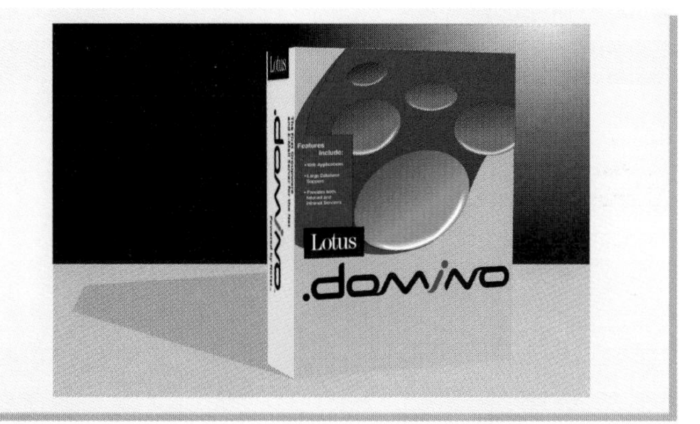

Microsoft BackOffice

Microsoft offers a suite of intranet software called BackOffice. Microsoft designed BackOffice for mid-sized companies that use a Windows operating system, such as Windows NT or Windows 2000. Besides the standard intranet programs, BackOffice includes an application called FrontPage, which helps users easily organize and manage a Web site.

Novell Small Business Suite

Novell is well known for its NetWare networking software and also offers intranet software, called Novell Small Business Suite (NSBS). NSBS is designed for small businesses with up to 50 intranet users. NSBS offers many basic intranet features, but the main advantage of the suite is its compatibility with Novell networking software.

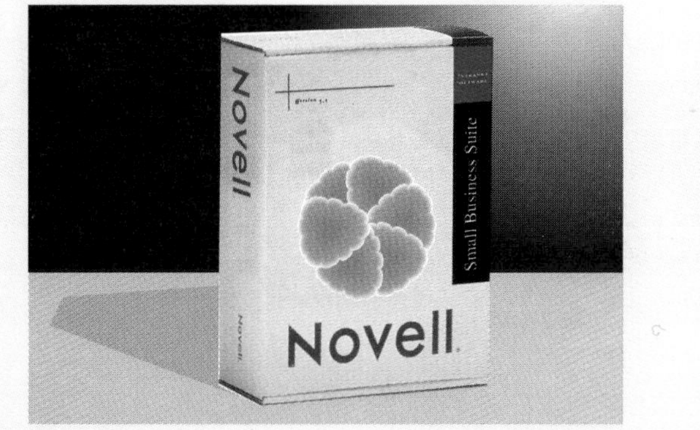

GROUPWARE

Groupware is software that allows network users to work together in groups. Groupware can be used to share information, track documents, coordinate resources and more.

Popular groupware products include Lotus Notes and Novell GroupWise.

Groups

In an organization or business, projects are often completed by teams or groups. A group is composed of individuals who are all working on a common project using the same information and resources. Most employees belong to at least one group. Groupware is used to track group activity and is particularly useful for organizing the activities of larger groups.

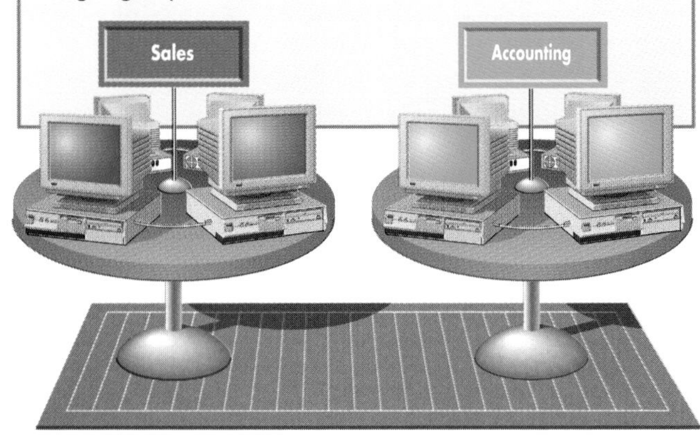

Collaboration

Groupware products allow people in a group to easily collaborate on projects. For example, when using groupware to work on a shared document, all group members can make changes, review changes made by other members or refer to earlier versions of the document. This type of collaboration enables groups to accomplish tasks and complete projects efficiently.

Communication

One of the most important features of groupware is its ability to allow group members to easily communicate with each other. Most groupware products include an e-mail feature. Some groupware products also allow users to communicate using text-based chat or videoconferencing.

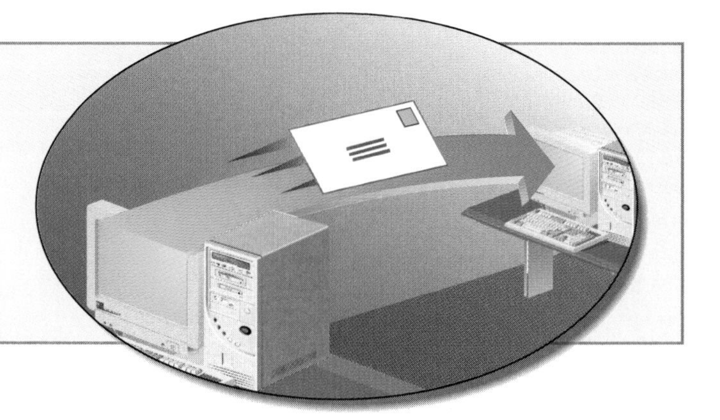

Scheduling

The scheduling feature included in groupware products allows group members to efficiently schedule meetings and organize events. Users can create personal schedules and then allow other group members to view their activities and availability. This allows meetings to be scheduled at a time convenient for everyone. Groupware can also be used to reserve company resources, such as printers and meeting rooms.

Document Tracking

Groupware software is useful for monitoring and organizing the circulation of documents within a company. The software can send a document to a series of users or to all members of a group at one time. The software can then track the document and produce a report that indicates the work done on the document by each user.

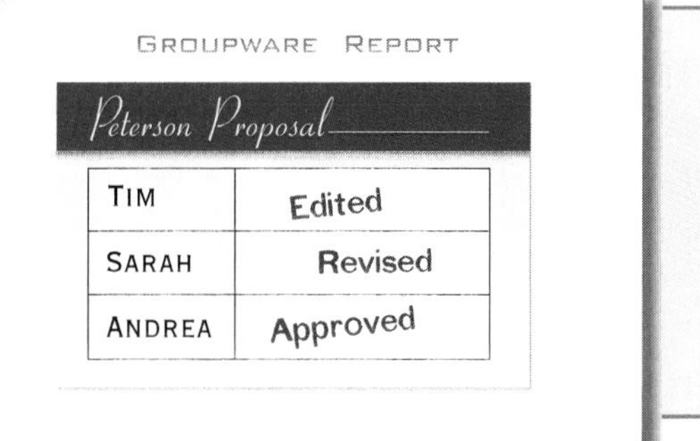

GROUPWARE REPORT
Peterson Proposal
TIM
Edited
SARAH
Revised
ANDREA
Approved

Voice over IP (VoIP) is a new technology that allows a company to use its network as the infrastructure for a telephone system.

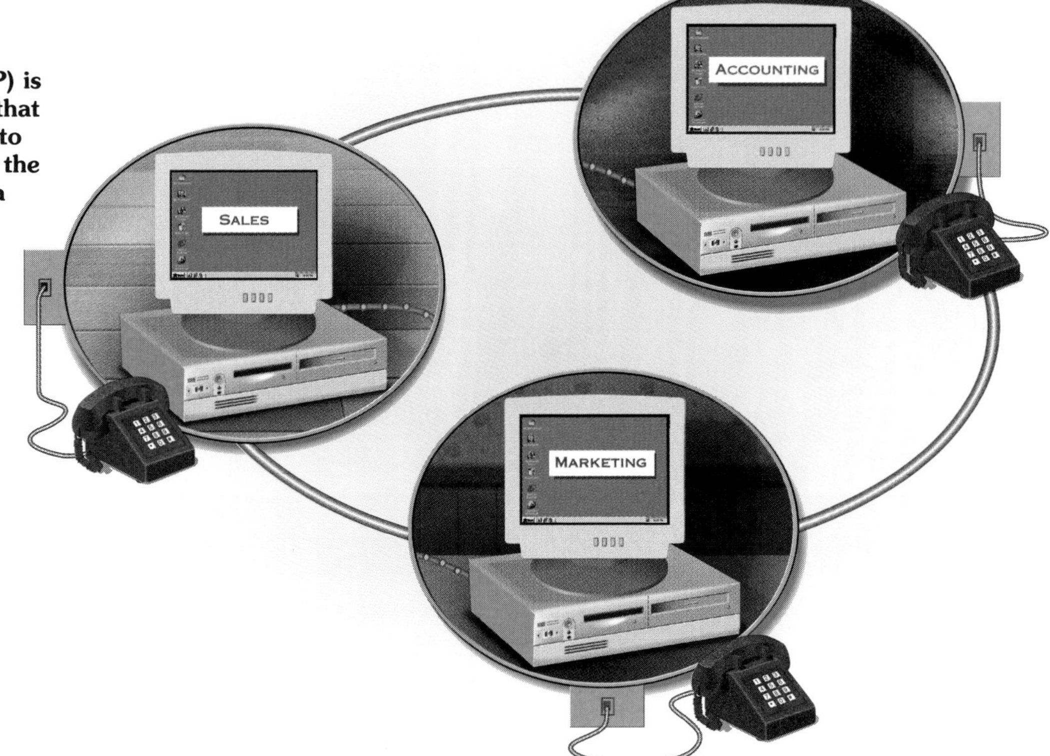

Telephone System

A VoIP system allows people on a network to place phone calls using the network instead of a traditional telephone system. A company can replace its entire telephone system with a VoIP system or integrate VoIP into its existing telephone system. Integrating VoIP into an existing telephone system allows people to use the VoIP system to call other network users and a traditional phone line to call people outside the network.

Hardware and Software

VoIP systems require dedicated hardware and specialized software in order to operate. A VoIP system typically uses a device similar to a hub to manage the phone calls made on the network. VoIP software is required to monitor and maintain the efficiency and quality of voice communications on the network.

Quality

When a VoIP system is used to place a phone call to another user on a local area network, the quality of the audio transmission is usually very good. Quality begins to decline, however, when a VoIP system must transmit information over a large wide area network or the Internet.

Advanced Features

VoIP systems can offer many advanced features. For example, some VoIP systems automatically distribute phone calls to network users. A VoIP system may also offer features such as voice mail and intercom messaging.

Save Money

A VoIP system can help a company save money by reducing long-distance telephone charges. For example, an employee can place a call free of charge to a branch office in another city using the company's wide area network. A VoIP system can also save a company money by allowing the company to expand and configure the system without having to pay for the services of a phone company.

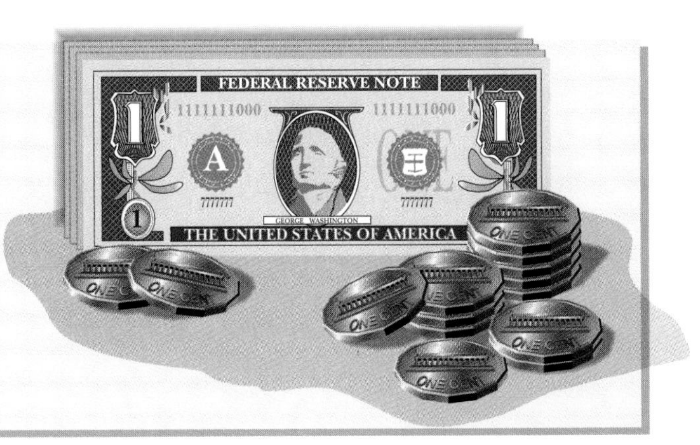

AltaVista - Welcome - Microsoft Internet Explorer
File Edit View Favorites Tools Help
Back Search Favorites History
Address http://www.altavista.com
Go Links
altavista:
IQ TRAINING
Click Here
Search Home
Comparison Shop
Channels
Rewards
Email & Tools
Sign Up! | AltaVista Members Sign In | Member Center
Super Searches
Shopping
Entertainment
News
ELECTION 2000: Judge OKs 5 P.M. Deadline, With Conditions
Search for:
Help | Customize Settings
Web Search
Power Search
Advanced Search
Raging Search
Today In:
Shopping
Entertainment
News
Holiday Shopping Guide
Win a Trip to D.C., $10,000
Gossip: Clooney in Love
Harrison Attacker in Court
Both Sides Praise Ruling
N.M Tilts Toward Gore
Multimedia Search
Hot Fashion Searches
Hot Celebrity Searches
Today's News Searches
Done
Internet
Start
AltaVista - Welcome -...
12:00 PM

CHAPTER 15

Wireless Networks

Mobile devices can access information on a wireless network without being physically connected to the network. Read this chapter to find out about wireless applications, devices, operating systems and technologies.

Introduction to Wireless Networks 254

Wireless Applications 256

Wireless Devices 258

Wireless Operating Systems 260

Wireless Technologies......................262

A wireless network allows devices, such as notebook computers and Personal Digital Assistants (PDAs), to access information on a network without being physically connected to the network.

A wireless network eliminates the cables that connect devices on a traditional network. Wireless networks allow mobile devices to remain connected to the network when they are moved from one area to another.

Radio Signals

Most wireless networks use radio signals to transmit information between devices. Wireless networks usually operate on radio channels between 800 megahertz (MHz) and 1.9 gigahertz (GHz). Information on a wireless network can be transferred at speeds of up to 11 Mbps.

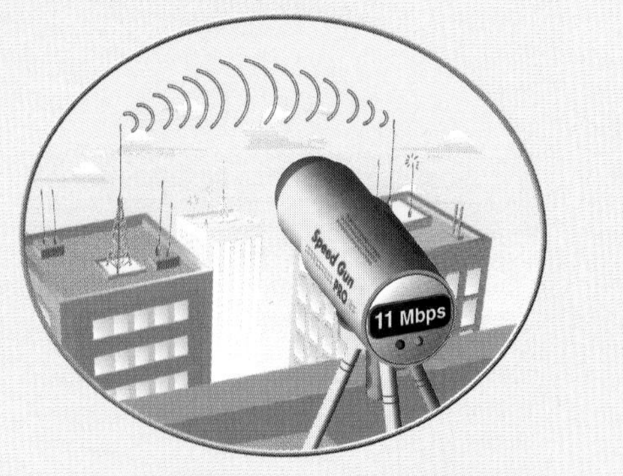

Radio Transceivers

Most wireless devices use a radio transceiver to exchange information on a network. Some wireless devices have transceivers connected to the outside of the device, while other wireless devices have built-in transceivers.

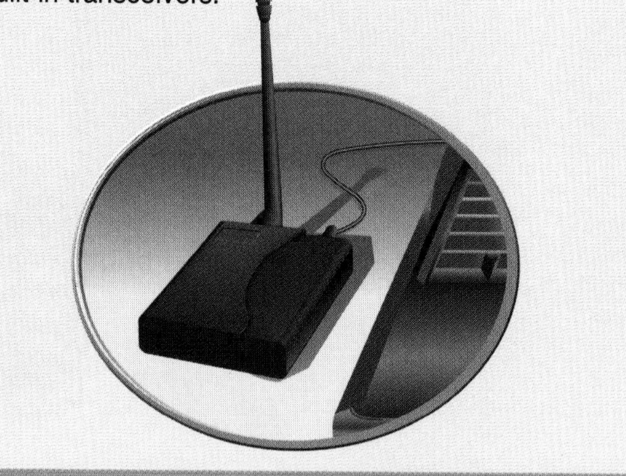

RADIO TRANSMISSION TECHNOLOGIES

There are three different ways radio signals can be used to transfer information on a wireless network.

GSM

Global System for Mobile communication (GSM) is the most popular transmission technology used on wireless networks and is the wireless standard in Europe. GSM transfers information by compressing the information and then using a single radio channel from the available channels to transmit the data.

CDMA

Code Division Multiple Access (CDMA) is a popular transmission technology that is used most often in North America. CDMA transfers information between wireless devices by distributing the data over all the available radio channels.

TDMA

Time Division Multiple Access (TDMA) is a transmission technology that divides one radio channel between multiple devices. Each device takes turns using the channel. TDMA is used most often by businesses that offer digital cellular communications.

There are many uses for wireless devices, including browsing the Web, storing personal information and sending e-mail messages.

Synchronize Information

Most wireless devices can connect to a computer so users can synchronize the data on the wireless device with the data on the computer. For example, users can synchronize the e-mail messages stored on their PDA with the messages stored on their desktop computer.

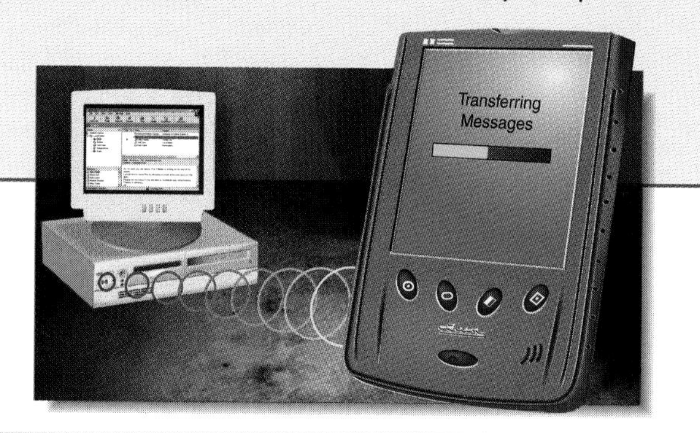

Web Browsing

Many wireless devices can be used to access information on the World Wide Web. Most devices, however, can display only Web pages specifically designed for wireless devices.

www.yahoo.com, www.amazon.com and www.cnn.com are examples of Web sites that contain Web pages designed for wireless devices.

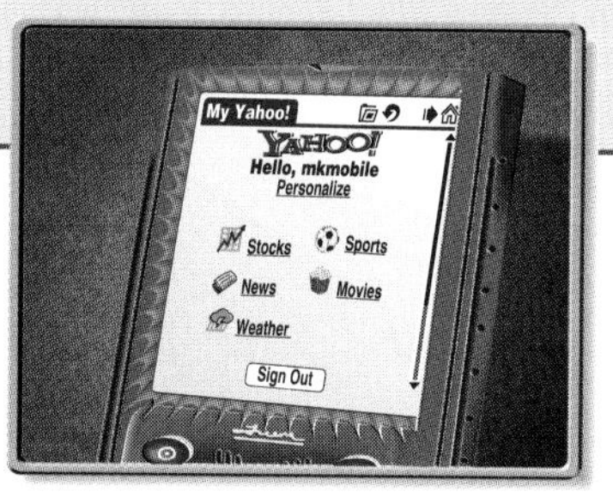

E-mail and Instant Messaging

Most wireless devices allow users to exchange e-mail messages to communicate with friends and colleagues. Some wireless devices offer instant messaging capabilities. Instant messaging allows users to see when their friends are online and send them instant text messages.

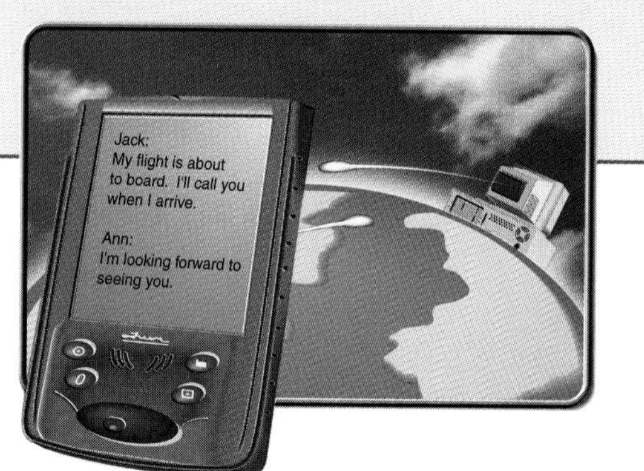

Electronic Organizers

Most wireless devices offer electronic organizer capabilities. These devices allow users to store contact information, schedule meetings, create to-do lists and more.

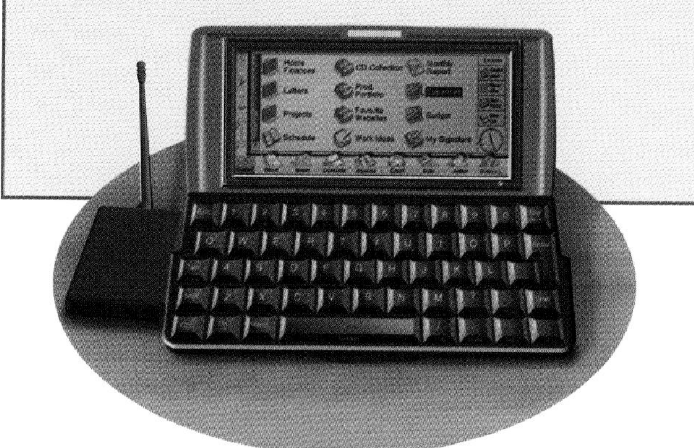

Navigation

Some wireless devices, such as PDAs and notebook computers, can display maps of cities and streets to help users navigate around an unfamiliar area. Wireless devices can also access traffic reports from the Internet and suggest alternative routes to avoid traffic congestion.

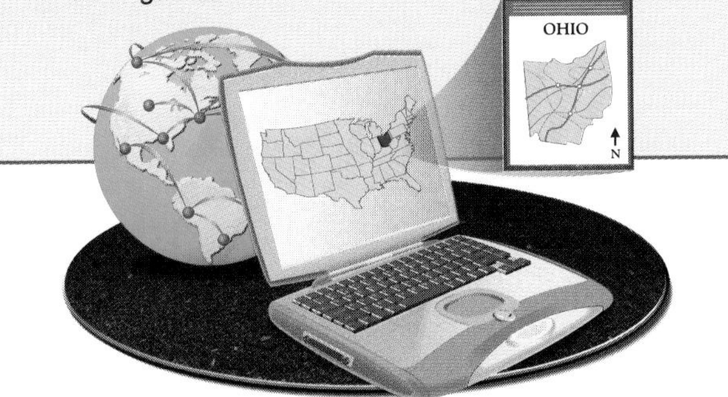

mCommerce

mCommerce, or mobile commerce, is a system that allows people to use a wireless device to purchase products and services on the Internet. mCommerce is useful for purchasing airline tickets and hotel accommodations, although almost any product or service can be purchased online.

Network Applications

Many large companies have developed their own network applications, such as invoicing programs. Adapting these applications to work on wireless devices provides employees with immediate access to the applications from almost anywhere. For example, a salesperson can use a wireless device to access network applications while traveling.

Multimedia

Some wireless devices, such as mobile phones and PDAs, now include multimedia software that allows users to access, store and play multimedia files, such as MP3 music files. There are many music Web sites, such as www.mp3.com, which allow users to download music files to a wireless device.

WIRELESS DEVICES

Wireless devices can access information on a network, such as the Internet, without a physical connection.

Personal Digital Assistants

Personal Digital Assistants (PDAs) are small, mobile, handheld devices that provide computing and data storage capabilities. PDAs usually use touch screens and an electronic pen, called a stylus, to input information. PDAs often include features such as a calendar, address book, electronic mail support and Internet access. Most PDAs connect to wireless networks using a radio transceiver. Companies that manufacture PDAs include Palm Inc., Handspring and Casio.

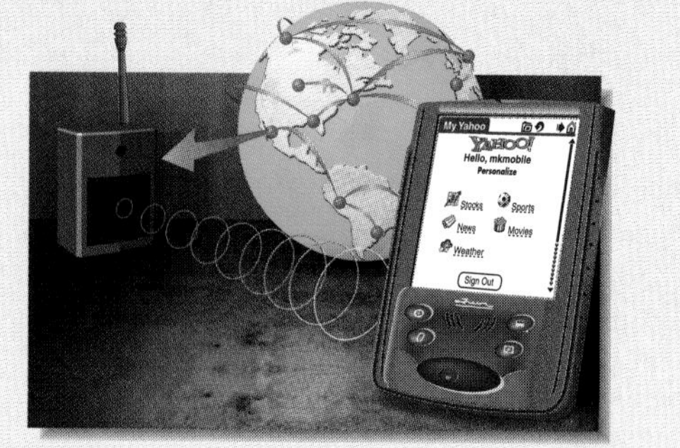

Mobile Phones

Mobile phones have built-in radio transceivers and are quickly becoming one of the easiest and most popular ways to wirelessly access the Internet. Most new mobile phones include electronic mail and Web browsing capabilities. Internet access for a mobile phone can be expensive and is provided by the same company that provides the telephone service. Mobile phones cannot display a large amount of information at once due to small display areas.

Two-way Pagers

Two-way pagers are small, handheld devices that allow users to exchange messages with other people. Two-way pagers have a small, built-in keyboard and screen. These devices specialize in text messaging, though they can sometimes perform more complex functions such as browsing the Web. RIM's BlackBerry is a popular two-way pager.

Laptop and Notebook Computers

A laptop is a small, lightweight, portable computer. Notebooks are similar to laptop computers, but are smaller in size. Notebook and laptop computers typically use the same operating systems as desktop computers, such as Windows 2000. Notebook and laptop computers have a built-in keyboard, pointing device and screen. These computers usually connect to wireless networks using a modem and a mobile telephone.

Automobile Devices

One of the newest developments in wireless technology is wireless Internet access for the automobile. Some companies are now creating wireless devices that work in conjunction with, or even replace, the radio and audio systems found in automobiles. These new devices will allow automobile occupants to use voice commands to access Internet information, such as stock quotes, music and traffic news, while driving.

An operating system is the software that controls the overall activity of a wireless device. All wireless devices require an operating system to function.

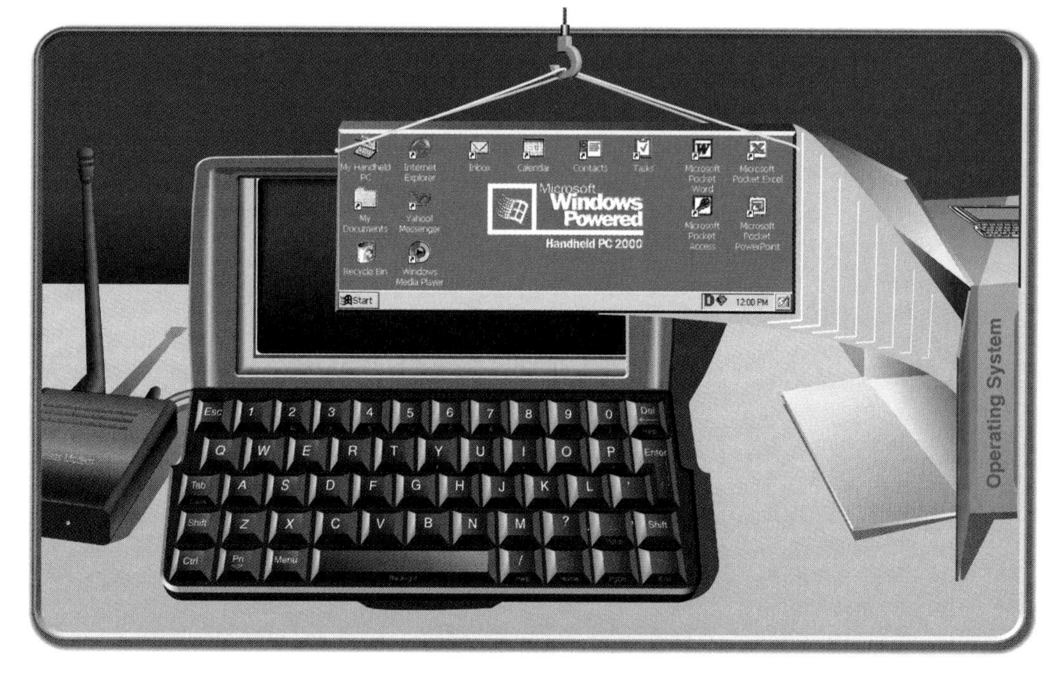

Embedded

Most wireless devices use an embedded operating system. An embedded operating system is stored on a microchip inside the device, instead of on an erasable storage device, such as a hard drive. Embedded operating systems usually cannot be upgraded without replacing the entire device.

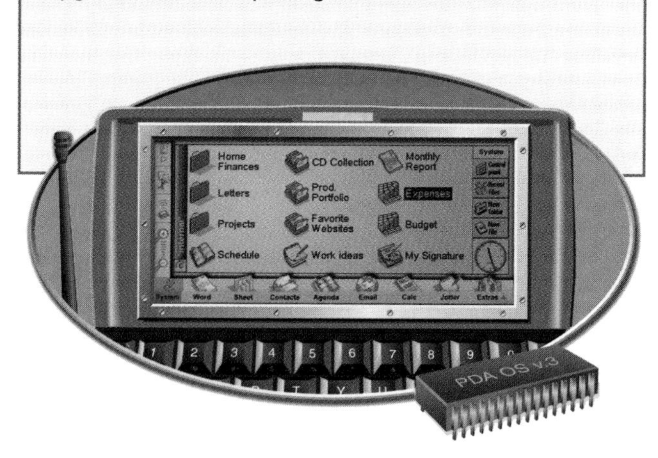

Software

An operating system runs all the software for a device, such as scheduling and messaging programs. Software designed for one wireless operating system will not work with another wireless operating system. Depending on the wireless operating system you use, you may be able to install additional software to add features to the device.

POPULAR WIRELESS OPERATING SYSTEMS

Palm OS

Palm OS is the most popular operating system for Personal Digital Assistants (PDAs). The Palm OS operating system was developed by Palm Inc. with a special focus on features that were important to PDA users. PDAs manufactured by other companies, such as Handspring and Casio, can also use Palm OS.

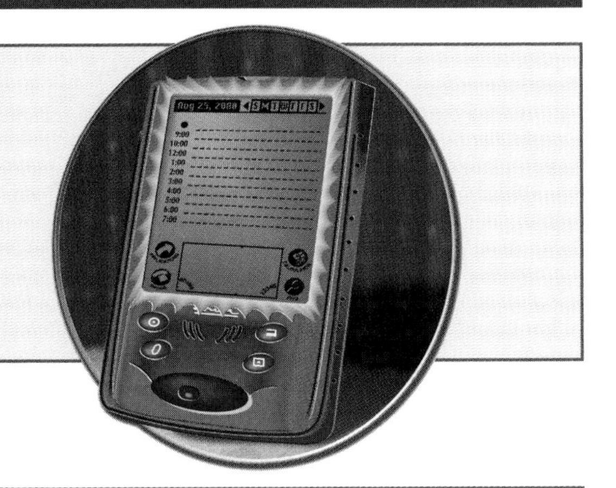

Windows CE

Windows CE is a version of the Microsoft Windows operating system developed specifically for PDAs. The main advantage of using Windows CE is that information can be easily exchanged with Microsoft programs that are commonly found on desktop computers, such as Microsoft Word. PDAs that use Windows CE are often referred to as PocketPCs.

EPOC

The EPOC operating system was developed by manufacturers of mobile phones and is commonly used on mobile phones that have Internet access capabilities. The EPOC operating system is now available for other devices, such as PDAs.

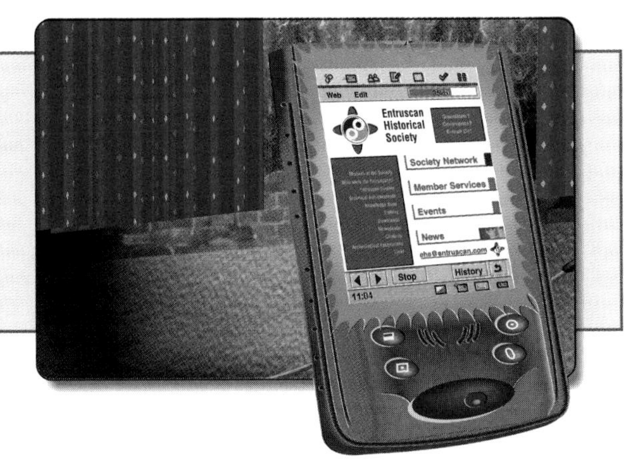

Although using wireless devices to access a network relies on relatively new technology, there are several standards in place to ensure that wireless networks function properly.

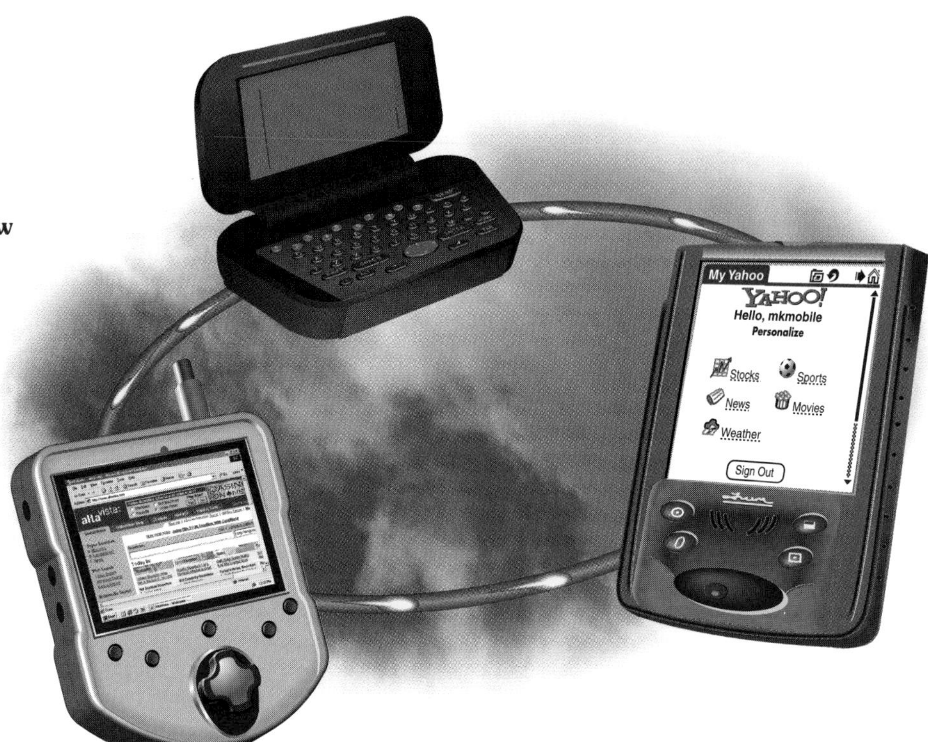

Bluetooth

Bluetooth is a new short-range wireless technology that allows wireless devices to exchange data with each other, with desktop computers and with networks. Currently, Bluetooth is most often used to synchronize the data on a wireless device with the information on a desktop computer. Bluetooth technology may eventually be used by businesses to build wireless networks that allow employees to remain connected to the Internet and corporate network while they move around an office building.

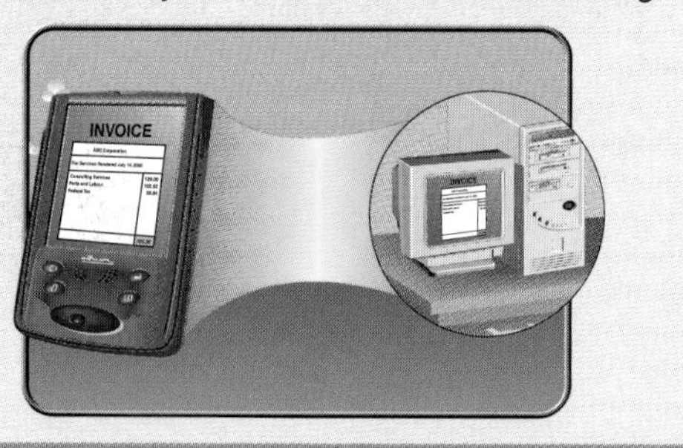

802.11, 802.11a and 802.11b

802.11, 802.11a and 802.11b are standards defined by the Institute of Electrical and Electronics Engineers (IEEE) that specify how information should transfer on a wireless Ethernet local area network. The 802.11 standard specifies transfer speeds of up to 2 Mbps and is used by most wireless transmission technologies, such as Bluetooth. The 802.11a standard specifies transfer speeds of up to 54 Mbps and 802.11b specifies transfer speeds of up to 11 Mbps.

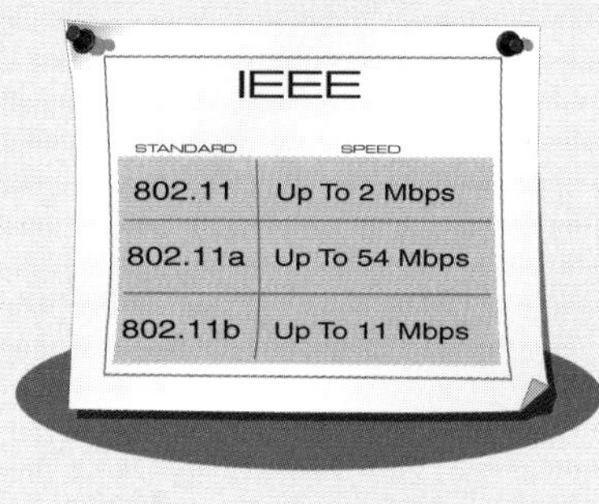
IEEE

STANDARD	SPEED
802.11	Up To 2 Mbps
802.11a	Up To 54 Mbps
802.11b	Up To 11 Mbps

Ricochet

Ricochet is a new network architecture designed for high-speed wireless networks.

A Ricochet network is created by placing wireless radio devices in various locations throughout an area, such as on street corners in a city. Wireless devices using Ricochet modems can then access the radio devices to connect to the network. The Ricochet network architecture can transfer information at speeds of up to 128 Kbps. Ricochet networks are used in many metropolitan areas in North America. More information about Ricochet is available at the www.ricochet.com Web site.

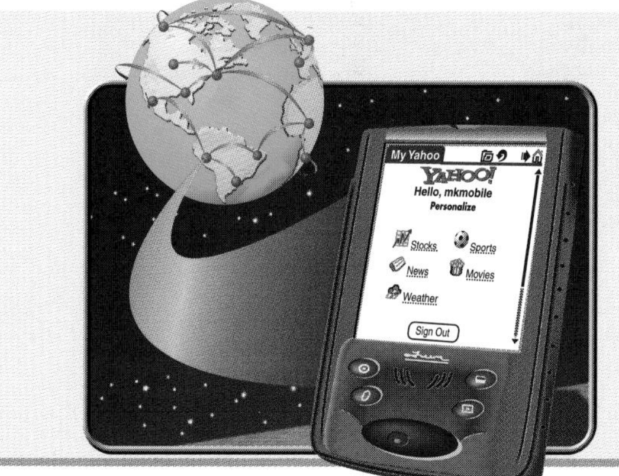

WAP

Wireless Application Protocol (WAP) is a new protocol suite that allows wireless devices to access the Internet. WAP works with several existing Internet standards, including the IP protocol, to transfer information over the Internet. WAP was developed by several large manufacturers of wireless products to ensure that products created by different companies would be able to work together.

WML

Wireless Markup Language (WML) is similar to HyperText Markup Language (HTML) and is used to create Web pages that can be displayed on wireless devices. WML is based on the Extensible Markup Language (XML). Only wireless devices that use the WAP protocol can display Web pages created using WML.

CHAPTER 16

Home Networks

Multiple computers in a home can be connected to share information and resources. Read this chapter to discover which devices and protocols are required to set up a home network and how to connect the network to the Internet.

Introduction to Home Networks 266

Ethernet Network Interface Cards......268

Ethernet Hubs 270

Network Protocols 272

Connect a Home Network
to the Internet................................274

INTRODUCTION TO HOME NETWORKS

A network can be set up to share information and resources among multiple computers in a home. Home networks are less complicated than business networks.

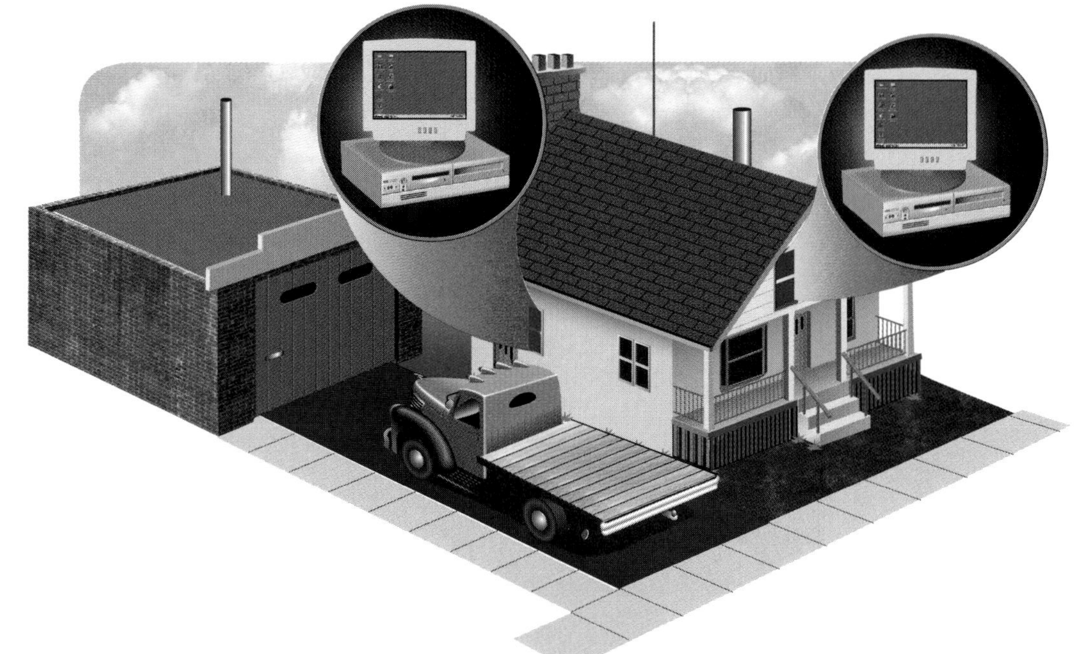

Set Up

Each computer connected to a home network must have a Network Interface Card (NIC) installed. Cables are also needed to physically connect each computer to the network. Some home networks may require a hub. If computers on the network are to connect to the Internet, one computer will need a modem or an additional network interface card.

Alternatives

There are alternatives to using network interface cards to create a network. If two computers that use a Windows operating system are being connected, a network can be created using the Direct Cable Connection feature. This feature allows two computers to be connected using a cable attached to their printer ports. While this network alternative is useful for simple file sharing, it is not appropriate for tasks such as accessing the Internet or playing multi-player games.

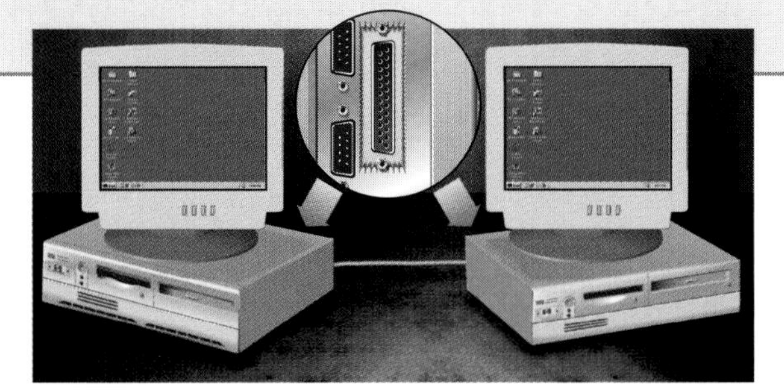

ADVANTAGES

Share Information and Resources

A home network enables family members to share information, such as schedules, and resources, such as storage devices, among their computers. Home networks are also useful for re-using old computers and equipment. While an older computer may not have the power to play the latest games, it may still be adequate for tasks such as printer sharing.

Share an Internet Connection

If one computer on a home network has a connection to the Internet, the other computers attached to the network can share the connection to access the Internet at the same time. This is especially useful if the Internet connection is a high-speed connection, such as a DSL line.

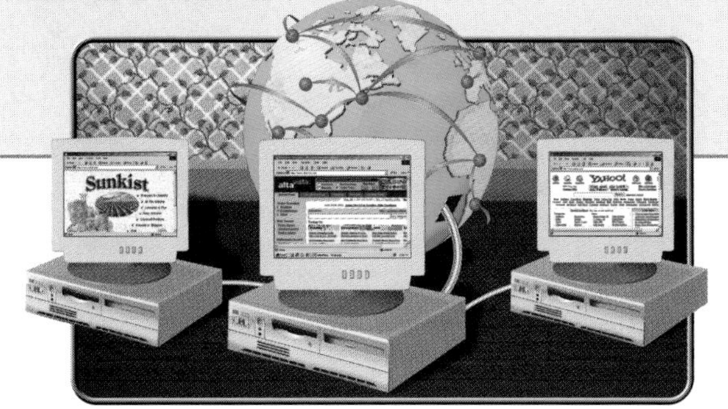

Games

One of the most popular reasons for creating a home network is to take advantage of today's games that allow multiple people to play a game on a network.

Intelligent Devices

One future trend is the use of home networks to control intelligent devices in the home. For example, items such as lighting and security systems can be easily managed using a home network.

ETHERNET NETWORK INTERFACE CARDS

Each computer that will be connected to a home network must have a Network Interface Card (NIC) installed. Most home networks use Ethernet network interface cards.

An Ethernet network interface card must be compatible with the type of cable a network will use. Home networks offer more flexibility than business networks when choosing a type of cable.

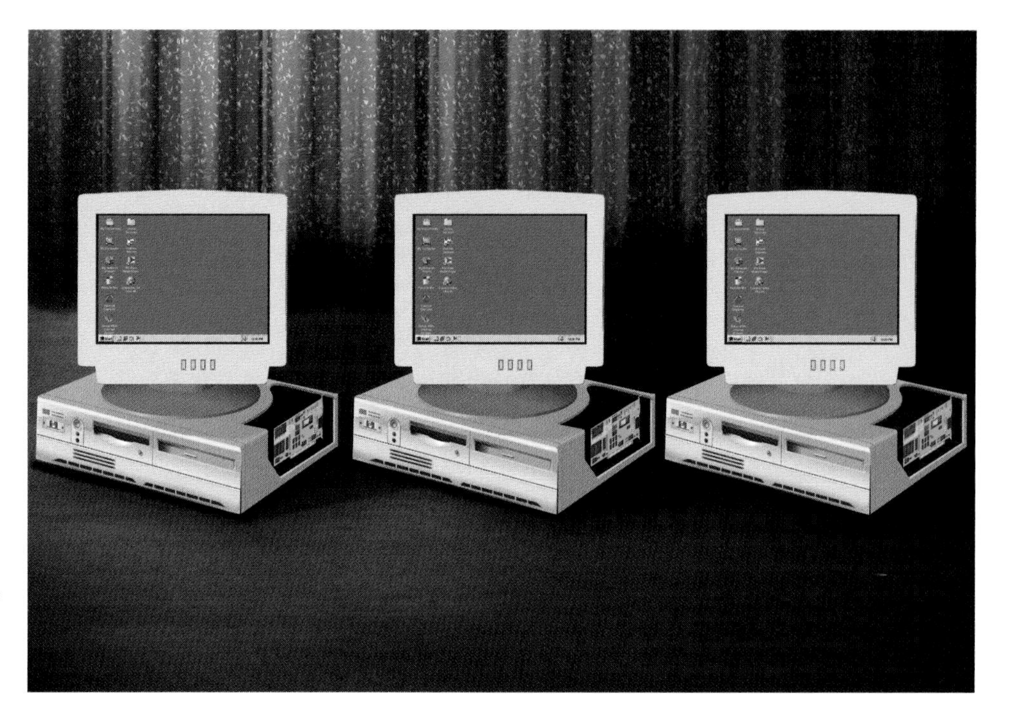

CABLE TYPES

Coaxial Cable

Home networks connected by coaxial cable do not require any other hardware besides network interface cards. However, it can be difficult to connect computers in different parts of a house using coaxial cable.

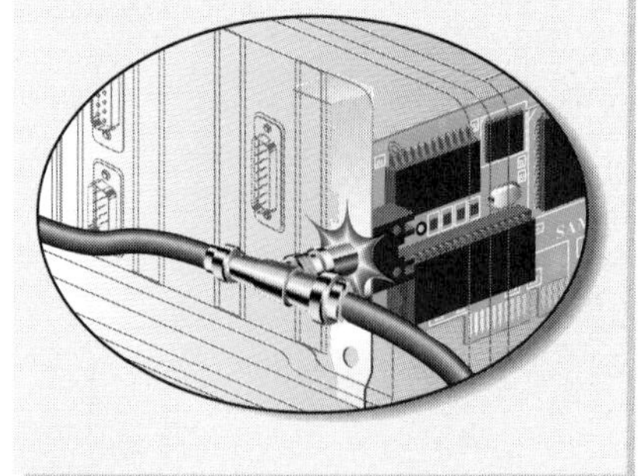

Twisted Pair Cable

Twisted pair cable requires the use of a network hub to connect multiple computers. Although a network created using twisted pair cable is initially more expensive, it is easier to manage and expand than a network that uses coaxial cable.

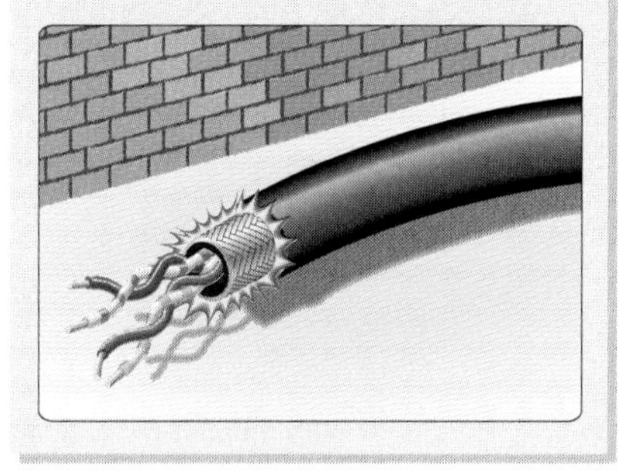

Crossover Cable

Crossover cable is a type of twisted pair cable that can connect two computers without the use of a hub. Crossover cables are available at most good electronics stores.

CHOOSE AN ETHERNET NETWORK INTERFACE CARD

Network Interface Card Types

The type of network interface card a computer requires depends on several factors. The network interface card must be compatible with the expansion slot the card will use in the computer. If a computer requires a network interface card to be removable, a card that connects to the computer's printer port instead of being installed in the computer can be used. A notebook computer can use a built-in network interface card or a PC Card network interface card.

Speed

Ethernet network interface cards can operate at speeds up to 100 Mbps, but a speed of 10 Mbps is more than adequate for most home networks.

Using Multiple Network Interface Cards

A computer may need to have more than one network interface card installed. For example, many high-speed Internet connections require a dedicated network interface card. If a computer will be connected to more than one network, a network interface card will be needed for each network connection.

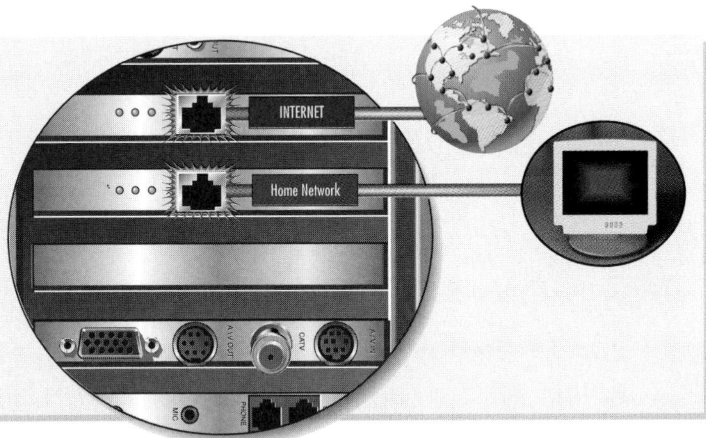

ETHERNET HUBS

An Ethernet hub provides a central location where all the cables on a home network come together.

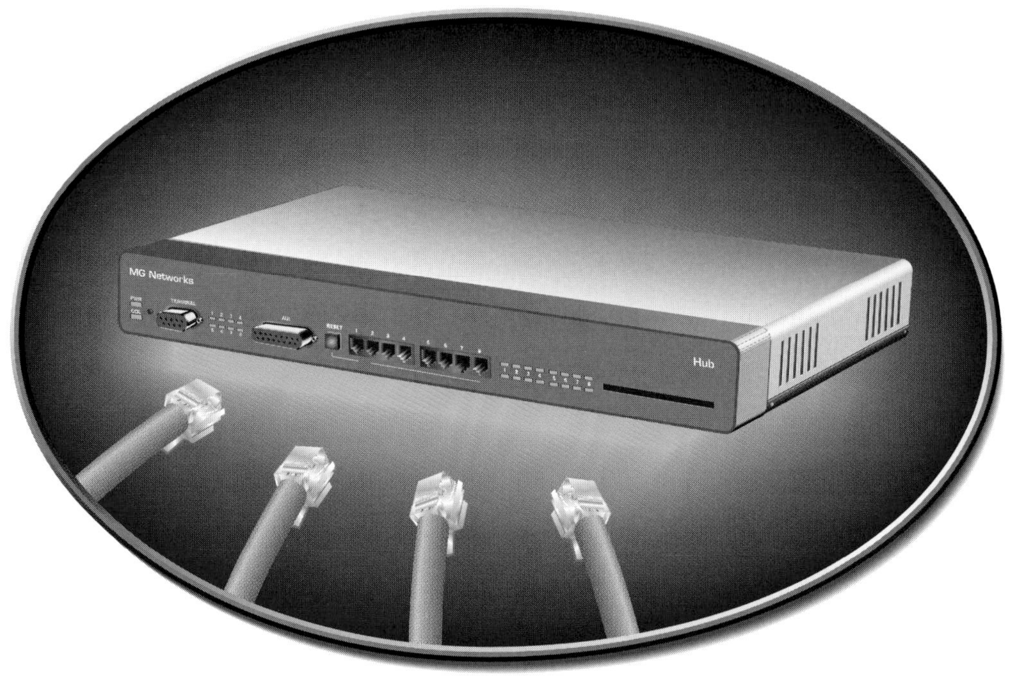

Hubs and High-speed Connections

Most transmission media that are used to connect a home network to the Internet, such as a Digital Subscriber Line (DSL), cannot simply be connected to a hub on a home network. The transmission media must be attached to a computer that is connected to the hub. Some specialized high-speed connection devices, however, can incorporate an Ethernet hub. For information about the availability of these combined devices, contact a local Internet service provider, cable company or telecommunications company.

Wiring a House

It is relatively easy to run network cable through the walls of newer houses to create network connections in different locations in the house. Each connection allows a computer to connect to the hub. Connectors and cabling are available at most good electronics stores. For difficult installations, a professional cable installer should be consulted. There are also wireless networking technologies, such as Bluetooth, which can be used when wiring is difficult. For more information about wireless technologies, see page 262.

CHOOSE AN ETHERNET HUB

Speed

The speed of a hub determines the speed of the network interface cards that can be used on a home network. The speed of the network interface cards must not exceed the speed of the hub. A speed of 10 Mbps is suitable for most home networks.

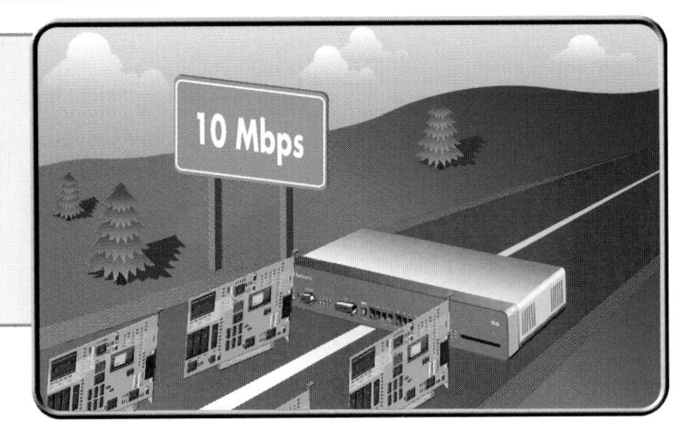

Ports

Hubs commonly have 4, 8, 16 or 24 ports where cables from computer devices can be plugged in. The number of ports on a hub should meet the current and future needs of the home network.

Cable Rating

Home networks use twisted pair cable and RJ-45 connectors to connect the Ethernet hub and the network interface cards. Twisted pair cable is rated for different speeds. Category 5 rated cable is capable of transmitting information at speeds of up to 100 Mbps. Using Category 5 cables and connectors ensures that the network will be easy to upgrade in the future.

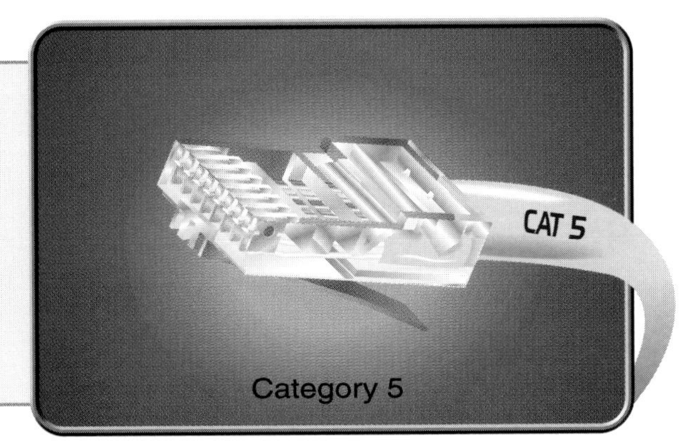

NETWORK PROTOCOLS

Once the computers and hub on a home network are connected, protocols must be installed to allow the devices to exchange information. Most operating systems come with the required protocols.

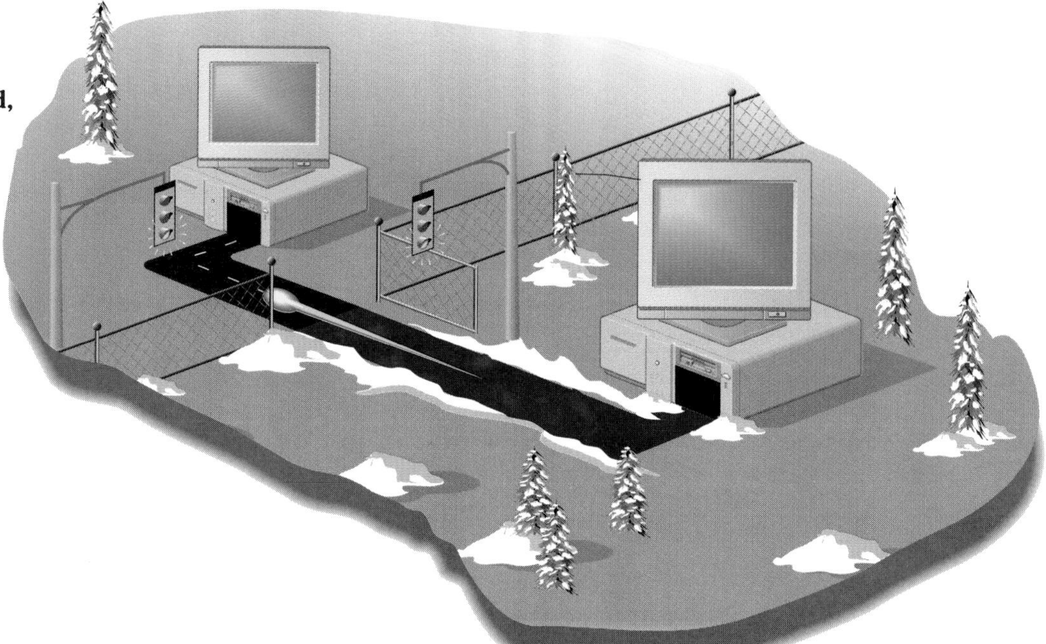

TYPES OF PROTOCOLS

TCP/IP

Transmission Control Protocol/Internet Protocol (TCP/IP) is a suite of protocols that allows computers and devices to connect to the Internet. Even networks and devices that are not connected to the Internet now use TCP/IP as a standard protocol. TCP/IP should be installed to ensure that the home network will be compatible with future devices. For more information about the TCP/IP protocol, see pages 130 to 135.

NetBEUI

NetBIOS Extended User Interface (NetBEUI) is a small and efficient protocol that allows computers on a Windows network to communicate. One of the benefits of using the NetBEUI protocol is that it requires very little configuration. When setting up network computers using NetBEUI, usually only a computer and workgroup name needs to be assigned to each computer. For more information about the NetBEUI protocol, see page 128.

CONFIGURE TCP/IP PROTOCOLS

IP Addresses

On a home network that uses TCP/IP protocols, IP addresses must be assigned to each computer to identify the computers on the network. The first three parts of the IP address should be the same for each computer on the home network. The last part of the address should be unique for each computer. For example, the first computer on the network could have the IP address 192.168.52.1. The second computer could have the IP address 192.168.52.2.

Subnet Mask

A subnet mask must be assigned to a home network. The subnet mask for most home networks should be set to 255.255.255.0. If a home network will be connected to the Internet, the Internet service provider may provide a subnet mask for the network.

Domain Name Server and Gateway

If a home network will be connected to the Internet, the IP addresses of the Internet service provider's Domain Name Server (DNS) and gateway may have to be specified. The required IP addresses can be obtained from the Internet service provider.

CONNECT A HOME NETWORK TO THE INTERNET

A computer on a home network can be set up to share its Internet connection with other computers on the network. There is a wide variety of software available to simplify connecting a home network to the Internet.

INTERNET CONNECTION SHARING

Windows Operating Systems

The Internet Connection Sharing (ICS) feature is included with the Windows 98 Second Edition, Windows 2000 and Windows Me operating systems. ICS allows users of a Microsoft network to access the Internet using a single Internet connection.

UNIX

A single UNIX computer can easily be configured to connect a network to the Internet without any additional hardware or software. Many UNIX-based operating systems, such as Red Hat Linux, are now available to the home user free of charge or at a low cost.

Third-party Applications

Programs, such as Qbik's WinGate or Sygate Home Network, allow a home network to connect to the Internet. These types of programs are useful if the network operating system does not have built-in Internet connection sharing capabilities.

INTERNET CONNECTION SHARING CONSIDERATIONS

Share a Modem

Internet connection sharing allows multiple computers connected to a network to share a single modem that is connected to the Internet. This allows any computer on the network to access the Internet without having to have its own modem and Internet connection.

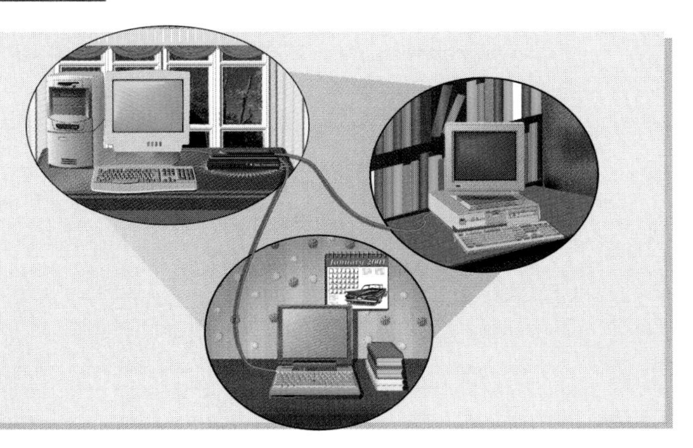

Share a High-speed Connection

Computers on a home network can share a high-speed connection, such as DSL or ISDN, to access the Internet. High-speed connections often require a network interface card. The computer with the Internet connection may require two network interface cards—one for the home network and another for the high-speed connection.

Internet Service Provider Account

Only one Internet service provider account is needed to connect a home network to the Internet. If users on the network wish to have their own e-mail accounts, each person will have to set up an e-mail address with the Internet service provider.

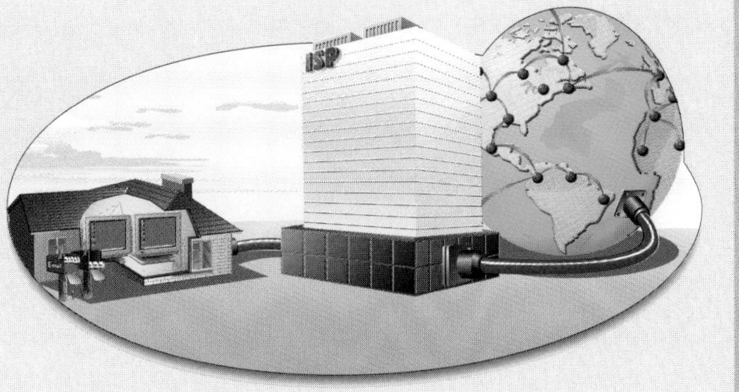

CONNECT A HOME NETWORK TO THE INTERNET (CONTINUED)

SET UP

Gateway

The computer that has the Internet connection sharing program and connects to the Internet is called the gateway computer. The gateway computer must be turned on and connected to the Internet whenever another computer on the network wants to access the Internet. Most gateway computers can be configured to connect to the Internet automatically when another computer tries to access the Internet and disconnect when there is no activity.

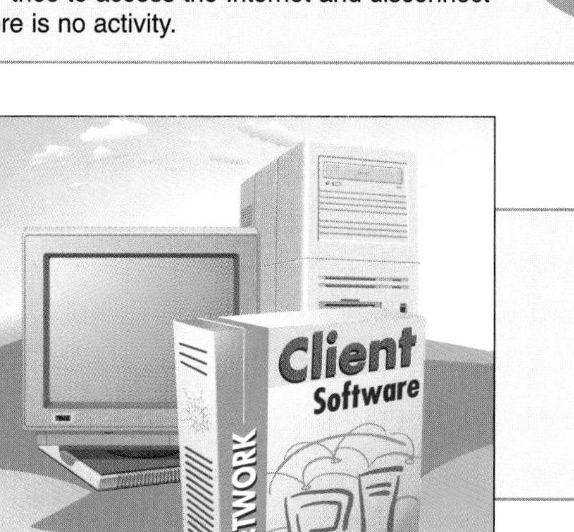

Client Software

Client software should be installed on any computer that accesses the gateway computer and connects to the Internet. The client software is used to configure the computer's TCP/IP settings and communicate with the gateway computer.

IP Addresses

Each computer that accesses the Internet requires its own unique IP address. The Internet connection sharing program typically sets up the IP addresses for each computer on the home network.

Multiple Operating Systems

Once a gateway computer has been set up to access the Internet, other computers using different operating systems can use the gateway computer to access the Internet. Computers running the Macintosh, DOS, UNIX and Windows operating systems can all share an Internet connection.

Firewalls

Home networks that are connected to the Internet can be vulnerable to unauthorized access from other Internet users. To prevent unauthorized access to a home network, Internet connection sharing programs usually include some firewall features. Home network users can also install separate firewall software on the gateway computer.

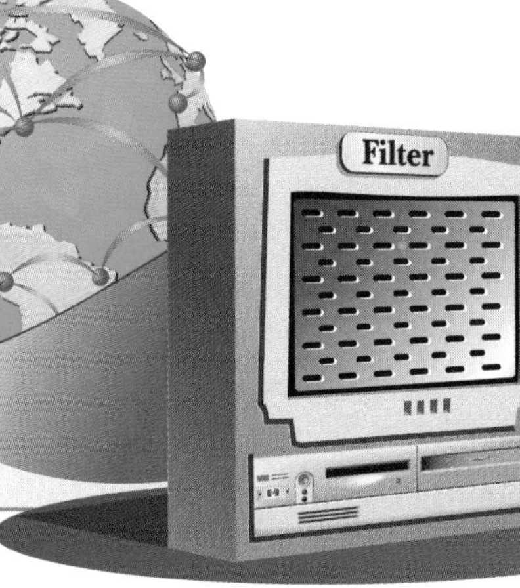

Filters

When using a single Internet connection for all the computers on a home network, access to specific areas of the Internet can be restricted. Some Internet connection sharing programs can be used to define which Web sites users on the home network can access. This is useful if children are accessing the Internet using the home network and access to inappropriate Web sites must be restricted.

C and C++
Perl
Java
JavaServer Pages
XML
CORBA

permission - Notepad
File Edit Search Help
<HTML>
<HEAD>
<TITLE>ABC Corporation</TITLE>
</HEAD>
<BODY>
<H2>You have successfully logged on to
the ABC Corporation Web site.</H2>
<P>
<%
Set objPchecker=Server.CreateObject("MSWC.PermissionChecker")
If objPchecker.HasAccess("\News\index.txt") = "True" Then
Response.Write("You have access to the file.
")
Response.Write("<A HREF='../News/passwords.html'>Click here to view the file.</A>")
Else
Response.Write("Sorry, you do not have permission to access the file.")
End If
%>
</BODY>
</HTML>
COLOR VIEW
zip
TRAVAN

CHAPTER 17

Network Programming

Programming languages can be used to create applications that function across networks. This chapter examines several programming languages, including Active Server Pages, Perl and Java.

Introduction to Network Programming 280

Scripting Languages 282

C and C++ 283

Active Server Pages 284

Perl 285

Java 286

JavaServer Pages 287

XML 288

CORBA 289

Network programming languages are becoming more widely used due to the increasing popularity of networks.

Network Programming

Network programming involves the creation of applications that function across networks and provide services to users. With the introduction of the Internet, different types of networks were connected and users needed a way to access resources and run applications on the different networks. Programs created using network programming languages make it possible for large, complex networks to work efficiently.

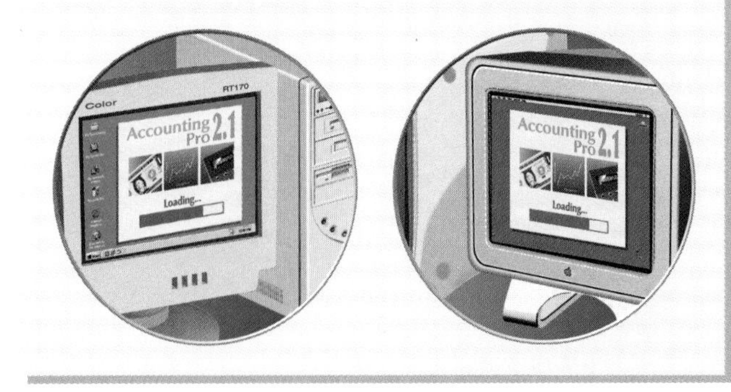

Object-Oriented Programming

Object-Oriented Programming (OOP) is a programming concept developed to make programs more understandable and easier to correct and modify. In this programming concept, a program is made up of one or more objects, which are small, re-usable chunks of code. Each object is used to perform a specific task and can be shared with other programs. For example, a sales program and a shipping program can use the same object to print invoices.

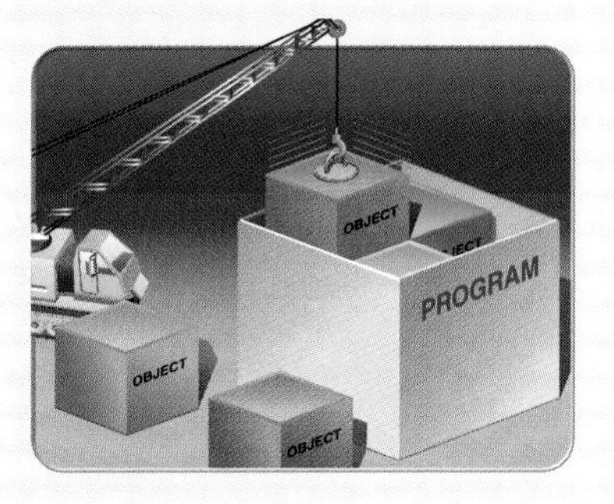

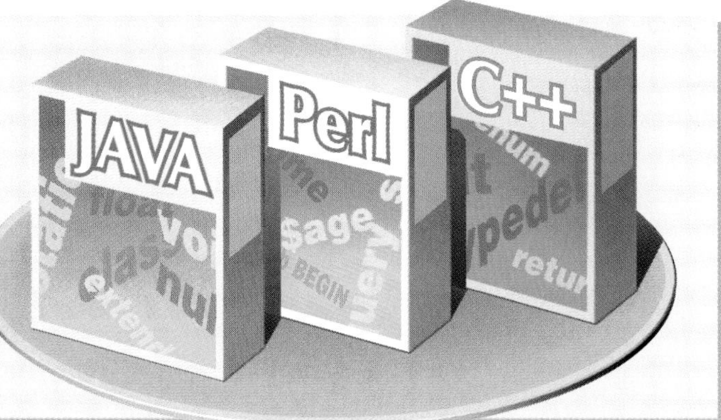

High-level Languages

Early programming languages were very difficult to use and understand. High-level programming languages that closely resemble human languages have been developed to make it easier for programmers to read, write and maintain their programs. Most programming languages in use today are considered high-level languages.

Dynamic Web Pages

A programmer can use network programming languages to create Web pages with content that changes depending on different factors. For example, a page may automatically present different content to users depending on the current date or the user's location. Dynamic Web pages are more useful to each individual user than static Web pages.

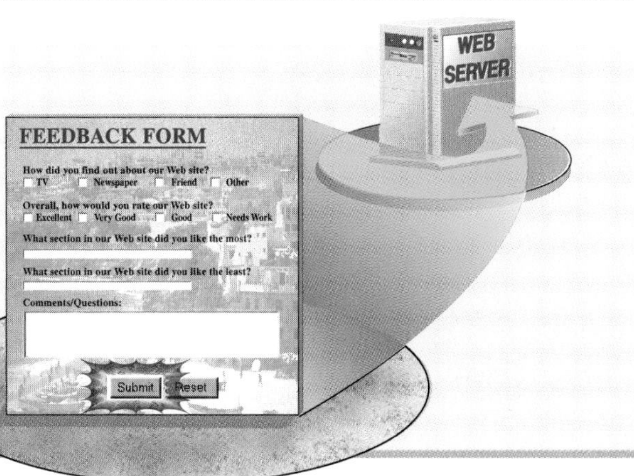

Interactive Web Pages

Interactive Web pages exchange information between a server and a user. Programmers can use network programming languages to easily create Web pages that process information from a user and then generate content depending on the information submitted by the user. Interactive Web pages allow programmers to tailor the content of Web pages to better appeal to the user.

A scripting language is a programming language that instructs a computer to perform a specific task. Scripting languages are often used to create simple programs.

Popular scripting languages include JavaScript, VBScript and PerlScript.

Web Pages

Scripting languages are relatively easy to learn and allow programmers to create programs using a small amount of code. This makes scripting languages ideal for Web pages, where file size is an important consideration. For example, using JavaScript lets a programmer add animated elements to a Web page without substantially increasing the file size of the page.

Interpreted Language

Scripting languages are interpreted languages, which means they are executed by a computer one line of code at a time. For this reason, scripting languages usually take longer to run than compiled languages, such as C or C++, in which all the code is interpreted by a computer before the program is executed.

C AND C++

C and C++ are high-level programming languages used to create large applications, including operating systems such as UNIX and Windows.

C

C is an older programming language that was initially used to create the UNIX operating system. Although C is an efficient and flexible programming language, it is complicated and difficult to learn. C forms the basis of many other languages, such as C++, Perl and Java.

C++

C++ builds on the C programming language and is used to create large-scale applications, such as the Windows and Macintosh operating systems. C++ is an object-oriented language that divides programs into small, manageable components, called objects. Using objects allows programmers to create complex and high-quality programs. C++ is one of the most popular languages used to create new programs.

ACTIVE SERVER PAGES

Active Server Pages (ASP) is technology developed by Microsoft that is used to create interactive Web sites and sophisticated network applications.

ASP is a server-side technology. This means that ASP pages are stored and processed on a Web server.

Scripting Languages

Scripting languages form the basis of ASP technology. There are many scripting languages that can be used to write ASP code. ASP supports VBScript and JScript by default. The scripting language code can be embedded in a Web page or stored in an external component.

Work With Databases

An important feature of ASP is its ability to connect to a database. ASP pages can be used to make information stored in a database available to the people who visit a Web site. Using databases to store information and ASP pages to access the information is an efficient method of displaying up-to-date information in a Web site.

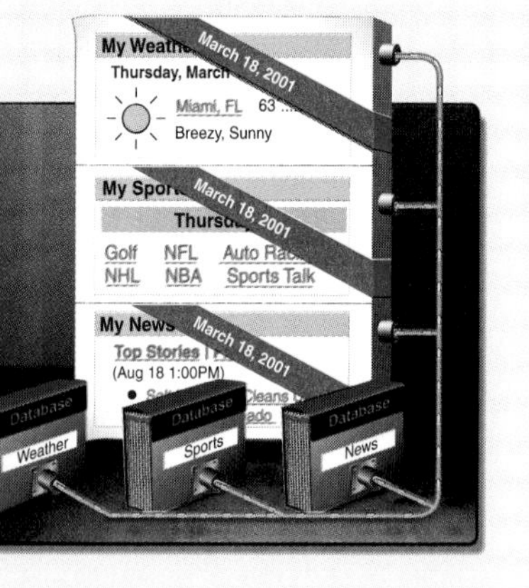

Perl (Practical Extraction and Reporting Language) is a programming language that was initially created to automate repetitive tasks on a network, but has become commonly used for Web programming.

Perl is based on several UNIX utilities and languages and is used on most Web servers running the UNIX operating system.

Text Manipulation

One of the main features of Perl is its ability to manipulate text. Perl can efficiently search text files, extract the necessary information and even create new text files. This is useful for computers running the UNIX operating system, since UNIX stores most information and settings in text format.

CGI Scripts

Perl is often used to create CGI (Common Gateway Interface) scripts. CGI is a technology used by Web servers to process information and pass information back to users. For example, CGI scripts commonly process information submitted using a form on a Web page. The text manipulation features of Perl make it an ideal choice for creating CGI scripts.

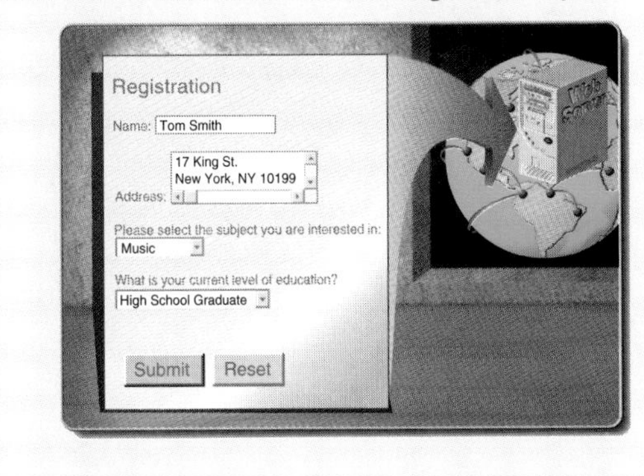

Java is a programming language developed by Sun Microsystems that is used to create client and server applications. Java is modeled after the C++ programming language.

Java can also be used to create small programs, called applets, which add animated and interactive elements to Web pages.

Portability

Most programs created on a particular operating system must be converted, or ported, before they can run on a different operating system. A major advantage of the Java programming language is that users can run the same Java programs on computers using different operating systems. The phrase 'write once, run anywhere' is often used to describe Java programming.

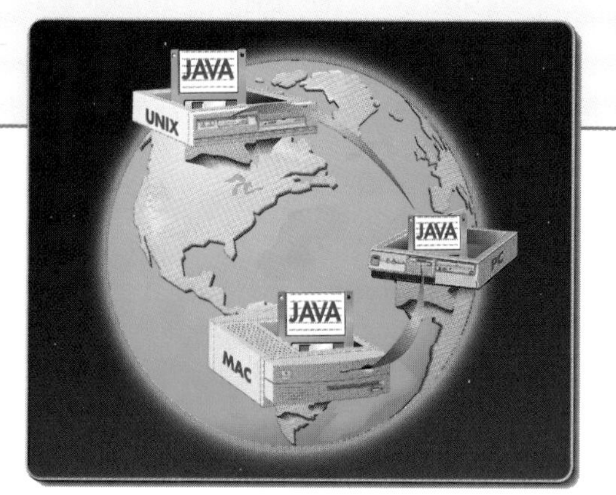

Java Virtual Machine

Java Virtual Machine is software that runs Java programs. The virtual machine creates a simulated software environment on a computer, which allows Java programs to run outside of the computer's operating system. This helps prevent malfunctioning Java programs from crashing a computer system and makes it possible for Java programs to run on computers using different operating systems.

JAVASERVER PAGES

JavaServer Pages (JSP) was developed by Sun Microsystems and is used to create powerful Web pages.

JSP is a server-side technology. This means that the dynamic content in a JSP page is processed by a server before it is displayed.

Java

A JSP page contains code written in the Java programming language. One of the benefits of using JSP is that it enables programmers familiar with Java to develop powerful Web sites without having to learn a new programming language.

Dynamic Web Pages

JSP allows programmers to create Web pages that display constantly changing data. For example, a JSP page can be used to display up-to-date stock quotes or weather information. JSP pages are also useful for retrieving data from databases and placing the information in dynamically created Web pages.

XML (Extensible Markup Language) is a flexible language that allows users to effectively exchange information on a network, such as an intranet.

Markup Languages

XML allows programmers to create their own markup languages. Markup languages consist of tags that provide instructions about the information in a document. XML offers more flexibility than predefined markup languages like HTML, since programmers can create custom tags that are suited to the information in their documents. For example, when creating a document that lists addresses, a programmer may create tags such as <street>, <city>, <country> and <zip>.

Exchange Information

A custom markup language created using XML can help people exchange information more effectively, since the language is specifically designed to suit the type of information being exchanged. For example, a supplier can use a custom markup language to create a Web page that clients can use to more accurately request information about the supplier's products.

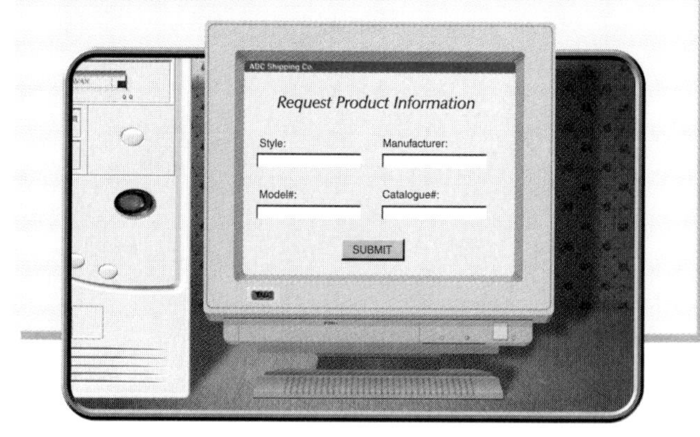

Common Object Request Broker Architecture (CORBA) is software that simplifies the way applications exchange data on a network.

CORBA was developed by the Object Management Group (OMG), which is an organization consisting of over 500 network manufacturers.

Exchange Information

CORBA allows programs located in different parts of a network and written in different programming languages to communicate with each other. For example, CORBA can allow an invoicing application to quickly retrieve customer information from a database located elsewhere on a network.

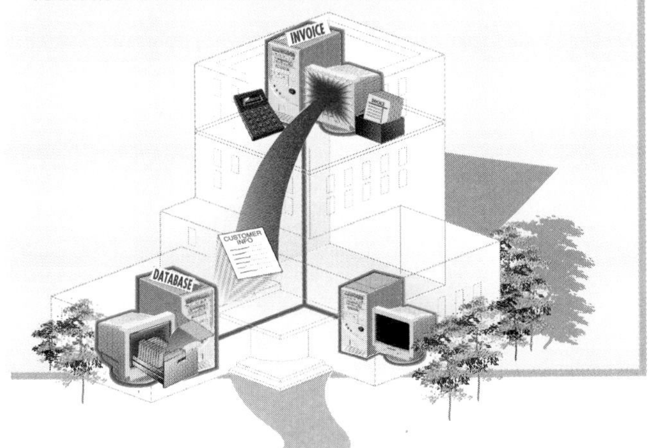

DCOM

Microsoft has developed its own version of CORBA, called Distributed Component Object Model (DCOM), which is used on Microsoft-based networks. CORBA and DCOM are compatible technologies, allowing them to exchange information. This is useful if one department in a large company uses a Windows operating system and other departments use the UNIX operating system.

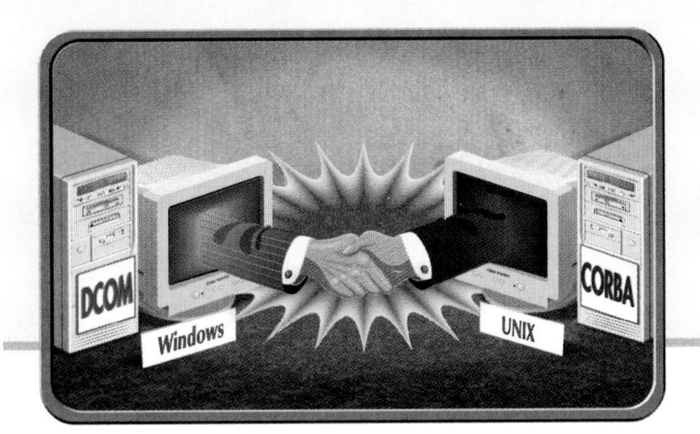

STUVWXYZ
Visual Glossary
Middleware
Middleware refers to software that allows different applications on a network to communicate. For example, a UNIX-based database may need middleware software to communicate with a Windows-based Web server. Middleware is often referred to as the 'glue' that holds a network together.
Mirror Site
A mirror site stores an exact copy of information stored at another site. Mirror sites are most often used to reduce heavy traffic on popular sites. Many file distribution sites, such as FTP sites on the Internet, use mirror sites.
Multistation Access Unit
A Multistation Access Unit (MSAU) is a device that connects multiple computers to a Token-Ring network. MSAUs allow Token-Ring networks to use a physical star structure and a logical ring structure. An MSAU automatically bypasses malfunctioning computers on a network. This prevents a malfunctioning computer from affecting the rest of the network.
Network Access Point
A Network Access Point (NAP) is a location where large communication companies connect their networks together, creating the Internet. There are several NAPs in the United States, typically located in major cities.
Network File System
Network File System (NFS) is a TCP/IP application created by Sun Microsystems that allows a computer to access storage space on a network as if the storage space were located on the computer. WebNFS is a version of the Network File System that is being developed for use on the Internet.
Null Modem
A null modem is a cable that can connect two computers using their serial ports. Once connected, the computers can exchange information as if they were connected using modems. Typically, a null modem cable should not exceed 30 feet in length. Null modem cables are often referred to as crossover cables, but should not be confused with Ethernet crossover cables.
294
Server Farm

CHAPTER 18

Visual Glossary

Find the definitions for interesting and useful computer terms, such as "cache server" and "infrastructure," in this glossary.

Visual Glossary 292

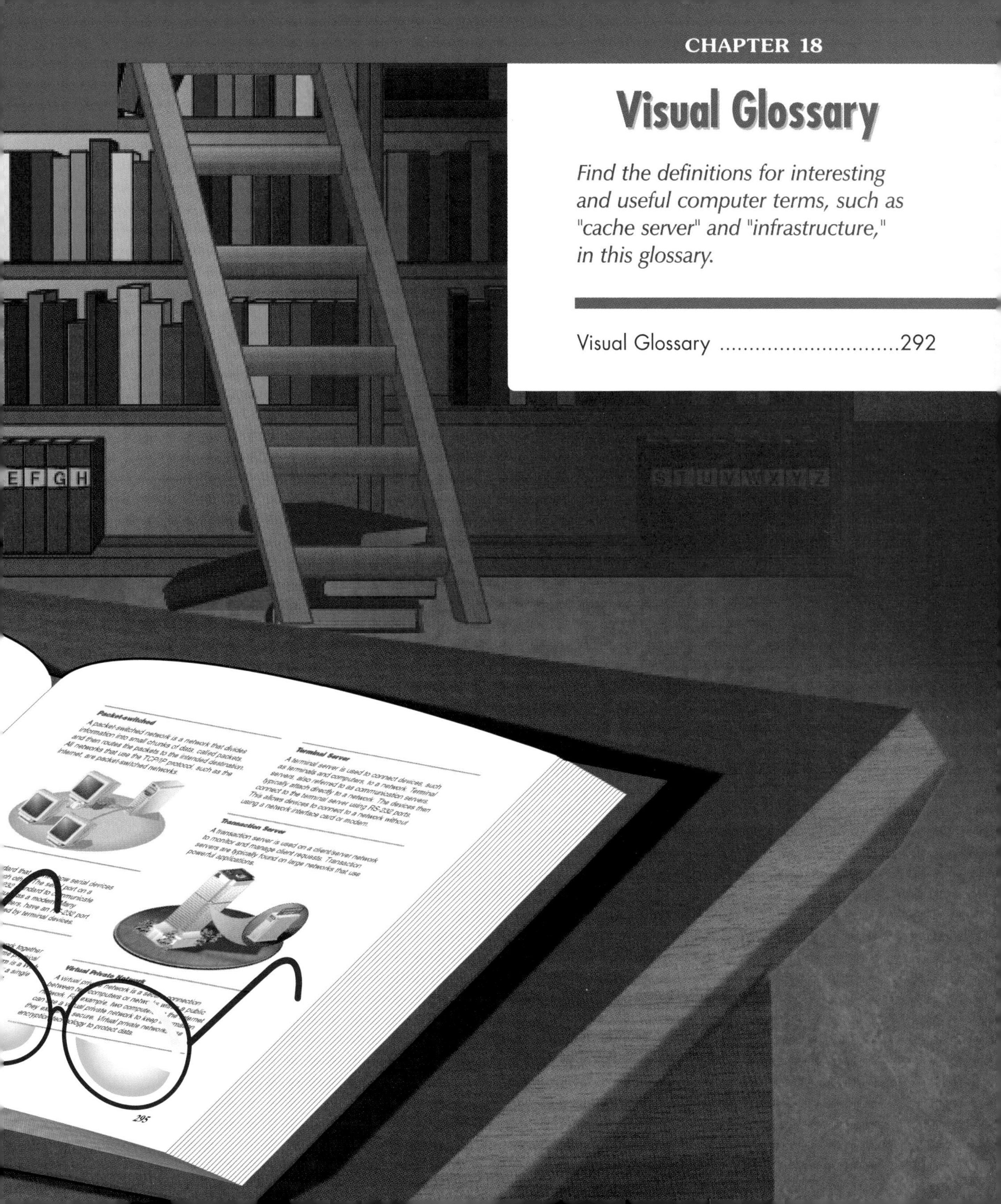

AS/400

AS/400 is a powerful computer manufactured by IBM. Originally intended for use as a server on large networks, the AS/400 is often used as a Web server. The AS/400 server provides up to 1.5 terabytes (TB) of hard disk space and up to 20 GB of memory.

Backbone

On the Internet, the backbone is the collection of high-speed transmission media used to transfer information between major networks. On a local area network, the backbone is the transmission media used to transfer information from one part of the network to another. For example, the hubs on a network may be connected by a fiber-optic cable backbone.

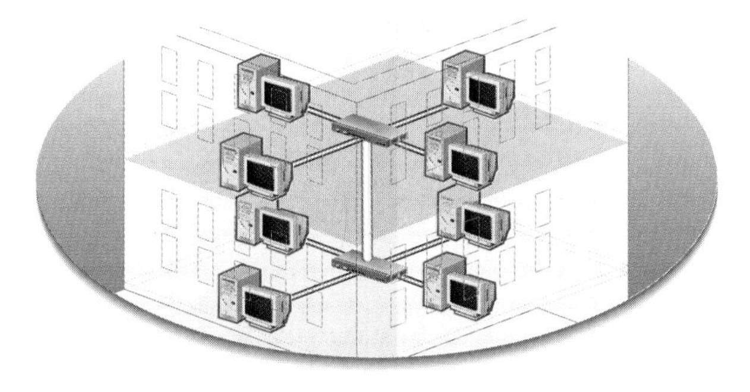

Cache Server

A cache server is a computer that stores frequently accessed information on a network. Typically, cache servers are used to store Web pages. A cache server copies requested files from the original source and then makes the copies available to all network users. This allows users to quickly access information and helps reduce network traffic.

Co-location

Many Web hosting companies, or companies that make Web pages available on the Internet, will store Web servers that belong to a client. This allows a client to maintain control over their Web servers without having to have a high-speed Internet connection.

Directory Services

Large networks can be difficult to maintain and administer. Directory services centralize information on a network, allowing a network administrator to manage the network from one location. Most network operating systems include directory services.

Enterprise

The term enterprise usually refers to large companies that have complex networks. When a device or application is marketed as an enterprise product, it usually means that it can be used on large networks.

Full-duplex

Full-duplex is a type of information transmission in which information can move in two directions at once. This allows a device to send and receive information at the same time. When information transmission is possible in only one direction at a time, it is referred to as half-duplex.

Handshake

When two communication devices connect to each other, they establish the protocol, speed and data format they will use to exchange information. This process is called a handshake. Handshakes are very common between modems, which can use a variety of different settings and speeds.

Hop

On networks that use the TCP/IP protocol suite, a hop refers to each device that information must pass through to transfer from one network segment to another. TCP/IP networks monitor the number of hops each piece of information encounters and remove any information with an excessively high hop count. This prevents 'lost' information from being continuously transferred around a network.

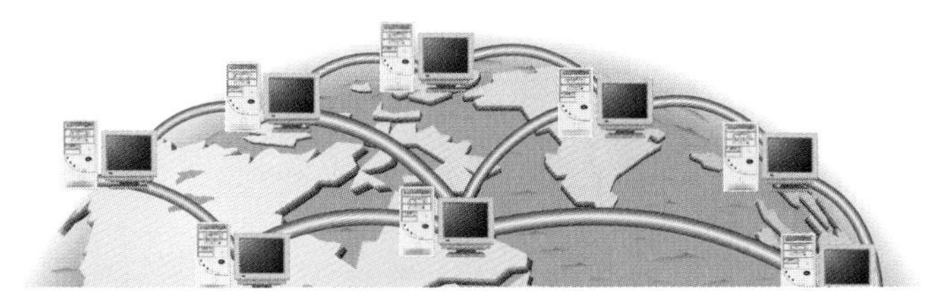

Infrastructure

A network's infrastructure is the hardware and software components that make up the network, including cables, hubs and the network operating system. Generally, the term infrastructure does not refer to the computers on a network.

Maximum Transmission Unit

A Maximum Transmission Unit (MTU) is the maximum size, in bytes, that information can be split into before being transmitted on a packet-based network. Most new operating systems can automatically adjust the size of the MTU to ensure optimal network performance.

Media Access Control Number

A Media Access Control (MAC) number is a unique physical address assigned to each device on a network. Older network devices allow users to set the MAC number for the device, while newer Ethernet devices have preset MAC numbers that are assigned when the devices are manufactured.

Middleware

Middleware refers to software that allows different applications on a network to communicate. For example, a UNIX-based database may need middleware software to communicate with a Windows-based Web server. Middleware is often referred to as the 'glue' that holds a network together.

Mirror Site

A mirror site stores an exact copy of information stored at another site. Mirror sites are most often used to reduce heavy traffic on popular sites. Many file distribution sites, such as FTP sites on the Internet, use mirror sites.

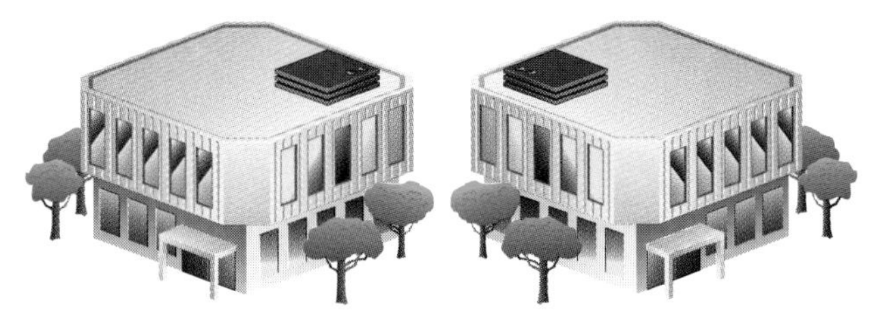

Multistation Access Unit

A Multistation Access Unit (MSAU) is a device that connects multiple computers to a Token-Ring network. MSAUs allow Token-Ring networks to use a physical star structure and a logical ring structure. An MSAU automatically bypasses malfunctioning computers on a network. This prevents a malfunctioning computer from affecting the rest of the network.

Network Access Point

A Network Access Point (NAP) is a location where large communication companies connect their networks together, creating the Internet. There are several NAPs in the United States, typically located in major cities.

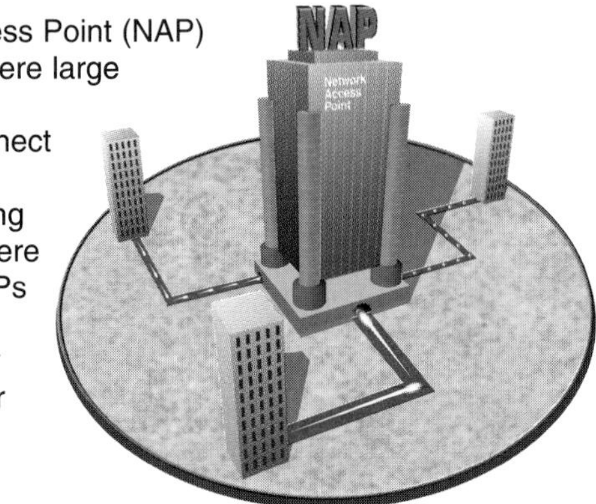

Network File System

Network File System (NFS) is a TCP/IP application created by Sun Microsystems that allows a computer to access storage space on a network as if the storage space were located on the computer. WebNFS is a version of the Network File System that is being developed for use on the Internet.

Null Modem

A null modem is a cable that can connect two computers using their serial ports. Once connected, the computers can exchange information as if they were connected using modems. Typically, a null modem cable should not exceed 30 feet in length. Null modem cables are often referred to as crossover cables, but should not be confused with Ethernet crossover cables.

Packet-switched

A packet-switched network is a network that divides information into small chunks of data, called packets, and then routes the packets to the intended destination. All networks that use the TCP/IP protocol, such as the Internet, are packet-switched networks.

RS-232

RS-232 is the standard that defines how serial devices communicate with each other. The serial port on a computer uses the RS-232 standard to communicate with an attached device, such as a modem. Many network devices, including routers, have an RS-232 port that allows them to be configured by terminal devices.

Server Farm

A server farm is a group of servers that work together to perform a task and are located in the same physical location. The most common type of server farm is a Web server farm, where multiple servers are used for a single Web site. Most busy Web sites have a server farm.

Terminal Server

A terminal server is used to connect devices, such as terminals and computers, to a network. Terminal servers, also referred to as communication servers, typically attach directly to a network. The devices then connect to the terminal server using RS-232 ports. This allows devices to connect to a network without using a network interface card or modem.

Transaction Server

A transaction server is used on a client/server network to monitor and manage client requests. Transaction servers are typically found on large networks that use powerful applications.

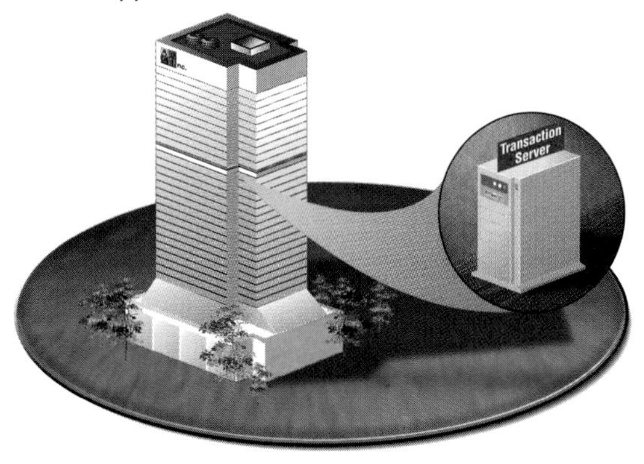

Virtual Private Network

A virtual private network is a secure connection between two computers or networks within a public network. For example, two computers on the Internet can use a virtual private network to keep information they exchange secure. Virtual private networks use encryption technology to protect data.

INDEX

Numbers and Symbols

100Base FX, 193
100BaseT cable, 89
100BaseT4 cable, 193
100BaseTX cable, 193
100VG-AnyLAN, 193
1000BaseLX cable, 193
1000BaseSX cable, 193
1000BaseT cable, 193
802.3, IEEE standard, 88
802.5, IEEE standard, 93
802.11, IEEE standard, 262
802.11a, IEEE standard, 262
802.11b, IEEE standard, 262

A

A+, 181
access
  information, connect to Internet, 211
  print services, 100
  resources, peer-to-peer network, 14
active hub, 94
adaptive certification exam, 171
address
  book, intranet e-mail, 238
  IP, assigning, using TCP/IP, 225
  network interface card, 49
  router, 58
administration
  centralized network layout, 36
  client/server network, 18
    operating system, 109
  distributed network layout, 37
  network, 156-157
    management software, 162
    upgrade, 187
  peer-to-peer network, 14
administration team, 156
administrator, network, 156-157
advanced features
  peer-to-peer network, 15
  VoIP, 251
advantages, home network, 267
alert, using network management software, 163
algorithm, router, 58
anonymous FTP, 245
anti-virus software, 221
AppleTalk architecture, 95
Application layer, OSI model, 122
applications. *See also* program; software.
  built-in, Internet, 220
  configure client computer to use, 205
  services, 102
  software
    Internet, 221
    network, 11
  use to determine network design, 191
  wireless, 256-257
architecture
  AppleTalk, 95
  ARCnet, 94
  considerations, 87
  Ethernet, 88-91
  network
    overview, 86-87
    upgrade, 192-193
  Token-Ring, 92-93
ARCnet architecture, 94
AS/400, 292
ASP (Active Server Pages), 284
ASP (Application Service Provider), 102
attachment, intranet e-mail, 239
automatic
  scheduling, 235
  shutdown, 151
automobile device, wireless, 259

B

backbone, 292
  network, 30
backup
  connection, 213
  file service, 99
  network, 21
    data, 146-147
  tape device, 148-149. *See also specific backup tape device.*
  types, 147. *See also specific backup type.*
bandwidth
  cable
    coaxial, 73
    fiber-optic, 79
    shielded twisted pair, 77
    unshielded twisted pair, 75
  Ethernet architecture, 89
  information transfer, network architecture, 87
  satellite system, 83
  transmission media, 71
  use to plan a network, 184
  videoconferencing, 233
battery, UPS, 150
benefits, network, 20-21
Bluetooth, 262
BNCs (British Naval Connectors), coaxial cable, 72
boot chip, network interface card, 49
breaks, cable, 207
bridge, 55
  information, brouter, 60
broadcast, test network, 207
brouter, 60
budget, consideration for connecting to Internet, 214
built-in application, Internet software, 220
bus network, 30-31

C

C, 283
C++, 283
cable
  coaxial, 72-73, 268
  crossover, 268
  Ethernet, 89
  fiber-optic, 78-79
  install, 196-197

length
shielded twisted pair, 77
unshielded twisted pair, 75
network hardware, 9
rating, 271
shielded twisted pair, 76-77
tester, 207
transmission media, 69
twisted pair, 268
unshielded twisted pair, 74-75
cache server, 292
CAD (Computer Aided Design) program, 102
carrier sense, Ethernet architecture, 91
categories, unshielded twisted pair, 75
CDE (Certified Directory Engineer), 172
CDMA (Code Division Multiple Access), 255
CD-ROM drive, 45
central network connector, 28
centralized network layout, 36
certification, 170-171. *See also specific certification.*
CGI (Common Gateway Interface) script, 285
channel service unit, 64
chat, on intranet, 242-243
chip, boot, 49
CIP (Certified Internet Professional), 172
Cisco Systems, Inc., 53
client
computer
configure, 204-205
install network hardware, 201
database, 101
software, 276
client/server network, 16-19
operating system, 108-109, 110-111
Windows NT, 112
clustering, Windows 2000, 115
CNA (Certified Novell Administrator), 172
CNE (Certified Novell Engineer), 172
CNI (Certified Novell Instructor), 172
CNS (Certified Novell Salesperson), 172
coaxial cable, 72-73
Ethernet network interface card, compatibility, 268
upgrade, 195
Cobalt Networks, Inc., 42
collaboration
groupware, 248
message service, 103
collision on Ethernet network
avoidance, 91
detection, 91
co-location, 292
combined
information, 65
media, 68
network structure, 27
common TCP/IP protocols, 132-135
communication
connect to Internet, 211
groupware, 249
company growth, upgrade network, 186
compatibility
Ethernet architecture, 88
intranet Web system, 236
NetWare, 111
network hardware, 199
OSI model, 125
TCP/IP protocol, 131
Token-Ring architecture, 93
transmission media, 68
using network monitoring, 160
CompTIA (Computing Technology Industry Association) certification, 180-181
computer
client, configure, 204-205
crime, 140
location
when choosing network hardware, 199
when planning a network, 185
network hardware, 8
computer-based training, certification, 170
conduit, install cable, 197
configure
client computer, 204-205
NetBEUI protocol, 129
TCP/IP protocol, 273
congestion, switch, 52
connect
devices, when installing a network operating system, 202
different network types, router, 59
home network to Internet, 274-277
to Internet, 210-211
considerations, 212-215
using TCP/IP, 224-225
printer to network, 46
connection types, Internet, 222-223. *See also specific connection type.*
troubleshoot, 226-227
connector
network hardware, 9
shielded twisted pair, 77
unshielded twisted pair, 74
considerations
for connecting to Internet, 212-215
Internet connection sharing, 275
network, 22-23
architecture, 87
transmission media, 70-71
constant updates, using network monitoring, 161
constraints, network administration, 157
consultant, network, 166-167
use to install network hardware, 200
use to plan a network, 185
contract, ISP, 216
CORBA (Common Object Request Broker Architecture), 289
cost
cable
coaxial, 73
fiber-optic, 78
shielded twisted pair, 76
unshielded twisted pair, 74
connect to the Internet, 214
modem, 63
network, 6
architecture, 87
Ethernet, 89
Token-Ring, 93
client/server, 19
hardware, 198

layout
centralized, 36
distributed, 37
peer-to-peer, 15
print services, 100
structure
bus, 31
hybrid, 80
ring, 33
star, 29
system
infrared , 80
microwave 82
radio, 81
transmission media, 70
create, Web page, 237
crossover cable, 268
CSMA/CA (Carrier Sense Multiple Access with Collision Avoidance), 90
CSMA/CD (Carrier Sense Multiple Access with Collision Detection), 90
CSU (Channel Service Unit), 64
current network, evaluate, 188-189
curriculum tracks, Linux certification, 177

D

daisy chaining, hub, 51
DAT (Digital Audio Tape) drive, 149
data conversion, 64
Data Link layer, OSI model, 123
database
ASP, 284
service, 101
DCOM (Distributed Component Object Model), 289
default gateway, 61
delay, satellite system, 83
department Web page, 237
determine
network design, 190-191
router route, 58
development, TCP/IP protocol, 130
device
driver, network interface card, 49
intelligent, 267
storage, 44-45
server, 41
tape backup, 148-149
wireless, 258-259
DHCP (Dynamic Host Configuration Protocol), 133
digital service unit, 64
directory services, 292
distributed network layout, 37
divide, network, 55
DLT (Digital Linear Tape) drive, 149
DNS (Domain Name System), 133
TCP/IP protocol, configure, 273
DNSs (Domain Name Servers), 225
document tracking, 249
downtime, network, 189
dpi (dots per inch), network printer, 47
drive
CD-ROM, 45
DAT, 149
DLT, 149
DVD-ROM, 45
hard disk, 44
LTO, 149
Travan, 149
driver
install, client computer, 204
network interface card, 49
TCP/IP, 225
DSL (Digital Subscriber Line)
Ethernet hub, home network, connect, 270
high-speed Internet connection type, 223
DSU (Digital Service Unit), 64
DVD-ROM drive, storage device, 45
dynamic
router, 58
Web page, 281, 287

E

efficiency
client/server network, 17
electrical resistance, coaxial cable, 73
electronic
mail (e-mail). *See* e-mail.
organizer, 256
e-mail, 103
intranet, 238-239
wireless, application, 256
embedded, wireless operating system, 260
employee
productivity, 214
schedule, 234
Web page, 237
enterprise, 292
EPOC, wireless operating system, 261
equipment, videoconferencing, 233
errors
checking, RAID level, 153
monitor, 159
Ethernet
architecture, 88-91
Gigabit, 89
switch, 53
hub, 270-271
network interface card, 268-269
switched, network, 192
evaluate, current network, 188-189
expansion
bus network, 31
client/server network, 18
network management software, 163
peer-to-peer network, 14
ring network, 33
star network, 29
transmission media consideration, 70
experience
network consultant, 167
vs. certification, 171
external modem, 63

F

face to face, videoconferencing, 232
Fast Ethernet, 89
    upgrade, 193
fault tolerance, 152-153
    hub, 50
    server, 43
FCC (Federal Communications Commission), 82-83
feature, network printer, 47
fiber-optic cable, 78-79
    upgrade, 195
file
    activity log, 145
    permission, 145
    services, 99
    transfer
        intranet, 244-245
            chat, 243
filter
    firewall, 143
    setup, 277
filtering, bridge, 55
firewall, 142-143, 219
    set up, home network, 277
FTP (File Transfer Protocol), 244-245
    as part of TCP/IP protocol suite, 132
full backup, 147
full-duplex, 293
future needs
    determine network design, 191
    hardware consideration, when connecting to Internet, 215
    server, 40

G

games, home network, 267
gateway, 61
    firewall, 143
    hardware, 61
    setup, home network, 276
    software, 61
get, IP address, 224
Gigabit Ethernet, 89
    switch, 53
    upgrade, 193
group
    groupware, 248
    password, 144
groupware, software, 248-249
GSM (Global System for Mobile), 255
GUI (Graphical User Interface), Windows NT, 113

H

handshake, 293
hard disk drive, 44
hardware
    consideration, 41
        connect to Internet, 215
    firewall, 142
    function, 199
    gateway, 61
    Internet, 218-219
    NetWare, 111
    network, 8-9
        choose, 198-199
        install, 200-201
        monitoring, 161
        upgrade, 194
    testing, 200
    troubleshoot, 226
    VoIP, 250
high-level programming language, 281
high-speed
    backbone, 53
    Internet connection, share, 275
    Internet connection types, 223. *See also specific Internet connection type.*
home network, 266-267
    connect to Internet, 274-277
    network protocols, 272-273
hop, 293
HTML (HyperText Markup Language), 237
HTTP (HyperText Transfer Protocol), 132
HTTPS (Secure HyperText Transfer Protocol), 134
hub, 50-51
    active, 94
    daisy chaining, 51
    Ethernet, 270-271
    fault tolerance, 50
    passive, 94
    port, 51
    signal regeneration, 50
    smart, 94
hybrid network, 34-35

I

ICMP (Internet Control Message Protocol), 134
ICS (Internet Connection Sharing), 274
    considerations, 275
    setup, 276-277
IEEE (Institute of Electrical and Electronics Engineers), 88, 93, 262
IGP/EGP (Interior Gateway Protocol and Exterior Gateway Protocol), 135
incremental backup, 147
i-Net+, 181
information
    bridge, 60
    configure, on client computer, 205
    route, 60
    share, on home networks, 267
    transfer
        AppleTalk architecture, 95
        ARCnet architecture, 94
        on bus network, 30-31
        Ethernet architecture, 88
        logical, 27
        network architecture, 87
        physical, 26
        on ring network, 32-33
        on star network, 28

types, mulitplexer, 65
infrared system, 80
infrastructure, 293
install
cable, 196-197
network
hardware, 200-201
operating system, 202-203
installation
cable
fiber-optic, 78
shielded twisted pair, 77
unshielded twisted pair, 75
infrared system, 80
Internet connection types, 222
microwave system, 82
peer-to-peer network, 14
satellite system, 83
transmission media, 70
intelligent
device, 267
router, 56
interactive Web page, 281
interference
cable, installation consideration, 197
coaxial cable, 72
fiber-optic cable, 79
infrared system, 80
install cable, 197
microwave system, 82
radio system, 81
shielded twisted pair, 76
transmission media, 71
internal modem, 63
Internet
access
intranet
e-mail, 239
file transfer, 245
backup, 146
connect
considerations, 212-215
home network, 274-277
network, 210-211
connection
considerations, 212-215
share, home network, 267
troubleshoot, 226-227
types, 222-223
hardware, 218-219
NetBEUI, 129
ready, Windows 2000, 115
software, 220-221
technology, on intranets, 230
Internet Service Provider (ISP), 216-217
account, 275
interpreted language, scripting, 282
intranet, 230-231
chat, 242-243
e-mail, 238-239
file transfer, 244-245
newsgroup, 240-241
scheduling, 234-235
software, 246-247
videoconferencing, 232-233
Web system, 236-237
inventory, evaluate current network, 188
IP (Internet Protocol), 132
IP address
to setup home network, 276
TCP/IP connection, 224-225
configure, 273-274
IPX (Internetwork Packet Exchange) protocol, 126-127
ISDN (Integrated Services Digital Network), 223
ISO (International Organization for Standardization), 121
ISP (Internet Service Provider), 216-217

J

jack, 196
Java, 286
Java Virtual Machine, 286
join network, bridge, 55
JSP (Java Server Pages), 287

L

LAN (Local Area Network), 7
LANtastic, peer-to-peer network operating system, 107
laptop, wireless device, 259
layer, OSI model, 122-123. *See also specific layer type.*
layout
centralized network, 36
distributed network, 37
LED (Light Emitting Diode), 51
level
logical, 27
physical, 26
light, transmission media, 69
line-interactive, UPS, 150
Linux, 117
certification, 177
log
chat, 243
evaluate on current network, 188
file activity, 145
use to plan a network, 185
logging on, network, 4
logical level, 26-27
Lotus Domino, 247
LTO (Linear Tape-Open) drive, 149

M

MAC (Media Access Control), 293
mail server, intranet, 238
maintenance, server, 43
MAN (Metropolitan Area Network), 7
manage users, network operating system, 203
management software, 11
manufacturer certification, 179
maximize network performance, 158
MCDBA (Microsoft Certified Database Administrator), 174
MCNE (Master Certified Novell Engineer), 172
mCommerce, 257

MCP (Microsoft Certified Professional), 174
MCSD (Microsoft Certified Solution Developer), 174
MCSE (Microsoft Certified Systems Engineer), 174
MCT (Microsoft Certified Trainer), 174
media
    care of tape backup, 148
    transmission, 68-69
memory, server, 41
message filter, 239
message service, 103
methods, fault tolerance, 153
Microsoft
    BackOffice, 247
    certification, 174-175
    NetBEUI protocol, 129
microwave system, 82
middleware, 294
mirror site, 294
mirroring, RAID level, 153
mobile phone, 258
model, OSI, 120-121
modem, 62-63, 218
    null, 294
    share, on home network, 275
module, NetWare, 110
monitor
    intranet resource, 235
    network, 160-161
MSAU (Multistation Access Unit), 294
MTU (Maximum Transmission Unit), 293
multimedia, wireless application, 257
multiple
    access, Ethernet architecture, 91
    Ethernet network interface cards, using, 269
    operating system, setup, 277
    participants, videoconferencing, 232
    recipients, intranet e-mail, 239
multiplexer, 65
multitasking, UNIX, 116

N

name, user, 144
NAP (Network Access Point), 217, 294
NAS (Network Attached Storage) device
    file service, 99
    storage device, 45
navigation, wireless application, 257
NetBEUI (NetBIOS Extended User Interface) protocol, 128-129
    on home network, 272
NetWare, 110-111
    certification, 172
network, 4-5
    administration, 156-157
    application, 257
    architecture, 86-87
        AppleTalk, 95
        ARCnet, 94
        Ethernet, 88-91
        Token-Ring, 92-93
        upgrade, 192-193
    backbone, 30-31
    benefits, 20-21
    centralized layout, 36
    certifications. *See specific certification.*
    client/server, 16-19
    considerations, 22-23
    consultant, 166-167
    cost, 6
    data
        backup, 146-147
        threats, 138-141
    defined, 4
    design, determine, 190-191
    distributed layout, 37
    divide, 55
    driver, 10
    evaluate, current, 188-189
    extension, 54
    guidelines, 164
    hardware, 8-9
        choose, 198-199
        install, 200-201
    home, 266-267
        connect to Internet, 274-277
        protocols, 272-273
    hybrid structure, 34-35
    interface card, 9, 48-49
        Ethernet, 268-269
    Internet, connect, 210-211
    join, 55
    layer, OSI model, 123
    layout, types, 36-37
    management software, 162-163
    monitoring, 160-161
    operating system. *See specific network operating system.*
        install, 202-203
        wireless, 260-261
    overview, 4-5
    peer-to-peer, 12-15
    performance, 158-159
    plan, 184-185
    policy, 164-165
    printer, 46-47
    program, 10-11
    programming, 280-281. *See also specific network programming language.*
    resource, 8
    services, 98
    size, 4
        consideration, when planning a network, 184
        Ethernet architecture, 89
        network
            architecture, 87
            types, 6
        peer-to-peer network, 12
        Token-Ring architecture, 93
    software, 10-11
    standards, 86
    structure, 26-27, 34
        bus, 30-31
        ring, 32-33
        star, 28-29

test, 206-207
topology, 26
types, 6-7
connect different, 59
TCP/IP protocol, 131
upgrade, 186-187
virtual private, 295
wireless, 254-255
Network+, CompTIA certification, 181
newsgroup, intranet, 240-241
NFS (Network File System), 294
NIC (Network Interface Card), 9, 48-49
on home network, 266
non-routable protocol, 129
NOS (Network Operating System), 10
notebook computer, 259
notes
use to troubleshoot, Internet connection, 226
while testing, network, 206
Novell certification, 172-173
NSBS (Novell Small Business Suite), software, 247
null modem, 294

O

OCP (Oracle Certified Professional), 178
OMG (Object Management Group), 289
online, UPS, 150
OOP (Object-Oriented Programming), 280
open
source code, Linux, 117
standard, TCP/IP protocol, 131
operating system
client/server, 19, 108-109
Linux, 117
multiple, setup, 277
network, install, 202-203
peer-to-peer, 15, 106-107
server, 42
UNIX, 116
Windows 2000, 114-115
Windows NT, 112-113
wireless, 260-261
optical drive, 45
Oracle certification, 178
OSI (Open Systems Interconnection) model, 120-121
layers, 20, 122-123
protocol, 124-125

P

packet-switched, 295
page, Web. *See* Web page.
Palm OS, 261
parity, RAID level, 153
passive hub, 94
password, 144
PC MACLAN, 107
PDA (Personal Digital Assistant), 252, 258
peer-to-peer network, 12-15
operating system, 106-107
Windows NT Workstation, 112
performance
evaluate current network, 189
management software, 162
NetBEUI protocol, 128
network, 158-159
peer-to-peer network, 13
Perl (Practical Extraction and Reporting Language), 285
permission, file, 145
Physical layer, OSI model, 123
physical parts, network, 26
PING, 227
planning
a network, 184-185
connection to the Internet, 210
policy, network, 164-165
POP3 (Post Office Protocol 3), 134
port
hub, 51
Ethernet, 271
IPX/SPX protocol, 127
network interface card, 48
power backup, UPS, 151
PPP (Point-to-Point Protocol), 135
Presentation layer, OSI model, 122
prevent loop, router, 57
print
network, 46-47
services, 100
privacy, intranet Web system, 236
private FTP, 245
professional cable installation, 196
program
backup, 146
database, 101
network benefit, 20
peer-to-peer network, 13
videoconferencing, intranet, 233
programming, network, 280-281. *See also specific network programming language.*
project newsgroup, 240
protection, upgrade network, 187
protocol
analyzer, 227
home network, 272
IPX/SPX, 126-127
NetBEUI, 128-129
OSI model, 124-125
router, 59
stack, 124
TCP/IP, 130-131
public telephone network, 64
purchase hardware, 198
purchased article, intranet, 241

Q

quality
network printer, 47
VoIP, 251

R

rack, 201
radio
  signal, 254
  system, 81
  transceiver, 254
RAID (Redundant Array of Inexpensive Disks) system, 152
Rapid Track curriculum, 177
read-only newsgroup, 241
records, network administration, 157
redundant path, router, 56
remote access
  hybrid network, 34
  modem, 62
  network management software, 163
  print services, 100
  server, 219
repair, server, 43
repeater, 54
reroute, TCP/IP protocol, 131
resource
  configure, client computer, 205
  password, 144
  peer-to-peer network, 13
  share, on a home network, 267
responsibility, network administrator, 156
restrict access, print services, 100
RG number, 72
RHCE (Red Hat Certified Engineer), 177
Ricochet, wireless technology, 263
ring network, 32-33
RIP/OSPF (Routing Information Protocol and Open Shortest Path First), 135
RJ-45 connector, unshielded twisted pair, 74
route information, brouter, 60
router, 56-59, 218
routing switch, 53

S

satellite system, 83
save money
  VoIP, 251
  when connecting to Internet, 214
scalability, NetWare, 111
scalable hardware, 215
schedule
  backup, 147
scheduling
  intranet, 234-235
  using groupware, 249
scripting language, 282
security
  client/server, 18
    network operating system, 109
  file service, 99
  guidelines, 164
  on network operating system, 203
  peer-to-peer, 15
    network operating system, 106
  software, 221
  switch, 53
  when connecting to Internet, 213
selective backup, 147
server, 40-43
  cache, 292
  client/server network, 16, 108
  farm, 295
  Internet, 219
  network interface card, 48
  network services, 98
  print, 46
  protection, 152
  software
    Internet, 220
    network, 11
  terminal, 295
  transaction, 295
  Web, 236
services
  application, 102
  client/server network, 17
  database, 101
  directory, 292
  file, 99
  ISP, 216
  message, 103
  network, 98
  print, 100
Session layer, OSI model, 123
set up
  bus network, 31
  home network connection to Internet, 276-277
  hybrid network, 35
  ring network, 32
  router, 57
  star network, 28
share
  home network
    information, 267
    Internet connection
      high-speed, 275
  modem, 275
  peer-to-peer network, 106
signal
  amplification, 54
  degradation
    fiber-optic cable, 79
    transmission media, 71
  regeneration
    hub, 50
    repeater, 54
site
  mirror, 294
  Web, 236
size
  client/server network, 17
  ISP, 217
  network, 4
    peer-to-peer, 12
    plan, 184
    types, 6
skill levels, Novell certification, 172
SLIP (Serial Line Internet Protocol), 135

smart hub, 94
SMTP (Simple Mail Transfer Protocol), as part of TCP/IP protocol suite, 134
SNMP (Simple Network Management Protocol), 160
socket, hub, 51
software
  client, set up, 276
  firewall, 142
  gateway, 61
  groupware, 248
  Internet, 220-221
  intranet, 246-247
  network, 10-11
    management, 162-163
    monitoring, 161
    peer-to-peer, 13
  scheduling, 234-235
  upgrades, 187
  VoIP, 250
  wireless operating system, 260
Solaris certification, 176
sophisticated filter, 143
speed
  bandwidth, fiber-optic cable, 79
  Ethernet
    hub, 271
    network interface card, 269
  information transfer, 87
  infrared system, 80
  network printer, 47
  radio system, 81
  router, 57
  server, 40
  switch, 52
  upgrade transmission media, 194
spike, UPS, 151
SPX (Sequenced Packet Exchange) protocol, 126
SQL (Structured Query Language), 101
Standard Track curriculum, 177
standards
  network, 86
  OSI model, 121, 125
standby, UPS, 150
star network, 28-29
static router, 58
storage device, 44-45
  file service, 99
  server, 41
STP (Shielded Twisted Pair) cable, 76-77
strategy, backup, 147
striping, RAID level, 153
structure, network, 26-27. *See also specific network type.*
subnet mask, 273
Sun Certified Network Administrator, 176
Sun Certified System Administrator, 176
Sun Microsystems, 176, 286, 287
support
  and equipment, ISP, 217
  consideration for connecting to Internet, 212
  NetWare, 111
  Windows NT, 113
surge protection, UPS, 151
switch, 52-53
switched Ethernet, 192
synchronize information, on a wireless device, 256
system
  infrared, 80
  intranet, Web, 236-237
  microwave, 82
  radio, 81
  satellite, 83

T

T1, 223
T3, 223
T-connector, 72
tape
  backup device, 148-149
  drive, 44
TCP (Transmission Control Protocol), 132
TCP/IP (Transmission Control Protocol/Internet Protocol), 130-131, 272-273
  common protocols, 132-135. *See also specific TCP/IP protocol type.*
  use, to connect to Internet, 224-225
TDMA (Time Division Multiple Access), 255
technical support
  evaluate current network, 189
  intranet chat, 243
  newsgroup, 240
  troubleshoot Internet connection, 227
technologies, wireless, 262-263
telephone
  line, use to connect to Internet, 222
  system, VoIP, 250
terminal server, 295
terminator
  bus network, 31
  coaxial cable, 73
testing
  certification, 171
  CompTIA, 180
  network, 206-207
tests, types, certification, 171
third-party application, 274
throughput, 159
Token-Ring architecture, 92-93
topology, network, 26
traffic simulator, 207
training
  Microsoft certification, 174-175
  network
    administrator, 157
    policy, 165
  Novell certification, 172-173
  Oracle certification, 178
  when connecting to Internet, 212
transaction server, 295
transfer
  information
    AppleTalk architecture, 95
    ARCnet architecture, 94
    on bus network, 30

Ethernet architecture, 88
install network operating system, 202-203
logical, 27
network architecture, 87
physical, 26
on ring network, 32
on star network, 28
speed, intranet file transfer, 245
transmission media, 68-69
considerations, 70-71
Token-Ring architecture, 92
upgrade, 194-195
Transport layer, OSI model, 123
Travan drive, 149
troubleshoot
bus network, 31
client/server network, 19
hybrid network, 35
Internet connection, 226-227
ring network, 33
star network, 29
Token-Ring architecture, 93
tunnelling, 127
twisted pair cable
with Ethernet network interface card, 268
upgrade transmission media, 195
two-way pager, 259

U

UDP (User Datagram Protocol), 133
unique address
hardware, network interface card, 49
router, 58
unit
channel service, 64
digital service, 64
UNIX, 116
Internet connection sharing, 274
update network policy, 165
upgrade
network, 186-187
architecture, 192-193
transmission media, 194-195
Windows 2000, 115
UPS (Uninterruptible Power Supply), 150-151
up-to-date certification, 175
User Datagram Protocol (UDP), 133
user name, 144
utilization level, 159
UTP (Unshielded Twisted Pair) cable, 74-75

V

version
NetWare, 110
UNIX, 116
videoconferencing, on intranets, 232-233
virtual private network, 295
virus, network, 141
VoIP (Voice over IP), 250-251

W

WAN (Wide Area Network), 7, 34
hybrid network, 34
modem, 62
router, 59
WAP (Wireless Application Protocol), 263
web browsing, wireless application, 256
Web
page, 236, 281
create, 237
scripting language, 282
server, 236
site, 236
system, intranet, 236-237
Windows
95, 107
98, 107
2000, 114-115
CE, 261
Me, 107
NT, 112-113
WINS (Windows Internet Naming Service), 133
wireless
application, 256-257
device, 258-259
networking, 254-255
operating system, 260-261
technology, 262-263
transmission media, 69
upgrade, 195
WML (Wireless Markup Language), 263

X

XML (Extensible Markup Language), 288
XNS (Xerox Network System), 126

Z

zone, AppleTalk architecture, 95

Read Less, Learn More™

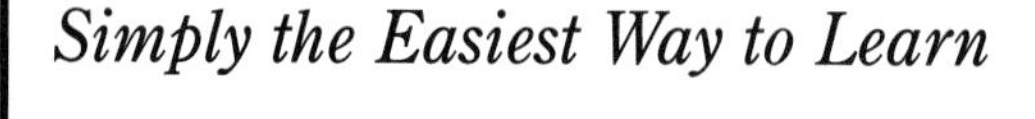

For visual learners who are brand-new to a topic and want to be shown, not told, how to solve a problem in a friendly, approachable way.

All *Simplified*® books feature friendly Disk characters who demonstrate and explain the purpose of each task.

Title	ISBN	Price
America Online® Simplified®, 2nd Ed.	0-7645-3433-5	$24.99
Computers Simplified®, 4th Ed.	0-7645-6042-5	$24.99
Creating Web Pages with HTML Simplified®, 2nd Ed.	0-7645-6067-0	$24.99
Excel 97 Simplified®	0-7645-6022-0	$24.99
Excel for Windows® 95 Simpified®	1-56884-682-7	$19.99
FrontPage® 2000® Simplified®	0-7645-3450-5	$24.99
Internet and World Wide Web Simplified®, 3rd Ed.	0-7645-3409-2	$24.99
Lotus® 1-2-3® Release 5 for Windows® Simplified®	1-56884-670-3	$19.99
Microsoft® Access 2000 Simplified®	0-7645-6058-1	$24.99
Microsoft® Excel 2000 Simplified®	0-7645-6053-0	$24.99
Microsoft® Office 2000 Simplified®	0-7645-6052-2	$29.99
Microsoft® Word 2000 Simplified®	0-7645-6054-9	$24.99
More Windows® 95 Simplified®	1-56884-689-4	$19.99
More Windows® 98 Simplified®	0-7645-6037-9	$24.99
Office 97 Simplified®	0-7645-6009-3	$29.99
PC Upgrade and Repair Simplified®	0-7645-6049-2	$24.99
Windows® 95 Simplified®	1-56884-662-2	$19.99
Windows® 98 Simplified®	0-7645-6030-1	$24.99
Windows® 2000 Professional Simplified®	0-7645-3422-X	$24.99
Windows® Me Millennium Edition Simplified®	0-7645-3494-7	$24.99
Word 97 Simplified®	0-7645-6011-5	$24.99

Over 10 million *Visual* books in print!

with these full-color Visual™ guides

The Fast and Easy Way to Learn

For visual learners who want to guide themselves through the basics of any technology topic. *Teach Yourself VISUALLY* offers more expanded coverage than our bestselling *Simplified* series.

Discover how to use what you learn with "Teach Yourself" tips

Title	ISBN	Price
Teach Yourself Access 97 VISUALLY™	0-7645-6026-3	$29.99
Teach Yourself Computers and the Internet VISUALLY™, 2nd Ed.	0-7645-6041-7	$29.99
Teach Yourself FrontPage® 2000 VISUALLY™	0-7645-3451-3	$29.99
Teach Yourself HTML VISUALLY™	0-7645-3423-8	$29.99
Teach Yourself the Internet and World Wide Web VISUALLY™, 2nd Ed.	0-7645-3410-6	$29.99
Teach Yourself Microsoft® Access 2000 VISUALLY™	0-7645-6059-X	$29.99
Teach Yourself Microsoft® Excel 97 VISUALLY™	0-7645-6063-8	$29.99
Teach Yourself Microsoft® Excel 2000 VISUALLY™	0-7645-6056-5	$29.99
Teach Yourself Microsoft® Office 2000 VISUALLY™	0-7645-6051-4	$29.99
Teach Yourself Microsoft® PowerPoint® 97 VISUALLY™	0-7645-6062-X	$29.99
Teach Yourself Microsoft® PowerPoint® 2000 VISUALLY™	0-7645-6060-3	$29.99
Teach Yourself More Windows® 98 VISUALLY™	0-7645-6044-1	$29.99
Teach Yourself Netscape Navigator® 4 VISUALLY™	0-7645-6028-X	$29.99
Teach Yourself Networking VISUALLY™	0-7645-6023-9	$29.99
Teach Yourself Office 97 VISUALLY™	0-7645-6018-2	$29.99
Teach Yourself Red Hat® Linux® VISUALLY™	0-7645-3430-0	$29.99
Teach Yourself VISUALLY™ Dreamweaver® 3	0-7645-3470-X	$29.99
Teach Yourself VISUALLY™ Flash™ 5	0-7645-3540-4	$29.99
Teach Yourself VISUALLY™ iMac™	0-7645-3453-X	$29.99
Teach Yourself VISUALLY™ Investing Online	0-7645-3459-9	$29.99
Teach Yourself VISUALLY™ Windows® Me Millennium Edition	0-7645-3495-5	$29.99
Teach Yourself VISUALLY™ Windows® 2000 Server	0-7645-3428-9	$29.99
Teach Yourself Windows® 95 VISUALLY™	0-7645-6001-8	$29.99
Teach Yourself Windows® 98 VISUALLY™	0-7645-6025-5	$29.99
Teach Yourself Windows® 2000 Professional VISUALLY	0-7645-6040-9	$29.99
Teach Yourself Word® 97 VISUALLY™	0-7645-6032-8	$29.99

The Visual™ series is available wherever books are sold, or call 1-800-762-2974. Outside the US, call 317-572-3993

ORDER FORM

TRADE & INDIVIDUAL ORDERS
Phone: **(800) 762-2974**
or **(317) 572-3993**
(8 a.m. – 6 p.m., CST, weekdays)
FAX : **(800) 550-2747**
or **(317) 572-4002**

EDUCATIONAL ORDERS & DISCOUNTS
Phone: **(800) 434-2086**
(8:30 a.m.–5:00 p.m., CST, weekdays)
FAX : **(317) 572-4005**

CORPORATE ORDERS FOR 3-D VISUAL™ SERIES
Phone: **(800) 469-6616**
(8 a.m.–5 p.m., EST, weekdays)
FAX : **(905) 890-9434**

Qty	ISBN	Title	Price	Total

Shipping & Handling Charges

	Description	First book	Each add'l. book	Total
Domestic	Normal	$4.50	$1.50	$
	Two Day Air	$8.50	$2.50	$
	Overnight	$18.00	$3.00	$
International	Surface	$8.00	$8.00	$
	Airmail	$16.00	$16.00	$
	DHL Air	$17.00	$17.00	$

Subtotal ____________

CA residents add applicable sales tax ____________

IN, MA and MD residents add 5% sales tax ____________

IL residents add 6.25% sales tax ____________

RI residents add 7% sales tax ____________

TX residents add 8.25% sales tax ____________

Shipping ____________

Total ____________

Ship to:

Name ____________________

Address ____________________

Company ____________________

City/State/Zip ____________________

Daytime Phone ____________________

Payment: □ Check to IDG Books (US Funds Only)

□ Visa □ Mastercard □ American Express

Card # ____________ Exp. ________ Signature ____________